W9-AHP-735

Soviet and Chinese Communism

SIMILARITIES AND DIFFERENCES

Soviet and Chinese Communism

SIMILARITIES AND DIFFERENCES

EDITED BY

DONALD W. TREADGOLD

SEATTLE   University of Washington Press   LONDON

Contents

Soviet Society and Communist Party Controls: A Case of
"Constricted" Development

PART FOUR: FREEDOM AND CONTROL

Introduction

Artificial "Flowers" during a Natural "Thaw"

The Revelation of St. Boris: Russian Literature and
Individual Autonomy

PART FIVE: STRATEGIES AND TACTICS OF ECONOMIC DEVELOPMENT

Introduction

Politics and Economics in Russia and China

Soviet and Communist Chinese Industrialization Strategies

PART SIX: RUSSIA AND CHINA IN INTERNATIONAL AFFAIRS

Introduction

Soviet and Chinese Communist World Views

Russia, China, and the New States

PART SEVEN: RUSSIA AND CHINA IN A MODERNIZING WORLD

Russia and China in a Modernizing World: A
Concluding Note

Introduction: The Comparative Study of Russian and Chinese Communism

I

ARE THE Union of Soviet Socialist Republics and the Chinese People's Republic to be understood as simply two particular cases of realization of the universal ideals of Communist theorists? Or are both regimes best approached as today's heirs of the millennia-long history of Russia and China? Widely-read popularizers and a number of scholars have argued both these opposed positions. More cautious investigators have avoided identifying themselves entirely with either extreme. However, until the conference held at Lake Tahoe, California, on June 13–17, 1965, no group of Western scholars including both Russia and China specialists had assembled to begin to examine and analyze the available facts, on the basis of which alone can come authoritative comparisons of the two governments and societies. Several different disciplines were represented—economics, history, law, literature, political science, and sociology. Most sessions consisted of papers comparing communism in the two areas, Russia and China, within a single discipline; the intention was thus to provide for intradisciplinary discussion within an interdisciplinary context.

The idea of such a conference was approved by the Joint Committee on Slavic Studies in November 1962 and accepted by the Joint Committee on Contemporary China[1] shortly afterward.

[1] Both committees are "joint" between the American Council of Learned Societies and the Social Science Research Council, the federations of the national organizations of scholars in the humanities and social sciences respectively. Gratitude is expressed to both councils for the financial sup-

In April 1963 a planning committee representing both met in New Orleans. It was decided that the purpose of the conference should be to "attempt a systematic if summary examination of the recent past and present of communism (viewed as both ideology and as political, economic, and social system) in Russia and China on a comparative basis, in order to gain better understanding of the main structural and developmental features of the two regimes and their doctrines and systems." Over two years of preparation resulted in the Tahoe conference. This book consists of the papers prepared as a basis for discussion there, with introductions to several sections added by some of those who were most active in the planning process and led the discussions at Tahoe. It may be claimed that the stage of development reached by the American (and perhaps the Western) scholarly community in comparative analysis of Russian and Chinese communism to date is reflected in this volume.

II

The problematics which occupy the forefront of the scholars' attention today have their own history, in part related to the great events of our own time. Three decades elapsed after the Russian Revolution of 1917 before Western studies of the USSR began to produce serious results. Before World War II there had not been any very large number of specialists on prerevolutionary Russia to help or hinder this development. There was no particular vested interest in holding that Russian communism was either completely new or fundamentally old in relation to the Russia of the Muscovite tsars or Petersburg emperors; some Russian émigrés most sharply opposed to communism still held that it represented a recrudescence of ancient habits in a modern guise, while certain admirers of communism justified its bloodshed on the basis of approximately the same contention. As a result, the theme of "continuity and change"[2] could be approached with a reasonable amount of detachment, as an empirical question to be resolved by careful study. The problem of Russia's kinship with

---

port that made the conference possible and to their officers, in particular Dr. Gordon B. Turner and Dr. Bryce Wood, for their advice and encouragement.

[2] See the volume based on the first significant conference of postwar Russian specialists: Ernest J. Simmons (ed.), *Continuity and Change in Russian and Soviet Thought* (Cambridge: Harvard University Press, 1955).

the West or divergence from it, that of whether Russia exhibited some traits common to all "modernizing" states,[3] that of whether Soviet totalitarianism marked the emergence of a new and unique kind of political system[4]—all these and others were discussed in an atmosphere which was affected by the Soviet-American antagonisms of the postwar period, but was not marked by particularly strong political passions or polarizations of viewpoint about what United States policy toward the USSR ought to be. A large share of the attention of American specialists on Russia was directed toward the modern period. Although Russian history loomed large in the spectacular academic growth of American Slavic studies after 1945, it was to a large extent history dealing with the Revolution and its more or less immediate background, and the rest of the disciplines, except to some extent for literature, tended to concentrate strongly on the Soviet present. Neither the proper topics of study nor the proper interpretations of these topics were very sharply at issue, and so it has remained to this day. What seems remarkable to many is not that American studies of Russia were influenced by the so-called "cold war," which brought Soviet-supported armies and United States armies into armed struggles in Korea and Vietnam and seemed to threaten war between America and the Soviet Union in Iran in 1946, in Cuba in 1962, and at other moments, but rather that in spite of these alarums and excursions the scholars managed to maintain the detachment they did, sharing despite their differences the conviction that scholarship has its own standards and imperatives.

In several respects American studies of China were in a different position. For roughly a century Sinology has had its distinguished American and other Western practitioners, who pursued the investigation of the creation of ancient Chinese culture and its subsequent literary, philosophical, and philological permutations. In part the missionary background of many Sinologists, in part the character of the written sources available helped to dictate a relative emphasis on thought and a relative neglect of institutional history and socio-political systems. Moreover, the greater

[3] Cyril E. Black (ed.), *The Transformation of Russian Society: Aspects of Social Change since 1861* (Cambridge: Harvard University Press, 1960).

[4] See the essays of Zbigniew Brzezinski, Alfred G. Meyer, and Robert C. Tucker, in Donald W. Treadgold (ed.), *The Development of the USSR* (Seattle: University of Washington Press, 1964).

degree of direct American involvement in Chinese affairs than in Russian during modern times produced strong if differing emotional responses; some Americans suffered from pangs of conscience about Western, if not so much American, imperialism and its interference in Chinese affairs after 1840; other regretted mistakes missionaries (sometimes including themselves) had made; still others thought that the United States, having committed itself to an "Open Door" in Chinese international relations and supported the establishment of a republic on Chinese soil, had failed to keep faith with that sort of liberal vision for China and had to some degree betrayed the republicans to the Communists before and during the 1940's.

The fact that United States policy toward China was moot in public discussion in the 1940's, and at least from time to time since, produced cleavages in scholarly opinion and political position deeper than any with which the Sovietists had to reckon. The apparently vast intellectual distance—as well as the clear chronological and geographical chasm—between Confucius and Marx, Lenin, and Mao was not easily traversed, and the study of Communist Party organizational charts and economic directives was a very different thing from study of the variants of Confucian texts. For the student of Communist China, Russian became a more important auxiliary language than Sanskrit, while the immediate need to command the old Chinese literary language waned in favor of the requirement of understanding Communist jargon as used in the colloquial tongue. The very height of achievements of the old Sinology thus paradoxically helped to produce the seriousness of problems of adaptation to the post-1949 scene with which specialists have had to wrestle. It was tempting for the Sinologist, harassed by journalists or beginning students, to retort that the new China was nothing but the old China that he knew so well. At the same time, however, the students of Chinese Communist affairs who were beginning to appear might be unable to judge whether new and old were the same because they were apt to know so little about the old.

The student of Russia was thus in some respects more fortunate than the student of China. Russia's revolution was long past, and there was only one entity that claimed to be Russia in international affairs; the Russian past had not been extensively studied, and in any event was at least 1,500 or 2,000 years shorter than that of China; the social scientists were influential in

Russian studies almost from their beginning, and had no need to ask whether it was wise to shed established habits of looking at their subject. At the same time the Russia specialists may have suffered from some handicaps. Their less solid acquaintance with the Russian past put them in peril of concluding too quickly that the Russian tradition was dead; their none too firm understanding of Russian Orthodox Christianity gave them scant basis for comprehending what difference communism had made in Russian culture, high and low; their relative detachment from political debates had in part been paid for by the fact that few had spent much or any time in Russia, knew many Russians (either in the USSR or in emigration), or had any clear sense of direct involvement through experience with the country they were studying. (In the last few years, of course, the trend has reversed; the Sinologist's memory of the mainland has dimmed, and the Sovietist has been making a few friends in the USSR.)

III

The problems of whether Communist Russia is more or less Communist than Russian and of whether Communist China is more or less Communist than Chinese, and if so or not so in what precise sense, were therefore far from being solved by the two groups of scholars who assembled at Lake Tahoe. Sharing the results of their studies with one another was expected to produce a clearer perception of what was peculiar to each country and what it had in common with the other, a better comprehension of the similarities and differences. In preparation for the conference the planners were conscious that few if any persons anywhere were prepared to speak as experts on both Russia and China, past or present. In encouragement of the ambition of those still to complete or indeed begin their training, the planning committee invited seven graduate students who were attempting double specialization to attend the conference as rapporteurs.

The intention of the planning committee was thus based on the assumption that specialists on one or the other country might be urged to attempt the beginnings of comparative analysis in their papers rather than completing it for the topic in question. Coupling commentaries from China specialists with papers from Russia specialists, and vice versa, would supplement the efforts of the authors of papers. Finally, endeavors to summarize what could be learned from the whole proceedings were invited from some persons not primarily specialists in either country. All these devices are exemplified in the pages that follow, though space did not permit the reproduction of even a substantial share of the commentaries or a record of discussions. The scholars who attended the conference had come to learn from each other. All of us knew we had much to learn, and few if any left the conference reassured by a feeling that our level of ignorance had been drastically reduced or that reducing it would be rather simply achieved in the near future. Definition of the limits of ignorance may be not only the mark of wisdom, however, but the prerequisite to sound planning for future study. What is striking to the editors of the volume is not the failure to solve all problems, but rather the noteworthy advances made in the direction of solution as shown in the essays which follow.

Thirty-nine participating scholars attended, from the United States, Great Britain, Germany, and Hong Kong, not including observers. They were a distinguished group, representing fifteen major universities and four research institutions. All came with a great deal to say of substance and relevance; the pity was that time permitted only a small fraction of that to be said. This volume assembles a record of the larger share of the data gathered and analyzed and of the major efforts at interpretation presented there. The editors take this opportunity to express their gratitude to all the participants and admiration for their thought and work, which produced this volume.

I V

The organization of the book follows the sequence of topics considered at the conference. First comes a discussion of the antecedents of communism in Russia and China, or more precisely, of elements in pre-Communist thought and institutions relevant to the establishment of Communist rule in both countries. Richard Pipes' essay confines itself to Russia. It begins with an examination of the historiography of the Bolshevik Revolution, contrasting "neo-Slavophile" with "Westerner" interpretations. History has dealt harshly with the former, while the latter has become transmuted into a part of the general notion of "modernization." The process of *raskreposhchenie,* of the liberation of the various segments of Russian society from state tutelage, had proceeded a fair distance, but society was not yet ready to replace the state. Therefore, Pipes concludes, Bolshevism (communism) in Russia might be considered accidental, but the restoration of an authoritarian regime was not. George E. Taylor undertakes to consider the relevance of the issues as posed by Pipes' discussion of Russia to the situation in China. He finds developments there, especially during the decade of effective Nationalist power beginning in 1927, comparable to many in Russia during the last decades or more of Tsarism. In both countries Western ideas and institutions provided inspiration to those indigenous leaders who were determined to break decisively out of the paths inherited from the old systems. It was a difficult task to attempt, hampered by the persistence of old and ingrained attitudes as well as the tenderness of new social and political tissue. In neither country was the non-Communist leadership able to hold the reins of power when faced by the shock of world war and the effectiveness of the Communist opposition.

The next section deals with the changes experienced by the two Communist parties after they were transformed from revolutionary undergrounds or regional cliques into national ruling authorities. Lucian W. Pye goes so far as to claim that the central theme of the whole conference was "the degree to which traditions of party organization and practices are now impeding developments in both countries." Many participants might agree. In any event Merle Fainsod's and J. M. H. Lindbeck's papers bring out clearly the magnitude of the alterations which the leaders made in party structure and function in order to assume the burdens not only of governing two vast nations but of undertaking revolutionary transformation of the societies and the economies. Fainsod concentrates on Russia, Lindbeck on China, but each paper ends by comparative discussions of developments in the other country. The Bolsheviks assumed power more swiftly, even considering the uncertain period of the civil war, but were slower to embark on reshaping the social order; the Chinese Communists' path to national power was more tortuous, but when they were established in Peking they moved more rapidly into revolutionary reconstruction of society. Although a paradigm of much Chinese Communist development is to be found in the earlier story of Russian communism under Lenin and Stalin, the different national settings dictated some divergences in the courses taken. The Chinese Communists sought to avoid the bloodshed of Stalin's purges by early introduction of methods of mass mobilization and integration of the individual in the party-led campaigns (including "brainwashing") which broke some new ground in the history of international communism. The imperatives of national power, despite all "fraternal" ties and similarities of pattern of development, created differences of organization and operation as well as, ultimately, disagreements and mutual denunciation. The problems of "redness" versus expertise, political reliability versus technical competence, had dogged both parties from the start, and remained at least partly unsolved.

The third section comprises materials first planned for a single session, divided into two for the conference, and joined together again in the book. It ranges over questions of law and social structure in the context of the controls adopted by the two parties and altered as policies changed. Jerome Alan Cohen distinguishes various periods in the development of Chinese Communist law, especially criminal law. After four years, Mao's regime introduced limited legal reforms based on Soviet models during the 1953–57 period. Since that time, however, there has been sharp retrogression in legal safeguards, and a new system of sanctions has been introduced, based on residents' committees and informal punishments. It may be that the Soviets have borrowed some of these devices from the Chinese. Leon Lipson analyzes the pattern of extra-judicial mechanisms developed by the Russian Communists during recent years, such as the comrades' courts, anti-parasite laws, and *druzhiny,* and shows how they supplement the regular criminal penalties. Extra-legal sanctions and pressures of a wider kind are the subject of Ezra Vogel's essay. He introduces the concept of "voluntarism," by which is meant the Chinese Communist practice of combining the use of non-material incentives with covert compulsion or the threat of compulsion to produce results which the regime desires but the people do not. He warns against considering the custom of "volunteering" to be pure sham, and explores the psychological techniques used to evoke it. Mark Field's essay is an effort to survey the chief clusters of theories that have been offered in the West of the entire system of social control used in the USSR. He distinguishes three: the first regards totalitarianism as the motivation of the rulers and their strategy as one of "protracted conflict"; the second argues that industrialism is the basic force at work; a third attempts to reduce communism to nationalism or the national heritage. No single explanation is found adequate, although each refers to real phenomena; moreover, the analysis of Stalin's Russia needs modification in view of the beginnings of social differentiation and evolution that have been observed since Stalin's death.

The fourth section is entitled, "Freedom and Control," and concentrates on the relationship between the regimes and the intellectuals. Victor Erlich points out that Shih-hsiang Chen's essay explores "control" more extensively, whereas Sidney Monas' probes more vigorously the meaning of "freedom" within Communist systems. Chen contrasts the contrived and controlled course of the "Hundred Flowers" movement in China in 1956 with the spontaneous and elusive character of the "thaw" that began in 1954 and has continued, with intermittent "freezes," since that time. The very brevity of the "Hundred Flowers," which bloomed no more than six weeks, accounts for its superficiality. Chen develops this comparison with rich detail. Monas investigates certain aspects of the entirety of modern Russian literature. He first contrasts the two different "muses" of the poet Alexander Pushkin, the "imperial" and "private" ones. Since then two opposing sets of images have persisted in Russian literature, one connoting the city, power, rank, and vanity, the other nature, family, community, and the free play of emotions. Pasternak's *Doctor Zhivago* draws on the latter set of images, and with this force Soviet literary policy may yet have to reckon.

"Strategies and Tactics of Economic Development" is the subject of the fifth section. In his introduction Gregory Grossman notes that similar "doctrinal political matrices" provide the rationale for a comparison of the Russian and Chinese economies, but prepares us for some surprises in their different paths. The Chinese Communists, with both regional experience of their own and the national experience of the Soviets to draw upon, still have executed sharp changes of strategy which contrast with the long persistence of the Stalinist economic system in Russia. Franz Schurmann in his paper speaks of the development of "bureaucratic pluralism" in China, though he notes that real decentralization runs against fixed habits and structures to be found in both the bureaucracy and the party. The influence of the Soviet model on the organization of the economy is considered, and the stages of party policy and economic change in the two countries are compared. K. C. Yeh probes into the specifics of party policy in the two countries. China, like the USSR, was at first the scene of economic development concentrating on heavy industry at the expense of investment in light industry and agriculture. The basic Soviet strategy was to convert agricultural surplus into industrial capital, whereas the Chinese aimed at converting labor into industrial capital. The economic collapse of 1960–62 led to a significant Chinese deviation from the Soviet model in placing heavy industry far down on the list of priorities. Whether this change is to last remains to be seen.

The sixth section is concerned with "Russia and China in International Affairs." Alexander Dallin stresses that the papers treat the actually operative side of the world view of the Soviet and Chinese Communist leaders rather than chiliastic hopes for the future. However, he cautions against neglecting the importance of ideological presuppositions on the common assumption that the Communists are concerned merely with practical problems like everybody else. Ideology is neither all nor nothing in Moscow's and Peking's approach to international affairs. Richard Lowenthal emphasizes that the two groups of leaders began with a common framework of Marxism-Leninism as interpreted by Stalin. However, their consciousness of difference in the roles of the two parties came increasingly to affect their ideological posture. There had been differences in the force of anti-colonial nationalism, in the function of organized military force, and in the degree of reliance on revolutionary will in the absence of economic prerequisites, which formed the background of the Peking-Moscow dispute over the relative importance of violent revolution and the risks which may attend it. The result is a Chinese Communist outlook apt to be less susceptible to Western influence than that of the Soviets. Donald Zagoria begins by recognizing much similarity between Soviet and Chinese Communist revolutionary strategies in underdeveloped areas, and then proceeds to explore the significant differences, especially as they emerged after 1959. Peking came to support a "Maoist-right" strategy, seeking in the first stage of revolution to subordinate Communist demands to "national democratic" ones but maintaining Communist independence and if possible hegemony by a "united front from below." Moscow settled on a "classical, coalition-right" strategy, based on a more optimistic assessment of the Communists' potential to tolerate in the short run nationalist leadership in a "united front from above." Peking's sense of urgency and danger is shown by its stress on armed struggle and guerrilla warfare. In the last few years the Soviets have gone far toward seeming to approve non-Communist one-party regimes—a further step in the "classical" direction. Peking profits from the extent to which leaders in underdeveloped countries can identify with its efforts to lift China by the bootstraps and from adroit use of the racial issue, but Moscow's greater wealth and power offset the former's appeal. Zagoria concludes that there are limitations on what either can be expected to achieve in the "third world."

The final section of the book consists of an essay written by Harold D. Lasswell, whose special field is defined less by concentration on either Russia or China as an area of study than by concern with the theoretical relationship between institutions and values and its practical consequences in differing societies. He stresses the problem of how far the imperatives of science and technology may affect the process of creating Communist systems and investigates it briefly with reference to both countries. His final note is a query regarding the probable fate of human dignity as a value in the sort of systems under study in Russia and China, anticipating that the continuation of comparative analysis of the two systems will illuminate this and other problems only briefly explored in the essays that precede his own.

v

The conference and therefore to a large extent the volume (though all of the papers have been revised, some extensively, during the months following the conference) suggest that the field of comparative study of Soviet and Chinese communism has been invaded in force, but scarcely occupied. A great quantity of factual material was examined and a number of important conclusions were at least tentatively advanced. Differences between Russia and China may seem to the reader to be much more in the foreground of what follows than similarities. Probably the majority of contributors would agree that the two societies have much in common; that the two great Communist parties in power were more like each other than like organizations existing anywhere else on the planet (the parties of the smaller Communist-ruled states differing at least in scale); and that the leaders had similar concepts of the nature of power and the function of ideology, of the purposes of controls, the objectives of economic planning, the goals of cultural management. At the conference many students of either country, assuming many common features to exist and knowing at least something about them in detail, were struck by the significance of the differences, even if they did not seem to affect fundamental structures or aims. When two institutional or ideological patterns have nearly coincided in history, it has often been apparently minor or trivial divergences which have had the greatest consequences. There is a constant temptation to shift from the comparative analysis of two systems as closely related as those of Russia and China to the examination of the actual Sino-Soviet relationship. In this volume this temptation is largely avoided; its tentative conclusions do not rest on any particular assessment of the Moscow-Peking dispute as of 1965/66 or its probable future course.

The Sino-Soviet border in Western scholarship, which was of greater concern to the conference than the territorial boundary between China and the USSR, was breached at many points. The indispensability of considering the comparison of the two great Communist powers if adequate analysis is to be made of developments in either one will scarcely need demonstration additional to the essays in this volume. None of the participants seemed to doubt the necessity of the comparison if either system is to be sufficiently understood, and readers may draw their own conclusions. It may be confidently expected that the problems of comparison will be in the minds of both Russia and China specialists for a long time to come, as indeed they were before the conference was held and this volume written—or neither would have been possible.

If any obstacle to the continuation of such comparative studies needs to be singled out, it may be one related to the development of Sinological and Sovietological scholarship in the West as summarized at the outset of this essay. The comparative treatment of the two systems presently lies to a considerable extent in the hands of the social scientists, with notable exceptions in the field of literature. The humanities have yet to make their full contribution. In part this means that the distinguished body of Sinologists (that is, literary, philosophical, and philological scholars) have yet to turn sustained attention to the contemporary scene; some might argue that there has not yet been the proper opportunity for them to contribute what they are already prepared to do. In part the reason lies in the fact that the humanities have tended to lag from the start of serious study of the USSR in this country and the West. If, as Lasswell argues, values and commitments of the leaders and the led must loom large in any successful pursuit of the analysis of the two systems, surely the disciplines of philosophy, religion (including the examination of the notion of a secular religion), and the fine arts can hope to add their own insights to those provided by the historians, political scientists, economists, and sociologists in this volume. This is far from saying that the social scientists are prepared to rest on their laurels or would be justified in so doing. The very progress they have made in identifying the issues makes advancement toward their solution seem more pressing.

In any event it might be contended that a volume of this kind, frankly concerned with breaking new ground rather than announcing the completion of construction work, ought to err, if anywhere, on the side of tentativeness of hypothesis, limitation of the scope of conclusion, and modesty of claims in the realm of theory and speculation. The implications of what Soviet and Chinese communism have to teach us about previously held views of human nature, its limitations and aspirations, its biological roots and its spiritual branches, are yet to be thoroughly explored. There was, of course, never any danger that such problems would be exhausted by any single conference or volume now or in the future.

PART ONE

Antecedents of Communism in Russia and China

Communism and Russian History

RICHARD PIPES

THE question implied in the title of this paper arose almost the instant the Bolsheviks had assumed authority over Russia. Already in the summer of 1918 a group of scholars and publicists, mostly of a moderately conservative persuasion, brought out in Moscow a volume of essays devoted to this very problem.[1] But it was only after 1920, that is, after the Bolsheviks had firmly ensconced themselves, that the historical roots of Russian communism attracted the intense attention of both émigré and foreign observers. The vast literature on this subject produced in the 1920's and 1930's has not yet been adequately surveyed; indeed, serious scholars have shied away from it, because so much that has been written on the connections between communism and Russia consists of wild pseudo-historical philosophizing. Generalizations about the historiography of the problem must of necessity, therefore, be very tentative. It does appear, however, that the interpretations formulated in the inter-war period fall into two principal schools corresponding to intellectual trends familiar from prerevolutionary Russian history: Slavophile (or, to be precise, neo-Slavophile) and Westerner.[2]

[1] *Iz glubiny* (Moscow, 1918). This book was put together on the initiative of Peter Struve, and included many contributors to the well-known symposia, *Problemy idealizma* (1902–3) and *Vekhi* (1909). The opening of the Red Terror in August 1918 prevented its publication. Later on, the stock was distributed by the printers, and at least two copies found their way abroad.

[2] I do not include, of course, theories concerning the Revolution of 1917 as such; nor theories which ascribe communism either to a plot (German, Jewish, etc.) or to historical inevitability.

3

The Slavophile view, whose most articulate exponent was Nicholas Berdiaev, assumed the uniqueness of Russian culture, laying particular stress on the alleged religiosity of the Russian people, or its "soul." "In the Russian soul," Berdiaev wrote, "there is a sort of immensity, a vagueness, a predilection for the infinite, such as is suggested by the great plain of Russia."[3] These spiritual qualities attract the Russian toward all kinds of chiliastic movements. In modern times, Russian religiosity has chosen secular outlets: a transposition has taken place "of religious motives and religious psychology into a non-religious and anti-religious sphere, into the region of social problems, so that the spiritual energy of religion has come to flow into social channels, which thereby took on a religious character."[4] To Berdiaev, the Third International was merely a modern counterpart of the Third Rome, the two ideas sharing a common messianic and chiliastic spirit. Communism to him was, of course, an evil, but not an unmitigated one. The movement performed a moral cathartic function in that it liberated humanity from the illusions of a terrestrial paradise. A similar view was advanced by Fedor Stepun, who considered Bolshevism "a historically comprehensible aberration of the religious energy of the Russian people."[5]

The Westerner argument was most convincingly put forward by Peter Struve. Even in the 1890's, when still a Marxist, Struve felt that Russia needed most of all freedom, for only through freedom could she acquire internal stability and the means to develop her potential. He opposed the patriarchal political and agrarian system of autocratic Russia as preventing the emergence among the people of a sense of civic responsibility, respect for law and property, industriousness and thrift (what the Germans call *Tüchtigkeit*), and all the other qualities which he subsumed under "culture" and considered the cause of Europe's greatness. Struve attached particular importance in this connection to capitalism. Capitalism to him was not merely or even primarily an economic phenomenon. It was a cultural phenomenon performing a necessary civilizing function. Despite his (partly deserved) reputation for intellectual inconstancy, Struve remained loyal to

[3] N. Berdyaev, *The Russian Idea* (New York, 1948), p. 2. Has any theory ever been formulated to ascribe "immensity, vagueness, and a predilection for the infinite" to the inhabitants of the plains of Nebraska?

[4] N. Berdyaev, *The Russian Revolution* (London, 1932), p. 10.

[5] F. Stepun, *The Russian Soul and the Revolution* (New York–London, 1935), p. 9.

this particular view throughout his life. He considered communism to be the consequence of the lack of economic and political freedom in prerevolutionary Russia and therefore of "culture" in the broadest sense of the word. For this he blamed mainly the Imperial government, and secondarily the intelligentsia.[6] The Russian Revolution, as Boris Nolde, a historian of views similar to Struve's, once put it, was the work not of "citizens" but of "subjects."[7]

The two hypotheses rested on different premises. One held that Russia had turned Communist because she was inherently predisposed that way; the other explained communism by Russia's lack of opportunity to reach a sufficient level of westernization.

In the 1920's and 1930's, the Slavophile view enjoyed for good reasons greater acceptance of the two. To Russian émigrés, it held out the hope that the tragedy which they and their country had experienced had not been in vain; odious as it was, communism fulfilled a great historic task—it was Russia's contribution, her "word." To foreigners, it offered an equally comforting message to the effect that the rest of the world enjoyed immunity from communism since it was a peculiarly national, Russian disease. This argument gained added strength from an old predisposition of Westerners to regard Russia as special and exotic. The writings of Berdiaev on this subject, for all their looseness and confusion, enjoyed for a time great popularity and appeared in many translations.

But history has been unkind to the Slavophiles, and since the end of World War II their views have been steadily losing ground. The spread of communism outside Russia—its conquest of China, and penetration into southeast Asia, the Middle East, Africa, and Latin America—inevitably discredited a theory which treated communism as a by-product of Russian national character. In the late 1940's, one could still read prophecies that communism, as a specifically Russian movement, stood no chance in China, being incompatible with Chinese traditions and habits of thought. But

[6] Among Struve's many scattered writings on the subject, the most important is *Razmyshleniia o Russkoi Revoliutsii*, originally delivered as a talk to officers and sympathizers of the Volunteer Army in Rostov on Don (Nov., 1919), and subsequently (1921) published in Sofia as a pamphlet.

[7] B. Nolde, *L'ancien régime et la Revolution russe* (Paris, 1928), p. viii. The views of P. Miliukov also belong to this school, although Miliukov was less philosophical in his interpretations, preferring to deal with concrete historical factors. See his *Rossiia na perelome* (Paris, 1927), I, 1–121.

after the Communists had established firm authority in Peking, Chinese traditions and habits of thought notwithstanding, such arguments lost force. For it would be certainly a hopeless task to seek common elements conducive to communism in the national tradition or national ethos of such different countries as Russia, China, and Cuba.

One consequence of this experience has been a shift of consensus from a neo-Slavophile to a modified Westerner position. The theory which may be said to enjoy widest support at present derives from the concept of "modernization," a rather vague term by which is meant the totality of phenomena attending the transition of a society from a traditional (i.e., predominantly agrarian and rural) to a modern (i.e., industrial and urban) one. Some consider communism to be a natural and perhaps even inevitable by-product of this process of modernization; others treat communism as its aberration and the Communists as "scavengers" who take advantage of the upheavals attending it to seize power. This theory tends to minimize the national factor, and in this respect it differs from the customary Slavophile as well as Westerner views presented in the older Russian works, each of which rested in its own way on a view of Russia's historic past. Insofar, however, as this theory, too, views communism as a product of specific and to some extent predictable historical factors, it may be regarded as a variant of the Westerner approach. Westerners like Struve and Nolde always denied that communism could or would remain confined to Russia.

We may begin our discussion by stating our acceptance of the concept of "modernization" in a qualified form to allow for national divergences. Like any major historic movement—feudalism, absolutism, liberalism, nationalism—"modernization" takes different forms in different countries, and in the long run the differences are as important as the similarities.

It is clear that since the outbreak of the French Revolution, forces have been set in motion which alter radically the quality of social life. A kind of dynamism has appeared which unsettles institutions, habits, and attitudes of considerable antiquity and wide acceptance. The virtue of the term "modernization" lies in the fact that for all its imprecision, it does suggest the dominant direction which modern life takes: against tradition, against everything that exists simply because it is and always has been. "Modernization" involves the application of some objective criteria to question the worth of institutions, customs, or values. No one has stated this outlook more succinctly than the leader of the Russian so-called nihilists, Dmitrii Pisarev, who in the 1860's advised his followers: "What can be broken should be broken; that which withstands the blow is worthwhile; that which shatters into smithereens is rubbish. In any event, strike right and left, for this cannot and will not cause any harm."

The dynamism implicit in "modernization" places society and state under severe strain. It is evident that some countries withstand this strain better than others. Japan industrialized quickly, westernized its population, waged and lost a major war, and yet managed to preserve its social stability and political continuity. Her neighbor, China, did not. The great powers of Western Europe have, on the whole, weathered the great transformations attending "modernization" surprisingly well, and managed in the nineteenth century—the century of revolutionary changes—to avoid revolution. This is even truer of the smaller states of western and northern Europe, such as the Low Countries and Scandinavia. On the other hand, the countries on the southern and eastern peripheries of Europe, such as Spain and Russia, have had a very difficult time of it.

Whether a given country will or will not go Communist (or, for that matter, Fascist) seems ultimately to depend on its capacity to absorb and assimilate the shocks engendered by "modernization" —in other words, on its viability. The critical question, therefore, is: what makes some political organisms more viable than others? Obviously, a question of such scope cannot be dealt with in this paper, and yet it cannot be altogether avoided, since it is central to the topic.

In premodern conditions, the viability of a political organism depended on factors very different from those that count today. What mattered then was the wealth of the reigning house, its dynastic connections, and its ability to administer. The well-ordered traditional state, that of a Louis XIV and a Frederick II, sought to attain stability through the exercise of control from above. How to achieve such control was one of the principal concerns of applied political science in the age of absolutism. This conception of politics, naturally, tended to deprecate the need for society's participation in affairs of state.

The French Revolution radically altered this traditional conception of the strong and efficient state. It did so less by the force of argument than by the argument of force: less by the cogency of its claims on behalf of the individual than by the effectiveness of its armies. Napoleon proved beyond doubt that a citizen army, organized by mass conscription, could beat the best trained professional regiments. The traditional monarchies of Europe were slow to draw the obvious consequences from this experience, but sooner or later learn they did. The reform movement of vom Stein and his Prussian colleagues, designed to bring the citizenry into more active participation in running the country, were particularly efficacious and laid the foundations of subsequent German hegemony on the continent. They were carried out, it must be noted, not as concessions to popular pressures, let alone to the abstract ideals of liberty and equality, but from considerations of power politics pure and simple.

The defeat of Napoleon and the triumph of old-style absolutism dampened for a while European enthusiasm for reform, but not for long. The revolutions of 1830 and especially those of 1848 paved the way, both in England and on much of the continent, for large-scale reform undertakings. The sixty or seventy years preceding the outbreak of World War I witnessed changes which transformed the mass of the Western population from passive subjects into active citizens. These reforms are generally depicted —and rightly—as "liberal" in the sense that they increased the voice of the ordinary man in public affairs. But it would be a mistake to interpret the increased participation of the citizenry in matters previously reserved for the ruling elite as resulting in a diminution in the power of the state. Quite on the contrary: liberal political and social reform everywhere *increased the power of the state both internally and externally;* and indeed, it was often deliberately undertaken for this purpose.

Space limitations prevent us from citing more than two examples illustrating this contention.

First as concerns the effects of political reform, that is, the introduction of representative government and the extension of the franchise. Already Napoleon I showed how the popular vote, skillfully exploited, could enhance the power of the sovereign: how to manipulate referenda to secure majorities of 99.99 per cent (the referendum on the Constitution of the year VIII held in 1799), and to structure representative institutions so that they became useful adjuncts of the administration. Napoleon III demonstrated even more impressively the authoritarian uses of "liberal" processes and institutions by employing all the then known paraphernalia of political liberalism to establish a personal dictatorship. This example was not lost on Bismarck, whose constitutional reforms, notably the extension of the suffrage to all male Germans—on the face of it, a measure so alien to his authoritarian temper—had been coldly calculated to strengthen the hand of the monarchy against its liberal and socialist opponents. (That his calculation did not quite work out is another matter.) Other European countries also gradually extended the franchise for similar reasons: either to forestall rebellion, or to gain mass support against internal and external enemies. The English Reform Bill of 1867 resulted from a political maneuver of the Conservatives to win public support against the Liberals. Wherever it was introduced, democratic franchise greatly enhanced the stability and power of a country, for it made possible the participation of the mass of citizens in activities, such as war, where it had become essential. It is unlikely that England, France, and Germany could have fought the First World War with quite the same suicidal determination had they been directed by governments of the old absolutist kind.

Education provides another example of the stabilizing consequences of liberalization. The notion that the state was obligated to furnish instruction to its citizenry may have been conceived by religious reformers and philosophers, but it was realized by politicians. The public school system, originated in Prussia and France and adopted by the 1870's in some measure by most European countries, owed its spread, at least in part, to an awareness that an educated citizenry was a source of national strength. Public education could and was used not only to provide the skills required by the modern economic and military establishments but also to imbue the citizenry with a sense of patriotism and respect for law. Through it, the modern state has been able to mold minds in a way that would have been entirely beyond the reach of the traditional absolutist state. By means of its school system, France stimulated a sense of national identity among its peasants and helped produce in 1870–71 popular resistance against the German invaders. The Ottoman government failed when it tried at the same time to promote the ideal of an all-embracing "Ottoman" nationality, for its schools were in the hands of religious groups opposed to modern nationalism.

Political reform and public education are only two forms out of the many that the process of political rejuvenation through liberalism took in the leading countries of Western Europe. One may also mention the establishment of universal military service, political parties, social legislation, labor unions, and consumer cooperatives. These, and similar devices, involved to an unprecedented degree the citizen of the advanced Western countries in the total life of society and state. To appreciate how radical these reforms were, one must abandon some rather prevalent conceptions of the pre-nineteenth-century West. As late as the eighteenth century, the vast majority of Westerners led in the rural areas lives of squalor and brutality, and had virtually no contact with the centers of "Western civilization" located in the cities and manors. How bad things were may be gathered from the fact that at the time of the Industrial Revolution hundreds of thousands of Englishmen preferred to move from the country into the city slums to put themselves at the disposal of a ruthless industrial machine. Bad as conditions were in the early industrial towns, they must have been preferable to those in the villages where the majority of the population resided.[8]

It is this silent, unspectacular upheaval, made possible by nineteenth-century wealth and peace, that saved Western Europe from the violent revolutions which Marx and Engels had prophesied in 1847–48. By 1895, even Engels had to concede that such revolutions were unlikely, and that the road to a better social order lay not by way of the barricade but the voting booth.[9] By pulling the citizenry into partnership, the liberalized European state averted revolution: for were he to destroy the state, the citizen of post-1870 Western Europe would in effect destroy himself.

The transformation of subjects into citizens did not altogether bypass Russia. But here (as in other countries outside the industrial West) the task was greater, the means smaller, and the will weaker; so that in 1914–17, when put to the ultimate test, Russia proved unequal to the challenge.

In the course of the sixteenth and seventeenth centuries, the Muscovite state had evolved a system of monarchial absolutism, which, given the responsibilities confronting the country and the

[8] The older view that the mass migration of Englishmen into the cities in the late eighteenth and early nineteenth centuries resulted from the Enclosure Acts is no longer tenable in the light of modern research.

[9] Introduction to Marx's *Class Struggle in France*, in K. Marx and F. Engels' *Sochineniia*, Vol. XVI, Part 2 (Moscow, 1936), pp. 463–86.

paucity of the means at its disposal, worked surprisingly well. The system rested on the principle of universal service. In theory, and to a large extent in practice, every inhabitant of Muscovite Russia, from the highest to the basest, had to serve the state, either directly (the nobility and to some extent the merchants) or indirectly (the peasants). It was not only the peasant who was enserfed in the sixteenth and seventeenth centuries—it was all of society. According to the service system, the rights of Russian subjects were the function of their obligations: rights derived from duties and did not exist outside of them.[10] Naturally, such a system could not tolerate "society" as a counterpart to state; society as a whole and in its parts constituted an element of the state machine. The social reforms of Peter the Great, notably his Table of Ranks, were from this point of view not innovations, but efforts to improve the operations of the traditional Muscovite manner of government.[11]

The main reason for this system of government must be sought probably in the immensity of the task confronting the Russian medieval monarchy. The Muscovite state was the largest empire in the world, the territory over which it claimed sovereignty being several times the size of all Europe. The administration of such a vast area would have taxed the resources of the richest government. Russia's means were quite inadequate for this purpose, the country being short of capital and civil servants. To collect taxes and to raise an army, the monarchy had to have recourse to a variety of drastic measures designed to keep the population in place and mutually responsible for the fulfillment of its state obligations. To make matters worse, the long eastern and southern frontiers of the empire were wide open to incursions of Turkic groups, some of which claimed title as successors to the Mongols and, as such, sovereigns of Russia. The Crimean Tatars time and again invaded the territory of Muscovite Rus', looting and burning it with impunity. Because of this vulnerable frontier, Muscovite Russia may be said to have been in a state of constant siege. The system of state service was evolved to meet these problems. It was generally accepted as indispensable. Even the so-called boyar opposition to autocracy did not clamor for exemption from service but merely for the right to be consulted.

[10] The only significant exception to this rule were monasteries.
[11] "Service" in this context is different from that familiar in feudalism, since it was an instrument of royal absolutism.

The dissolution of this brand of absolutism may be said to have begun with the death of Peter the Great (1725). By this time the eastern and southern frontiers had become stabilized, the Turkic inhabitants no longer offering a serious threat to the modernized Russian army garrisoned in chains of fortress towns. At the same time, the monarchy weakened because Peter had abolished the law of succession, and thereby made the Russian throne a tool of guard regiments and court intriguers, often financed by interested foreign parties. The choice of these groups usually fell on children and women, neither of whom were likely to make full use of the enormous prerogatives vested in the Russian crown. As a result, from 1730 onward, Russian society underwent a process of *"raskreposhchenie"* or "emancipation" from state control. The process proceeded by fits and starts, the monarchy sometimes taking back what it had given, but its general course was unmistakable and irreversible.[12]

The first social group to win emancipation was the gentry. The gentry took advantage of every crisis in St. Petersburg, and especially those attending changes of monarchs, to win easements of their obligations. In 1762 they finally secured complete release from all compulsory service. Catherine the Great, being foreign and lacking a good claim to the crown, had special reason to please this group. Her Charter to the Nobility of 1785, confirming the gentry's freedom from service obligations as well as their ownership of land (originally given them on condition of service) and granting them new privileges (e.g., trial by peers, exemption from corporal punishment, freedom to travel abroad, etc.), created in Russia the first social group with rights independent of duties. The year 1762 and 1785 marked thus the beginning of Russian "society" as a counterpoise to the Russian state.

The process of social emancipation resumed in the 1860's in the guise of the so-called Great Reforms. The defeat in the Crimean War had persuaded the monarchy and some of its conservative officials that a state which accorded society no place was intrinsically weak. The reforms were intended to remedy this situation by creating for private citizens a narrow but well-defined sphere of public activity. In this sense, the reforms are rightly regarded as liberal. Had they been continued, imperial Russia

[12] This subject constitutes the major theme of V. Leontovitsch's provocative *Geschichte des Liberalismus in Russland* (Frankfurt am Main, 1957).

might well have acquired the requisite stability and made a more or less peaceful transition to modern statehood.[13] But the fact is they were not continued. Indeed, the tendency in the last four decades of the nineteenth century was to limit even those rights which had been granted to society. In the end, the reforms of Alexander II did not bring society into partnership with the state or even develop in it a sense of genuine involvement in the state. Among the educated, having at first whetted appetites they produced frustration and resentment, while among the mass of inhabitants they failed to shake the traditional indifference to public affairs.

It is not my intention to belittle the reforms of Alexander II. The reforms fulfilled an important role if only because having done away with serfdom they made possible the emergence of a common Russian citizenship. In the *zemstva* and city councils, as well as in the courts, the ordinary citizen for the first time in Russian history received an opportunity of working for his country's benefit: earlier, the very demand for such an opportunity had been considered seditious. But surely the reforms did not go far enough to have been of significant political benefit.

The liberation of the serfs in 1861 completed the process of *raskreposhchenie* of society begun ninety-nine years earlier with the gentry. An act of bold statesmanship, it contained, however, safeguards which vitiated its political value. The worst of these was the subordination of the peasant to the commune. The economic drawbacks of communal landholding are too familiar to require elaboration. But the political effects of this measure were no less debilitating. By denying the peasant the opportunity to own his land, the government deprived him also of the best school of political education. For the average citizen everywhere, the management of property, especially real estate, represents the main and sometimes only exercise in practical politics. It brings him in direct contact with legislatures and courts, local as well as central, and develops in him a sense of political pragmatism: a

[13] It may be argued, of course, that the Hapsburg Empire did undergo liberalization in the second half of the nineteenth century, and yet it too in the end collapsed. But the Hapsburg Empire was intrinsically weaker than the Russian Empire because of the antagonisms among its nationalities. Russia's nationality problem was much less critical because the Great Russians constituted some 45 per cent of the population, and with the kindred Ukrainians and Belorussians, 65 per cent, whereas in the Austro-Hungarian Empire, the Germans constituted only 24 per cent. Moreover, Austria lost the war.

property owner may not like the authorities who tax him but he cannot help being concerned with their activities. Furthermore, by being tied to the commune, the peasant remained in an inferior social condition: he was still a peasant rather than a Russian. When the country entered World War I, a large proportion of its rural population lacked an elementary sense of citizenship or of national identity. Some peasants even wondered in August 1914 whether the declaration of war affected their own villages. The full consequences of this immaturity became apparent only after two and a half years of war when military discipline dissolved. At that time, Lenin, Trotsky, and Bolshevik agitators could persuade the peasant to desert the ranks and head back for the village, whereas those who appealed to his sense of patriotism met with little success.

The organs of self-rule, the *zemstva* and city councils established in 1864, also proved inadequate to the task. These institutions had been introduced to secure society's assistance in carrying out responsibilities of local government for which St. Petersburg lacked the means. Although their competence was restricted to nonpolitical concerns, they might still have performed an important political function had they not been hamstrung in every possible way both in their original constitution and in subsequent performance. The mere fact that the leaders of the *zemstva* and city councils were forbidden to organize nationally indicated the mistrust the authorities felt toward them. In the 1880's and 1890's their sphere of competence, narrow to begin with, was further limited by the bureaucracy. The imperial government, instead of availing itself of the good will available in the provinces to bolster its position, constantly antagonized the organs of self-rule, and in the end transformed them into centers of resistance. It is only thanks to the innate moderation of the men who ran these institutions that the friction between the organs of self-rule and the bureaucracy did not break out in the open before 1904.

Even the judiciary reform, by all accounts the best of the reforms of Alexander II, was not allowed to become an effective instrument of civic education. Having tasted defeat before jury courts the government transferred trials involving the broad category of political crimes to the jurisdiction of administrative courts. As a result, Russian society was excluded from participating in judiciary proceedings involving the security of the state.

Even more pernicious from this point of view was the practice introduced in 1892 of placing vast areas of the country under martial law as a means of suspending the normal operation of the courts.[14]

But the worst sin of the government lay in its adamant refusal to concede the country a constitution and a parliament. Its position on this issue was quite untenable. By the end of the nineteenth century all the European countries, including conservative Germany and Austria, operated under constitutional and parliamentary regimes. Even the Ottoman Empire, that synonym for backwardness and despotism, had made an attempt in this direction in 1876—a whole thirty years before Russia! The Russian government's commitment to autocratic monarchy went so far that it rejected out of hand even the innocuous Slavophile proposals for a consultative assembly to inform the tsar of the wishes of the "land." By this policy, the government punished itself much more than society. From 1874 on, it came under constant attack from a small but determined group of revolutionaries. Had Russia possessed a parliament of some kind, the government would have certainly enjoyed its support in the struggle against sedition of the overwhelming majority of the deputies. Instead, the government had to fight the revolution alone and unaided. Even if the public rejected the methods and aims of the revolutionaries, it did not feel affected, and perhaps derived some satisfaction from the discomfiture of the authorities.

All the political flaws of the Great Reforms—those of commission no less than those of omission—derived ultimately from a deep-seated mistrust of the population. Centuries of treating the country as a "command" and its inhabitants as servitors had accustomed the government to regard any sign of vitality on the part of its subjects as a threat to its existence. It was convinced the emancipated peasants would turn into bandits unless tied to the commune, that the *zemstva* and city councils would encroach on its sovereign authority unless strictly controlled, that juries would always decide in favor of the defendants, and that parliament would stand in permanent opposition. The government sensed the need for society's support, but did not really dare to

[14] See Marc Szeftel, "Personal Inviolability in the Legislation of the Russian Absolute Monarchy," *American Slavic and East European Review*, Feb., 1958, pp. 1–24.

invite it. The spectacle of social and political conflict in Western Europe reinforced this negative attitude.

The necessity of bringing the Russian state and society together is apparent not only by hindsight. In the second half of the nineteenth century a number of prominent Russian publicists realized it and constantly clamored for it. Among them was Iurii Samarin, a leading Slavophile, who pleaded for closer ties between the monarchy and the mass of the population, especially the peasantry. His philosophy of "revolutionary conservatism," derived in large measure from the German State Socialists, called for an authoritarian but dynamic monarchy committed to social reform. Another was Boris Chicherin. As a Right Hegelian, Chicherin believed in the strong state; but he also felt that a state could not be strong when it encroached upon spheres of activity best left to society and the individual citizen. But neither Samarin nor Chicherin was listened to. The former died in emigration an embittered man, while Chicherin suffered oblivion in his own lifetime (as well as since), being rejected by the conservatives for wanting to weaken the state, and by the liberals for wanting to strengthen it.

Had the imperial regime followed Leont'ev's advice and "frozen" itself, it might have succeeded for a long time with this policy. But the government felt itself committed to westernization, and allowed dynamic "modernizing" forces to penetrate and undermine its authority. Aspiring to the status of a major world power, it reformed its army, introduced public education, constructed railroads, and did many other things incompatible with its rigid and conservative political philosophy. It both westernized the country and refused to let westernization take its course.

The inconsistency of the imperial policy appeared most vividly in the realm of cultural policy. The government never made a serious effort to prevent the influx into Russia of Western ideas, including those of an unmistakably radical tendency. (It is common knowledge, for example, that the translation of Marx's *Capital* appeared in Russia with the imprimatur of the censorship, but it is perhaps less known that both the first [1872] and the second [1885] volumes were printed in the typography of the Imperial Ministry of Transport.) Utilitarianism, positivism, anarchism, socialism, social Darwinism, and other ideologies were freely allowed to penetrate into Russia; and being in stark contrast to the official policy of the regime, inevitably widened the cleavage between state and society.[15] On the one hand stood the regime with its officialdom, on the other that amorphous body of public-minded citizens known as the intelligentsia. The regime made no attempt to conciliate the intelligentsia by attracting it into positions of responsibility. Deprived of a chance to acquire a sense of political realism, the intelligentsia tended to become more and more estranged, and to view its relationship to the government as one of irreconcilable hostility. The irresponsibility of the educated combined with the anarchism of the uneducated created an obvious threat to national survival—a fact noted by the contributors to the celebrated symposium *Vekhi* in 1909.

The advent of industrialization compounded the problems created by the estrangement of the peasantry and the intelligentsia. In a single decade—1890–1900—the numbers of Russian industrial workers doubled. These workers were not the grey mass they are often assumed to be. In 1897, 58 per cent of Russian industrial workers could read; among the skilled workers, such as the St. Petersburg metallurgists, the percentage of literates reached 73 per cent.[16] (It may be noted that the ratio of literates among recruits entering the Russian army in 1913 exceeded 70 per cent.) These workers, especially the first generation, do not seem to have been interested in politics of any sort, let alone in revolution. But the restrictions under which they lived drove them inexorably into opposition. They were forbidden to organize trade unions or even to form circles for mutual assistance and self-education. By trying to keep workers in a condition similar to that of the peasants, the government in effect opened the doors of factories to socialists. Much as the workers distrusted the socialists, they had no other allies in their struggle for better wages and working conditions, and secondary education. Had Russian labor been given an opportunity to develop in the open, there is every reason to expect that it would have evolved in as moderate a fashion as its counterparts in England or Germany. The enor-

[15] The frontiers of imperial Russia were open to travel, and many Russians took advantage of this fact to make extensive trips in foreign countries. In one decade (1872–81) three million Russian citizens went abroad; in the year 1900, 200,000 Russians traveled outside their country for an average of eighty days. See B. Ischchanian, *Die ausländischen Elemente in der russischen Volkswirtschaft* (Berlin, 1913), p. 5n. I am indebted to Mr. Robert C. Williams for calling my attention to this source.

[16] A. G. Rashin, *Formirovanie rabochego klassa Rossii* (Moscow, 1958), pp. 584, 591.

mous success of the police-sponsored labor unions (*zubatov-shchina*) provides adequate proof of the essentially pacific, apolitical trend of Russian labor.

We could compound such illustrations showing the conflict between the government's principles and attitudes on the one hand, and the practical consequences of its commitment to westernization on the other. They stood behind the tug-of-war between the regime and all elements of society that erupted after 1900 and culminated in the Revolution of 1905.

The Revolution of 1905 appeared to the government as a calamity and the end of Russia; but it could have well marked the salvation of the imperial government, as the revolutions of 1848 had saved Europe in the long run from greater upheavals. The Constitution of 1906, given as a concession to avoid the complete breakdown of authority, was a workable arrangement. For all its limitations, it was not a "sham," as has been claimed.[17] It gave society, through its elected representatives, a voice in domestic legislation, as well as a forum from which the government and its officials could be criticized without fear of reprisals. The Duma had no precedent in the Russian past, but the country took to it with enthusiasm. By giving in the first election in its history a majority to Constitutional-Democrats, the party of constitutional action *par excellence,* it demonstrated its acceptance of the system.

But the imperial government and the bureaucracy treated the Duma from the beginning as an affront, a living reminder of its humiliation in October 1905. The premature dissolution of the first two Dumas, even if permitted by the fundamental laws, was a display of contempt for the nation's representatives. Even more so was the unconstitutional reform of the electoral law carried out in 1907 to assure the preponderance of conservative deputies. Such actions encouraged extreme groups, especially on the left, who from the start had maintained that the constitution was a fraud.

Already in 1906, when the government's bad faith became apparent, farsighted Russians predicted dire consequences. The following passage, written by Struve in the spring of 1906, bears eloquent testimony of this fear:

[17] Max Weber, *Russlands Übergang zum Scheinkonstitutionalismus, Beilage, Archiv für Sozialwissenschaft und Sozialpolitik,* Vol. XXIII, No. 1 (1906).

As before, the leading, most powerful, and immense revolutionary force is the government itself. In its stubborn refusal to concede authority to the only element still capable of reviving the country and establishing in it a stable order, the government broadcasts in the country sparks of indignation, decomposition, and anarchy. These people do not know the most important thing about the art of politics —to make decisions in time and with bold and direct *actions* to anticipate and regulate *events*. The leading party in the Duma [i.e., the Constitutional Democrats] still enjoys enough moral and political respect in the country to be able to furnish authority; it still—and this is important—believes in itself. Ignoring this unique constructive power in the country, the government aggravates anarchy, and in this anarchy may exhaust itself, burn out and perish that force which still has the capacity to organize the country and save the monarchy.

The Constitutional Democratic Party may yet suffer in the course of the Russian Revolution the fate of the other, more moderate movement [i.e., landed conservatives]. Now it is too late to call to power Shipov. On January 9, 1905 it was still possible. Similarly, the moment has not yet come, but it may, or, more precisely, must come when it will be too late to call to power [the Constitutional-Democrats] Muromtsev, Petrunkevich, and Miliukov, when they, too, will be powerless to keep the stream of the revolution within the confines of normal development, when the future waves of an irrepressible anger of the masses, accumulated over the centuries, boiling and foaming, will inundate the ancient structures of the Russian monarchy.

There is one additional dangerous symptom. Earlier, there had been blind faith in the political omnipotence of the Tsar; he could do anything. But this faith, if not entirely calm, was at least passive. It helped the people not to move mountains, but patiently to bear the misery of political and social oppression.

It was a conservative faith and on it rested immovable autocratic Russia. Today, this passive, blind faith has been extinguished in the soul of the people; it has been replaced by another faith, also blind, but active. The people still believe in political miracles, but they do so not with the quiet, passive faith of a child, but with the active, violent faith of a youth, inflamed by passion. Yesterday, this youth believed, and perhaps even today he still believes, that the Duma can do everything; tomorrow, he will believe that he himself, or his creation, the Constituent Assembly, will accomplish miracles. One may contemptuously shrug one's shoulders at such a simple faith in the miraculous force of political institutions; one can and even must refute and fight it; but one cannot fail to see in it a mighty destructive force capable of sweeping everything from its path. This destructive force can be fought only through the most rapid possible transition

to political forms capable of giving the people in the shortest time
the maximum of political education and self-education.[18]

If, despite this inherent weakness, Russia carried on the war as
long as it did, the reason must be sought in the conciliatory
attitude of the Duma and moderate public leaders. Carried away
by patriotic zeal, they buried their disagreements with the imperial government, and threw their prestige behind it. The committees formed by the Duma in 1914–15 to organize production
and supply proved essential to the war effort. Yet even now, in the
midst of the war which had exposed the woeful inadequacy of its
means, the government chose to snub the elected representatives
of its citizenry. When, in the autumn of 1915, it prorogued the
Duma, it sealed its own fate. The abdication of Nicholas II a year
and a half later was, from the perspective of history, an inevitable
consequence of the government's refusal to take the Duma into
partnership in the conduct of war.

The tsar's abdication threw Russia into anarchy. Deprived of
direction from above, the bureaucratic apparatus simply dissolved; there was no one to replace it, because the country had
not been permitted to develop institutions capable of assuming
responsibility for its administration in time of need. The peasantry, in and out of uniform, now gave vent to all its suppressed
resentments. Its destructive fury in 1917–18 was directed not so
much against the imperial regime, nobility, or church, as against
all that had been created in Russia since the early eighteenth
century: cities, industry, learning, manners—in a word, all that
Western "culture" they had not been able to share. Memoirs of
participants in the Revolution abound in incidents illustrating this
mood. In late 1917, General Denikin, traveling in disguise to the
Don to join the Volunteer Army, was astonished and terrified
by it:

First of all [I noticed] everywhere a flood of boundless hatred for people as well as ideas; for everything that was socially and intellectually
above the mob, that carried the smallest trace of prosperity, even for
inanimate objects that betokened some level of culture alien or inac-
cessible to the mob. In this feeling one could discern direct anger accumulated over the centuries, brutalization caused by three years of
war, and hysteria stimulated by revolutionary leaders . . . The psy-

[18] P. Struve, "Skazka po belogo bychka," *Svoboda i kul 'tura*, No. 8, May
31, 1906, pp. 606–7.

chology of the mob gave no indication of striving to rise to a higher level of life; dominant was one desire: to grab or destroy.[19]

Awareness of this temper had a very discouraging effect on all those interested in re-establishing law and order. Had the mass revolt aspired to concrete aims, it might have been satisfied and soon stilled. But there was something elemental in this anti-Western, anti-modern explosion, and many felt that it had to spend itself before order could be reimposed.

There were in Russia in 1917–20 three potential contenders for power: the liberals (among them, moderate conservatives and socialists), the generals, and the Jacobin radicals. The *ancien régime*, it may be noted, never offered the slightest threat of a restoration. In 1917, its innumerable Grand Dukes simply retired from public life to their estates or to the West, and consistently spurned invitations to join the anti-Bolshevik struggle. The unconcern of the members of the imperial family for the fate of Russia is one of the more striking features of the Revolution.

The liberals tried to hold the authority which had devolved upon them with the abdication of the tsar, and failed. The story of the Provisional Government is familiar and requires no recapitulation. Ultimately, the liberals may be said to have lost out because they lacked the will to power: precisely because they wanted to hold power, not to exercise it. Russian liberals, like their counterparts in other authoritarian states, had been so accustomed to fighting the government that they failed to develop the political instincts necessary to run a country. The collapse of Russian liberalism in 1917 was not so different from that of German liberalism in the 1920's, or Spanish liberalism in the 1930's. Liberalism, as a theory of freedom, by its very nature operates best within a stable political environment; it is not well suited to the task of establishing political stability.

The generals seemed to have a better chance. Indeed, from the summer of 1917 onward, the country expected a "Bonapartist" coup. Russian intellectuals liked to believe in the "inexorable laws of history," and, being well versed in the story of the French Revolution, looked for a repetition of the 18th Brumaire. This historical miscalculation accounted in large measure for Kerensky's worst error: the alliance in late summer 1917 with the radicals against the so-called "danger from the right." But the anticipated coup never came (the Kornilov incident hardly de-

[19] A. Denikin, *Ocherki russkoi smuty* (Paris, 1922), II, 147–48.

serves the name), and Bonapartism proved to have been largely an imaginary threat. The Russian generals turned out to be remarkably apolitical. The leaders of the White Armies displayed neither political acumen nor interest, being content to leave politics to the casual assortment of intellectuals, mostly liberal or liberal-socialist, who had gathered around them. Had there been an effective Russian conservative movement, the generals undoubtedly would have rallied behind it. They had neither the ability nor the ambition to create such a movement themselves.[20]

There is another factor to keep in mind in connection with the army. In dealing with the Russian Revolution, one concentrates so heavily on its internal aspects that one forgets the preoccupation of the time with war. The officers were concerned not with Russia's political regime as such, but with fighting the Germans, Austrians, and Turks. When they first organized the Volunteer Army, it was with the intention of reactivating the front. (Later on, they joined the Red Army in droves for similar patriotic reasons to expel the Poles.) Their anti-German feeling was very strong, one may almost say obsessive. Now, in 1918, the Germans were the only force capable of dislodging the Bolsheviks. They were at the point of doing so (June–July, 1918) and even put out various feelers to army leaders and right-wing politicians. But these feelers were rejected out of hand, and the Germans had no choice but to continue backing, militarily and financially, the Bolshevik government in which they were losing confidence. The anti-German nationalism of the army at a time when alliance with the Germans offered the only hope of overthrowing the Soviet government was no mean factor in the ultimate outcome of the Revolution.

When we survey the political situation in 1917 and 1918, we find no one in Russia except Lenin willing to assume political responsibility. The moderates reigned but did not rule, preferring to entrust all decisions to a future Constituent Assembly. The generals wanted to continue the war at all costs, and left politics to the politicians. The imperial family withdrew, turning its back on Russia. The question was not so much who would succeed in the struggle for power, as who would engage in it—who would assume the authority that lay unclaimed and unwanted.[21] The

---

[20] It would be interesting to find what factors in the social background or professional training of Russian generals accounted for their disinterest in politics.
[21] The absence of any formal "power seizure" in October 1917 is par-

celebrated incident in the early summer of 1917 when Lenin, hearing an orator assert that no party in Russia wanted to assume responsibility, shouted, "There is such a party!", illustrates better than any generalization the political vacuum of the time.

It is tempting to discover in Lenin deep Russian traits, but close analysis of his actions and thoughts reveals little that can be described as typically Russian. He had undoubtedly learned a great deal from the terrorists of the *Narodnaia volia,* and his loathing of compromise reveals a characteristic trait of the Russian intelligentsia. But he lacked the really fundamental qualities of a Russian *intelligent:* love for the "people," respect for learning (he detested "professors" most of all), belief in progress, kindness and generosity. His temperament and outlook had in them more of Wilhelmian Germany than imperial Russia. Of course, one can find in Russian revolutionary history individual forerunners of Lenin; but there are even more of them in the revolutionary history of nineteenth-century France.

The question of the relationship of communism to Russian history contains really two questions: why did the imperial state collapse? and, why did the successor state assume the form that it did? To the first question one may formulate the following answer: The imperial government, having initiated for reasons of power and prestige technical, economic, and educational modernization, refused to soften the resultant shocks by allowing corresponding modernization of society and the political apparatus. To the second question it may be replied that when the imperial government collapsed, anarchy was inevitable, because the state had no political underpinnings to support it once the monarchy was gone; and that the only way out of anarchy in Russia, as elsewhere, was an authoritarian regime. The authoritarian regime inevitably, unconsciously slipped back into the habits and institutions which had prevailed in Muscovite Russia, its only available model. It reharnessed society back into the service of the state. Communism undid two centuries of slow emergence of Russian society as a counterpoise to the government. It is in this sense, it seems to me, and only in this sense that one can speak of the historic roots of Russian communism.

ticularly stressed in S. Melgunov's excellent but paradoxically titled monograph, *Kak Bol'sheviki zakhvatili vlast'* ("How the Bolsheviks Seized Power"; Paris, 1953).

Communism and Chinese History

GEORGE E. TAYLOR

I

COMMUNIST writers have explained the failure of the dialectical historical process to work itself out in the industrial countries by saying that the capitalist chain broke at its weakest link—imperial Russia. But once the Russian base had been established, communism spread to the East rather than to the West. The self-appointed leaders of the European proletariat have marched steadily backwards into Asia bringing with them many of the worst features of European industrialism and most of those of oriental despotism. The student of history will recall other doctrines which have died in the land of their birth and flourished elsewhere. In this case he may be less interested in making a debating point than in isolating the reasons why the militant wing of European socialism was more successful outside Europe than within it.

Putting the matter in terms of modern social science, Mr. Pipes has argued that communism in Russia was a product not of the positive but of the negative factors in Russian history, not of what Russia had experienced but of what she had failed to experience. The main thrust of Mr. Pipes' paper is that communism arose in Russia as an aftermath of modernization and that the Bolsheviks succeeded mainly because state and society were not integrated into an organic and viable whole. Political and social modernization had not kept up with the efforts of the imperial government to strengthen itself; the "imperial government refused to complete the task." In this view the history of modern Russia is the story of two centuries of a slow and partial emergence of Russian society as a counterpoise to the state. With the hegemony of communism this work has been undone. The state once more is stronger than society. This view takes account of the fact that communism has spread into countries outside Russia, thus proving that it is not a by-product of the Russian national character, as the Slavophiles have held. It leans more to a "modified Westerner position." Mr. Pipes, in essence, explains the expansion of communism outside the boundaries of Russia by accepting the concept of "modernization" in a qualified form to allow for national divergences, an event that takes different forms in different countries. At the same time he concludes that it would be a hopeless task "to seek common elements conducive to communism in the national tradition or national ethos of such different countries as Russia, China, and Cuba." The main argument is that under the pressures of war the structure of the state broke down, that the state was authoritarian in character and therefore could hardly give birth to anything different. In other words, Pipes is arguing that Russia was the weakest link in the chain of modern-style representative governments rather than in the chain of capitalism.

The point is well taken. It draws our attention to political institutions and therefore to the specific character of the Russian state. It was the agrarian system that gave to the Russian economic, social, and political order its distinctive characteristics and differentiated it from the rest of Europe. In spite of the considerable growth of the Russian economy during the period between 1900 and 1917, the process still had not gone far enough to eat into the agrarian order—which is another way of stating Mr. Pipes' argument that modernization had been frustrated.

The Bolsheviks themselves, in their own tortuous fashion, discussed this aspect of the problem as early as the Stockholm Congress of the Russian Social Democratic Party in 1906. Plekhanov attacked Lenin's proposal to nationalize the land as one that would leave untouched an old semi-Asiatic order and thus make possible the restoration of what Lenin himself referred to as the Asiatic mode of production or even a return to the *aziatchina*. Plekhanov warned against "Russian Wang An-shih's" (the Chinese statesman Wang An-shih of the eleventh century proposed making the state the owner of all land, and the state officials the managers of all production). "We want no *kitaishchina*—no Chinese system." One answer, said Lenin, was to have the support of the socialist revolution in the West, for this would be an "absolute guarantee" against an Asiatic restoration. The sophistries of Plekhanov and of Lenin are less important than the fact that the Bolsheviks were aware of the fantastic difficulties in the way of a new kind of state taking over the job of controlling millions of peasants as if they were workers. The Russian peasant was seen as a major problem for a socialist state.

It is idle to speculate on what might have happened if the Communist revolution had first succeeded in the West, but it is useful to keep in mind that the specific conditions in Russia are not sufficient in themselves to explain the rise of communism in that country. The socialist movement, of which the Bolshevik wing was only one part, was European in origin and in action, as it continues to be to this very day. The impact of European socialism on the non-Western world has indeed continued to flow in two main streams, one by way of the Bolshevik revolution and the Soviet state system, and the other by way of the force of ideas and example in western Europe and for that matter the United States. European socialist ideas can be traced in the thinking of Sun Yat-sen long before the Bolshevik revolution. They entered the stream of Japanese political thinking soon after the middle of the nineteenth century.

The record would seem to suggest that as practically every country in the world was exposed to socialist ideas over the last century, the Communist deviant of European socialism has succeeded where socialist intellectual preparation was combined with the decay of a more or less despotic system of government and power was there for the taking. In the cases of both China and Russia a disastrous war was also a common element at the time when the Communists took control of the state. Although the break-through came first in Russia, there is a very real sense in which the Russian and Chinese revolutionary movements were from the first a part of the same sweep of world revolution—both were part of a world movement which was seeking to capture the heartlands of capitalism in western Europe. The Chinese Communist Party was organized as early as 1921, before the Bolshevik efforts to stimulate violent revolution in the West finally failed in Germany in 1923. Within a year Soviet advisers and materials were pouring into Canton in the expectation of capturing the leadership of the Chinese Nationalist movement and starting the flames of anticolonial war all over Asia. It was only after the failure of the attempt to envelop Europe from the colonial East that the Communist parties of China and Russia settled down to the tasks of capturing or consolidating power within their own countries. The Bolsheviks, who had hoped to have the weight of the European proletariat behind them in order to handle the Russian agrarian problem, were now committed to help solve the even more difficult one of China. The ratio of proletariat to peasants had changed beyond recognition.

It is not surprising that the Bolsheviks almost destroyed the chances for communism in China at a time when there was power for the taking and the intellectual preparation was favorable. When the Bolshevik revolution took place, Sun had already achieved his first objective of getting rid of the Manchus (in 1911), but he did not control the new republic. The Soviet Union played on Sun Yat-sen's socialist leanings and his anti-imperialist tendencies, and persuaded him that it wished to help carry out his national revolution. The Chinese Communist Party became a member of the Communist International in the summer of 1922, half a year after the first Congress of the Toilers of the East, at which Comintern representatives had discussed the idea of a national front with Chinese Nationalists and Communists. The National United Front was not an alliance of two parties. Dr. Sun agreed that Communists should join the Kuomintang as individuals, which they did and then proceeded to infiltrate mass organizations and dominate propaganda. Under close Moscow supervision the Chinese Communists worked with the left-wing elements in the KMT and attempted to polarize that party. It is quite clear that the Communists were working systematically to gain control of the Chinese Nationalist movement. This they failed to do. The first united front collapsed in the summer of 1927; the Communists were suppressed in the cities but survived in some of the more out-of-the-way parts of the countryside. During the next few years the Nationalists crushed the Kiangsi Soviet and drove the Communists into the northwest (the Long March). In 1935 for reasons of international politics the Soviet Communist Party advised the formation of a second united front. The decision was taken at the Seventh World Congress in Moscow in July–August, 1935, and in the spring of 1936 Mao Tse-tung, who by now was in control of the Chinese Communist movement, offered to cooperate with Chiang Kai-shek on condition that he oppose Japan. The story after 1945 is well known and need not be repeated. The Chinese Communist movement had been saved from defeat by the Japanese war, which smashed the social and economic basis of the National Government and polarized the KMT into the extreme right and the extreme left.

The significant part of the story is why the Soviets failed in China. Stalin applied in China a strategy that Lenin had laid down at the Second Congress of the Comintern in 1920 when he spoke on the National and Colonial Question. Lenin insisted that "the proletariat of the advanced countries can and must assist the backward toiling masses, and that the development of the backward countries can emerge from its present stage when the victorious proletariat of the Soviet republics stretches out a helping hand to these masses." The Soviet Union therefore was to provide the one essential condition for the success of Communists in colonial and backward countries, to wit, the support of the Soviet Union. Lenin even thought that with this assistance the backward countries could avoid the capitalist stage of development and move directly on toward socialism and communism. The character of the help that the Soviet Union should give to national and colonial liberation movements would depend upon the development of the proletariat and other classes in such countries. In the case of China, which was declared to be feudal and semi-colonial, Stalin's strategy was to cooperate with the national bourgeoisie but after squeezing the bourgeois lemon dry to throw it away. The strategy failed because the analysis was incorrect. The KMT leaders, especially the military, were far from being bourgeois, and they had little sympathy with the preparations for agrarian revolt and workers' unions. The essential condition—the assistance of the Soviet Union—had been provided and had failed abysmally. By 1935 the Chinese Communists were in a backwater of Chinese life, militarily contained and ready to be annihilated. But there was a hard core Communist Party and a small agrarian base and a small army. The Sino-Japanese War provided the essential precondition for the rise of Chinese communism by destroying, to all intents and purposes, the effectiveness of the Nationalist regime. War destroyed the slender but promising base for modernization.

Up to 1935 the story of China's modern development is not one of a predestined move toward communism. On the contrary. There is no one term that can be used to identify China in 1935, but it was far from being totalitarian. The government was committed to democratic and parliamentary development; it was strongly influenced by the military, but there were other power centers. The progress made in less than ten years in building up the institutions of a modern state was nothing short of phenomenal. Important steps had been taken toward recovering China's full administrative and territorial integrity. There most certainly existed the possibility of the growth of representative institutions and the peaceful transfer of power. It was a regime much more enlightened and self-confident than that of Nicholas II. It was ready to pay most of the price of modernization. China apparently was not preconditioned for communism.

II

Yet we still have to explain why it was possible for Mao Tse-tung, in spite of the ghastly mistakes and defeats of the twenties and the thirties, to keep a nucleus of dedicated followers together and when the balance of power shifted in 1944–45 to carry on to victory. The main reason was that the destruction brought about by the Sino-Japanese War broke the backbone of the Kuomintang and the National Government. The war put the clock back twenty years; the Communists were given a second chance. If it had been only the material achievements of the Nationalists which had been destroyed, these could have been rebuilt. The more serious aspect of the matter is that the doctrines, the morale, and the organization of the Nationalists were not equal to the postwar situation. There must have been latent attitudes and ideas which were in retreat during the rise of the Nationalists but which became important again when they were faced with the ruined country of 1945. What were these ideas and attitudes? Some are quite clear. One has an echo in Mr. Pipes' paper. That is the general lack of expectation on the part of the peasantry and even of the intellectuals that they could participate in government. Before the war the intellectuals, especially the Western-trained ones, were slowly reacquiring an influence in government to which they felt they were by right entitled. By the end of the war they were dependent upon the military, and the gap between them and the military widened to such an extent that it was unbridgeable. The separation of military and civil functions was not characteristic of traditional China; it was rather a phenomenon of China in transition. Before the war there was a division of powers or at least a division of labor between civil and military, but after the war the two groups were in uneasy relationship because the civil authority had lost its power base. The Communists had no such problem, for politics was always in control, as it was in imperial China. They may therefore have had more of an appeal to the nostalgic memories of the intellectuals than appeared on the surface, especially after the war, when the future for the intellectual seemed so bleak.

The Communists established their rule on the battlefield through military conquest. But there is no doubt that the intellectual climate after the war was a strategic factor of utmost importance to them. How did it come about? Hellmut Wilhelm has pointed out that we have to answer the question of what made mature and responsible scholars prepare the minds of youth for vociferous sloganizing and for the beliefs and attitudes which proved to be so helpful to the Communists. With the help of a construct based on concepts borrowed from Carl Jung and Ernst Neumann and following largely the theory of Ira Progoff's *The Dynamics of Hope and the Image of Utopia,* Wilhelm traces the intellectual processes leading to the normative, especially utopian, systems of thought that he thinks characterize the intellectual climate of the time.

According to Wilhelm the first stage in the intellectual process is that of daydreaming, induced by an urge to escape from a prevailing social or intellectual situation. The daydreaming conjures up the image of a desired (ideal) situation. Then comes a breaking point, when it is realized that this intellectual process is in reality meaningless. This leads to the second stage of soul-searching, an inward-directed movement in which the ideal images are confronted with archetypal, primordial images. This descent into the stockades of the soul conforms in itself to an archetypal situation, the descent into hell, with all the attending anxieties and agonies. Symptomatically, this process has all the appearances of an exercise in schizophrenia, but the process should not be considered pathological. It is necessary, and if uninterrupted, a normal stage. Validated by the process described, the utopian ideals become imbued with the dynamics of hope and thus acquire a new impetus.

Mr. Wilhelm applies this construct to the development of Chinese thought in late imperial and early republican times. He puts particular emphasis on Confucian thought, since many of the tenets of Confucianism, here taken as a system or systems of

philosophy, are deliberately normative, if not downright utopian.
Both the orthodox and heterodox trends in Confucianism share
the characteristics of utopianism, but in different ways.

To understand the orthodox trend, it is necessary to go back to
the beginning of the nineteenth century. At this time the discrepancy between normative, canonical values and the actual
situation was so great that the values were almost meaningless.
T'ang Chien was the prime representative of a movement to
revalidate the canonical values. T'ang, who was the revered
teacher of almost all the important thinkers of nineteenth-century
China, initiated this movement by reviving the concept of self-
cultivation, a concept which had served a similar purpose at other
times, especially after the introduction of neo-Confucianism of
the Ch'eng I school. As the process of self-exploration and searching self-criticism went into ever deepening layers of the self,
canonical reverence was reduced to stark fear. At this point in the
second stage of the process, at the moment of utter anguish,
historical developments cut off the process before the third stage
of creative confrontation had been consummated. The symptoms
of schizophrenia now took on a pathological character. The
intellectual challenge of the day could thus no longer be met by
the naive mind of unaffected traditionalism or by a mind newly
invigorated through the process of self-realization. The challenges
had to be met instead on an *ad hoc* basis, that is to say, by reflexes
rather than responses.

The heterodox trend worked itself out in an entirely different
manner. Heterodoxy, usually identified in Ch'ing time with the
school of Han learning, was free to move in intellectual areas
unrestricted by the responsibilities of the orthodox. The process of
reasoning was unfettered by the dictates of what was potentially
or existentially realistic; the mind was not exposed to the pressures that come from exploring its contents and its limits. The
school of Han learning has recently been rather heavily taken to
task for its nihilistic character. In view of its nineteenth-century
epigones and the fundamental Confucian vocation of state service, this judgment has some validity. At the same time, however,
Han learning had one function in the nineteenth century which
was of major practical importance. It trained the Chinese mind
along more rational lines. When the Han and the Sung schools,
under the pressure of outside challenges, came together for joint

action, the rational character of the reflexes was the contribution of the Han school.

Without going into the different phases and aspects that these ever more entangled reflexes went through as ever more layers of challenging thought were gradually unfolded in the Chinese mind, we should note two related phenomena that emerged from this process. One was the sham flower of nationalism which was coerced into blooming by the pressure of defensive reflexes which perverted the traditional Chinese attitude of patriotism into a combative and destructive weapon. The other was the frantic search for a formula which would leave a section at least of age-old Chinese prerogatives uncorrupted and uncorruptible. There was first the priority formula which tried to show that even in the field of science and technology the basic principles were known and applied by the Chinese first and that learning from the Westerners in these fields would be equivalent to a return to long-practiced lores of old. Then there was the substance and function formula which would concede to the Westerners pre-eminence in functionally useful knowledge, adoption of which, however, would not touch China's superiority in substantive and essential matters. And there was finally the most widespread and most commonly adopted formula which would see in the West a strictly material culture as opposed to the spiritual East. This formula was accepted as a matter of self-defense, forcibly, and almost against better insight.

The fallacy of all these formulas was eventually realized, a realization which found its most dramatic expression in the May Fourth Movement. This realization led to the conclusion that to live in the modern world meant to accept it wholeheartedly and without any mental reservations. Where, however, was the model of modernity to be found by which one had to recast himself if not in the West? Circumstances had denied China the time to develop her own modern period in her own terms. The only available model of modernity was thus the West, or rather, the then prevailing image of the West. And now it was that the fateful formulas came home to roost. The prevailing and generally accepted image of the West was that of the material West which denied room to spiritual values. This West became the mold then for the "modern" Chinese mind, embraced as a powerful if unvalidated utopia—the dynamic West and, ominously, the materialistic West. This explains, according to Wilhelm, the reason why the modern Chinese thinker is generally a materialist and a pragmatist, and why even those who were aware of, and attracted by, the so-called Faustian nature of Western civilization were dominated by its pragmatic features. And those who, against this torrent of modernization, came to a weak defense of "metaphysics" and "the tradition" had nothing more to offer than nostalgic reflections on once beautiful words.

Under normal circumstances this process might have worked out its positive potential. Again circumstance interfered and denied to the minds of Chinese thinkers the time needed to consummate a new act of self-realization. There was the war and there was the civil war, and by the time the civil war had ended in the triumph of the Communists, the Chinese mind was not only generally geared to think in materialistic terms but had embraced materialism as a matter of desperate hope.

III

Such an hypothesis suggests that traditional Chinese values were indeed a precondition for communism but in a specific manner. It would explain the apparent paradox that men who embraced a set of values utterly at variance with those of the past were yet able to wrest control away from the Nationalists, who openly appealed to certain traditional values. It also explains why the similarity between the institutions of Red China and Imperial China—the monopoly of "magic," the rule by a self-perpetuating elite, the lack of individual freedom or representative government, the theory of an all-powerful and all-embracing state—is misleading and superficial. There was no Restoration. In neither China nor Russia did the world view of communism emerge from the imperial past; it came from England, Germany, and France and was as foreign to Russia as to China.

This hypothesis also suggests why the Russians eventually succeeded in their efforts to cooperate with the Chinese Nationalist movement, where the Japanese had failed, by drawing attention to the importance of the changes in the intellectual climate between the early twenties and the early forties. This is important because so many assume that the Bolshevik break-through in 1917 had a decisive demonstration value in China. We have seen that far from promoting the cause of communism in China the Russian revolutionaries practically killed it.

Nor did the Chinese need to be shown that a small group of

disciplined men could seize power and remake a society. This was not unique, even in Asia. The Chinese Nationalists had already drawn inspiration from the example of the Meiji Restoration in Japan, a revolution that was carried out by a small group of disciplined men operating from a power base in the southwest, who built up a new kind of army, operated through a united front, seized power, monopolized it, and changed the values and institutions of Japanese society in a period of twenty years. Sun Yat-sen organized his nationalist movement to do for China what the Japanese had done for Japan long before 1917. The Japanese even gave assistance to Sun in carrying out his program in China. Two prominent members of the Black Dragon Society actually attended Sun's funeral in 1925 at a time when they must have known that their place had been taken by Borodin and his assistants.

The Russians succeeded where the Japanese failed partly because they were able to conceal their motives behind a strong anti-imperialist line and a universal theory of history in spite of the fact that Lenin's attitude toward nationalism in Asia was essentially instrumental. They were also able to offer superior organizational techniques. The concealment did not last long, but the universal theory, combined with organization, was kept alive during long years of failure and defeat. Then came the anti-Japanese struggle of 1937 to 1945 followed by civil war. Wilhelm's hypothesis suggests that the decade or more of war, much of it the direct result of Communist activities, helped prepare the Chinese mind for acceptance of the essential ingredient, the universal theory of history as currently applied and interpreted by the Communist Party of China.

The analysis of intellectual history is fraught with difficulties, but it is here that the key to an understanding of the preconditions of communism must be sought. Wilhelm's hypothesis is no more than an hypothesis, but it is useful in putting into proper perspective the suggestion that Russia and China are both cases of arrested modernization. Taken by itself, the arrested-modernization theory does not explain why communism did not succeed in other cases of a similar sort. The term "modernization," as Mr. Pipes points out, is admittedly vague; it is usually understood to mean the "totality of phenomena attending the transition of a society from a traditional (i.e., predominantly agrarian and rural) to a modern (i.e., industrial and urban) one." There is a good deal wrong with this definition, the main objection being that it implies the existence of a political system but says nothing about it. In this respect traditional societies differed greatly. There is also the troubling question of how much industrialization and urbanization is called for and of what sort? Has the Soviet Union completed the process of modernization? Over half the population still makes its living from the land. The difficulties of definition obviously arise from the fact that this is not a normative concept but a name for an historical process.

For the purposes of this analysis it is more useful to identify the term "modernization" with the expansion of western European civilization during the last two or three centuries. In this expansion across the face of the globe largely but not entirely through the channels of imperialism, this civilization itself changed almost beyond recognition. It took with it the forces that were bringing about the changes at home. The leading countries of western Europe, assisted in no small measure by the United States of America, compelled the rest of the world either to accept or to adjust to their own methods of doing trade and conducting international relations. The forces that were changing the world were the same ones that were changing Europe—the idea of progress, the belief in science, the concepts of representative government, the rule of law, capitalism, Christianity, militarism, nationalism, socialism, and communism.

There are not many generalizations to be made about the reasons why communism had its impact in some countries and not in others. Each case is unique. Russia and China had certain characteristics, some of them in common, that might be considered preconditions but only tentatively. Neither received the impact of Europe when under the complete domination of an imperial power, as India did. The modernizing process disturbed the old society, particularly the authority and institutions of government, but there was no external power to impose the institutions of the modern state. It may be no accident that nearly all of the ex-European colonies have successfully resisted communism. Both Russia and China got rid of their traditional regimes by their own efforts, but in each case the new institutions were crushed by war before they could take hold. Neither was given the opportunity to work things out in peace, not that peace would have necessarily guaranteed the establishment of an open society. In neither case did the Communists overthrow the old society. They destroyed the beginnings of the new, which would seem to argue that the process of modernization must be well advanced before this particular precondition for communism can be fully effective.

PART TWO

The Communist Parties:
Transformations after the Assumption of Power

Introduction

LUCIAN W. PYE

EVER since Lenin gave Marxism a disciplined organizational form it has been axiomatic that the concept of the party gave communism a universal political advantage. Whether the situation called for revolutionaries to band together in clandestine subversion or for triumphant Communist heroes to mobilize entire peoples to the tasks of economic development and social revolution, it was generally assumed by Communist and non-Communist alike that the distinctive characteristics of a Leninist party were uniformly positive assets. Presumably non-Communist competitors labor under a liability in not possessing such an "organizational weapon," and they cannot hope to match the mobilizing capabilities of "the party."

In the case of the CPSU and the CCP all of this may, however, belong in the past. For at the Tahoe Conference the central theme in the comparative analysis of the Communist parties in Russia and China was the degree to which traditions of party organization and practices are now impeding developments in both countries. There has, of course, been a long tradition of scholarly criticism of Marxism as ideology, but it is a relatively new departure to stress the organizational limits of Communist parties in dealing with the major problems of the contemporary world. Could it be that Leninism is becoming as old-fashioned as nineteenth-century Marxism?

In his comparative analysis of Communist parties Merle Fainsod raises the question whether the CPSU has not become an anachronism in a Russia concerned with space exploration and plagued with rising consumer tastes. He sees the end of the CPSU as a mobilizing party and heralds its transformation into an adaptive party that must accommodate and reconcile various conflicting but legitimate interests in modern Soviet society. The party will have to take on a radically new meaning if it is to continue to be a central element in the management of Soviet affairs.

It is striking that the crisis of adaptation in both the Russian and Chinese parties did not occur at the time of assuming power but only well after power was consolidated. Neither party altered radically its policies and practices when it became a ruling party, and, indeed, for the CCP the transition was exceedingly gradual, since it had been long engaged in governing at Yenan and even earlier in Kiangsi. In both societies changes occurred when public issues became more complex and demanded more specialized skills. Consequently, the essentially monolithic character of the traditional Communist Party organizations has become increasingly irrelevant.

Ironically the CPSU was nearly destroyed by the personal tyrannical rule of Stalin, and then after being amazingly revitalized by Khrushchev, it now seems to be in search of a justification for its existence. This is a shocking development for the most sacred institution of communism. In the next chapter Merle Fainsod directs our attention to some of the directions in which the CPSU may move.

In China at present the dilemma of mobilization versus routinization is only beginning to take shape, but it is likely to become even more acute. The CCP was a remarkably effective agent for all mobilization campaigns which have swept China and which culminated in the Great Leap, but the process of rule through campaigns has caused some "withering away of the state." Consequently, the Chinese now appear to have a weaker state apparatus than would be ideal for coping with persisting development problems, particularly with respect to their economy. John M. H. Lindbeck in his chapter describes the extent to which the CCP is now acting as a civil bureaucracy and performing both executive and administrative functions in the ruling of China. Thus, although it is far too early to say that the CCP has become an anachronism, the stage has been reached at which the old ideals of a Leninist revolutionary party have less pertinence. Needless to say, Mao Tse-tung and the old men who rule China cannot abandon those ideals or admit they are outmoded. The scholars at the Tahoe Conference had no such constraints, and they freely grappled with the question whether either of the two Communist parties is likely to adapt to the needs of its changing society and still preserve its essential characteristics.

The examination of what has been happening to these two Communist parties provides a unique opportunity for disciplined comparative analysis. The ideals of party life and party organization spring from a common source, and essentially they stress the possibility that all individuals, regardless of cultural or personal differences, can be molded into the same disciplined revolutionary.

In observing the differences which have emerged in the practices and even the ideals of the two parties, it is possible to note the most important differences in the social conditions and revolutionary experiences of Russia and China.

The interaction between party and society thus deals with the most vital dimensions of the revolutionary experiences in the two countries, and through comparative analysis of the transformation of the two parties after the assumption of power it is possible to distinguish both the potentialities and the limitations of communism in guiding national development.

Transformations in the Communist Party
of the Soviet Union

MERLE FAINSOD

PERHAPS the most haunting nightmare of revolutionaries who come to power is their gradual realization that they cannot dispense with the "cursed" legacy of the past. However much they may dream of a human nature which is infinitely plastic and malleable and of new institutions which will shape men like wax, once they assume power they discover that the reality which confronts them is obdurate and recalcitrant and that they must adapt to it if they are themselves to survive.

The transformation of a revolutionary party into a ruling party works changes in the nature of that party of which at first even its most perceptive leaders are only dimly aware. In the revolutionary phase there is a tendency to assume that once power is won all problems will disappear. Even such a spokesman of organizational realism as Lenin was not free of illusions on this score. A few months before the October Revolution, he proclaimed: "Capitalist culture has created large-scale production, factories, railways, the postal service, telephones, etc., and on this basis the great majority of the functions of the old 'state power' have become so simplified and can be reduced to such simple operations of registration, filing and checking that they can be easily performed by every literate person. . . . We ourselves, the workers, will organize large-scale production on the basis of what capitalism has already created, relying on our own experience as workers, establishing strict, iron discipline. Supported by the state

Parts of this chapter are adapted from the author's *How Russia is Ruled* (revised edition enlarged; Cambridge, Mass.: Harvard University Press, 1963), Chapters 8 and 10.

power of the armed workers, we shall reduce the role of the state officials to that of simply carrying out our instructions as responsible, revocable, modestly-paid 'managers' (of course, with the aid of technicians of all sorts, types and degrees). . . . Such a beginning, on the basis of large-scale production, will of itself lead to the gradual 'withering away' of all bureaucracy, to the gradual creation of an order in which the functions of control and accounting—becoming more and more simple—will be performed by each in turn, will then become a habit and will finally die out as the special functions of a special section of the population."[1]

These utopian notions did not long survive the trials of power. The euphoric expressions of confidence in the capacity of the proletariat to exercise control functions and to practice self-discipline gave way to sober second thoughts. While Lenin excused the backwardness and inefficiency of the Russian worker as a perhaps unavoidable carry-over from Tsarism, he now described the task of "civilizing" him as requiring "an entire era of cultural development for the whole mass of the people."[2] It was far easier, Lenin admitted, to expropriate and nationalize industry than to manage it. "Our work of organizing proletarian accounting and control has obviously . . . *lagged behind* the work of directly 'expropriating the expropriators.' " "The art of administration," he proclaimed, "is not an art that one is born to, it is acquired by experience. . . . Without the guidance of specialists in the various fields of knowledge, technology and experience, the transition to Socialism will be impossible." Because of the indispensability of the specialists, Lenin continued, "we have to resort to the old bourgeois method and to agree to pay a very high price for the 'services' of the biggest bourgeois specialists. . . . Clearly, such a measure is a compromise, a departure from the principles of the Paris Commune . . . a *step backward* on the part of our Socialist Soviet state power, which from the very outset proclaimed and pursued the policy of reducing high salaries to the level of the wages of the average worker."[3] Lenin justified the measure as a necessary "tribute" which the Soviet state was compelled to pay to

[1] V. I. Lenin, *Selected Works Two-Volume Edition* (London: Lawrence & Wishart, 1947), II, 170, 174.
[2] See A. G. Meyer, *Leninism* (Cambridge: Harvard University Press, 1957), p. 213.
[3] Merle Fainsod, *How Russia is Ruled* (rev. ed. enlarged; Cambridge: Harvard University Press, 1963), p. 89.

compensate for its backwardness. "The sooner we workers and peasants learn to acquire the most efficient labor discipline and the most modern techniques of labor, using the bourgeois specialists for the purpose, the sooner shall we liberate ourselves from having to pay any 'tribute' to these specialists."[4]

Nor was the party exempt from Lenin's strictures. Writing some five months after the Revolution, he sought to excuse its disappointing administrative performance. "It goes without saying that the Party which led the revolutionary proletariat could not acquire the experience and habits of large organizational undertakings embracing millions and tens of millions of citizens; the remolding of the old, almost exclusively agitators' habits is a very long process. But there is nothing impossible in this, and as soon as the necessity for a change is clearly appreciated . . . we shall achieve it."[5] Four years later he was more impatient. His report to the Eleventh Congress was a biting indictment: "Suppose we take Moscow with its 4,700 responsible Communists, and suppose we take that huge bureaucratic machine, that huge pile—who is directing whom? I doubt very much whether it can truthfully be said that the Communists are directing the pile. To tell the truth, they are not doing the directing, they are being directed. Something has happened here that is similar to what they used to tell us about history in our childhood. This is what they taught us: Sometimes it happens that one people conquers another people, and then the people who conquered are the conquerors, and the conquered ones are the defeated. That is very simple, and everyone can understand it. But what happens with the culture of these peoples? Here matters are not so simple. If the people who did the conquering are more cultured than the defeated people, then the former will impose their culture on the latter, but if it is the other way around, then what happens is that the defeated will impose their culture on the conqueror. Has not something similar happened in the capital of the RSFSR; is it not true that 4,700 Communists (almost an entire division, and all of them the very elite) turn out to have been subjugated by an alien culture? Indeed, we might even get the impression here that the defeated have a high culture. Nothing of the sort! Their culture is miserable and insignificant, and yet it is greater than ours. However pitiful, however miserable, it is nevertheless greater than

[4] *Ibid.*
[5] V. I. Lenin, *op. cit.*, II, 329.

that of our responsible Communist functionaries, because they do not have sufficient skill in governing."[6]

To understand the problems which the Bolsheviks faced in assuming the function of governance, one must begin by examining the roster and talents that they brought to the task. At the beginning of the revolutionary year 1917 the size of the Bolshevik Party was officially estimated as 23,600. At the Sixth Congress in August 1917 the party claimed a total strength of 200,000, though a subsequent estimate for January 1, 1918, scaled down party membership to 115,000. The top leadership of the party consisted predominantly of professional revolutionaries who had worked in the social-democratic movement for years, the great majority as Bolsheviks. At the Sixth Congress in August 1917, 171 of the 264 delegates to the Congress filled in questionnaires about themselves.[7] All, needless to say, were engaged in revolutionary activity as agitators, propagandists, journalists, organizers, and secretaries of party committees. Ninety-four, or more than half of those reporting, had received a higher or secondary education and could be classified as members of the intelligentsia. Seventy of the 171 reported their occupations as workers; of the remaining groups of 101, 23 had no defined professions, 22 had been white-collar employees, 20 had been engaged in literary pursuits, 12 were teachers, 7 doctors, 6 lawyers, 4 statisticians, 3 officers or cadets, 2 soldiers, and 2 technicians. Even these relatively precise figures are misleading. The overwhelming majority had in fact spent their adult lives as revolutionaries; most had at one time or another been in prison, exile, or emigration because of their revolutionary activities.

Around this core of professional revolutionaries was an undisciplined mass of recently recruited rank-and-file members, mainly from the army and the factories of Petrograd, Moscow, the Urals, the mines of the Donets Basin, and other industrial centers. The vast peasant population of Russia was virtually unrepresented within Bolshevik ranks. On January 1, 1918, the rural contingent in the party totaled less than 17,000, an insignificant fraction of the total peasant population. The power of the Bolsheviks in the initial days of the Revolution was largely concentrated in Petrograd, Moscow, and a few other industrial areas.

---

[6] A. G. Meyer, *op. cit.*, p. 215.

[7] The data yielded by these questionnaires are summarized in *VI S'ezd RSDRP (Bolshevikov)* (Moscow, 1958), pp. 291–300.

It is commonly assumed, and to a substantial degree correctly, that the skills and techniques that professional revolutionaries develop are different in kind from the qualifications that make for success in governmental administration. Yet the point can be pressed too far. Revolutions too require organizational talent, and there have been few revolutionary ideologies in history that placed such a high premium on organizational doctrine as Leninism did. Practice to be sure fell short of theoretical pretensions, but organizationally what most clearly distinguished the Bolsheviks from their political competitors was the notion of the party as a committed band of revolutionary professionals, subject to highly centralized control and disciplined to the core. For Lenin revolution was an art in which the capacity to discern the potential for insurrection had to be combined with the most minute attention to factors of timing, tactics, and organizational dispositions at the crucial points.

In the preparation for the seizure of power on November 7, 1917, these qualities were manifest. As Leonard Schapiro describes the process, "The organization of the rising was in the hands of the Military Revolutionary Committee of the Petrograd Soviet, which was formed on 25 October, and of which Trotsky was chairman. This improvised general staff of the revolution maintained control over the military units in the capital which were prepared to support the bolsheviks, and also controlled the Red Guard. . . . The Military Revolutionary Committee acted through commissars, of whom there were several hundred by the date of the rising. These commissars were mainly appointed to the military units in the capital, and to those factories, where, owing to the prevalence of menshevik or socialist revolutionary influence, the bolsheviks could not rely on their own factory committee to mobilize worker support. The work of the Military Revolutionary Committee and its commissars was under the general supervision of individual members of the Central Committee, each responsible for a particular sector of activity, such as the railways or posts and telegraphs, and one member was entrusted with the supervision of the rising in Moscow. . . ."[8]

Once power was seized in Petrograd, it remained to be consolidated in the country, and this required years of unremitting effort. The Bolsheviks confronted formidable obstacles. After ex-

[8] Leonard Schapiro, *The Communist Party of the Soviet Union* (New York: Random House, 1960), pp. 173–74.

tricating themselves from the German war through the Treaty of Brest-Litovsk (March 1918), which cost them dearly in territory and resources, they faced the onslaughts of the White generals, the Allied intervention armies, the Poles, and rebellious anti Bolshevik nationalist movements in the borderlands. Even though party membership more than quadrupled from 115,000 on January 1, 1918, to 576,000 on January 1, 1921, it still represented less than half of one per cent of the population. It fell to this small minority to assume the reins of government in a war-ravaged nation, to recruit armies and to prod and lead them into battle, to feed and clothe them, and to supply them with weapons, to organize production and to extract grain from the peasants, to crush opposition and to mobilize support for the Communist cause.

In retrospect it still remains something of a miracle that the Bolshevik regime was able to survive its first traumatic test. It is difficult to conceive of a group of leaders less suited by way of previous training for the responsibilities they assumed. There were very few among them who had had any military, technical, or administrative experience, and what they learned had to be painfully acquired on the job. What gave them their strength was their sense of mission, their willingness to make temporary concessions where they were required, their capacity to enlist the talent they needed and their ruthless determination to hold onto power at any cost. They disarmed rural opposition by confirming the peasant land seizures, though they did not hesitate to requisition grain from the peasants when the life of the regime was at stake. They enrolled thousands of bourgeois specialists and Tsarist officers in their service and enforced their loyalty by threatening the grimmest kind of retaliation against their families in the event of treachery or sabotage. They moved their most trusted cadres into key positions in the army, the police, and state administration and counted on their zeal and commitment to build firm bases of power.

Despite the most strenuous efforts of the Bolshevik leadership to impose central direction on the course of events, the first years of Soviet power were uniquely a period when the spontaneous and anarchic forces of the revolution had their way. Even the party itself was a battleground of competing opinion and factions, and the mass influx of new members brought with it a miscellaneous array of discordant and not readily disciplined personalities and views. While trusted Bolsheviks occupied strategic power positions in the administrative apparatus, the lower levels of the bureauracy were still composed predominantly of old regime carry-overs who sometimes worked at cross purposes with their party superiors.

What was true of Moscow was infinitely truer of the periphery. Localism flourished, and the effectiveness of Communist controls decreased in direct relation to the distance from the great urban centers. Even in the Red Army, the top command encountered the greatest difficulty in enforcing its authority on the armies in the field. The former Tsarist officers whom the Bolsheviks enrolled as military specialists often met defiance from Communist commanders and rank and file. Guerrilla units loosely attached to the army fought their own war in their own way.

For the Bolsheviks during the Civil War, there was only one determining priority—survival. And survival involved mobilizing the men and the material to defeat the enemy. Every other consideration gave way before this pressing necessity. In moments of crisis, Communists from the factories and offices were rushed to the front in hundreds and thousands to stiffen resistance. In every army unit, it was the party core that supplied the needed discipline and dedication. Communist commissars guarded the loyalty of the old-regime officers and carried on the agitation and propaganda that drove men to battle. Where bottlenecks in supply and communications occurred, Communist emissaries were dispatched to unravel the tangle.[9]

For the party leadership, the Civil War years were a school of administration in which aptitudes were developed and specialized knowledge and experience acquired. Assignments in the initial instance bore little or no relation to previous training, since in most cases those designated for positions of large responsibility were utterly unprepared for their jobs. During the war years, nevertheless, the party leadership began to form its own specialized cadres whose expertise derived from concentrating their energies on one or another administrative task. Necessarily military affairs claimed a commanding priority, but in the process of disposing of its forces the party also developed its specialists in foreign relations, in party management, in nationality policies, in journalism, in trade union organization, and in other fields of

[9] For a vivid first-hand description, see Jan M. Meijer (ed.), *The Trotsky Papers 1917–1922* (The Hague: Mouton & Co., 1964), Vol. I.

major concern. The economic sector was perhaps the party's greatest area of weakness. There were very few of its leaders who had either the background or disposition to devote themselves seriously to mastering economic affairs.

Meanwhile, the Red Army itself served as a school of communism. It played a particularly important role in recruiting soldiers of peasant origin into the party and in enabling the party to broaden its hitherto insignificant influence in rural districts. Between January 1, 1918, and January 1, 1921, the peasant element in the party rose from 14.5 per cent to 28.2 per cent. While this peasant contingent of less than 163,000 was still a very small fragment of the rural population, its effect in the post-civil-war years was to provide the party with substantially increased leverage in the countryside.

As the civil war drew to a close and the Soviet regime embarked on the NEP, or New Economic Policy, the party leadership undertook to eliminate the careerists and power seekers who had attached themselves to the party in its hour of victory. The purge of 1921, in the course of which approximately 175,000 members were expelled from the party, was aimed, in Lenin's words, at ridding the party "of rascals, bureaucrats, dishonest or wavering Communists, and of Mensheviks who have repainted their 'façade' but who have remained Mensheviks at heart."[10] Faced with the necessity of retreat and concessions to the peasantry and the private trader, the party sought to purify its ranks and root itself in the support of its proletarian formations.

At the Twelfth Party Conference in August 1922, the party rules were revised to discourage the admission of non-proletarian cadres. During the twenties, the party waged a vigorous campaign to increase its proletarian component. As a result of a series of recruitment drives, the worker element in the party increased from 41 per cent in 1921 to 61.4 per cent in 1929, while the peasant proportion declined from 28.2 per cent to 21.7 per cent, and the category of office employees and others fell even more sharply from 30.8 per cent to 16.9 per cent. By January 1, 1929, the size of the party had mounted to 1,090,508 members and 444,854 candidates.

The proletarianization of the party, however, was more apparent than real. Statistics on the social composition of the party registered the social origins of members, rather than the positions

[10] Fainsod, *op. cit.*, p. 250.

which they occupied in the social or political structure. A substantial proportion of party members who were classified as workers or peasants were actually engaged in administrative or other non-manual occupations. Party membership served to accelerate upward social mobility and provided a reservoir from which officialdom was recruited and replenished.

In the higher reaches of the party, Communists of intellectual or white-collar origin were still predominant. As Leonard Schapiro has noted, "an analysis of nearly 15,000 leading party officials made in 1921 showed that scarcely more than a third were of proletarian origin."[11] During the twenties, the Old Bolsheviks of pre-1917 seniority continued to dominate the key positions in the party and governmental apparatus. But more than a few found the transition from revolution and war to the routines of peacetime administration irksome and difficult and fell by the wayside. The prerevolutionary committeemen of Stalin's stripe moved readily and easily into secretarial posts in the party hierarchy. The more cosmopolitan and better-educated group who had spent years in emigration gravitated to positions in foreign affairs, the Comintern, the ideological sectors, and policy posts in state administration.

The party encountered its gravest difficulties in staffing managerial posts in trade and industry. Many party leaders found it all but impossible to adjust to Lenin's injunction, "Learn to trade." As Lenin put it in his report to the Eleventh Party Congress in 1922: "The whole point is that responsible Communists—even the best of them who are unquestionably honest and loyal, who in the old days suffered penal servitude and did not fear death—cannot trade, because they are not businessmen, they have not learned to trade, do not want to learn, and do not understand that they must start from the A B C. What! Communists, revolutionaries who have made the greatest revolution in the world . . . must they learn from ordinary salesmen? But these ordinary salesmen have had ten years' warehouse experience and know the business, whereas the responsible Communists and devoted revolutionaries do not know the business, and do not even realize that they do not know it."[12]

The party's deficiencies in the economic area were made graphically manifest in an analysis of the educational background of

[11] Schapiro, *op. cit.*, p. 237.
[12] Fainsod, *op. cit.*, pp. 98–99.

directors of state enterprises as of January 1, 1928.[13] Of the
directors studied, 89.3 per cent belonged to the party and 10.7 per
cent were non-party. Of the party directors, only 2.8 per cent had
a higher education, compared with 58 per cent of the non-party
directors. 78.6 per cent of the party directors had only a lower-
school education compared with 14.8 per cent for the non-party
directors. More than 70 per cent of the party directors were
former workers who had been promoted to managerial posts. On
the eve of the First Five-Year Plan the problem of training party
cadres for high technical and managerial responsibilities remained unsolved.

Meanwhile, important changes were taking place in the character of the ruling elite. The purge of the left and right-wing
oppositions eliminated many whom Stalin called "the old leaders
from among the literati." Their places were taken by the organization men, the "practical" workers of the party apparatus, many of
whom began their careers as underground committeemen in the
prerevolutionary period. The way was also opened for a replen-
ishment of the leadership group, and a new generation of Civil
War veterans began to make its way into leading posts. At lower
levels of the party apparatus the claims of a still younger generation were beginning to be heard. An analysis of more than 31,000
secretaries of party cells at the end of 1927 indicated that more
than 50 per cent joined the party after 1923.[14] These new men
were increasingly to depend on Stalin for their advancement and
to become part of his supporting entourage.

By the late twenties the mass membership of the party consisted overwhelmingly of postrevolutionary recruits. The primary
strength of the party was concentrated in urban industrial centers; its rural representation remained woefully weak. In terms of
social origin, its membership was predominantly working class,
but many who were classified as workers were actually discharging administrative or other non-manual duties. The nationality
weight of the party was distributed among its Great Russian,
Jewish, Latvian, Estonian, Polish, Armenian, and Georgian contingents. The Ukrainians, the Central Asian groups, and the other
minority nationalities of European Russia were still very inade-
quately represented. The educational level of the party was low.
The 1927 party census revealed that less than 1 per cent of the

13 *Ibid.*, p. 258.
14 *Ibid.*, p. 259.

membership had graduated from a higher educational institution, and the total of those with a higher or middle education was less than 9 per cent.[15] As a result there was a serious deficiency in trained party personnel capable of discharging the large managerial tasks which industrialization and collectivization imposed.

The decision in the late twenties to embark on a program of rapid industrialization and collectivization strained the administrative resources of the party to the utmost. As in the Civil War period, improvisation became the order of the day. Lacking members equipped with agricultural skills, the party mobilized thousands of party workers in the industrial centers and dispatched them to the countryside to lead the collectivization drive. Ambitious Communist workers were encouraged to enroll in *tekhnikums* in order to raise their technical qualifications, and great emphasis was placed on home study as well as on factory schools to prepare cadres of skilled workers. Responsible Communist Party officials such as Khrushchev who had demonstrated administrative aptitude were assigned to a newly established Industrial Academy in Moscow, where they were subjected to intensive training designed to fit them for managerial posts. In order to fill quickly the crying need for engineers of all types, rather narrowly oriented technical institutes were organized to provide accelerated courses in the engineering specialities most in demand. Such old regime specialists as were still available were pressed into service, though they also on occasion were subjected to charges of sabotage and espionage when scapegoats were needed for the mistakes and difficulties which inevitably attended the industrialization drive. Foreign engineers and technicians were also enlisted in large numbers, though their services were dispensed with as soon as they could be replaced.

Meanwhile, longer-range efforts were launched to satisfy the growing demand for highly qualified engineers, technicians, and scientific workers. The curriculum of the lower and middle schools was reorganized to place major emphasis on mathematical and scientific disciplines. The network of universities and higher technical institutes was greatly expanded, and their courses revised to provide more broadly based engineering and scientific training. The new technical intelligentsia produced by this intensive educational effort was to play an increasingly important role in Soviet society.

[15] *Ibid.,* p. 258.

A crucial question was how they would relate to the party. During the early and mid-thirties admission to the party was still regulated by discriminatory rules which placed industrial workers in the most favored category and relegated the technical intelligentsia to an inferior position. As the industrialization program gathered momentum, hints were thrown out that the party would welcome members of the technical intelligentsia into its ranks and that the party rules might have to be modified to facilitate their entry. A revision of the party rules in 1934 eased the conditions of admission for engineers and technicians working directly in production, but until 1939 formal barriers to the admission of other technical and managerial personnel still remained substantial.

Meanwhile, beginning in 1933 the party was rocked by a series of purges which culminated in the Great Purge of 1936–38. Its effect on the party elite was shattering. As Khrushchev noted in his secret speech to the Twentieth Party Congress, "of the 139 members and candidates of the Party's Central Committee who were elected at the Seventeenth Congress, 98 were arrested and shot (mostly in 1937–38)," and of 1,966 delegates with either voting or advisory rights at the same Congress, "1,108 persons were arrested on charges of anti-revolutionary crimes. . . ."[16] The Bolshevik Old Guard was virtually destroyed. The roll of Stalin's victims included members of his own entourage as well as former oppositionists. No sphere of Soviet life was left untouched. The senior officer corps of both army and navy suffered severely. The removal of Yagoda and later Yezhov from the NKVD was accompanied by the arrest of their leading collaborators. The Comintern, the Commissariat of Foreign Affairs, and the diplomatic service were particularly hard hit. Among the victims were leading officials in the union republics, secretaries of the party, Komsomol and trade union apparatus, leading writers, scholars, and scientists, and heads of departments, industrial trusts, and enterprises.

Tragedy for the older generation of Communist functionaries spelled opportunity for the new technical intelligentsia. Even before the 1939 Party Congress threw party membership open to intellectuals on an equal basis with workers and peasants, the

[16] Russian Institute, Columbia University (ed.), *The Anti-Stalin Campaign and International Communism* (New York: Columbia University Press, 1956), pp. 22–23.

new technical intelligentsia was being eagerly welcomed into party ranks. When the party resumed large-scale recruitment in 1938, the enlistment of the technical intelligentsia assumed the character of a campaign. The reports of local party organizations gave primacy to the number of engineering-technical personnel that they had succeeded in recruiting for the party. A profound shift in the social base of the party was set in motion. The problem of the relationship of the new Soviet intelligentsia to the party was "solved" by assimilating them into the party. The younger cadres of bureaucrats, engineers, and plant directors turned out to be the primary beneficiaries of the Great Purge.

The changes in the character of the party elite were already dramatically evident by 1939. As Schapiro has pointed out, "Over a quarter of the delegates to the Eighteenth Congress had completed higher education, and a further quarter secondary education. In 1930 the equivalent percentages were 4.4 and 15.7."[17] By 1939 the preponderant majority of party secretaries were under forty years of age and had joined the party after 1923. Among the secretaries of regional, territorial, and republic party committees, 28.6 per cent had a complete university education and an additional 30 per cent had either a complete secondary school education or an incomplete university education.[18] There were also impressive gains in the educational qualifications of Soviet administrative and economic personnel. As Andreyev noted in his speech to the Eighteenth Congress: "The proportion of university graduates among the People's Commissars of the U.S.S.R. and the R.S.F.S.R. is 53 per cent, among the Assistant People's Commissars 68 per cent, among the directors of the chief boards and syndicates of the People's Commissariats 60 per cent and among the directors of economic establishments 27.6 per cent."[19] Comparable gains were reported at lower levels of the economic and administrative hierarchy. These developments represented a response to the overriding need for qualified personnel in responsible positions. The absorption of the new Soviet intelligentsia into the party was followed by its rapid elevation to leading posts.

The transformations in the nature of the party during the thirties can be briefly summarized. After a period of rapid expansion at the beginning of the decade, the party underwent a series

[17] Schapiro, *op. cit.*, p. 439.
[18] Fainsod, *op. cit.*, p. 268.
[19] *Ibid.*

of traumatic purges which reduced its membership by almost one-half. In 1938 growth began again, and by the beginning of 1940 the party had almost reached the peak membership of 3½ million registered in 1933. As a result of the purges, the power of Stalin was securely consolidated. The most significant social change was the reception of the new Soviet-trained intelligentsia into the party. The industrial worker lost his preferred position, and after 1934 peasant strength also shrank. Although the party remained predominantly urban in composition, the newly favored categories both in town and country were the administrators, engineers, technicians, and the so-called leading workers, the shop chiefs, foremen, brigadiers, and Stakhanovites who represented the aristocracy of labor. Among the nationalities the Great Russian and Transcaucasian Communists maintained their strong position, while the Jewish party membership declined in importance and Ukrainians and Belorussians continued to be underrepresented. Communist weight in the Central Asian republics remained weak, although some progress was registered in comparison with the twenties. The recruitment of youth in the wake of the purges resulted in a rejuvenation of the party and was accompanied by a considerable improvement in the educational backgrounds of party members.

With the end of the Great Purge, the party entered a phase of rapid expansion. In the three years from 1938 to 1941 the party doubled in size. During the war years party membership soared to a new peak as the party relaxed its standards of admission in order to encourage Red Army men, and particularly front-line fighters, to apply for entrance. The party's first concern was to strengthen its base in the crucial military formations. By January 1, 1945, the party attained the unprecedented total of 5,760,369 members and candidates. During the immediate postwar years expansion continued, though at a much slower rate. On the eve of the Nineteenth Party Congress (October 1, 1952), the total membership of the party was 6,882,145, of whom 6,013,259 were full members and 868,886 candidates.

At the end of Stalin's reign, the party, along with much else in Soviet society, appeared to be fixed in a relatively rigid mold. Few new members were being admitted, and there was little disposition to "chase after numerical growth." Despite some efforts to broaden the party's social base by recruiting "leading" workers and collective farmers into the party, the administrative, managerial, and technical intelligentsia provided the hard elite core around which the party was built. The party's representation in rural areas increased but still had far to go to match its urban strength. One of the effects of the war was to create greater opportunities for women in the party. Their numbers in the party increased from 14.9 per cent in 1941 to 19.2 per cent in October 1952. Although very few penetrated the upper reaches of the party hierarchy, they were increasingly represented in the middle and lower party apparatus as compared with prewar days. The national-ethnic composition of the party remained much as it was during the late thirties, with the Great Russian and Transcaucasian areas registering high rates of party membership, while the Central Asian republics, Belorussia, the Ukraine, and some of the newly acquired regions lagged far behind. The educational level of the party continued its upward trend. By 1947 more than a fifth of the party could claim a completed secondary school education compared with 14.2 per cent in 1939. By 1952 the members and candidates with either a complete or incomplete higher education accounted for 11.8 per cent of the party total. The rise in the educational qualifications of the party elite was dramatic. At the Nineteenth Congress in 1952 more than 58 per cent of the voting delegates had a higher education compared with 26.5 per cent at the Eighteenth Congress in 1939. Of the 709 delegates at the Nineteenth Congress with a higher education, 282 were engineers. The absorption of the new Soviet technical cadres into the inner cadres of the party was strikingly manifest.

The death of Stalin cleared the way for a re-examination of the party's membership policy. Seeking to strengthen their link with the masses, the new leaders decided both to enlarge the size of the party and to widen its social base. Starting in 1954, there was a renewed emphasis on party growth. By the Twenty-Second Congress, held in October 1961, the party numbered 8,872,516 members and 843,489 candidates and by mid-1965 the total passed the 12,000,000 mark.

The determination to broaden the social composition of the party assumed the character of a campaign. Khrushchev in 1954 expressed special concern at the lagging rate of party recruitment among collective farmers. At the Twentieth Party Congress in 1956, Suslov, who delivered the main speech on party organizational work, declared: "Party organizations must . . . radically increase the proportion of workers and collective farmers among new recruits."[20] Of those admitted to membership in the party between the Twentieth Congress in 1956 and the Twenty-Second Congress in 1961, workers constituted 40.7 per cent, collective farmers 22.7 per cent, employees 35.3 per cent, and students 1 per cent. In undertaking to strengthen its link with the masses, however, the party still emphasized the recruitment of "leading" rather than rank-and-file workers and collective farmers. The definition of both workers and collective farmers was apparently elastic enough to embrace foremen, brigadiers, and other administrative and specialist personnel who were not themselves engaged in physical labor. Despite the seeming intensity of the drive to enroll workers and collective farmers, in the period between 1956 and 1964 the collective-farmer contingent in the party declined from 17.1 per cent to 16.5 per cent, the worker component increased from 32 to 37.3 per cent, while the "employee and other" category dropped from 50.9 per cent to 46.2 per cent.[21] By December 1, 1960, of a total of 8,784,000 Soviet citizens classified as specialists working in the national economy, 2,495,200, or 28.5 per cent, were party members. As might be expected, the continued rapid industrialization of Soviet society served to emphasize the indispensable role of the technical intelligentsia. Between January 1, 1956, and July 1, 1961, the number of party engineers, technicians, agricultural specialists, architects, and economists nearly doubled from 685,470 to 1,233,448, far outstripping the rate of increase shown by other groups in the employee category, as well as by workers and collective farmers. The administrative, managerial, and technical intelligentsia continued to represent the preponderant element in the party, and their predominance was particularly marked in leading posts.

The national-ethnic composition of the party also underwent changes in the post-Stalinist years. The new leadership made special efforts to build up the weaker union republic party organizations. Between January 1, 1957, and October 1, 1961, when party membership as a whole increased by nearly a third, the party organizations of a number of republics expanded at a far greater rate: the Ukraine 59 per cent, Belorussia 55 per cent, Lithuania 54 per cent, Moldavia 50 per cent, Tadjikistan 49 per cent, Uzbekistan 48 per cent, and Kirghizia 42 per cent. On the

---

[20] *Ibid.*, p. 276.
[21] For the most recent data on party membership, see *Partiinaya Zhizn,* No. 10, May, 1965, pp. 8–17.

other hand, such traditional strongholds as the Armenian and Georgian party organizations increased by only 22 per cent and 13 per cent respectively.[22]

Despite these efforts, traditional disparities persisted. The RSFSR, Georgia, and Armenia continued to boast particularly high membership rates. Moldavia and Lithuania were still at the bottom of the ladder. The Belorussian party organization remained small in proportion to population, and the Ukrainian party, despite the acceleration in its rate of growth, was still well below the USSR average. In Central Asia, the Uzbek and Tadjik organizations were the greatest laggards. The Turkmen and Kirghiz organizations claimed somewhat higher membership rates, though still substantially below the national average. The relative strength of the Kazakhstan party organization reflected an influx of Russian and other non-indigenous party personnel who had moved into the area as an accompaniment of its rapid industrialization and the development of its virgin lands.

The educational qualifications of party members continued to rise in the post-Stalinist years. The proportion of party members and candidates with a complete secondary school education or better increased from 37 per cent in January 1956 to 47.7 per cent in January 1964. The same trends were visible in the higher party apparatus. As a result, however, of a deliberate effort to feature the participation of leading collective farmers and workers in the post-Stalinist party congresses, the percentage of delegates with a higher education declined from 59.5 per cent at the Nineteenth Congress to approximately 55.8 per cent at both the Twentieth and Twenty-First Congresses and 52.5 per cent at the Twenty-Second. Of the delegates with a higher education, the largest single occupational group remained those trained as engineers.

Perhaps the most dramatic way to illustrate the changes which have taken place in the top party elite is to compare the membership of the Politburo and Presidium at various stages of their development.[23] After the death of Lenin in 1924, the Politburo consisted of Stalin, Trotsky, Kamenev, Zinoviev, Rykov, Tomsky, and Bukharin. All belonged to the generation of professional revolutionaries, and all except Trotsky were Old Bolsheviks of long standing. Of this group, four—Kamenev, Zinoviev, Rykov,

---

[22] *Ibid.*, p. 279.
[23] See Fainsod, *op. cit.*, pp. 307–45.

and Bukharin—were executed on Stalin's orders during the Great Purge, one—Tomsky—committed suicide while awaiting arrest, and the sixth—Trotsky—was assassinated in Mexico in 1940 by one of Stalin's agents. With the exception of Tomsky, all of those whom Stalin destroyed were intellectuals of cosmopolitan interests and experience derived from years spent in emigration. Even Tomsky, who began his career as a lithographic worker and quickly became a Bolshevik trade union organizer, attended the London Congress as a delegate in 1907 and participated in the Paris conference of the editors of *Proletarii* in 1909. As a group they were articulate, argumentative, and independent; all of them including Tomsky had opposed Lenin at one time or another in the course of their party careers. During the period of revolutionary preparation, they had functioned primarily as agitators, propagandists, and journalists; they were men of the word and the pen with a talent for oratorical and agitational pursuits.

After the Bolshevik conquest of power, they moved quickly into positions of prominence in public life. Trotsky, Kamenev, Rykov, and Tomsky all displayed great organizing talents, but as a group they found themselves attracted to policy posts in military, state, and trade union administration and tended to avoid the drabber responsibilities of internal party management which represented Stalin's primary concern. Zinoviev, to be sure, took responsibility for the Leningrad Party organization, but his energies were largely devoted to the management of the Communist International. Bukharin's assignments included the editorship of *Pravda* (1917–29), responsibility for the Comintern after Zinoviev's downfall, and the editorship of *Izvestia* after his own decline in power. Perhaps the most striking common characteristic of the group (and an important cause of their failure) was the fact that not a single one of them was concerned in an important way with the central management of the party organization and its secretariat. By 1930 all of them had been eliminated from the Politburo.

The reorganized Politburo of 1931 consisted of Stalin, Molotov, Voroshilov, Kalinin, Rudzutak, Kuibyshev, L. M. Kaganovich, Kirov, Kossior, and Ordjonikidze. All shared with Stalin the distinction of having served their apprenticeships as "practical" workers in the party apparatus. Only three of the ten—Molotov, Kuibyshev, and Ordjonikidze—can be positively identified as of middle- or upper-class origin, and even these three were organization men rather than cosmopolitan intellectuals with an interest in ideas. Stalin found himself most at ease with *apparatchiki* like himself, who were frequently of lowly origin, who had had limited opportunities for education and foreign travel, who had little interest in theoretical disputations, and whose primary gifts were organizational. The career profiles of the 1931 Politburo reveal that loyal, disciplined service in the apparatus served as the highroad to admission into Stalin's inner circle.

Yet even this seemingly closely-knit group failed to provide the servility which Stalin demanded. Of Stalin's nine Politburo associates in 1931, only four—Molotov, Kaganovich, Voroshilov, and Kalinin—survived the Great Purge. Kirov was assassinated in 1934 under circumstances which Khrushchev later described as "inexplicable and mysterious"; he implied, if he did not say, that the order came from Stalin. The death of Kuibyshev in 1935 involved its own still unresolved mystery. Ordjonikidze's death in 1937 was announced as due to a "paralytic stroke," but, according to Khrushchev, "Stalin allowed the liquidation of Ordjonikidze's brother and brought Ordjonikidze himself to such a state that he was forced to shoot himself." Rudzutak and Kossior, according to Khrushchev, were executed on the basis of "false . . . slanderous materials."[24]

The four new persons added to the Politburo during the thirties who managed to survive the purge were Andreyev, admitted in 1932, Mikoyan, admitted in 1935, and Zhdanov and Khrushchev, both admitted in 1939. Their careers followed the traditional Stalinist course of upward mobility through the party apparatus. Khrushchev was the harbinger of a new Politburo generation, the first member of the inner circle to enter the party after the revolution. In other respects, however, his career was that of the typical *apparatchik*.

During the forties, five new members were added to the Politburo: Beria and Malenkov in 1946, Voznesensky in 1947, Bulganin in 1948, and Kosygin in 1949. Of the five, only Malenkov and Beria fell more or less clearly into the pattern of *apparatchiki* who rose to power through the secretarial hierarchy. In the case of Beria, however, a long period of service in the security police both preceded and succeeded his tour of duty as a party secretary. The three others, Bulganin, Kosygin, and Voznesensky, were primarily state and economic administrators rather than party

[24] *Ibid.*, p. 314.

figures. Their appointments were a marked break with the earlier practice of reserving Politburo membership for successful party *apparatchiki*. As a response to the complex urgencies which the Soviet high command faced in managing a society in process of rapid industrialization, this new departure was not without long-range significance.

The background of technical training or experience which characterized the group of new appointees is worth emphasis. Beria received a higher education at the Baku Polytechnic Institute. Malenkov spent three years at an engineering institute in Moscow between 1922 and 1925. Kosygin was trained as a textile engineer. Voznesensky completed a postgraduate course in economics at the Institute of Red Professors in Moscow and became an economic planner. Bulganin made his reputation as a competent factory manager during the twenties; in those years, one of his official biographies reports, he "completed his education 'on the run' from the technical experts under him."[25]

No one of the group was an Old Bolshevik. Beria and Bulganin joined the party in 1917, Voznesensky in 1919, Malenkov in 1920, and Kosygin, the youngest of the group, in 1927. Kosygin, who was a mere boy of twelve when the Bolsheviks seized power in 1917, was completely a product of the Soviet era. Except for Kosygin, none of the group derived from a working-class family.

The period between the Eighteenth Party Congress in 1939 and the Nineteenth Congress in 1952 was characterized by relatively stable Politburo membership. Kalinin died in 1946 under normal circumstances. The death of Zhdanov in 1948, however, was followed by a purge of his Leningrad entourage, and in the course of the so-called Leningrad Affair, Voznesensky, one of Zhdanov's protégés, was arrested and executed. Even though the remaining members of the Politburo retained their posts, all of them, according to Khrushchev, lived in dread of "annihilation." In Khrushchev's words, "Stalin evidently had plans to finish off the old members of the Politburo." His decision at the Nineteenth Congress to abolish both the Politburo and the Orgburo and to replace them by a greatly enlarged Presidium was interpreted by Khrushchev as "aimed at the removal of the old Politburo members. . . ."[26] If Khrushchev's testimony is to be credited, only the death of Stalin in March 1953 saved them from extinction.

[25] *Ibid.*, p. 316.
[26] Russian Institute (ed.), *op. cit.*, pp. 84–85.

The reorganized Presidium after Stalin's death was built around the old Politburo core of Malenkov, Beria, Molotov, Voroshilov, Khrushchev, Bulganin, Kaganovich, and Mikoyan. Andreyev and Kosygin were dropped from membership and their places taken by Saburov and Pervukhin, both talented economic administrators whose careers were devoted to state rather than party work. Their inclusion in the inner group testified to the importance of the skills which they represented. Of the ten 1953 Presidium members, only one, Mikoyan, was to survive Khrushchev's ouster in 1964. Beria was executed in 1953 when his control of the police loomed as a threat to his colleagues. The remaining seven—Malenkov, Molotov, Kaganovich, Voroshilov, Bulganin, Pervukhin, and Saburov—joined in a plot to oust Khrushchev in 1957; in the wake of their failure they were dropped from the Presidium.

At the end of 1965 the Presidium consisted of twelve members: Brezhnev, Kosygin, Podgorny, Mikoyan, Suslov, Shvernik, Polyansky, Voronov, Kirilenko, Shelepin, Shelest, and Mazurov. Within this group at least four distinct party generations were represented: the Old Bolsheviks, the Civil War band, the generation of the late twenties and early thirties, and the youngest members who dated their party affiliations from the post-purge period. The two Old Bolsheviks—Shvernik aged seventy-seven and Mikoyan aged seventy—were obviously passing from the center of the stage. The only representative of the Civil War generation, Suslov, who joined the party in 1921, still played an important role. By far the largest group were the six members who joined the party between 1927 and 1931—Brezhnev, Kosygin, Podgorny, Voronov, Kirilenko, and Shelest—who ranged in age from fifty-five to sixty-two. Well behind them, skipping the missing generation of the years of the Great Purge, were Polyansky, aged forty-eight, who joined the party in 1939, Shelepin, forty-seven, who was admitted to party membership in 1940, and Mazurov, who also joined the party in 1940.

A close look at the biographies of the group reveals some interesting common characteristics. Most were of humble social origin, children of workers and peasants, whose rise to eminence was deeply intertwined with the opportunities made available to them by the Soviet system. Of the group of twelve, eight were Great Russians, three Ukrainians, and one Armenian. With the exception of Kosygin, every member of the group could point to long periods of service in the party apparatus. Within the newer members of the group was to be found a degree of technical training and competence that was noticeably lacking in the earlier generation of party functionaries recruited by Stalin. Shelepin, a graduate of the Moscow Institute of History, Philosophy, and Literature, was the only non-technician in the group. Brezhnev and Shelest were both graduates of metallurgical institutes, Kirilenko of an aviation institute, Podgorny of a technical institute for the food industry, Voronov of an industrial institute, Polyansky of an agricultural institute, and Mazurov of a highway *tekhnikum*. Brezhnev, Kosygin, Podgorny, Shelest, and Kirilenko had all served in industry as engineers or factory directors. Despite the fact that most of them made their real careers in the party apparatus, they brought a technical background to their party assignments which helped them to cope with the problems of directing an increasingly complex industrial society.

The same tendencies were visible at lower levels of the party apparatus. Responsible secretarial posts in the party hierarchy appear increasingly to be reserved for party functionaries with a higher education, usually of a technical variety. According to M. Polekkin of the Central Committee secretariat, in the RSFSR in 1963 98.6 per cent of the secretaries of oblast and krai industrial party committees and 96.2 per cent of secretaries of oblast and krai agricultural party committees had a higher education.[27] More than half the secretaries of city and urban region party committees and industrial production party committees were "specialists with a higher and secondary technical education." The staffing of key posts in the party apparatus with technically trained personnel reflected an increasing technocratic and economic emphasis in party management.

Advancing industrialization brought new burdens for the party elite. Among the marks of a mature industrialized society are the complexity of the functions which it must discharge, the multiplication of professionalisms and specialties to perform them, and the increasing difficulty of ordering their interrelationships. A ruling party such as the Communist Party of the Soviet Union which assumes the awesome responsibility of guiding the whole life of society faces a particularly troublesome problem in coordinating these multiplying functions and professionalisms.

The response of the party to this challenge has taken various

[27] See *Partiinaya Zhizn*, No. 1, 1965, pp. 24–30.

forms. Within the Presidium itself, the trend in recruitment has been to draw on party secretaries with technical training whose assignments in the party apparatus in the regions, republics, and at the center have tested their coordinating capacities. The staff which serves the Presidium, the Central Committee secretariat, reflects the specialization and differentiation which increasingly characterizes Soviet society. Organized to oversee every sector of Soviet life, its members provide a pool of expertise on which the Presidium can draw. They also usually possess the professional backgrounds which enable them to communicate with and appraise the performance of their opposite numbers in state administration. The Central Committee itself, though a large and somewhat unwieldy body, provides still another point of policy coordination. The core of its membership consists of the top stratum of the party and state elite; party secretaries from the center, the union republics, and the more important regions, and leading members of the USSR Council of Ministers and chairmen of the Councils of Ministers of the union republic. In addition, there is a sprinkling of representation from the high military command, the police, and the foreign service as well as outstanding party ideologists, scientists, and intellectuals.

Serving the central organs of the party is a network of party organizations, committees, and secretaries reaching down from the republics through the regions, cities, and districts to the primary party units. At every level of the party hierarchy, the party first secretary plays a key role as mobilizer, coordinator, and expediter to ensure that party policies are executed. Within the party apparatus itself, functions differentiate. There are indoctrination specialists who are responsible for "ideological work" and whose task it is to ensure the political loyalty of both party and non-party members. There are specialists in party organization and cadres, or personnel work, whose responsibilities embrace both appointments to party and state office and supervision of party, Komsomol, and trade union organizations. There are also specialists in agriculture and in the major branches of industry and trade whose function it is to observe, to check, to report on, and to assist the cluster of enterprises for which they are responsible.

By absorbing key members of every professional and skill group into the party, the leadership undertakes to project its controls into every sector of Soviet society. Here, however, certain limitations operate. There are important differences in attitude and degree of commitment between party functionaries for whom party work is the whole of life and other party members who make their careers through the technical or professional skills which they have mastered. Whether the latter be professional army officers, scientists, or factory managers, their tendency is to assume that they can be trusted to do their jobs, and they resent excessive tutelage and supervision by party functionaries who cannot match them in professional qualifications. Such attitudes are calculated to make party functionaries uneasy, but even they recognize the problem. The more technocratically minded of the party leaders know that future Soviet power rests on technical and scientific progress, and that their task is to tap professional competence without stultifying it.

As the Soviet Union becomes a more and more highly industrialized society, dependent on its scientists, engineers, and managers to maintain its on-going technological and economic momentum, some redefinition of influence within the society appears probable. The authority of scientific knowledge cannot be denied without doing damage to the society's prospects. This need not challenge the party's monopoly of political power. It does mean that party functionaries must possess sufficient scientific and technical knowledge to exercise their leadership role intelligently. It also means that the scientific and technological community is likely to exert an increasing influence over decision-making in areas where a high level of sophisticated technical knowledge is the decisive component. More importantly, it opens up the prospect of the gradual erosion, adaptation, and even outright rejection of ideological dogmas which operate as barriers to future progress. A party which embraced forced draft industrialization as a key to its salvation promises to be transformed by its own handiwork.

Since Stalin's death the Soviet Union has moved into a more mature stage of development in which the party puts less reliance on coercive mobilization and more on incentives, welfare benefits, and social pressure to achieve its objectives. Despite prophecies to the contrary, the result has not been to produce a more homogenized society, but rather one in which the plural energies of Soviet society find easier expression. The diverse interests which the party seeks to contain have assumed increasingly visible political form. In a one-party system of the Soviet type, interest representation expresses itself in ways quite different from those which prevail in political systems where interest groups are free to organize, to appeal to the electorate, and voice their demands before legislative and executive bodies. Soviet politics tend to be bureaucratic politics, and bureaucratic politics typically take the form of intra-elite struggles which reflect conflicting institutional interests and group views. Party functionaries may unite in fending off challenges to their predominance, but since their responsibilities encompass the whole of Soviet society, they also mirror the variety of interests represented in that society. Thus, those party functionaries charged with responsibility for agriculture may plead the case for agricultural investments, while those responsible for various industrial sectors may identify with the interests in their charge. Regional and republic secretaries assert the claims of their localities, and each section of the party apparatus tends to become the guardian of its own preserve.

The armed forces have their own interests to safeguard. Like military establishments elsewhere, the Soviet armed forces press for a high level of military expenditures and have their own internal problem of allocating resources between the older, more conventional arms and the newer strategic nuclear missiles forces.[28] There are built-in institutional frictions between the military professionals and the party representatives in the army who play a watch-dog role. The security police no longer exercise the awesome power which they enjoyed under Stalin, and like the armed forces, they are party-controlled and penetrated. But they too have their vested bureaucratic interests and are naturally concerned to expand their power and influence. Since they live and grow by crisis and vigilance, they are under constant temptation to create the incidents which will testify to their indispensability.

The state bureaucracy represents another identifiable interest formation. While it may be joined together by a common desire to fend off undue interference by party functionaries, it is actually divided and fragmented among various economic and other sectors, each of which seeks maximum support at the expense of its bureaucratic competitors. Nowhere is the process of bureaucratic politics more visible than in the continuing battle for the allocation of scarce resources as spokesmen for the military, heavy

[28] See Thomas W. Wolfe, *Soviet Strategy at the Cross Roads* (Cambridge: Harvard University Press, 1964).

industry, light industry, agriculture, and other interests press their rival claims.

Factory and other enterprise managers in trade and agriculture constitute still another source of pressure. As Soviet press reports make amply clear, the thrust of their demands for many years has been more autonomy in decision-making and freedom to marshal their internal resources in the interests of efficient production. Given the growing complexity of the Soviet economy, accommodation to their aspirations appears increasingly essential to rational management.

The scientists too represent an influential group with growing influence. The leverage which they exert is maximized because they hold the key to technological progress. Their crucial indispensability lends force to their demands for scientific freedom and for adequate supporting resources.

The cultural elite makes up still another cluster of interests. It is expected by the regime to serve as an instrument of indoctrination in official party values, but the cultural elite is itself divided between those who are prepared to accept the role of custodians of party orthodoxy and others who aspire to function as critics and innovators. The literary and artistic debates of the Khrushchevian years mirror these divergent tendencies. While the party leaders have been willing to make room for and even encourage so-called orthodox dissent or within-system criticism, they have sternly rebuffed and are likely to continue to condemn any challenge to the party's infallibility.

Even at the base of the Soviet social pyramid, rank-and-file peasants and workers are now in a position to exert greater influence on the course of elite decision-making. When collective or state farm workers respond to inadequate incentives by listless performance in the public sector, by transferring their energies to private plots, or by abandoning their jobs to seek better-paid work in the industrial centers, they in effect bargain to improve their position. In the absence of large-scale terror, there is a point beyond which they cannot be driven. If more production is to be extracted from them, improved incentives have to be provided. The state and party functionaries responsible for increasing agricultural output find themselves forced to plead the case of their peasant clients. In a perhaps perverted form, what takes place is a form of indirect representation.

The same principle applies more or less to the industrial

worker. In the absence of forced labor, workers abandon unattractive jobs in search of better opportunities. Those who are
responsible for the recruitment of labor in difficult circumstances
—whether they be enterprise directors or party secretaries—
recognize that they must provide incentives and amenities if they
are to attract a work force. Willingly or unwillingly, they become
spokesmen for the workers' needs and demands when they argue
the case for greater incentives as a key to increased production.

The emergence of a process of group interplay, even though in
a political form quite different from the Western constitutional
pattern, represents an important new stage in the history of the
Soviet Communist Party. In the Stalinist phase of high totalitarianism, as the Soviet Union accelerated its program of forced
draft industrialization and collectivization, primary emphasis was
given to the mobilizing role of the party. While educational
opportunities and incentives were made available to build up the
technical intelligentsia and cadres of skilled workers, there was
extensive reliance on terror and forced labor to enforce a regime
of austerity and sacrifice for most of the population. Stalin's
system of intensive mobilization and calculated insecurity tended
to fragment both elite and masses and was successful in discouraging any form of independent group activity.

While it would be incorrect to suggest that the party has
abandoned its mobilizing role, some modification is apparent.
With the abandonment of large-scale terror, there is greater
dependence on indoctrination, persuasion, and such forms of
social pressure as the comrades' courts, the *druzhiny,* or people's
guards, and the anti-parasite tribunals to discourage deviant social behavior and to enforce prescribed conduct. But perhaps
more important, there is much greater reliance on economic
incentives to induce responses which the party leadership deems
essential. The result has been to introduce a strong adaptive
ingredient into the party's mobilizing role. As the diverse interests
which the party seeks to manipulate begin to exercise greater
leverage, the party leaders find themselves mediating and balancing the claims of the functional and professional groups whose
synchronized efforts arc required to maintain the system's forward momentum. Whether the transformation of a mobilizing
party into an adaptive party will operate as a threat to the
system's dynamism is not easily determinable. It may well be that

the successful management and direction of a complex and sophisticated industrial society offer no other alternative.

The road which the Soviet Communist Party has traversed differs in important respects from that which the Chinese Communist Party has so far traveled.[29] Comparisons of the character and commitments of their respective memberships must necessarily take these differences into account. The Bolshevik seizure of power came with dramatic suddenness; within the space of months a small and relatively insignificant conspiratorial party leaning largely on worker support in industrial areas and with no experience of governance captured authority at the center, and after another three years of civil war managed to consolidate its control. The Chinese Communist march to power, by contrast, was a much more protracted affair. The first attempts under Russian tutelage and direction to collaborate with the Kuomintang, and then to seize power in the cities and industrial areas resulted in a series of disasters. Forced to retreat to the countryside, the Chinese Communists under Mao's leadership made a virtue out of necessity, built their bases in the rural areas, shaped their appeals and policies to win peasant support, organized peasant armies, recruited the mass of their membership from the peasantry, and transferred the party into a militarized vanguard for the conquest of power. Where the Bolsheviks were virtually catapulted to power in 1917, more than fourteen years elapsed between Mao's assumption of party leadership at the Tsun-yi conference in 1935 and the final defeat of Chiang Kai-shek in 1949. Unlike the Russians, the Chinese Communists had a long period of apprenticeship during which they exercised governing responsibilities over substantial parts of their future domain. They were able to use this interval to build large contingents of trusted cadres, to acquire considerable experience in rural administration, and to mold a disciplined body of party officials and army officers to serve as a nucleus for a future governing class.

Once power was won, the two parties pursued different strategies of membership recruitment. During the Civil War, the Bolsheviks inducted peasant soldiers into party ranks in order to strengthen their links with the countryside, where they were virtually unrepresented. The Chinese Communists, on the other

[29] A reading of the preliminary draft of John Lindbeck's companion paper on the Chinese Communist Party contributed importantly to the formulation of these comparisons.

hand, emphasized the recruitment of workers and intellectuals, since the task which they faced involved extending their authority to the cities and industrial centers.

With civil war behind them, the policies pursued by both parties also differed markedly. Bolshevik weakness in the rural areas was reflected in the NEP retreat, which in effect left the peasants in possession of their land while the Bolsheviks concentrated their energies on restoring production, on perfecting their control system, and orienting their recruitment policies toward the urban workers. The radical restructuring of Soviet society did not really begin until the launching of the collectivization and industrialization programs in 1928. By contrast the Chinese experience was much more telescoped. After a relatively cautious three-year period of transition and rehabilitation, the Chinese Communist leadership launched its ambitious First Five-Year Plan in 1953, at the same time initiated the first phase of its collectivization program, and then followed by announcing that the full stage of agricultural collectivization would be completed by 1958. That same year came the call for the Great Leap Forward with its introduction of agricultural communes and its gigantic efforts to mobilize the total energies of a nation to perform unprecedented production feats. While the disorganization which ensued and the subsequent retreat from full-fledged communes recall a somewhat parallel development in Russia in the early thirties when the "excesses" of collectivization were officially condemned and repudiated, it remains true that the Chinese Communist effort to transform its society proceeded at a pace and with an intensity that has no equivalent in Soviet history.

This difference may also offer a partial clue to the rather diverse approaches of the two parties to the task of molding the character and shaping the commitments of their respective memberships. The model of the dedicated and disciplined Communist activist is one which the Chinese Communists inherited from their Soviet colleagues. So too the institution of criticism and self-criticism has its precedents in Soviet prescriptions. But the thoroughness and depth of the Chinese Communist effort to integrate the individual into the collective by using the small group as an instrument of rectification and manipulation go well beyond Soviet practice. Whether the pattern be rooted in the cultural and social structure of historical China or be traceable to new techniques devised by the Chinese leadership to achieve a rapid and radical restructuring of traditional attitudes, the result has been to produce a form of pervasive group control and a degree of ideological involvement and commitment that cannot be found to the same degree in Soviet society.

The continuity and stability of the Chinese party leadership provide still another striking contrast with Soviet experience. Had Lenin not died prematurely, it is possible that the contrast would not have been so striking. It is also possible that the cohesiveness of the Chinese leadership group will not survive Mao's death. Meanwhile, the capacity of the Chinese leaders to maintain their esprit de corps remains an impressive feat which has contributed to the unity and strength of the party. Whether the phenomenon be attributable to the years of comradeship in adversity, or to the central and transcendent role assigned to Mao and his doctrines, the solidarity of the ruling group has been impressive. It has ensured forceful direction of China's vast experiments in social engineering and given Mao and the group around him a position of unmatched prestige in the international Communist movement. By comparison, the Soviet record since Lenin's death with its bitter factional struggles, its bloody internal party purges, and the denigrations to which both Stalin and Khrushchev have been subjected have had their inevitable effect in undermining confidence in both Soviet leadership and doctrine.

It is, of course, hazardous to compare a party like the Chinese which is still led by its revolutionary generation and which presides over the destinies of a poor underdeveloped country with the Soviet party which has been in power for nearly half a century and which directs the fortunes of a relatively affluent and mature industrial society. Developments which have already taken place in the Soviet Union may well foreshadow experiences which Communist China will repeat at a later point in its history. The impact of modernization and industrialization on the Soviet party has been to raise the importance of the technical intelligentsia at the expense of workers and peasants and to transform large parts of the ruling elite into a technically educated managerial group which dedicates much of its energy to the rational management of an increasingly complex industrial society. As Communist China embarks on the path of industrialization, a somewhat similar pattern of development may be anticipated. The first faint signs of such a transformation have already become visible. The drive to modernize has been reflected in a considerable strengthening of the intellectual contingent in the party, and particular emphasis has been placed in recent years on the recruitment of students, teachers, engineers, technicians, and other professional personnel. The poorly educated older party veterans, while still entrenched in military, police, and party organizational activities, have been shunted aside when managerial posts requiring technical or other educational qualifications have had to be filled. While top party and governmental posts still remain securely in the hands of the revolutionary generation, a more literate and better educated younger generation has been working its way up the secretarial echelons of the party and taking over the management of economic enterprises and other posts where professional competence is required. Should this trend continue over the next decades, it may augur an inner transformation in the character of the Chinese Communist Party resembling that which the Communist Party of the Soviet Union has undergone.

There is a final difference between the two parties which is perhaps most fundamental of all. When a Communist party takes power and sinks its roots in national soil, its perception of its needs and the nature of its commitments cannot avoid being colored by the national interests which it has inherited and the pressures of the milieu in which it is compelled to function. A common ideological legacy does not of itself ensure that it will be applied in precisely the same way regardless of time, place, and circumstance. Indeed, the history of most faiths and creeds suggests that they undergo substantial mutations as they are domesticated. If Leninism in its Soviet variant has developed to a point where Russian national interests and Soviet Communist objectives have become virtually indistinguishable, so Leninism in its Maoist version has been subjected to a comparable process of sinification. Over the long run, the results are likely to be visible, not merely in the clashing interests already dramatized by the Sino-Soviet dispute, but also in a continuing process of accommodation in which each party is increasingly shaped by its own environment.

Transformations in the Chinese Communist Party

J. M. H. LINDBECK

THE impact of the assumption of power in 1949 on the character and commitments of the membership of the Chinese Communist Party, that is to say, on the composition and functions of the party, can be understood only in terms of its earlier history. The party's role in Chinese politics, its organizational forms, its leadership, its working style, its objectives and programs all, in varying degrees, were fashioned and took shape during the Maoist period after 1935, when it relentlessly fought to achieve national power. This history cannot be reviewed here, but it is useful, indeed necessary, to note a few of the salient features of the party's experience and development in this earlier period in order to put the post-1949 transformation of the party into perspective.

The Chinese Communist Party was both the product and instrument of revolution. Like its competitor, the Nationalist Party (Kuomintang), it was the outgrowth of revolutionary movements fostered by a combination of Western influences and the disorders of a polity and society that were no longer able to meet the domestic and foreign needs of their people. Its founders in 1921 belonged to the literate minority who were alienated from the past and despaired of the present. They were, like the leaders of the Kuomintang, participants in and strongly affected by the revolutionary social and political activities that took form after the turn of the century and became increasingly intense and organized after the First World War. The party leadership was, in short, a part of the larger movement of those who were out to remake and modernize China—to create a new political system, to find a new ideological and constitutional basis for establishing a national consensus, to develop new social values and relationships, to industrialize the country, and to expand China's international influence and power.

The Communist Party was the creation of minority radical elements in the Chinese nationalist revolutionary movement. Not only were its leaders prepared to make a sharp and violent break with China's past, but they also were committed to the introduction of a particular and prescribed revolutionary system drawn from Marxist-Leninist concepts and Russian experience. This special commitment led to separate organizations which, in turn, finally produced a major division within the Chinese revolutionary movement. United by common antipathy to foreign intrusions and to the warlord coalitions which dominated the country, the Communist Party worked closely at first with the more broadly based revolutionary forces under the Kuomintang which were seeking to introduce a united national government. After a period of collaboration, the two parties—Communist and Kuomintang—broke in 1927 over the issue of control of the new nationalist government they had brought to power in China. Thereafter the Communist Party competed openly with the Kuomintang for control of the country.

The break with the Kuomintang had tremendous consequences for Chinese politics. The competition between rival revolutionary elites, Nationalist and Communist, increasingly dominated Chinese affairs. In time, competition between the two major parties led to a gradual reduction of the power and influence of all other political groups, both national and regional, and the absorption of larger and larger parts of the country into the orbit of one or the other rival party.

The contest for power drove both parties toward increasing reliance on military force. In the Chinese setting of the time this tendency may have been almost inescapable, because there was no integrated political system through which divergent and minority interests could seek orderly expression and fulfillment. China was fragmented into a host of unstable political administrations bolstered by military forces. The main task for the Communist leadership became the refashioning of the party for the military conquest of China. The wild revolutionism that was rampant in the period after 1927 and at times during the Kiangsi Soviet (1931–34) was replaced by Maoist pragmatism after

1935. The Maoist leadership set out to create a militarily effective force capable of competing with the warlords and the Kuomintang. Mao Tse-tung affirmed that "the army is the chief component of the political power of a state." The path to power in China was by way of military action not political activities, for "political power grows out of the barrel of a gun."[1]

The break with the Kuomintang exiled the Communists from the cities and industrial areas. They were compelled to revise their strategies and programs to accommodate to their rural environment and to remold the party into an instrument for mobilizing and directing peasant military forces. In order to win peasant support and maintain rural morale in the territory which it controlled, the party leadership sacrificed revolutionary agricultural schemes for reform measures which promised to satisfy critical peasant aspirations.

The Communist Party also needed to attract the support of educated and skilled men and women to provide leadership for the illiterate and parochial peasants. The party leadership needed both masses of peasant soldiers and a small but loyal core of officers. The programs it championed therefore had to combine nationalistic and revolutionary appeals capable of attracting, in competition with the Kuomintang, the allegiance of a sector of the country's urban and technically and educationally skilled population. Its rural, territorial policies were developed to mobilize peasant manpower and resources; its "united front" coalitional strategies, which kept them in touch with the revolutionary and modernizing urban youth, were designed to recruit the officers needed to man the party's military and administrative staffs.[2]

MILITARIZATION OF THE COMMUNIST MOVEMENT

In competition with warlord groups and the Nationalist government, the party won, not because of its effective political mobilization of the majority of the Chinese people, although it did have either the active or passive support of politically important groups, but because it built a more efficient military system. Mao Tse-tung and his associates became preoccupied with problems of

[1] Mao Tse-tung, "Problems of War and Strategy" (Nov. 6, 1938), in *Selected Works of Mao Tse-tung* (London: Lawrence & Wishart, 1954), II, 272.

[2] See Mao Tse-tung on "The Orientation of the Youth Movement" (May 4, 1939) and the Central Committee Resolution of Dec. 1, 1939, on "Draw in Large Numbers of Intellectuals," in *ibid*, III, 12–21, 69–71.

warfare.[3] In 1939 the "militarization of party members" was adopted as a basic slogan by the party, and this became the principle upon which the entire party was to be organized.[4] Beginning in 1937 with about 40,000 members who had survived the Long March and earlier guerrilla struggles, the party grew to 1,210,000 members by the end of the war with Japan in 1945. Of this number about 1,000,000 members of the party were under the so-called "military supply system," that is, working without salaries and under military-type discipline. As described by the Chinese Communists, they "led a life of strict military Communism."[5] A substantial percentage of these people, in turn, were regular members of the People's Liberation Army. In the army they not only served as combatants but also acted as the army's political and propaganda specialists and as the party's security agents. The party leadership depended upon party members in the 8th Route Army and the new 4th Army to act as "models of heroism in warfare and as models in the execution of orders, in their discipline, in political work, and in maintaining internal unity and solidarity."[6] These members enabled the leadership to maintain control and discipline over peasant troops and also provided the cadres for the local military governments which were established in Communist-occupied areas.

The result of the militarization policy was that dedication, fighting spirit, and responsiveness to discipline and orders became the hallmark of Communist Party members, as well as the harsher virtues of a soldier—ruthlessness, toughness, and a will to override and subdue other people. They held the guns out of which Mao's political power and everything else grew. By the time the party had conquered China, the bulk of its membership was made up of triumphant warriors.

This created problems. As Liu Shao-ch'i told his colleagues at

[3] For bibliography on the Communist Chinese army see Edward J. M. Rhoads, *The Chinese Red Army, 1927–1963: An Annotated Bibliography* (Cambridge: East Asian Research Center, Harvard University, 1964).

[4] "Remoulding the Party's Style of Work and Improving Its State of Organization," *Jen-min jih-pao* (*JMJP*), July 1, 1950, in Boyd Compton, *Mao's China: Party Reform Documents, 1942–44* (Seattle: University of Washington Press, 1952), pp. 272–78.

[5] Ch'en Yün, "How To Be a Communist Party Member," in Conrad Brandt, Benjamin Schwartz, and John Fairbank, *A Documentary History of Chinese Communism* (Cambridge: Harvard University Press, 1952), p. 335.

[6] *Ibid.*, p. 333.

the Seventh Party Congress on May 14, 1945, there was a tendency among some comrades to regard "the army as a special power standing outside or above the people." This manifested itself in a "purely military approach to the relationship between the revolutionary army and the revolutionary government, seeking to place the army above the government and to run the government by the army, just as the warlords would do."[7]

After coming to power, some of the Chinese Communist leaders noted that there were party members who felt they should enjoy the fruits of their victory—that since "the world is won by the peasants, peasants must rule the world"; that others complained that "those who win an empire do not rule; those who rule an empire [did] not win it."[8]

These attitudes were rather quickly attacked and eradicated by the party leaders. The army was not to be allowed by the party leaders to become an independent force or interest group in the new political system. The army had for the most part completed the task of military pacification and military government by 1952. Civilian agencies had been created as rapidly as possible and by that time had begun to function effectively. As a result, between 1952 and 1954 the political and administrative powers of the initial regional military-political party administrations were thoroughly displaced by those of new centralized administrative bureaus and departments. The army meantime was employed in the Korean War and as a reserve force in major policing operations. The original ambitions and expectations of the conquering troops were finally supplanted by the professionalism which accompanied the introduction of conscription and the regularization of the military organization.[9]

Military communism, however, left its mark on the post-1949 party. Military terms and figures of speech have been incorporated into the party's vocabulary and invest party communications with a highly militant and violent quality. The army has been held up at times as an organizational model to be emulated

---

[7] Liu Shao-ch'i, *On the Party* (Peking: Foreign Languages Press, 1950), pp. 50–51.

[8] Po I-po, "Strengthening the Party's Political Work in the Countryside," *JMJP*, June 29, 1951, in *Current Background* (*CB*), No. 161 (Feb. 20, 1952), p. 19; Tung Pi-wu, "On Strengthening Work Connected with Conference of Representatives of the People," *JMJP*, Jan. 30, 1952, in *CB*, No. 162 (Feb. 22, 1952), p. 12.

[9] Ellis Joffe, "The Conflict Between Old and New in the Chinese Army," *China Quarterly*, No. 15 (Apr.–June, 1964), pp. 118–40.

for its individual and group discipline, its political commitments, its accomplishment of set tasks, its well-defined leadership, and its morale and group solidarity based on the highly collectivized form of organization of its members. The Chinese people have had the unusual experience of being swept into the militia through a mass movement.[10]

CONTINUITY AND STABILITY OF PARTY LEADERSHIP

In the transition to becoming the party in power, the men on top stayed on top. They kept firm control of the party—a control which they successfully maintained to conduct a remarkably orderly transition, followed by a radical restructuring of Chinese society to fit prescribed revolutionary patterns. The continuity and stability of the party's leadership is striking. The political durability of this leadership has been greater than that of any other major Communist Party, including the Russian.

For thirty years Mao Tse-tung has firmly presided over the party and is its undisputed leader. Its key figures clearly are his men. Almost all of the senior men and the majority of the Central Committee members shared the Long March of 1934–35 with him. The "core group" at the top is composed of 24 men in the Political Bureau, 22 of whom were among the 43 regular members and 27 alternate members of the 7th Central Committee, first elected in 1945. Forty-one members of the 7th Central Committee survive as regular members of the present 8th Central Committee. By 1958 the Central Committee had been enlarged to 97 regular members and 96 alternates. So far as can be determined, all of these 193 persons joined the party before 1938 and with perhaps no exceptions attained prominence in party affairs before 1949. Only a few of Mao's leading lieutenants before 1949 have been dropped or removed from positions of importance (Kao Kang, Jao Shu-shih, Peng Te-huai are the most notable), except by illness or death from natural causes.[11]

[10] See T. A. Hsia, *Metaphor, Myth, Ritual and the People's Commune* (Berkeley: Center for Chinese Studies, University of California, 1961), pp. 1–15; John Gittings, "China's Militia" and "The 'Learn from the Army' Campaign," *China Quarterly*, No. 18 (Apr.–June, 1964), pp. 100–17, 153–59.
[11] For information on the party leadership see Robert C. North, *Kuomintang and Chinese Communist Elites* (Stanford: Stanford University Press, 1952); Franklin W. Houn, "The Eighth Central Committee of the Chinese Communist Party: A Study of an Elite," *The American Political Science Review*, LI (1957), 392–404; Chao Kuo-chün, "Leadership in the

Since acquiring his leading position at the Tsun-yi conference of the Political Bureau in 1935, Mao's continuity of tenure has had an immense impact on the party. It has been his authority, his statement of values and doctrines, and his men that have permeated the party and built it from a regional band of 40,000 members in 1937 to 17 million in 1962, and perhaps 20 million by 1965. Factionalism, regionalism, and competing loyalties have not been allowed to emerge or have been quickly suppressed by the determined and powerful group that runs the party. This continuity and solidarity are reinforced by the central place given to Mao and his "thoughts." Maoism is the only orthodox interpretation of communism. Maoist doctrines were developed in their essentials before the party came to power and have continued to provide ideological continuity between the rebel band at Yenan and the party cohorts who now govern all of China from Peking party palaces. Within the party, continuity of leadership and doctrine has produced a stable pattern of political relationships and loyalties, especially at the top but probably also down through the ranks.

All of these factors minimized the disruptive impact of the change of function and perspective which the party had to undergo to carry out the social and economic transformation of China sought by its leaders. At the same time, the isolation of the party leadership before 1949 from the areas and groups experiencing urbanization, industrialization, and related aspects of scientific and technological change, and the concentration of Mao and the party leadership on developing a corpus of doctrines and operational styles to meet the situation of rural China and military operations left the party a legacy of ideas, principles, practices, and leaders that were a drag if not a positive handicap in the drive to achieve China's full potentials for economic and social development in the post-1949 period. There has been no transition similar to the shift in Russia from Lenin to Stalin.

Chinese Communist Party," *The Annals of the American Academy of Political and Social Science*, Vol. 321 (Jan., 1959), pp. 40–50; Donald W. Klein, "The 'Next Generation' of Chinese Communist Leaders," *China Quarterly*, No. 12 (Oct.–Dec., 1962), pp. 57–74. Harold C. Hinton, "The Succession Problem in Communist China," *Current Scene* (Hong Kong), Vol. I, No. 7 (July 19, 1961); and biographies of several Communist leaders (Mao Tse-tung, Liu Shao-ch'i, Tung Pi-wu) by Howard L. Boorman appearing in the *China Quarterly*.

Mao's professional revolutionaries have not yet given way to a new elite group of professional rulers.[12]

PRE-1949 EXPERIENCE IN GOVERNMENT AND ADMINISTRATION

To cope with the problems of government after coming to power, the party leadership had the benefit of some early experience and the training received in its wartime power bases. As young men, many of the party leaders had served as administrators in the Kuomintang's Canton government or elsewhere. Almost all had a good deal of administrative experience, as had large numbers of party members at all levels, in managing the territorial bases the party controlled through its military forces. By 1945 the party claimed to rule 95 million people in these bases, which it thought of as "a pattern for the New China."[13] Primitive though the institutions and administrative agencies were, a fairly large number of party members did acquire some knowledge and rudimentary skills which could be applied to the provinces and cities they conquered in 1948 and 1949. They apparently relied on the standard military government principles and procedures practiced in occupied territory by conquering armies. Incumbent officials and the staffs of various agencies and enterprises were directed to remain at their posts and carry on their jobs.[14] By planting a small number of supervisors in existing agencies and enterprises, the party quickly restored local services and economic and social activities. Although the newly conquered areas were very different from the local and regional peasant enclaves they had been administering, party groups were

[12] See Zbigniew Brzezinski and Samuel P. Huntington, *Political Power: USA/USSR* (New York: Viking Press, 1963), p. 141. Compare the Chinese experience with the Russian: "Most of the Russian revolutionary leaders lived in exile; they had neither fought nor shared the same hardships. They spent much of their time hurling abuse and polemics at one another. The second generation of Soviet leaders who now rule are not even welded together by the struggle against the old regime, since most of them joined the Party after it had taken power." Donald S. Zagoria, "Some Comparisons Between the Russian and Chinese Models," in A. Doak Barnett (ed.), *Communist Strategies in Asia: A Comparative Analysis of Governments and Parties* (New York and London: Praeger, 1963), p. 26.

[13] Liu Shao-ch'i, *On the Party*, pp. 7–8; John W. Lewis, *Leadership in Communist China* (Ithaca: Cornell University Press, 1963), p. 166, believes the territory under Communist control was somewhat smaller—91 million square miles.

[14] See "Proclamation of the Chinese People's Liberation Army, April 25, 1949," in *Selected Works of Mao Tse-tung*, IV (Peking: Foreign Languages Press, 1961), 397–400.

able to staff and run urban centers, large enterprises such as banks, and communication and transport services.[15] On coming to power the Chinese Communist Party had the twin advantage of solid administrative control over millions of people and thousands of square miles, and the plans and the corps of partially trained administrators necessary to govern the rest of the country.

Thus, the Chinese Communist Party faced the problems of running China with strong assets. It possessed powerful and victorious military forces; a stable, united, and competent leadership group sufficiently reliable to permit wide delegation of authority; a membership large enough in its mobile and quasi-military and military units to blanket key centers throughout the country; existing administrative control of important territories which served as base areas; and a corps of men with some administrative experience and competence. Moreover, the party leadership was already anticipating the exercise of nation-wide power and preparing the party for its new tasks to be performed directly or through willing and unwilling collaborators. The Chinese Communist Party had a shadow government, including a National Assembly (the People's Political Consultative Conference), ready in the wings to legitimize its rule over China.[16]

It has been said that Russia's Communist leaders came to power "by a combination of fortune and accident during a domestic revolution caused by an external military defeat."[17] China's Communist leaders came to power by careful planning and by prolonged military operations conducted with large and trained military forces and party units operating from their own territorial bases against a government debilitated by internal corrosion and war against an external enemy. When the Chinese Communist leaders came to power they had at their command what Lenin lacked: a large, well-organized, and highly disciplined party with administrative experience and well-developed operating principles. The latter were well adapted to accommodate

[15] See A. Doak Barnett, *China on the Eve of Communist Takeover* (New York: Praeger, 1963), pp. 338–57.

[16] See, for example, Mao Tse-tung, "On Coalition Government," *Selected Works of Mao Tse-tung*, IV, 244–315; also "On the September Meeting," pp. 269–76; "Turn the Army into a Working Force," pp. 337–39; "Report to the Second Plenary Session of the 7th Central Committee," pp. 361–75.

[17] Brzezinski and Huntington, *Political Power*, pp. 28–29.

rapid expansion of membership and to integrate large groups of newcomers into the party through the Chinese Party control mechanisms of "rectification," "thought reform," and "struggle meetings."

In addition, the Chinese Communists had the Soviet model and experience in administration to guide them. Not only had some Chinese had experience in Russia, but the Soviet Union also sent thousands of technicians and specialists to China to help the party get specialized services and key industries working efficiently.

PARTY REDEVELOPMENT AFTER 1949

Since coming to power, Communist China's leaders have had to deal with the continuous problem of fashioning ways of translating their goals, programs, and decisions into policy.

In the process they have transformed the party from a politically organized force of peasants and soldiers into a complex institution performing a variety of executive, administrative, and political functions. The principal tasks set for the party have undergone, in rough sequence, these major changes: (1) military victory; (2) consolidation of political power through destroying political opponents and empowering new political groups; (3) creation of a new structure of government; (4) "socialist transformation"—social modernization through the destruction of old and creation of new institutions of property, production, and social relationships; and (5) "socialist construction"—economic development. The size, structure, composition, and functions of the party have been substantially altered with these changes in objectives. The transformation of the party is the result of the change in the party's role in the execution and administration of national policy.

Party membership was built up to over seventeen million by 1962 and by 1965 perhaps to twenty million people—a number exceeding the population of Taiwan by four or five million and almost equal to the population of Canada or East Germany. To this number must be added more than twenty-five million members of the Young Communist League, whose ages range from fourteen to twenty-five years. The League, described as the "party's assistant," is a branch of the party controlled by a department of the Central Committee. Although there is some overlapping of membership, together, the party and the league, with their forty-two million members, represented about 6 per cent of the population in 1962 and formed the organized political forces upon which the party leadership principally relied to exercise control and influence.

"Party building" is not a haphazard process. It is directly related to the role or functions assigned to the party by its leaders. The first priority and underlying condition for membership is, of course, political: strong, if not absolute, support of the leadership. This support is measured by knowledge, sometimes very rudimentary, and acceptance of the essentials of a complex and prescribed belief system—the Maoist version of the Marxist-Leninist world view; a personal record of social or group activity in support of the party's programs; a demonstration of some leadership capacity; willingness to comply with party rituals and group behavior patterns; and submission to organizational discipline and to the authority of higher party officials.[18] These criteria have been very unevenly interpreted and applied at times; standards differ markedly for simple working people inducted into low-level rural branches and those admitted to party organizations for intellectuals and administrative and professional specialists. High political qualifications alone, however, do not ensure admission to the party. Nor do relatively poor political qualifications necessarily exclude a person from membership. At times local politics and personal influence affect the selection of members.[19]

The significant factor in shaping recruitment, however, is the systematic effort of Chinese leaders to develop the party as an effective national agency to carry out assigned functions. Membership targets are periodically established by the leadership, calling for expansion in areas where party strength is needed or establishing restrictive quotas in areas of less need. Periodic surveys are made of the distribution of party strength in industrial, production, administrative, and cultural enterprises and in

[18] These requirements have been variously stated. See, for example, Articles 1 and 2 of the 1956 Party Constitution; An Tzu-wen, "Strengthen the Work of Party Reform and Party Expansion, etc.," *JMJP*, July 1, 1952, in *CB*, No. 191; "How We Manage and Educate Newly Recruited Party Members," *Honan jih-pao*, Dec. 29, 1958, in *Survey of the China Mainland Press (SCMP)*, No. 1959, p. 14; Lewis, *Leadership in Communist China*, pp. 101–7.
[19] Teng Hsiao-p'ing in *Eighth National Congress of the Communist Party of China (8th Party Congress)* (Peking: Foreign Languages Press, 1956), I, 214.

rural areas. Targets are then set for the recruitment of members from each social or institutional category by various party units.[20]

A number of criteria have been used in setting targets: comprehensive geographic distribution, coverage of all major segments of the population—including women, workers, farmers, teachers, soldiers, and youth—penetration of key institutions, and sufficiency of manpower to accomplish special tasks such as programs of collectivization or industrial reorganization.

TERRITORIAL COMPREHENSIVENESS

The organizational pattern of the party is tied to the land— territorially structured and rooted in rural administrative divisions. Geographic distribution of party members is therefore an operating principle for party building. Before 1949 party control was concentrated in the rural north. After coming to power, the party leadership first developed new party bases in industrial and administrative cities and towns down through the county seat and district (*ch'ü*) level. Next they extended the organization in regions yet to be covered. There were party units in only 170,000 of 220,000 *hsiang*, or administrative villages, in 1955. In large areas, in the absence of established local party organizations, land reform had had to be carried out by roving party teams and units, often drawn from district military forces. The party speeded its rural recruitment and organizational work in 1955 and 1956 in order to plant party branches in virtually every *hsiang*, making possible intensive collectivization and the launching of labor drives during the Great Leap and in the communes.[21]

The party's general policy was to recruit into membership politically alert opponents of the local elites and to create a new local elite (often drawn from less reputable elements) by conferring party memberships on a small nucleus of persons who might be counted upon to support the party in the locality. Less effort was made in areas under special minority group jurisdiction

[20] Extensive surveys and recruitment drives took place in 1955 and 1956. A typical case is that of Shensi which, after a provincial survey, set a target of 38,300 recruits for 1955. *Shensi jih-pao,* Mar. 6, 1955. Teng Hsiao-p'ing at the 8th Party Congress discussed the importance of "a planned way to admit those who apply for membership and are fully qualified for it." *8th Party Congress,* I, 216–17.
[21] *New China News Agency* (NCNA), Peking, Mar. 8, 1955, in *SCMP,* No. 1003, p. 12.

where social changes were being introduced less rapidly. The present pattern is one in which the party system is almost as complete in its coverage of China as the civil bureaucracy, or government. In a few places party members probably are the only local representatives of the present political order.

INSTITUTIONAL CONCENTRATIONS

The party has been especially careful to extend strong party organization to key functional institutions—civil administration, mass organizations, education, economic enterprises—and to maintain a substantial party membership in the military forces.

The army has some 2.5 million men; the Public Security Forces add another 1.7 million to the total.[22] The stated party policy in 1951 was set forth in a note appearing in the first volume of the *Selected Works of Mao Tse-tung:* "Experience has shown that it works out quite well when party members number about one-third of the complement of the Red Army. This proportion was generally maintained in the Red Army and in the People's Liberation Army."[23] With the introduction of military conscription in 1954 and 1955, the percentage of party members fluctuated, but there is no reason to believe that it has significantly declined. It might be estimated that 90 per cent of the field grade officers and above, 80 per cent of the junior officers, and 10 per cent of the noncommissioned officers are party members and that Youth League membership in the lower ranks is very widespread.

The focus of party attention and guidance is the government. The main component of government is the vast civil administration organized and directed by the State Council and reaching down through provincial, county, and *hsiang* governments to hamlets and towns and to municipal wards and streets. In this bureaucratic hierarchy the concentration of party members is heaviest at the top. The Standing Meeting of the State Council, which can exercise the full authority of that body, is composed almost entirely of members, full and alternate, of the Political Bureau, the others being members of the Central Committee.[24] About three-fourths of the members of the State Council are party members. Although so-called state organs at first had few party

[22] Edgar Snow, *The Other Side of the River: Red China Today* (New York: Random House, 1961), p. 350.

[23] I, 307, note 16.

[24] Article 4, Organic Law of the State Council of the People's Republic of China.

members, by 1956, according to An Tzu-wen, Director of the Organization Department of the Central Committee of the party, one-third of the cadres working at the county level and above were party or Youth League members.[25] In Shensi province 23.6 per cent of the government employees in 1955 were party members.[26] For the country as a whole, the actual proportion of party members in the administrative branches of the government at each level is unreported. However, there clearly is a heavy concentration of party members in the network of government agencies.

Party representation is organized in other kinds of institutions. In 1956 about one million party members worked in mass organizations. "Cultural and educational institutions"—those concerned with dissemination of information and the development of attitudes and social behavior—have received special attention: over 425,000 party members were in such institutions by 1956.[27] In the economic field large factories and major commercial and transportation enterprises all have substantial blocs of party members among their employees.

Since political qualifications are prerequisite to appointment in all public positions of authority or responsibility, and since the Communist Party has an exclusive mandate to determine the political eligibility or qualifications of all such appointees, the party performs a basic personnel function for all public institutions and organizations. The political orientation of employees of state agencies and of the leaders of all organized groups is thus guaranteed to be favorable to the regime and its leaders. Membership in the party and the Young Communist League, and to a lesser degree in the mass organizations, either confirms or enhances eligibility for official and leadership positions and is therefore valued both by the party in making personnel evaluations and by aspirants to advancement and leadership positions. As public and mass organizations have required manpower with an increasing variety of skills, the party has sought, as far as possible, to provide the key specialists from among its members.

[25] *Staffing Procedures and Problems in Communist China,* A Study Submitted by the Subcommittee on National Security, Staffing and Operations to the Committee on Government Operations, United States Senate (Washington, D.C.: U.S. Government Printing Office, 1963), p. 22.

[26] *Shensi jih-pao,* Mar. 9, 1955.

[27] *Staffing Procedures and Problems in Communist China,* from chart on p. 7.

This has led to a vast expansion of party membership, bringing into the party the most politically-minded, party-oriented representatives of many diverse groups.

PREFERRED SKILL GROUPS

The party is concerned with obtaining an effective presence among all strata of society. But all sectors of the population are not of equal importance for achieving the party's national goals. Despite the party leadership's doubts about the political reliability of intellectuals and its attacks on them, priority has been given to the recruitment of members from higher skill groups in order to staff and control key institutions and organizations.[28]

Since 1955, as modernization and rapid technological and economic growth have become prime party objectives, the leaders have evidenced dramatic, almost pathological, preoccupation with mobilizing intellectuals, although at the same time they fear them and therefore determinedly seek to transform their attitudes and values. The party leadership, on the basis of its record, appears to attach prime importance to enlisting members who have the training and capacity to assume managerial and sophisticated political assignments. Intellectuals have been presented with inducements, subjected to intensive pressures, and badgered with wide-ranging arguments to persuade them to accept the perspectives, values, policies, authority, and directives of the party leaders.[29] The non- or anti-intellectual members of the party have at the same time been urged to accept and work with the intellectuals. Party leaders have at times argued that standards of social origin and class status should not be rigidly applied in a puristic Marxist-Leninist fashion. Teng Hsiao-p'ing in 1956 reproved party members who opposed elimination from the party constitution of provisions applying social-class criteria and distinctions for admission to the party and who belittled the importance of

[28] See, for examples, *8th Party Congress.* I, 173; *JMJP*, Aug. 8, 1960, in *SCMP*, No. 2329, p. 4; *JMJP*, Mar. 27, 1963, in *SCMP*, No. 2959, p. 8.

[29] The problems of the party and the intellectuals have been much discussed. For example, see Roderick MacFarquhar, *The Hundred Flowers Campaign and the Chinese Intellectuals* (New York: Praeger, 1960); Theodore H. E. Chen, *Thought Reform of the Chinese Intellectual* (Hong Kong, 1960); Edgar Snow, *The Other Side of the River.* In his report to the National People's Congress on December 21 and 22, 1964, Chou En-lai proclaimed that "no intellectual can slacken his efforts at ideological remoulding."

white-collar workers and intellectuals.[30] In January 1956 Chou En-lai summarized at a national conference of party representatives the record of success and failure of the party in its work with intellectuals and alluded to "irrational features" of the party's treatment of intellectuals.[31] The purpose of the conference, he said, was "to strengthen the Party's leadership of intellectuals and of scientific and cultural work as a whole." The aim of the party was, Chou said, the development of a reorientation and recruitment program which by 1962 would ensure that "one third of the total number of higher intellectuals will be Party members," and that 75 rather than 40 per cent of the intellectuals would endorse the official ideology and be wholehearted supporters of the party and its program.

At that time, Chou said there were reported to be 3,840,000 intellectuals in China. In September 1956 the Organization Department of the Party's Central Committee classified 1,250,000 members as "intellectuals." Given comparable definitions, this would mean that already in 1956 about one-third of China's intellectuals were in the party. In the same year less than 18 per cent of the industrial workers and about 1.4 per cent of the peasants were party members. In proportional terms, educated and professional groups form the elite class or social stratum in the Chinese political system. It has been recognized, as the deputy director of the United Front Work Department of the Central Committee said in 1958, that in China intellectuals "monopolize cultural knowledge" and therefore their participation is essential for "organizing revolutionary forces and carrying on revolutionary work," and also for "social construction."[32]

[30] *8th Party Congress*, I, 213–15. The "Seventy Articles concerning Cultural and Educational Work," issued in December, 1961 (Union Research Service, Vol. XXIX, No. 22 [Dec. 14, 1962], pp. 337–47) attempted to create a favorable atmosphere for intellectuals, although political indoctrination and programs of reorientation through manual labor continued to bedevil the lives of students and intellectuals, and political discrimination against older, senior intellectuals continued.

[31] *Report on the Question of Intellectuals* (Peking: Foreign Languages Press, 1956).

[32] Chang Chih-i, "The Importance and Possibilities of the Reform of Intellectuals and Major Ways and Means of Reforming Intellectuals" (Peking: Chinese Home Service, in Mandarin, Oct. 12, 1958), *Foreign Broadcast Information Service* (*FBIS*), No. 19 (1958), BBB 1–13. Sixty per cent of college and university graduates in 1962 were party or Young Communist League members, and one half came from proletarian families. *JMJP*, Aug. 29, 1962, referred to in *China News Analysis* (Hong Kong), No. 476, p. 5.

The party has felt it was essential to continue to recruit large numbers of members from the rapidly increasing group of educated young people. The Second Five-Year Plan (1958–62) called for the turning out of half a million secondary-school graduates a year. A high proportion of these had to be drawn into the party if it was to meet its goals. To facilitate enlistment, the educational system was reshaped to promote favorable political attitudes among the students.[33] Thus far the problem facing the regime, however, is that of bringing a larger proportion of the present intellectual elite, the "higher intellectuals," into active participation in and support for the political system.

SHIFTS IN COMPOSITION OF MEMBERSHIP

Reflecting the changing functions of the party, shifts in the internal composition of the party up to about 1962[34] can be summarized as follows:

(1) Under the impetus of industrialization programs, there has been a marked shift in rural-urban ratios. In 1949 about 80 per cent of the party members were peasants; although the total rural membership has grown, the percentage has fallen to 69.1 per cent (7.4 million) in 1956, to 66.8 per cent (8.5 million) in 1957, and in 1961 to about 66 per cent (11.22 million). The rural-urban ratio in the total population in 1956 was 86 to 14. China's rural areas thus are "underrepresented" in the party in contrast to the period before the assumption of power. The proportion of industrial workers in the party increased from almost none in 1949 to 14 per cent (1.5 million) in 1956 and 15 per cent (2.55 million) in 1961. In 1950 about 73 per cent of the party members were engaged in agriculture; by 1956 only 58 per cent were in agriculture.[35] In 1950 and again in 1953 the

[33] Immanuel C. Y. Hsü, *Reorganization of Higher Education in Communist China* (Santa Barbara: General Electric Company, TEMPO, 1962), p. 23; Evelyn L. Narner, *Middle School Education as a Tool of Power in Communist China* (TEMPO, 1962), p. 47.

[34] There is very little data after 1961, but previous trends do not seem to have undergone major changes.

[35] The difference between the peasant members and those engaged in agriculture is about 1,200,000. Presumably these peasant members were in the army and security forces or in urban jobs, but not in industry where they would have been classified with industrial workers. It might be guessed that most of these were in the military forces. The growth in size and the changing composition of party membership is summarized in *Staffing Procedures and Problems in Communist China*, p. 15, but other sources have also been used for data presented here and in the following paragraphs.

admission of peasants in areas controlled by the party before 1949 was completely stopped and in other rural areas was restricted, while the party built up its membership in industrial enterprises.[36] There has been a notable and disproportionate growth of party organizations and members in urban and industrial areas which in 1949 had negligible representation in the party. In 1956, when 1.74 per cent of the total population of China were party members, the proportion in Peking was 5 per cent, in Tientsin 4.4 per cent, and in Shanghai 2.4 per cent.[37] Some of this urban growth represented the relocation of party administrative personnel in major industrial-administrative centers, but the main increase came through recruitment of urban "intellectuals," workers, and civil servants.

(2) The shift from military conquest to the civil tasks of nation-building have brought a striking change in the military-civilian ratio in party membership. In 1949 army members (1.0 million) made up about 22 per cent of the party. This proportion has declined. In 1950 military membership was reported by one source to be 1.2 million, or over 20 per cent of the total party membership.[38] The party leadership presumably has adhered to the pre-1949 principles of maintaining within the army a ratio of one party member to two non-party members. However, with the vast expansion of party members among other occupational groups, the percentage of military members in the party declined in 1956 to about 10 per cent and in 1961 to perhaps 6 per cent.

(3) The drive to modernize has led to an infusion of intellectuals into the party. The level of education and skill has been greatly improved. The proportion of educated members, defined as "teachers, students, engineers, technicians, and professional people" and collectively described as "intellectuals,"[39] has increased from a small number—one might guess as few as 5 per cent (0.22 million), the size of the party's administrative staff corps in 1949—to 11.7 per cent (1.25 million) in 1956, 14.8 per

[36] Compton, *Mao's China*, p. 276; An Tzu-wen, "The Consolidation of Party Organizations," *People's China*, July 1, 1953, in *SCMP*, No. 622, pp. 27–32. In Kansu, for example, a quota was established for membership in rural *hsiang*—not to exceed one per cent. At the same time, a party conference pointed to the need for more party members in the city of Lanchow, where they were "far from adequate to meet the needs of economic construction." *Kansu Jih-pao*, Feb. 12, 1955.
[37] *NCNA*, Sept. 13, 1956, in *CB*, No. 411, pp. 26–27.
[38] *JMJP* editorial reprinted in *Wen Hui Pao* (Hong Kong), July 1, 1950.
[39] Snow, *The Other Side of the River*, p. 344.

cent (1.88 million) in 1957, and about 15 per cent (2.55 million) in 1961. Nonetheless, these figures indicate that even yet over 80 per cent of the membership has less than high school training. Some of the local rural members are virtually illiterate; the better educated are described as "peasant intellectuals."

(4) A trend toward inclusiveness and "national" representativeness has produced other shifts in party composition. Among a variety of changes, the proportion of women has undoubtedly increased since 1949 and stood at about 10 per cent in 1953, 1956, and 1957. This percentage means gross underrepresentation for women. Although women party leaders have charged discrimination against women,[40] this has not, apparently, undermined party influence among women, the majority of whom probably accept for themselves traditional role images. Membership of non-Chinese ethnic and cultural groups has grown markedly from a small handful in 1949 to 0.84 per cent in 1956, and to 4 per cent (680,000) in 1961. Regionally, representation was predominantly from North China in 1949. Now membership as a ratio of the population is fairly evenly spread throughout the country except in areas where ethnic minorities predominate.

There are very few clues to the power position and the influence exerted on party policy and in factional disputes by these various groups in the party. The party leadership has thus far succeeded in maintaining unity and solidarity within the party, but has not altogether avoided major intra-party conflicts of interest.

As the size and composition of the party has changed, so has the organization of the party. There has been a tremendous expansion and elaboration of party organizations, a striking bureaucratization of party administration, and a rapid growth in functional specialization and status differentiation among party members.

PARTY ORGANIZATION

In order to ensure the solidarity and institutional effectiveness of this oversized party and, above all, to guarantee its responsiveness or subordination to direction from the top, the party leaders have had to devote a considerable part of their time and energies to party affairs. Size alone has made the management of party affairs a major undertaking requiring the skills of a professional

[40] *8th Party Congress*, pp. 281, 282.

service corps. The party has gone through a number of reorgani-
zations, some of a constitutional character, as in 1956 with the
adoption of a new constitution, and others administrative and
political in nature.

The basic change in party organization after 1949 was increased centralization of authority. By necessity, the Border Region and Red Army party committees before 1949 exercised
considerable independence and initiative. The Political Bureau
was often out of touch with local developments and problems and
depended primarily on the reliability of local party leaders and
units to maintain its authority in the guerrilla bases. A comparison of the 1945 party constitution with the 1956 constitution
reflects this difference. The pre-1949 constitution granted regional and local party committees the right to "modify" various
regulations and provisions. After the entire country was pacified
and reconstruction began, the regional political-military administrations retained a good deal of autonomy. However, between
1952 and 1954 the authority of these regional party groups was
thoroughly undercut with the limitation and final abolition of the
regional governments. The regional party bureaus themselves
were abolished in 1954 and 1955, and party affairs came under
the direct management of the departments of the Central Committee in Peking. Overcentralization produced problems. These
led finally to the reintroduction of regional bureaus of the Political Bureau in 1961, but these bureaus appear to function more as
administrative than policy bodies.

The party is organized geographically in a hierarchy of elected
congresses and corresponding committees, each of which has an
administrative corps consisting of a secretary, or a secretariat,
and a standing committee. At the lowest level, primary party
committees are organized both on a geographical basis and in
functional units—such as public institutions and organizations,
schools, industrial enterprises, cooperatives, and the army. The
party constitution attempts to resolve any conflicts of authority
between territorial and functional units by making the territorial
committee the "highest" of the party organizations in the area
within its jurisdiction.

Each congress and its correlative committee are subordinate to
the authority of the next higher congress and its committee.
Under the territorial principle the "highest leading body of the
Party is the National Party Congress" and the Central Committee

which it elects. The county is the basic administrative unit, both in the party system and for civil administration. The county-level committees control the bulk of the party's local organizations and the overwhelming majority of the members. At this level, under the territorial principle, party units in local administrative units and in functional industrial, institutional, and administrative organizations are drawn together under a common authority. Each county committee, on a statistical average, would have responsibility, either directly or through sub-county district (*ch'ü*) committees established "as its representative bodies within its area," for almost six hundred party branches; these branches are organized under some forty to fifty general branch committees, which are authorized to elect delegates directly to the county congresses.

In the last three years changes have occurred. The urban commune and the district (*ch'ü*) division apparently have not been discussed. The number of organizational units at each level of authority in 1962, however, is indicated in Chart 1.

THE PARTY BUREAUCRACY

Management of party affairs to a very considerable degree seems to have come into the hands of an administrative bureaucracy, territorially organized. The party is now so large and the activities and character of its organizations so varied that much of the regular business of the party must be handled by full-time administrative professionals. The constitutional powers of party congresses have been taken over by party committees; the duties of committees, which only meet intermittently, are now performed by Standing Committee members and secretaries. The latter, in turn, have such varied and comprehensive responsibilities in their own geographic jurisdictions or institutional settings that, at the county level and above, they have to entrust large responsibilities to staff and service departments. The staffs of these departments exercise the authority of the party and direct party activities on a day-to-day basis.

At the top of the party's administrative system is the Secretariat of the Central Committee, operating under the Political Bureau with Teng Hsiao-p'ing as Secretary-General. It presumably exercises administrative direction over the work of the Central Committee's departments, committees, and special agencies which control all lower segments of the party. The administration and

CHART 1
PARTY ORGANIZATIONAL STRUCTURE
1962

CENTRAL COMMITTEE

Political Bureau

Standing
Committee
Political
Bureau

6 Regional Bureaus

28 PROVINCIAL LEVEL COMMITTEES

21 Provinces
5 Autonomous Regions
2 Municipalities (Peking, Shanghai)

258 SPECIAL DISTRICTS (CH'ÜAN CH'Ü) AND
MUNICIPAL LEVEL COMMITTEES

196 Special Districts
32 Municipalities
30 Autonomous Chou

2,204 COUNTY (HSIEN) LEVEL COMMITTEES

1,952 Counties
125 Municipalities
20 Urban Wards
107 Autonomous Counties or Banners

DISTRICT (CH'Ü) COMMITTEES (15,000–16,000?)
[10,741 in 1956; 8,893 (388 municipal and 8,505 rural) in 1958]

74,000 RURAL AND 1,027 URBAN COMMUNES
AND 600 URBAN WARD COMMITTEES

1,300,000 BRANCH COMMITTEES (ESTIMATED)

17,000,000 Party Members

staffing of these central organs of the party are major undertakings in themselves. At the highest level of the party professional service are the members of the Grade I organs of the Central Committee. The organization and staffing of the party's central bureaus may be the responsibility of the administrative office of the Secretariat, of which Yang Shang-k'un is the Director. He is also the Secretary of the Committee for Party Organs Directly Subordinate to the Central Committee, which ranks with the other central departments and committees under the Secretariat. The Committee for Party Organs presumably includes the party's senior administrative professionals. It ranks with, but is distinct from, the party's Committee for Central State Organs, which represents committees and bodies made up of party members in the ministries and agencies of the State Council.

The size of the administrative staffs at the highest level is suggested by a decision of the Central Committee in 1957 to "transfer 1,000 higher and middle Party member cadres from the Party and government organs of the highest level [that of the CCP Central Committee and the Central Government]" to educational and cultural institutions. This meant the transfer of 200 officials with rank of department head and bureau chief or higher, and of 800 with the rank of office director, section chief, and higher.[41]

The Political Bureau through its Secretariat and departments directs the work of the provincial committees through six regional offices or bureaus: Northeast China, North China, Northwest China, East China, Southwest China, and Central-South China. Although information about these bureaus is sparse, it seems clear that these agencies are beginning to replicate the organization of the Central Committee, dividing their work into the same functional departments and offices which are maintained by the Central Committee. Thus they perform both executive and administrative functions. A similar organizational pattern prevails in the provincial party organization and apparently down through the county (*hsien*) and perhaps district (*ch'ü*) committees. This arrangement obviously facilitates communications and the possi-

41 "The CCP Central Committee Decides To Detail 1000 Party Member Cadres from the Highest-Level Party and Government Organs to Reinforce Cultural and Educational Front," *NCNA,* Oct. 22, 1957, in *SCMP,* No. 1641, pp. 10–11; "Training Class of Theoretical Teachers and Tutors for Intermediate Study Groups Organized by Grade 1 Organs of the CCP Central Committee and Central People's Government," *NCNA,* May 21, 1963, in *SCMP,* No. 578, pp. 19–21.

bility of close and efficient direction from above by maintaining a chain of uniform administrative and functional offices from the top to the bottom of the party bureaucracy.

The largest number of professional party administrators probably are employed at the county level. Under each of the county committees there exists a regularly established party administration, located, according to informants from several places, in the most imposing building in the town or city. The cost of maintaining these offices and employees seems to be charged to the regular county budgets. Reports from two counties in 1956 give the following figures on the party administration: Ting *hsien* (Hopei)—15 offices and 122 employees; T'ai-an (Shantung)— 22 offices, plus 5 semi-permanent offices and 20 offices located in *hsiang* and towns, and 369 employees.[42] On the basis of this fragmentary data a crude guess at the size of the bureaucracy might be made. If, on an average, each county administration employed 200 people, then in the 2100 rural counties of China in 1956 about 420,000 full-time paid employees were maintained in the party's county administrative offices.

The comprehensive scope of the responsibilities of party administrative units and the types of functional specialists required by the party are indicated in the organizational chart of a provincial party committee (Chart 2).

The power of the party is in the hands of its elite; the seventeen and more million members in the ranks are their instruments. A very sharp distinction exists between the party mandarinate and ordinary members, a distinction generally blurred or passed over in the ordinary run of publications issued in China. One differentiation between the ranks and the elite is made at the county level. Party committees at the county-regiment level are included in the circle of those kept informed on national party policies and problems and, conversely, the lower party ranks are excluded from access to such information. It is doubtful, however, that even members of provincial rank necessarily participate in high-level party policy formulation. The failure to convene a national Party Congress since 1958 may reflect as well as accentuate a

[42] Yao Kuang, "My View of the Problem of Consolidation," *Hsin-hua pan-yüeh-k'an*, No. 3 1957, pp. 16–18, in *U.S. Joint Publications Research Service (JPRS)*, Jan. 17, 1963, pp. 35–41; Chin Sha, "Too Many People at the Top Levels and Quite a Few at the Lower Levels," *Hsin-hua pan-yüeh-k'an*, No. 4 1957, pp. 52–53, in *JPRS*, Jan. 18, 1963, pp. 42–43.

CHART 2

ORGANIZATION OF PROVINCIAL PARTY COMMITTEES

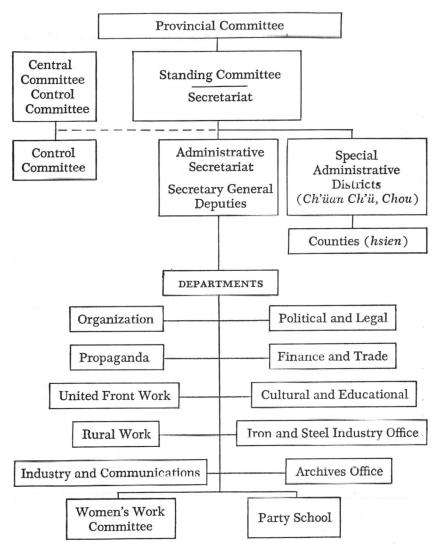

This is a composite chart, but each office or department has been identified in two or more provinces. The main departments, such as Organization . . . Archives Office, exist in all provincial-level committees. Additional departments and offices appear to reflect local conditions and problems. Peking, for example, has departments dealing with Building Work, Local Industry, University Scientific Work, Public Health, and Physical Culture. Shanghai also has Industrial Production and Labor Wage Committees; Inner Mongolia, a Department of Agriculture and Animal Husbandry; and Heilungkiang, a Department of Forestry. Many of the officials heading these departments and committees have been listed in the files of the East Asian Research Center's biographical project.

growing estrangement and lack of understanding and confidence between the leaders and the led.

For administrative purposes party members at and above the county level constitute an influential officer corps who guide and discipline the rank-and-file and give unity and direction to the organization as a whole. In 1956 the party had about 300,000 members in units at and above the county level. The ratio between the higher ranks and the sub-county membership at that time was one to thirty-six.[43] If the same general ratio prevails, in 1962 there would have been over 500,000 members with county rank and above. These members are described as key functionaries who enjoy "greater confidence from the Party" and thus have "greater responsibility to the Party and the people than the rank-and-file members."[44]

Because committees above the primary level have managerial and administrative responsibility for party units at lower levels, it is deemed essential to exercise tight control over selection of their members. In 1956 Teng Hsiao-p'ing, Secretary-General of the Central Committee, noted that "the quality of the work of these 300,000 people [at county level and above] is of decisive significance to the cause of the party" and called for improved methods of selection and promotion to produce a larger corps of upper-rank officials of ability. The criterion for promotion to important posts Teng stated to be "personal qualities and abilities,"[45] meaning political knowledge and reliability and technical or administrative competence. The needs of the party at this time dictated bypassing popular old party veterans in favor of "carefully selected" new cadres who could be trained in the techniques and professions essential to build socialism. Teng emphasized that cadres must be familiar with local conditions,[46] but he also noted later, in 1957, that their selection must be kept out of "local politics."[47]

In staffing committees at the national, provincial, and county levels, party leaders therefore seek: (1) to place their most reliable supporters in key positions; (2) to weed out semi-educated and parochial representatives of local bodies and to replace

[43] Lewis, *Leadership in Communist China*, p. 186.

[44] Teng Hsiao-p'ing, in *8th Party Congress*, I, 220.

[45] *8th Party Congress*, I, 220.

[46] *8th Party Congress*, I, 221.

[47] Teng Hsiao-p'ing, *Report on the Rectification Campaign* (Peking: Foreign Languages Press, 1957), p. 5.

them with persons possessing skills requisite for responsible posts; and (3) to provide promotional channels and incentives for able men and women.

PARTY AND STATE

Although the "Chinese Communist Party is the nucleus of leadership of the State,"[48] it is not a state, or official and public, institution. In governing the country the party leadership nonetheless has not fully resolved the question of the proper administrative role for the party. The party has created large administrative agencies to manage economic, social, and civic enterprises and activities. However, in the area of party-state relations, the party has wavered between direct and indirect control. The party's assumption of power shifted the primary concern of its leaders from the army to the state, from military operations to economic construction; but the control and use of state agencies for development and modernization has proved to be a far more complex and difficult undertaking than the problems of combat. Production and economic development require more than political organization and social mobilization, at which the party excels; they require, among other things, sustained incentives, the development of new patterns of group action (institutions), systematic accumulation of resources and skills, and efficient methods of coordinating numerous kinds of activities and resources. In a centrally planned and directed society and economy, a single and clear chain of command and responsibility would seem to be particularly important in order to avoid confusion. How far could the party, as a political organization, go in undertaking technical tasks?

The administrative functions of the party have gone through a series of major changes. In the period from 1949 to 1952 regional party groups governed the country directly. From 1952 to 1958 the party, as a separate bureaucracy parallel to the state, performed governmental services and staff functions—acting as a personnel and security agency for government institutions and as an information and supervisory staff for party leaders in government posts at various levels; during this period executive and administrative responsibility and control were in the hands of state agencies. From 1958 to 1961 the party exercised direct

[48] Liu Shao-ch'i, "Report on the Draft Constitution," *NCNA*, Peking, Sept. 15, 1954.

administrative authority over all but a few enterprises and operations reserved to government agencies; it absorbed most of the executive and administrative functions previously performed under the direction of the State Council. Since 1961 there seems to have been a partial return to the pre-1958 pattern in which at the national level and in the modern industrial sector of the economy, and perhaps in urban centers in general, the party once again performs only certain service and staff functions in the governmental system; however, in agriculture and throughout rural areas in general party organizations appear to be functioning as operating agencies, performing many of the administrative functions of government. To the degree that it performs direct managerial and administrative functions, the lower levels of the party tend to become quasi-public or semi-governmental agencies, administrative arms of higher levels of administrative and executive authority. This is especially the case where most of the local administrators are party members and party membership becomes virtually essential to performance of administrative tasks.

Why have stipulations for limiting the governmental functions of the party not been observed consistently in practice? The record suggests that questions of administrative rationality and jurisdictional clarity have had to take second place to urgent practical problems. On the practical side, there has been a shortage of administrative resources to achieve the goals set by the national leadership. The shortage consisted both of properly qualified and reliable personnel and of appropriate institutions. The party, therefore, has been pressed into service to perform technical functions and meet administrative problems which it was not intended or qualified to perform. This "misuse" of the party has been particularly apparent in connection with programs of manpower mobilization and in the implementation of programs in the field of agricultural management.

The determination of the regime to overhaul and modernize the Chinese political, economic, and social order under forced acceleration has required large numbers of supervisors and mobilizers working under close central direction. Major reform programs were instituted shortly after the party came to power, when governmental agencies were still in very primitive form, or nonexistent. Governmental agencies did not command either the manpower or the coercive power to carry through such drastic programs. The ineffectualness of government agencies may be partly due to the fact that the party has, through vast expansion and recruitment of large proportions of groups with higher skills and monopolization of leadership elements, weakened and pauperized other institutions; moreover, the party, itself, has acted in large measure as the regime's police and control force.

Perhaps for a variety of reasons—fear of political opposition, the continuous pace of rigorous and unpopular social and economic programs of change, the lack of stable and reliable non-party institutions, the necessity for imposing austerity and use of non-material incentives, the scale of programs for mobilizing manpower and the like—the process of governing has produced cleavages and strains among party members. In the upper echelons of the party there have been noticeable divisions between those members who run the territorial administration of the party and those who control the governmental bureaucracy. Party members within government agencies have been accused of acting not as "Communist Party members assigned by the party to work in non-party organizations," but as representatives of their own non-party organizations within the party.[49] Down the line there have been other problems. One cause for dissatisfaction at the local and intermediate levels among the older and more senior party members appears to have been the placement of young and better educated members in the party secretariats because of their ability to produce the reports and documents on which the management of the party depends. Interviews in Hong Kong suggest that the older, politically reliable but poorly educated, rural members with "revolutionary experience" from North China tend to be employed in organizational, security, and police activities, and the more literate younger members are placed in positions relating to "united front" work, economic and social enterprises, propaganda, and secretarial activities.[50] The latter are not only publicly visible, but on the basis of competence may also tend to be promoted more rapidly than the rank-and-file party veterans who fought the war and carried out the harsh programs of nationalization and agricultural collectivization.

[49] Liu Lan-t'ao, "The Chinese Communist Party is the Supreme Commander of the Chinese People in Building Socialism," *JMJP*, Sept. 28, 1959, in *Communist China 1955–1959: Policy Documents with Analysis* (Cambridge: Harvard University Press, 1963), p. 574.

[50] Ezra F. Vogel, unpublished manuscript.

THE PARTY AND ITS MEMBERS

Thus far we have been concerned with the effect of the assumption of power on the perspectives of the party leadership—its effort to build a party better able to cope with the problems of social and economic transformation of China, the development of more elaborate organizational and administrative mechanisms to handle a party of greater size and more complex functions, the increased bureaucratization of the party, and the role of the party in national administration. The perspectives of the party membership as a whole also have changed. These changes can only be ascertained in very general ways through deductions from Communist reports and party programs and from occasional refugee reports.

It seems evident that the party has been generally accepted by the bulk of the Chinese people as the dominant institution in the social and political life of the country and that it will continue to maintain its position. Membership in the party, therefore, is no longer the goal of only a revolutionary or dissatisfied minority but is desired by substantial numbers of the Chinese people in most walks of life. The former external risks of membership have been removed and only the personal and organizational risks of party discipline remain, and these tend to be outbalanced by the rewards—political, social, and economic—of membership.

The party's rectification campaigns reflect some of the attitudes which tend to permeate various sectors of the membership at different times. In the Cheng Feng movement of 1941 and 1942 the party leadership was particularly concerned with intra-party relations and problems: the acceptance of Communist attitudes and values, responsiveness to party control and discipline, and the development of working methods adapted to Chinese circumstances. Although the party leaders were also concerned about the relationship between the party and the "masses," the burden of their effort was to instill in the members an understanding of the organizational and ideological[51] requirements of party membership. The rectification movement of 1947 and 1948 was more specifically intended to improve the relations between party members and the population in order to facilitate agrarian reform and gain support for the army. The movement of 1950 seemed to

[51] Brandt, et al., *A Documentary History of Chinese Communism*, pp. 372–75.

have as its main aim the correction of "authoritarian methods of work."[52] From that time on, one of the constant preoccupations of the party leadership has been that "with the party in power, our comrades are liable to be tainted with bureaucracy."[53] Political authority in China, as in many countries, seems to produce the usual attitudes of "arrogance" and "self-complacency." Teng Hsiao-p'ing complained in 1956 that "commandism" was fairly widespread: "Quite a number of party organizations and cadres fail to consult the masses before they make decisions and issue instructions. Moreover, in the process of carrying out these decisions and instructions, they do not try to persuade and educate the masses, but simply resort to issuing orders to get things done. Such mistakes of commandism are more glaring among the primary party organizations and their cadres, but mistakes of this kind in the lower organizations are often inseparable from the subjectivist and bureaucratic methods of leadership employed by the leading bodies above them.[54] Once again after the setbacks of 1959–62, the party is preoccupied with the values, commitments, and responsiveness of party members to the programs and authority of the party leadership.

In the pre-1949 efforts to correct attitudes and stamp out undesirable habits, the party leaders concentrated on re-education, indoctrination, and "self-criticism" techniques. More than in most other Communist parties, the Chinese party leadership has stressed "redness," that is, political commitment rather than "expertise." It needs and wants experts, but insists that these experts prove that their basic motivations are political and their outlook ideological rather than professional. With the influx of blue- and white-collar workers and intellectuals into the party after 1949, the leadership has also introduced part-time manual labor as a method of checking the presumptions of party members and bringing them into closer and more cooperative relations with the general populace. Despite the personally humiliating features of party discipline and practice, it is clear that both the party member and his non-party associates are aware and act on the recognition that party membership confers real advantages— inside knowledge through party sources and meetings, influence with local or higher decision-makers, better opportunities for

[52] Compton, *Mao's China*, pp. 274–75.
[53] Teng Hsiao-p'ing, *8th Party Congress*, I, 173.
[54] Teng in *8th Party Congress*, I, 184.

superior positions and rewards, greater ability and opportunity to injure or assist others, and greater social and political security. Party leaders appear to have purged or corrected many of those who blatantly or rudely used their membership for personal advantages, but there is no thought of removing the real privileges which attach to party membership, because the party organization must not be reduced in its relations with other organizations, groups, and individuals to a subordinate position. Party membership therefore confers authority.

At the same time, there are party members who have been inclined to go too far in seeking comfortable relations with those among whom they live and work. These members presumably lack sufficient commitment to the party's goals and programs and seek to modify or to accommodate themselves and the party's policies to the wishes of the people. They are the "rightists" and "revisionists" who do not wish to push people too hard, who listen not to the party's leaders but to the people around them, and who seek to moderate the pace and direction of the party's policies for transforming China.

While size and variety of background, education, and specialization among its members mean that the party contains people of many types and commitments, the party leadership through constant disciplining seeks to keep them responsive to direction from above and committed to the specific programs and policies which it has laid down for China. Most of the party members probably understand and accept these conditions and the instrumental role assigned to them.

PART THREE

Communist Law and Social Change

The Criminal Process in China

JEROME ALAN COHEN

"Violation of socialist legality became a practice of state activity in China. Distorting Marxist-Leninist teaching on the role of the Party in the system of the dictatorship of the proletariat, the Chinese leaders assigned to Party organs not the role of organizers and teachers of the masses, but the role of a 'commanding force' determining and regulating all activities of local organs of power, of the courts and the procuracy. The persistently repeated conceptions that 'politics is the commanding force' and that the Party official is 'the commander of production' are served up as a kind of theoretical justification of such practices. Things have reached a curious state when the secretary of a county Party committee, having dispensed with the judge, himself sits in the judge's chair and begins to decide cases, and such facts are presented in the press as a positive experience." "Revolutionary theory is the guide to action—on the dictatorship of the proletariat." *Izvestia*, May 17, 1964, pp. 3-4.

THE trouble with you Westerners," the man said, wagging his finger at me before I could sit down, "is that you've never got beyond that primitive stage you call the 'rule of law.' You're all preoccupied with the 'rule of law.' China has always known that law is not enough to govern a society. She knew it twenty-five hundred years ago, and she knows it today." The man, interestingly enough, was a London-educated Chinese barrister who practices in Hong Kong and is known there as a principal, if unofficial, spokesman of the People's Republic of China. When properly deciphered, his cryptic defense of the regime in mainland China suggests much about the Communists' attitude toward the criminal process. They have been acutely sensitive to criticism that they have failed to adhere to the fundamental principles of fairness that Western—particularly Anglo-American—societies proclaim as ideals. Yet they have rejected those principles as Western and bourgeois and inapplicable to a Chinese Communist regime. And recently this rejection has been defended in part by an appeal to history and to the traditional Chinese attitude toward law and lawyers.

One should note that the barrister said that law is "not enough" to govern Chinese society—not that it is unimportant or irrelevant in that task. Confucius and his followers had advocated governing in accordance with approved social norms (*li*) through persuasion and moral example, rather than governing in accordance with positive law (*fa*) through coercion and deterrence. But even they had recognized that a penal system was a regrettable necessity, to be applied against those members of the community who proved to be unresponsive to the *li*. Although the leaders of the Chinese Communist Party have made masterful use of other measures of social control and still at times predict that the state will wither away, they have never had illusions that they could dispense with criminal sanctions. On the eve of assuming power over the mainland of China, Mao Tse-tung exhorted his party comrades to strengthen the police and the courts, as well as the army, on the ground that these agencies were the state's major institutions for enforcing the people's democratic dictatorship.[1] Much attention has since been lavished on perfecting the criminal process.

But, as the barrister's remark implies, while the Chinese have been unable to dispense with "law," they have not been preoccupied with the "rule of law." To Westerners that clouded phrase suggests not only a respect for state proscriptions but also that an accused should have an opportunity to defend himself effectively. In China the phrase that Westerners sometimes translate as "rule of law" (*fa-chih*) has been well known for over two thousand years,[2] but a more accurate translation would be "rule by law." Traditional Chinese law was mainly an instrument for enforcing status-oriented Confucian social norms and for bending the will of an unruly populace to achieve the purposes of an authoritarian government. When in 1912 imperial rule disintegrated and was

[1] Mao Tse-tung, "On the People's Democratic Dictatorship" (1949), republished in *Selected Works of Mao Tse-tung* (English ed.; Peking: Foreign Languages Press, 1961), IV, 411–18.

[2] See the exceptionally illuminating study by Benjamin Schwartz, "On Attitudes toward Law in China" in *Government under Law and the Individual* (Washington, 1957), p. 27.

succeeded by the Republic, there was in China no developed concept of "rights" of the accused as limitations upon the state.

Both of the rival party dictatorships that have subsequently sought to pick up the pieces, to reintegrate the shattered nation, and to convert it into a modern industrial power have consciously looked outside the Chinese tradition for legal models. After gaining control of the Republic of China in 1928, Chiang Kai-shek's Nationalist Party built upon the efforts of previous republican governments and perfected codes of criminal law and procedure similar to those of the European continental nations that Japan had earlier sought to emulate. Even before officially founding the People's Republic of China in 1949, during its two decades of rule over rural "liberated areas," the Communist Party began to borrow substantially from the Soviet Union, whose institutions for administering criminal justice also reflect important European influences. Yet, as the Stalinist experience proved, it is one thing for the leadership of a dictatorial regime to adopt legal forms, and quite another for that leadership to assimilate the values, attitudes, and assumptions that underlie the forms. In practice, both the rival Chinese governments have accorded low priority to the observance of safeguards for the accused that exist on paper. When one compares the uses of law in traditional China, in the Republic of China (located on Formosa since 1949), and in the People's Republic of China, significant differences, of course, appear. Yet, one major similarity exists—law and legal institutions still serve principally as instruments for enhancing the power of the state and for disciplining the people to perform its bidding. In the official Chinese value system the interests of the state and the group have always dwarfed those of the individual. Now, as in the past, this value preference is reflected at every stage of the criminal process.

The goals of the imperial dynasties and of the Nationalist Party were far more limited than those of the Communist Party. The Communists have been determined for the first time in Chinese history to extend the power of the central government to the grassroots level and to control virtually every aspect of human activity. Their avowed purpose is to bring about the rapid political, economic, and social transformation of the most populous country in the world, and one of the most backward, at whatever cost may be necessary. In these circumstances the burden that has fallen upon the criminal process has been immense.

Thus far I have treated the era of Chinese Communist rule as though it were a single period. Actually, the student of law should divide the fourteen years under review into three major stages.

A. *1949–53*. From 1949 to 1953 was a period of economic reconstruction and consolidation of political control, roughly comparable for our purposes to the period of War Communism in the Soviet Union (1917–21). During this period the criminal process served as a blunt instrument of terror as the party proceeded relentlessly to crush all sources of opposition and to rid society of apolitical but antisocial elements that plagued public order. The Nationalist legal apparatus, including the bar, was abolished at the outset, but it was not immediately replaced by a well-regulated system of criminal justice. Although the Communist government created a judicial structure, much criminal punishment was administered outside the regular courts; for it was not until the "judicial reform" of 1952–53 that the courts were sufficiently purged of holdovers from the Nationalist regime to inspire the confidence of the party.

In many kinds of cases the police had unfettered power to investigate, arrest, prosecute, and convict. The police also conducted large-scale "administrative" round-ups of many types of undesirable persons and subjected them to "noncriminal" reform measures during long confinement. In many areas of the country, punishment was meted out by military control commissions. In the course of the regime-sponsored mass movements or campaigns that swept the country, such as those to carry out the land reform and to suppress counterrevolution, *ad hoc* "people's tribunals," which were thinly veiled kangaroo courts, dispensed their own brand of justice. Although these various criminal processes usually functioned in secret, in major cases their verdicts were often dramatically pronounced in "mass trials" convened before hordes of onlookers. Hundreds of thousands of class enemies were sentenced to death, and many more were sentenced to long terms of "reform through labor." In short, the army, the police, and the courts implemented the directive of Chairman Mao to serve as the instruments for oppressing the hostile classes, inflicting "legalized" violence and lesser sanctions upon all those who were deemed to be "reactionaries" and "bad elements." The need for such an unattractive program was foreshadowed by Mao more than twenty years before he assumed national power: ". . . [A] revolution is not the same as inviting people to dinner, or painting a picture, or doing fancy needlework; it cannot be anything so refined, so calm and gentle, or so mild, kind, courteous, restrained and magnanimous. A revolution is an uprising, an act of violence whereby one class overthrows another."[3]

B. *1953–57.* The second stage in the development of the contemporary criminal process began in the spring of 1953, shortly after the initiation of the government's first Five-Year Plan for the development of the national economy, and ended with the launching of the "anti-rightist" movement in June 1957. From the Western viewpoint this period may, with some exaggeration, be called the "golden age" of law in the People's Republic. Having chosen to adopt the Soviet model for economic development, the Chinese leaders decided to develop a Soviet-style legal system. By the end of 1954 this decision had resulted in the promulgation of a constitution and a series of laws that established the framework of a regularized system for the administration of justice; apart from a few liberalizing touches, this system was similar to that which the Soviet Union had erected along European lines during the relatively moderate period of the New Economic Policy (1921–28) and which subsequently coexisted with Stalin's parallel structure of extrajudicial coercion.

Citizens were guaranteed against arbitrary detention, arrest, and search. The nationwide procuracy that had been organized shortly after the Communist takeover was authorized to fulfill those functions that we associate with a prosecutor's office, including review of police recommendations to arrest and prosecute. It was also to exercise general supervision over the legality of the action of all government organs including the police. Implicit in the constitutional grant of judicial power to the courts was the understanding that they were to serve as the exclusive agencies for the adjudication of criminal responsibility; this went far beyond the situation that prevailed in the Soviet Union until Stalin's death. At most trials in courts of first instance, a judge and two people's assessors were jointly to preside as a judicial college to decide all questions of fact and law; normally three judges were to hear appeals. Most trials were to be public, and the

---

[3] Mao, "Report of an Investigation into the Peasant Movement in Hunan" (1927), republished in *Selected Works of Mao Tse-tung* (English ed.; London, 1954), I, 21, 27.

accused was entitled to make a defense. It was contemplated that this defense would ordinarily be made for him by the new "people's lawyers" whom recently revamped law schools were beginning to train and who were to be organized to practice in Soviet-type collectives. Although individual judges were to serve at the pleasure of the political organs, in theory the courts were to be independent in administering justice, "subject only to the law." Plans were made to draft a criminal code that was to provide more guidance to the agencies of law enforcement and to the public than had been provided by a miscellany of isolated published proscriptions or by the policies of the party and the government from which those agencies were instructed to shape a substantive law of crimes in the absence of specific proscriptions. Rules of criminal procedure were to be devised for experimental use prior to formulation of a code. Scholars were called upon to write texts that were to guide both the administration of justice during the period prior to the completion of the projected legislation and the drafting of the legislation itself. All of this lawmaking effort was to be undertaken with the aid of Soviet legal experts who had come to help the Chinese understand the Soviet codes and the many treatises on Soviet law that were being translated into Chinese. The party line on law was the same as that for other aspects of the country's development—to adapt the advanced experiences of the Soviet Union to China's conditions.

These were not mere paper reforms. Another wave of terror—the movement to "liquidate counterrevolution"—almost swamped them in the second half of 1955; at that time, in a manner that was reminiscent of, but more successful than, Stalin's collectivization efforts of the late twenties and early thirties, the regime sought to prepare the ground for rapidly completing the "socialist transformation" of agriculture and industry. But shortly after Khrushchev publicly launched his program of de-Stalinization in early 1956, the pendulum returned to an emphasis upon "legality" in China and, at least in the larger cities, many of these reforms began to be implemented. Police power to detain, interrogate, and arrest was subjected to more regularized administrative checks against arbitrary action. Moreover, if the police did not always comply with the requirement of obtaining the procuracy's approval before issuing an arrest warrant and if general supervision of the legality of police conduct merely remained one of the procuracy's aspirations, nevertheless the procuracy was usually able to carry out conscientiously its obligation to review police recommendations to prosecute. Similarly, although certain relatively severe sanctions not deemed to be "criminal" continued to be meted out by agencies other than courts, these sanctions were used less often and less arbitrarily; and the courts did assume exclusive jurisdiction over the imposition of sanctions that were regarded as "criminal."

For the most part, adjudication, as in the past, continued to take place behind closed doors. Secret trials consisted of judicial interrogation of the defenderless accused in order to verify the evidence assembled by the investigating agencies. This was supplemented by *ex parte* interrogation of witnesses on occasions when the information in the file and the account of the accused left important questions in doubt. Yet even such truncated "trials" often provided a significant check upon the adequacy of the cases presented by the police and the procuracy. And increasingly there were experiments with public trials conducted according to tentative rules of procedure that closely resembled those in force in the Soviet Union. The lay assessors who sat with the judge in public trials were a façade designed to display the participation of the masses in the administration of justice. In these public trials innocence was not seriously at issue, since, if pre-trial judicial screening found proof of criminality to be insufficient, the case was not set down for public trial but was either dismissed or returned to the procuracy or police for further investigation. But it was not unusual for defense counsel to appear and to argue with spirit and ability for conviction of a lesser crime or for mitigation of sentence, and the defendant often had at least a formal opportunity to confront his accusers. If, initially, these experiments only constituted morality plays carefully staged for the education and edification of the masses, they later often served the purpose of determining the degree of the defendant's guilt and the appropriate punishment.

The courts, which were preponderantly staffed by members of the Communist Party and the Communist Youth League, were, of course, entirely dependent on the party. *Ad hoc* interference with individual cases by the local party apparatus was not an unknown phenomenon. Yet generally this was an era when the party's will was carried out "vertically" by means of party control of the formulation of national judicial policies rather than "horizontally" by means of local party control of actual decision-making. This arrangement allowed professional judicial considerations to begin to influence the disposition of individual cases. And the competence of members of the judiciary, most of whom had had little or no legal education, was gradually being nourished by study of the various laws, decrees, regulations, instructions, reports, and model cases that emanated from Peking; the spate of serious law review articles that were then being published on problems of criminal law and procedure; and the lectures that were originally delivered at the law schools and were subsequently distributed for the guidance of legal workers. It was anticipated that enactment of the draft criminal code that was before the National People's Congress in the spring of 1957 would provide substantial further impetus to the evolution of legality in a direction similar to that being followed by Soviet law reform of the same period.

These were modest beginnings. To Western lawyers they appear pitiably small. Certainly the pace was exasperatingly slow to a small but articulate group of Chinese intellectuals who were schooled in Western legal values. At the height of the movement to "let a hundred flowers bloom, let a hundred schools contend" in May and early June 1957, when Chairman Mao induced the intellectuals to help "rectify" the party by offering it criticisms, some legal scholars castigated the party on a variety of grounds. They accused it, for example, of assuming a "nihilist standpoint toward law," of maintaining an attitude of superiority to the law, of committing grave violations of legality during past mass movements, of overloading the judiciary with ignorant party members who imposed arbitrary punishments, of obliterating the distinction between party and government, and of being reluctant to enact the widely heralded draft criminal code. One critic said of the draft code, "One hears the sound of footsteps on the stairs without seeing anyone coming down."[4] Legal specialists were not the only intellectuals who responded to the invitation to help "rectify" the party. The depth and scope of this criticism apparently exceeded anything party leaders had expected and made it clear that intellectuals desired democratic reforms, including more drastic reform of the criminal process, which would end the party's monopoly of political power and fundamentally alter China's political structure. After a brief period of stunned inac-

[4] Chi Ch'ing-i (editor, Legal Publishing House), quoted in Roderick MacFarquhar, *The Hundred Flowers Campaign and the Chinese Intellectuals* (New York: Praeger, 1960), p. 115; other representative statements appear on pp. 114–16.

tion, the response of the party leaders was to initiate the "anti-rightist" movement, which savagely struck back at their critics both inside and outside party ranks and which radically transformed China's political climate. This ushered in the third period in the development of the criminal process.

C. *1957–64*. One of the principal targets and first casualties of the anti-rightist movement that began in mid-June 1957 was the evolving system for administering the criminal law along de-Stalinized Soviet lines. The party leaders had never felt comfortable about the decision to import Soviet law, which to them was essentially a Western product. As a result of the "hundred flowers" debacle, they came to fear that full implementation of this system would unduly curb the power of the party and would introduce bourgeois law and values. Therefore, during the second half of 1957 and 1958, while de-Stalinization was culminating in a series of reforms that brought Soviet criminal law and procedure closer to that of the West, in China principles of Western justice, such as the independence of the judiciary from political interference and the non-retroactivity of the criminal law, were being systematically denounced. Moreover, Chinese writers placed increasing emphasis upon the inapplicability to China of their wagon behind closed doors [i.e., are unrealistic], revere their the Soviet legal model and severely censured cadres who "build [Soviet] textbooks as 'classics,' copy everything, apply everything they read, and make a set of troublesome procedures"; it was said that this attitude of "only believing books" had become so serious that even the words of the party were not heeded.[5]

Drastic changes were deemed necessary. Procurators were warned to abandon the one-sided "favor the accused" mentality that emphasized "troublesome legal procedures and the rights and status of the criminal, opening the door of convenience to the criminal."[6] During the 1953–57 period, this had led many of them to refuse to approve arrests and prosecutions and instead to order the release of detained persons on a variety of technical grounds, such as that the act in question did not amount to a completed crime or was not committed with the requisite intent or

[5] T'an Cheng-wen, "Absorb Experience and Teaching, Propel a Great Leap Forward in the Work of the Procuracy," *Cheng-fa yen-chiu* (hereafter cited in English translation: *Political-Legal Research*), No. 3, 1958, pp. 34–35.
[6] *Ibid.*, p. 38.

did not result in serious consequences.[7] Defense lawyers were also admonished to act "in the interests of the state and the people" rather than to "favor the accused"; for example, if in consulting his lawyer, the defendant should reveal that he had committed crimes not yet attributed to him, it was said to be his lawyer's duty to inform the police with or without the defendant's consent.[8] Furthermore, at the trial no equality was to be tolerated between the procurator and the defendant, for the procurator represents the state, whereas most defendants are enemies of the people and should be allowed to defend themselves only insofar as they do not utter reactionary statements or distort the facts or the laws and policies. Generally, it was asserted, the only purpose of the constitutional provision that the defendant has the right to make a defense is to assist the law enforcement agencies to assess the evidence of his crime and the degree of his repentance and thus "more fiercely, accurately, and firmly to attack the enemy."[9] Nor can the court be permitted to serve as a fair and impartial arbiter between procurator and defendant, because a clear separation between accusation and adjudication is helpful to the defendant and harmful to that harmonious cooperation among police, procuracy, and court that is the hallmark of true socialist legality. Similarly, the principle of an uninterrupted trial was held to be unacceptable, for criminal cases were said often to require a number of court sessions over a considerable period of time to ascertain the facts. And the principles of "directness" and "orality" in adjudication were condemned, because they require those who decide the case to hear it and are therefore inconsistent with the newly enunciated policy that openly called upon the trial judge to submit his proposed decision not only to the chief judge of the court's criminal division and the president of the entire court but also, in cases of any importance, to the local, territorial party committee.[10]

It is this explicitly articulated, persistently avowed espousal of local party control over concrete judicial decisions that in recent years has set Chinese justice most sharply apart from Soviet

[7] *Ibid.*

[8] Su I, "Should a Defender Attack or Protect Crime?", *Political-Legal Research*, No. 2, 1958, pp. 76–77.

[9] Shen Ch'i-ssu, "Censure the 'Principle of Debate' in the Criminal Litigation of the Bourgeoisie," *Political-Legal Research*, No. 1, 1960, pp. 30, 34.

[10] Chang Hui, Li Ch'ang-ch'un, and Chang Tzu-p'ei, "These Are Not the Basic Principles of Our Country's Criminal Litigation," *Political-Legal Research*, No. 4, 1958, pp. 76, 77–78.

justice. Even under Stalin, whatever the realities of practice, party control of judicial adjudication was not publicly advocated, and in the post-Stalin era the Soviet press has occasionally reprimanded local party secretaries for attempting to interfere with individual court decisions.[11] In China since the anti-rightist movement, the judge who is held out as a model is one who consults the local party secretary on any case of importance.[12]

This sudden change in "legal philosophy" that began with the anti-rightist movement was accompanied by profound practical changes. Theoretically, no inroads were made upon the principle that only the courts impose criminal sanctions. But the significance of that principle was undermined because the regime perfected a highly punitive system of police-imposed "administrative" sanctions. The actual jurisdiction of the procuracy and the courts was thus severely circumscribed. Large numbers of party and non-party persons were declared "rightists" and were removed from their jobs in the judiciary and the procuracy for having "indulged criminals" and "opposed party leadership." This group included the chief judge and two associate chief judges of the Criminal Division of the Supreme Court and the Director of Research for the Supreme Court, as well as major figures at the provincial level.[13] Virtually all the remaining non-party members of the procuracy and the courts were reassigned to less sensitive work in other branches of the government. The draft code of criminal law was never promulgated by the National People's Congress, and, because "judicial work has made new progress along the mass line," the Supreme Court directed the lower courts "to revise, enrich, and improve" the existing rules of criminal procedure in order "to meet the demands of the progress of our work."[14] A number of changes were immediately put into effect to "simplify" the system of mutual restraints which the framers of the constitution and organizational laws had expected to exist

[11] See, e.g., A. Popov, "Under Fire of Criticism: Impermissible Interference," *Pravda*, Jan. 23, 1963, p. 2; English translation in *Current Digest of the Soviet Press*, Vol. XV, No. 4 (1963), p. 27.
[12] See Liu Tse-chün, "Realizations from My Experience in Adjudication Work," *Political-Legal Research*, No. 1, 1959, p. 48.
[13] "Smash the Dream of Rightists Who Try to Change the Nature of the Court," *Jen-min jih-pao*, Dec. 12, 1957, p. 4, col. 1. Wu Te-feng, "Struggle to Defend the Socialist Legal System," *Political-Legal Research*, No. 1, 1958, p. 10.
[14] Kao K'o-lin, "Crimes of Treason by Reactionary Groups in Tibet Are Something the Law of the State Does Not Tolerate," *Hsin-hua pan-yüeh-k'an* (*New China Semi-monthly*), No. 9, 1959, pp. 64, 65.

among the police, procuracy, and courts. The public-trial system that had begun to evolve virtually came to an end except in the relatively rare instances when trial in a public courtroom was deemed unusually educational or it was desired to accede to a foreign delegation's request to attend a trial. Defense counsel became largely obsolescent, and the recently organized lawyers' collectives soon were operating with skeleton staffs. Control by the local, territorial party apparatus over the decision-making processes of the police, procuracy, and courts was strengthened so that "internally . . . the three departments have become one fist, attacking the enemy with even more strength."[15]

During the Great Leap Forward that began in the spring of 1958, law enforcement agencies, like all other agencies of government, were called upon to make their own "great leap." Law review essays, newspaper articles, and the work reports of provincial high courts of that era were replete with boasts of extraordinary numbers of arrests, prosecutions, and convictions achieved in remarkably short time spans. These accomplishments were usually attributed to the observance by legal workers of the newly re-emphasized "mass line," which required them to leave their offices and to go down to the people in order to dispose of cases "on the spot." A typical description depicted a "work group" that was composed of several police officers, a procurator, and a judge leaving the county seat to swoop down on a village shortly after receiving a report of a crime there. By shrewd and assiduous questioning of local party and government officials and the masses, it quickly ferreted out the identity of the offender and then detained him. After jointly interrogating him to verify the accuracy of the suspicion, the group promptly filled out legal forms such as the arrest warrant and the indictment, consulted the local officials about what the sentence should be, and, during a rest period in the production day, took the defendant before a large assembly of peasants in the fields. There, "under face-to-face exposure by the masses" even the most impenitent offender "could not but bow his head and admit his guilt" and receive his sentence. These steps were carried out in jig time. Such techniques of "smashing permanent rules" and "having the courage to innovate" "not only reduced the time wasted in traveling [of witnesses to the city] and greatly improved the speed of handling the

[15] Chang Wu-yün, "Smash Permanent Rules, Go 1,000 *Li* in a Single Day," *Political-Legal Research*, No. 5, 1958, pp. 58, 60.

case but also punished criminals promptly and powerfully, made propaganda for the legal system, and educated the masses." In addition, it was emphasized, they elicited more reliable evidence and brought judicial officials into contact with the life of the masses, who did not like cases to be tried as the mysterious preserve of specialists in distant city courthouses. All this was hailed as both "a new creative experience" and "a traditional method of handling cases that has a national style."[16]

Interviews with former police officials indicate that these published accounts of the "Great Leap" era have to be treated with caution. Although they appear to represent the manner in which the criminal process often functioned in cases of relatively minor crimes, seldom in cases of importance were law enforcement cadres allowed to act with such dispatch and unreviewed abandon. Certainly these accounts cannot be taken as typical of the authorized procedures that have prevailed since that national paroxysm subsided in 1960, although the problem of how to persuade low-level cadres to adhere to authorized procedures has proved to be troublesome and persistent, particularly in rural areas.

How then should we characterize the post-1957 criminal process? Although this third stage aborted the constitutional era of 1953–57, it did not represent a return to the rather unregulated reign of terror of 1949–53. The anti-rightist movement spurred the party to produce a more integrated and well-ordered system of imposing sanctions than had previously been developed. Because this system neatly meshes "administrative" and "criminal" sanctions and because many of the "administrative" sanctions and the acts that they punish would be deemed "criminal" in many other countries, it is necessary to treat the system as a whole rather than confine ourselves to the process for imposing "criminal" sanctions. It is feasible here only to sketch the major components of the system: the actors in the sanctioning apparatus, the sanctions they apply, the substantive standards that guide them, and the procedures used.

SANCTIONING APPARATUS

To identify all the actors in the sanctioning apparatus one would need to describe the diverse patterns of their organization within the work units and residential units of the cities and

16 *Ibid.,* pp. 58–59.

within the rural communes, which since 1958 have integrated
work and residential units in the countryside. Here I will merely
take as an illustration a standard urban residential apparatus of a
large city.

China is a national state that is subdivided into provinces and
two major cities and a number of autonomous regions that are
treated as the equivalent of provinces. Other large cities are
usually directly under provincial governments. The ordinary large
city is subdivided into districts. Each district government has
several suboffices, called street offices, which are the lowest level
for government units in the city. In each district there is a Basic
Level People's Court (hereafter called the Basic Court), a Basic
Level People's Procuracy (hereafter called the Basic Procuracy),
and often a public security subbureau.[17] Respectively, these
agencies are under the Intermediate Level People's Court, the
Intermediate Level People's Procuracy, and the public security
bureau that serve the entire city. Of these three agencies, only the
public security structure has an organized unit—the public security station—at the street office level. A dozen or more patrolmen
work out of the public security station, each treading a specific
"beat" within the area.

Less conventional is the semiofficial substructure that not only
feeds information into the official apparatus but also participates
in the administration of relatively minor sanctions. The area
under the jurisdiction of each street office and public security
station is organized in numerous residents' committees, which are
"autonomous organizations of the masses" that are mainly staffed
by elected, unpaid volunteers. According to the authorizing legislation[18] a residents' committee may be responsible for activities
relating to from one hundred to six hundred households and is
subdivided into residents' groups, each of which is responsible for
from fifteen to forty households. In many areas residents' committees perform their variety of functions through specialized

[17] In the People's Republic of China the "people's police," who are
uniformed, visible law enforcement officers, and the plain-clothes or secret
police are integrated under the administration of the Ministry of Public
Security. For convenience in this article the term "police" is used generally
to include all personnel of the Ministry of Public Security and its subdivi-
sions.

[18] Act for the Organization of City Residents' Committees, *Chung-hua
jen-min kung-ho-kuo fa-kuei hui-pien* (Collection of Laws and Regulations
of the People's Republic of China) (hereafter cited as *FKHP*), I (1954),
173.

committees, two of which—the mediation committee and the security defense committee, and especially the latter—are of principal assistance in the criminal process. There are usually one or more members of the security defense committee in each residents' group; their major job is to discover and to report to the police all suspicious activities in the neighborhood. Thus, surveillance of the teeming urban masses is brought down to the level of the individual household, a task which the single patrolman who is usually assigned to the area of a residents' committee would find it impossible to carry out. The patrolman works closely with the chairmen and other responsible members of the residents' committee, the security defense committee, and the mediation committee; if there are party or Youth League units within the residents' committee, he also cooperates with their leaders. Together with the patrolman this group forms the power elite in the life of the ordinary urban resident.

SANCTIONS

The sanctions imposed by the apparatus range from private "criticism-education" to the death penalty. I have already emphasized that there are "administrative" as well as "criminal" sanctions. The former embrace "informal" as well as "formal" sanctions.

The hierarchy of "informal" sanctions generally includes, in ascending order of severity: (1) private "criticism-education" by members of the local power elite; (2) private warnings and threats to impose sanctions by such persons; (3) criticism before a small group of one's peers, for example, his residents' group; (4) similar criticism before a larger body, such as a meeting of all residents within the jurisdiction of one's residents' committee; (5) "censure," which is a harsher degree of criticism before such groups; it requires a correspondingly greater degree of positive response from its object, such as thorough oral or written statements of "self-accusation," "self-examination," and "repentance," with written statements often posted at prominent places in the vicinity; (6) "speak reason struggle," which seeks to "help" its object by means of exposure to intense vituperation from those in attendance, amid shaking fists, shouts, and accusing fingers; and (7) ordinary "struggle," which reaches an even higher emotional pitch than the "speak reason" type and subjects its object to even graver degrees of public humiliation and physical intimidation, with people often rushing at him, forcing him to kneel and to bow his head and even hitting or kicking him.

The principal "administrative" sanctions of a "formal" nature, which are all imposed by the police, are: (1) the formal warning, modest fine, and short period of detention (up to a maximum of fifteen days) that are prescribed by the Security Administration Punishment Act[19] for a variety of minor offenses roughly comparable to our misdemeanors, as well as the Act's supplementary sanctions of requiring offenders to compensate their victims and of confiscating both instruments used to commit offenses and property obtained from offenses; (2) "supervised labor," which is also known as "controlled production" or "supervised production"; it permits the offender to remain in society, but for a long, indefinite period subjects him to a severe stigma and requires him to engage in appropriate labor and special indoctrination programs, to report periodically on his activities to the police and mass organizations, to obtain the permission of the police before traveling, and to abide by other humiliating and burdensome restraints and obligations; and (3) "rehabilitation through labor," which also imposes a severe stigma and moreover separates the offender from society and resettles him in the harsh conditions of a labor camp for what until 1962 was a lengthy, indefinite period;[20] subsequently, according to several former police officials, this period may have been limited to three years.

The major "criminal" sanctions are: (1) "control," which in actual content is the same as "supervised labor" and is sometimes confused with it, but which is deemed to be a different and more severe sanction because since 1956 it has been imposed by a court for the commission of a crime;[21] (2) imprisonment for a fixed number of years; (3) imprisonment for life; (4) the death sentence, with execution suspended for a period of two years in which the condemned person may earn commutation through self-reform; and (5) death.

All imprisonment is known as "reform through labor" and may

[19] *FKHP*, VI (1957), 245.

[20] *FKHP*, VI (1957), 243.

[21] See "Provisional Measures for Control of Counterrevolutionaries," *Chung-yang jen-min cheng-fu fa-ling hui-pien* (Collection of Laws and Decrees of the Central People's Government) (hereafter cited as *FLHP*) 1952, p. 53; and "Decision of the Standing Committee of the National People's Congress Relating to Control of Counterrevolutionaries in All Cases [Being Decided] by Judgment of a People's Court," *FKHP*, IV (1956), 246.

actually be served in a prison or in a labor camp whose regimen is somewhat harsher than that of a "rehabilitation" camp. Confiscation of property and deprivation of political rights are supplementary criminal punishments. Formal reprimand, fine, short term detention, conditional suspension of the execution of a prison sentence, and, in the case of foreigners, deportation are also criminal punishments. But of late they have been more rarely imposed, because in recent years cases that warrant the imposition of such mild punishment are often disposed of by "administrative" means.

GUIDING STANDARDS

Some of the standards that guide the application of these sanctions are published, and therefore are available both to the Chinese public and to us. Many others are communicated exclusively for the confidential use of certain officials. The failure to enact a criminal code and the fact that there is no systematic publication of judicial decisions have already been mentioned. Apart from the broad provisions of the Act for the Punishment of Counter-revolution,[22] "criminal" conduct is publicly defined only by a miscellany of specialized regulatory statutes and decrees. Some of these are merely vague statements about what acts shall be deemed criminal and what punishment shall attach to criminality, and others are fairly precise. What is particularly striking is the absence of any published proscriptions relating to the major common crimes, such as murder, rape, and robbery.

Official doctrine states that in the absence of express proscriptions, "the relevant resolutions, decisions, orders, instructions and policies of the Party and the government shall be taken as the basis for determining whether or not a crime has been committed."[23] Not surprisingly, to the extent that they have been published, such generalized "sources of law" have been so unspecific that they have failed to provide adequate guidance for either the law enforcement agencies or the public. For example, no speech is more relevant to the criminal process than Mao's "On the Correct Handling of Contradictions among the People," and no distinction in it is more fundamental than the one he elabo-

[22] *FLHP*, 1951 (1), p. 3.
[23] *Lectures on the General Principles of Criminal Law of the People's Republic of China*, edited by the Teaching and Research Office for Criminal Law of the Central Political-Legal Cadres' School (Peking, 1957), p. 58.

rately draws between cases that involve "contradictions between the enemy and us" and cases that involve "contradictions among the people." Yet the attempt to extrapolate concrete rules from Mao's precepts has led to considerable confusion both in theory and practice.

Interviews with former legal officials have established that the law enforcement agencies' need for guidance is met by a vast body of unpublished regulations, rules, orders, instructions, policies, reports, interpretations, and syntheses of judicial decisions that attempt systematically and specifically to define both political and nonpolitical crimes and that set forth applicable ranges of punishments and criteria for their imposition. There are also unpublished handbooks that contain judicial decisions, selected as models to illustrate how these standards are to be applied. These unpublished materials are subject to continuing revision in the light of experience and China's evolving needs. In order to prevent legal standards from lagging behind the policy demands of the day and previously unproscribed but socially dangerous acts from going unpunished, the People's Republic permits criminal proscriptions to be applied both analogically and retroactively on those occasions when the process of revision fails to keep pace with China's rapid political, economic, and social changes.

The public is not considered to require the guidance of legal standards to the same extent as those who administer the system. Nor is it thought desirable to facilitate its access to written rules and thereby limit the flexibility with which those rules can be administered. Yet the public is not entirely neglected, for its compliance is, after all, what is sought. As supplemented by accumulated post-1949 experience, community notions of right and wrong are thought to be a satisfactory substitute for published proscriptions of the major common crimes. With respect to other crimes, which reflect values that the Communist government is seeking to impose upon the community, apart from published proscriptions and experience with their enforcement, the regime relies upon informal, especially oral, communication of relevant norms. Thus, when a new policy is initiated and the use of criminal sanctions is contemplated to assure its enforcement, the requisite rules of behavior to implement that policy are in large part communicated and reiterated in the frequent small group meetings that virtually every Chinese is supposed to attend, either at work or in his residential area. Related techniques are also used, such as stimulating the masses "democratically" to adopt "patriotic pacts," which embody "norms for the conduct of the masses," telling them "what to advocate and what to praise, what to oppose and what to prohibit." Newspaper editorials, posters, radio broadcasts, large rallies, and other media of mass communication all disseminate in nontechnical fashion the substance of official norms that have not been published. Such techniques have been used by the regime since its inception. Even those substantive criminal standards that have been promulgated have tended to appear at or toward the end of a mass movement.

A similar picture can be drawn of the guidelines that exist for the application of "administrative" sanctions. Although one runs across frequent reference to the need to subject people who engage in certain kinds of antisocial behavior to sanctions such as "criticism-education" and "struggle," published sources do not systematically articulate the full hierarchy of these "informal" sanctions and the circumstances in which they are to be applied. Published documents do purport to regulate the application of the "administrative" sanctions of a "formal" nature. The Security Administration Punishment Act[24] is the nearest thing to a criminal code that Communist China has produced. It sets forth with considerable specificity many types of violations of public order which are closely akin to our misdemeanors but which the Chinese do not consider "crimes." For each type of violation the Act prescribes a range of sanctions and criteria for their imposition. It also deals with problems that are usually covered by the general part of a continental criminal code, such as questions of the responsibility of the mentally ill, the young, and the intoxicated, of mitigation and aggravation of punishment and of time limitations upon accusation and punishment.

Published rules that provide for the most severe "administrative" sanctions are far more sketchy. The documents that govern the imposition of supervised labor provide that it shall be applicable to unregenerate former landlords, rich peasants, and counterrevolutionaries and to certain "bad elements" such as persons who persistently refuse to take part in production.[25] Through

[24] *FKHP*, VI (1957), 245.
[25] See "National Agricultural Development Outline for 1956–57" (Revised Draft), *FKHP*, VI (1957), 37, 57–58; and "Instructions of the Central Committee of the Chinese Communist Party and the State Council on Checking the Blind Outflow of the Population of Rural Villages," *FKHP*, VI (1957), 229.

unpublished directives the category of "bad elements" has been extended to include such diverse types as hooligans, recidivist petty offenders, "unlawful bourgeois elements," and others who resist the commune movement. For a few years, the more serious "rightists" represented a fifth category to which this sanction could be applied. By its terms the Decision of the State Council establishing "rehabilitation through labor" embraces similar types of "bad elements" as well as minor counterrevolutionaries and reactionaries and those who persistently violate labor discipline and work assignments.[26] And its definitions too have been supplemented through internal documents.

THE PROCESS

The hierarchical structure of the sanctioning apparatus and the formulation of standards to guide those who staff the apparatus suggest the central government's interest in curbing the potential for arbitrary action of law enforcement cadres at the working level. Yet, plainly enough, the applicable standards permit those cadres a considerable amount of discretion. Moreover, the central government frequently emphasizes the importance of applying its rules flexibly and sensibly in the light of local conditions. By illustrating the process of imposing sanctions, it is possible to provide some insight into the scope of the discretion exercised and the factors that condition, and the procedures for reviewing, its exercise.

If we continue to take a residential area of a large city as our example, we note that very minor cases are often disposed of below the level of the official police organization by the semi-official, grass-roots elite. Members of the mediation committee are explicitly authorized to mediate disputes that involve minor criminal infractions as well as civil matters. In performing this function they engage in a good deal of persuasion, criticism-education, and warning of one or more of the parties, both in private and, when necessary, before small or large groups. Members of the security defense committee and the residents' committee and officials of any party and Youth League units in the area also perform similar functions, and such informal sanctioning is a staple in the routine of the patrolman on the beat. This informal processing of large numbers of petty violations relieves the formal process of an enormous burden and thereby enhances its re-

[26] *FKHP*, VI (1957), 243.

sources for dealing with important cases. It also does much to supplement generalized modes of informing the public about what conduct is prohibited.

When sanctions of greater magnitude are contemplated, the problem usually ceases to be one that can be disposed of by the low-level elite. The police organization identifies, at least preliminarily, conduct that warrants sanctions of any consequence, and it determines whether that conduct should be deemed noncriminal or criminal, that is, whether it alone will decide the offender's fate or whether it will invoke the participation of the procuracy and the court. Details of the process of imposing the more severe sanctions vary somewhat from city to city, even within cities. They also depend upon the offense involved, the difference between political and other offenses being fundamental. Yet the essential features of this process can be presented by describing typical methods of handling a number of representative cases of theft by laborers who are temporarily unemployed because of urban economic dislocations.[27]

Case A. A is caught in the act of stealing a small amount of rice from the local government storehouse. He is searched and is taken to the neighborhood police station. After the station chief (or his deputy) informally questions A, any witnesses, and the patrolman who apprehended him, it becomes clear that A stole out of hunger, that he has never previously run afoul of the law, that he is duly repentant, and that there is no reason to suspect him of other misconduct. The station chief therefore decides to lecture him severely and to release him on condition that he write out, for posting in public places, several copies of a "guarantee" not to repeat the offense and that he make an oral "self-examination" before his residents' group. Although the Security Administration Punishment Act [SAPA] authorizes the issuance of a formal warning, a fine and detention, the first two sanctions are seldom applied, and in this case detention is deemed too harsh. Even in these circumstances, if A were a member of the bourgeoisie, his act of stealing public property would take on a sinister aspect and would usually be classified as a "contradiction between the enemy and ourselves." A would then be treated as an "object of dictatorship" subject not to mere detention but to severe crimi-

[27] These illustrations derive from extensive interviewing that sought to ascertain the extent to which published laws and other documentary sources correspond to "law in action."

nal punishment. Because A belongs to the proletariat, however, his act is viewed as a "contradiction among the people" and therefore relatively innocuous.

Case B. B is caught committing the same petty offense as A in similar circumstances, but, unlike A, he has had two such minor brushes with the law before. Because previous resort to "guarantee" and "self-examination" does not appear to have stimulated B to reform, the station chief believes that B deserves seven days of SAPA detention. But because detention is a relatively severe punishment, the station chief is not permitted to decide to impose it himself but must obtain the approval of the chief of the Public Security Subbureau's Security Section, which handles nonpolitical violations of public order. If there is no reason to suspect B of misconduct more serious than petty theft, while B remains at the station, the station chief may either telephone the Security Section and discuss his recommendation with the section chief (or his deputy) or he may send a policeman to the Subbureau to submit the detention application papers for the section chief's perusal. In either event, if the recommendation is approved, as it normally is, B is informed of this decision and is asked whether he has "any opinion" about it, that is, whether he wants to seek a review of the decision by the city Public Security Bureau. Persons in this situation rarely seek review, and if they do are unlikely to obtain relief. They usually accept the decision and serve their terms in the station's detention quarters, either because of a felt inability to comprehend legal processes or an awareness that they might well receive heavier sanctions and that a petition for review might be taken as a sign of an unrepentant attitude.

Case C. C is caught committing the same petty theft as A and B in similar circumstances but, unlike them, he has thrice previously been subjected to SAPA detention for offenses of this type. Thus, short-term detention has failed to educate him, and more extensive exposure to reform is thought to be required. Yet the offense is too minor for criminal punishment to be deemed appropriate, and C is not suspected of any graver misconduct. In these circumstances the station chief recommends to the Subbureau's Security Section not only that C receive the maximum fifteen days of detention authorized by SAPA, but also that, on completion of this term, he be subjected to supervised labor or rehabilitation through labor as a "bad element." While C is serving his new detention term at the station house, the section chief reviews C's entire file to consider whether his record justifies imposing either of these severe administrative sanctions. Although, from the point of view of the individual, remaining in society under a strict and stigmatizing regimen is a lesser depriva tion than being confined in a rehabilitation camp, from the point of view of the regime the two are generally of comparable magnitude. Whether one or the other is meted out is ordinarily a matter of administrative convenience that is determined by such factors as whether the "bad element" is a family man or a floater, whether the need for his labor is greater locally or at a rehabilitation camp, and whether or not those camps are overcrowded at the time. Because of the severity of these two sanctions, if the chief of the Security Section finds that C requires either of them, he cannot himself make the final determination but must submit a recommendation to the chief of the Subbureau.

Although "struggle meetings" are not as readily convened against ordinary urban residents as they are against government or factory personnel or rural people, if the case has particular educational significance, the station chief and the section chief may also recommend that imposition of the major sanction of supervised labor or rehabilitation through labor be preceded by a "speak reason struggle." If these recommendations are approved, at the end of the period of SAPA detention, C is "struggled" before a meeting of his neighbors or of residents of the area in which he committed the theft, and at the climax the major sanction is announced. The simplicity of these procedures makes it easy to understand why, as one former police official put it, the regime finds these administrative sanctions to be "very convenient."

Case D. A police patrolman catches D sneaking out of the local government rationing office with hundreds of new grain ration booklets. Because these circumstances suggest that he has committed a major crime, D is taken to the Subbureau rather than to the local police station.

1. *Detention.* At the Subbureau D is detained on suspicion of the crime of theft. This detention for purposes of criminal investigation must not be confused with detention authorized by SAPA as administrative punishment for an offense that does not amount to a crime, as in cases A, B and C. There are two methods for apprehending and confining persons who are suspected of crime: detention and arrest. Detention is the emergency appre-

hension and confinement of a suspect without a warrant for the purpose of determining whether there is sufficient evidence to justify his arrest. Arrest is the apprehension and confinement or the continuing confinement of a suspect on the basis of an arrest warrant. The Arrest and Detention Act[28] requires the police, within twenty-four hours after a suspect is detained under its broad "emergency measures," to question him and either release him unconditionally or request the procuracy's authorization of an arrest. The procuracy must within forty-eight hours after receiving this request either authorize arrest or disapprove it and order the suspect's release. Frequently, however, these statutory requirements are not observed by the police, and the procuracy does not become aware of the case until the police investigation is completed.

The Subbureau's Trial Preparation Section is responsible for D's case. After studying the file, one of its staff orders D up from his cell to a small interview room. There, often with a clerk present to record D's statements, the staff member subjects D to the first of a number of intensive interrogations. In the course of these, the interrogator resorts to a variety of tactics. Most prominent among them is persistent reiteration of the much-publicized Chinese Communist policy of "leniency for those who confess, severity for those who resist." Other standard techniques also have a familiar ring to a student of criminal law. The interrogator frequently alternates between a harsh, threatening, impatient manner and a kind, helpful, and understanding one. Often, holding a stack of papers up for D to see at a distance, he resorts to the "We've got the goods, so you might as well come clean" approach. And if others are thought to be implicated, D may be told: "Your companions have talked—only you look like you're going to be the 'fall guy'." The tactics are chosen on the basis of the interrogator's evaluation of D's weaknesses. Physical coercion has played only a minor part in the interrogation process in the past ten years. Official policy has long prohibited it, although in practice a certain amount is winked at as "necessary." For example, leg irons and/or handcuffs are placed on suspects who stubbornly "resist" in the face of what is deemed to be convincing evidence.

A record is made of the substance of D's statements, and, while D waits in his cell, the interrogator and others seek to verify this

[28] *FKHP*, I (1954), 239.

information from other sources. Their investigation provides material for further interrogation, which in turn leads to further investigation. This process often requires weeks and months. In some cities, at the end of D's first ten days of detention, the Trial Preparation Section must obtain approval of a ten-day extension from the Subbureau chief, and a series of such extensions may be necessary. Where it exists, this procedure, which is designed to permit higher level cadres to check periodically upon the processing of detained suspects, is prescribed by internal police regulations rather than by the Arrest and Detention Act.

2. *Arrest.* When from the materials gathered, the interrogator believes there is reliable evidence that D has committed one or more crimes, even though investigation of the suspected crimes may not have been completed, he will draw up a "conclusion to arrest." This contains a summary of the evidence supporting the charges upon which arrest is recommended, and describes D's class status, family background, past record, and various identifying facts. If this document is approved by the chief of the Trial Preparation Section and the chief of the Subbureau, an arrest warrant is issued, often without obtaining the legally required approval of the procuracy. In some cities, however, especially in cases in which the suspect is an important person or the crime is a grave one, this application for an arrest warrant must also be approved by the chief of the Basic Procuracy and the president of the Basic Court, who personally or through representatives meet with the Subbureau chief or his representatives to work out a joint decision with respect to arrest.

Arrest relieves the interrogator of the annoyance of having to seek repeated extensions of D's detention term (the Chinese system appears to observe no fixed limits upon the length of time following arrest that a person may be confined prior to adjudication). Arrest also facilitates the remainder of the interrogation process, because it makes clear to D that prosecution is probable and that he would do well to cooperate in an effort to obtain leniency. And it makes clear to the interrogator that D is unlikely soon to be released and to be in a position to complain about mistreatment, thereby giving the interrogator more freedom to expose D to pressures including overt coercion.

3. *Recommendation to prosecute.* Police interrogation ends when D has been exhaustively questioned about each of the crimes of which he is suspected and outside investigation has

ceased to turn up new relevant evidence. If, on the basis of the recorded statements of D and the witnesses and the other materials in the case, there appears to be comprehensive trustworthy evidence that D has committed one or more crimes, the interrogator draws up a "conclusion to prosecute," which summarizes all the information thought necessary to a thorough analysis of each charge. This is submitted to the chief of the Trial Preparation Section for review. If he approves, the "conclusion to prosecute" and the entire file in the case are sent to the district office of the procuracy.

4. *Indictment.* The case is assigned to an individual procurator, who studies the file and then proceeds to the detention house to interview D, often in the presence of the interrogator who handled the matter for the police. The procurator questions D closely about each charge of the "conclusion to prosecute." He then returns to his office to study the case further. If the evidence is complete and there is nothing suspicious about D's answers, the procurator usually does not make an independent investigation of those charges that D has admitted to be correct. But if D has denied any of the charges or significant facts relating to them or if the evidence appears incomplete or open to doubt, the procurator personally interviews the principal witnesses, and he may question D again. He also discusses any problems in the case with the police interrogator, sometimes persuading him to undertake further investigation of certain charges or to drop them or to dispose of the case through noncriminal processes.

If there are serious problems with the charges and the procurator and the police interrogator cannot agree informally upon disposition of the case, the procurator may recommend that his chief not approve prosecution. If his chief agrees, the case is returned to the police, who may acquiesce and release D or substitute administrative measures for criminal punishment or continue the investigation and interrogation in order to gather necessary evidence. Or the police may challenge the Basic Procuracy's adverse determination in a variety of ways. For example, the chief of the Subbureau or the chief of the Trial Preparation Section may enter into direct negotiations with the chief procurator, or he may take the problem to the secretary of the party unit that guides the district law enforcement agencies, or he may complain to the city Public Security Bureau and have it raise the question with the Intermediate Procuracy. Often, several of these procedures may be invoked in the same case until a solution is arrived at either through consultation and compromise or through a decision of the party secretary or the Intermediate Procuracy. Contradictions of such seriousness are relatively rare at present, and those that arise tend to be resolved in favor of the police. Although procurators are concerned about risking criticism for professional incompetence or overzealousness that allows improperly prepared cases to reach the courts, they are aware that the risks of "rightist" errors that frustrate the police are far more substantial.

If the procurator who handles the case finds it appropriate for prosecution, he draws up an indictment, which is a revised version of the "conclusion to prosecute," and submits it to the chief procurator. With the approval of the latter the indictment and the file are transferred to the court.

5. *Adjudication.* The procedures of the court are similar to those of the procuracy. The case is assigned to a judge, who studies the materials and then, usually in the company of his clerk, goes to question D at the detention house. If the basic facts of a charge are admitted in detail, the judge usually considers it to be confirmed. If D does not admit all the important facts, the judge or his clerk may subsequently interview witnesses and investigate any points of importance that require clarification. When the limited investigation permitted by judicial resources fails to reveal sufficient reliable evidence to support the major charges of the indictment, the judge usually discusses the case with the relevant procurator and police interrogator and suggests that they take the case back and either continue the investigation or dispose of the case by noncriminal means. Those agencies often acquiesce. Sometimes an informal compromise is reached, the judge, for example, agreeing to recommend to his superior within the court that D be convicted on a minor charge and that he merely be sentenced to "control" rather than to reform through labor. If no such solution is arrived at, one of the judge's superiors, either the chief judge of the court's criminal division or the president of the court, may discuss the case with the chief procurator and a responsible police official. Should it be necessary in order to solve the problem, the secretary of the district party committee may also be consulted.

When the major charges of the indictment appear to be supported by reliable evidence, the judge writes out a draft judgment that includes the sentence and submits it for the scrutiny of the chief judge of the criminal division, who may approve it, modify it, or disapprove it and send the case back to the procuracy and police. If the sentence is to be a substantial one, e.g., over three years, the proposed judgment will be cleared with the court president and often with the district party secretary. Once approved, the judgment is put into final form and made public, perhaps only by posting copies in prominent places in the district or perhaps by announcing it at a public meeting. If the latter course is taken, people's assessors are selected to appear with the judge who pronounces sentence. In either event D is notified of the judgment and is told that he has a right to appeal within a certain number of days.

6. *Appeal.* Whether out of ignorance or a legitimate fear of seeming to manifest an unrepentant attitude that might result in a heavier sentence or harsher prison treatment, D seldom appeals. Yet there is a fair amount of evidence that, at least at certain times, appeals have proved beneficial to convicted persons. Should he wish to appeal, D may simply indicate his dissatisfaction at the time that sentence is pronounced or, when back in his cell, he, or another prisoner acting at his request, may write an informal letter asking for appellate review. Upon receipt of D's request and the file, the Intermediate Court assigns the case to one of its judges. If, after study, the appeal appears frivolous, the judge rejects it without further inquiry. Otherwise, he goes down to the Basic Court to discuss the case with the judges who handled it. If satisfied with their analysis, he rejects the appeal at that point. If not, he and his clerk may talk with the procurator, the police interrogator, important witnesses, and D himself in an effort to clear up doubtful points. At the conclusion of this investigation, the assigned judge submits his recommendation to the chief judge of the Intermediate Court's criminal division, and frequently the case is discussed with the court president and perhaps a secretary of the city party committee before a decision is made.

Thus, appellate review, like adjudication in the first instance, is ordinarily a secret, informal, *ex parte* administrative inquiry. It normally reaches one of four conclusions: it voids the judgment of conviction and orders retrial below, which usually implies antecedent reinvestigation by the police; more rarely, it voids the conviction and dismisses the case; it affirms both the conviction and the sentence; or it affirms the conviction but modifies the sentence to make it more lenient or more harsh. Since 1958 a sentence can be increased on appeal not only when review is initiated by the procuracy or a complaining witness but also when it is initiated by or for the accused.

7. *Postconviction review.* Chinese law allows only one appeal. The judgment of the court of second instance is a legally effective judgment. If no appeal is taken, the judgment of the court of first instance becomes legally effective after the period for appeal has expired. But in either event D may still resort to other modes of securing reappraisal of his conviction. In death sentence cases, special procedures provide automatic review by both the High Court of the province and the Supreme Court in Peking. In all other cases D or someone acting on his behalf may directly request the sentencing court or an appellate court to subject the case to "adjudication supervision," a postconviction review proceeding that permits consideration of all substantial questions. Or they may ask the procuracy or local party officials to suggest such review to the courts. If, while D is undergoing reform through labor, new evidence is discovered that may materially alter the outcome of his case, it must be communicated to the sentencing court, or to the court that serves the labor camp area, for reopening of the case.

In reviewing the validity of a legally effective judgment, a court often consults representatives of the police and procuracy. If extensive further investigation is necessary before a decision is reached, a joint-work group of officials from the three departments may be formed to undertake the task. In addition to review on an isolated basis, sometimes the courts and their sister departments jointly reconsider entire classes of previously adjudicated cases, especially in conjunction with shifts in policy that call for harsher or more lenient handling of certain categories of criminals. For example, in 1957, in response to widespread discontent over the severe and often unjust punishments meted out during earlier mass movements, Mao Tse-tung proposed "a comprehensive examination of the work of liquidating counterrevolution."[29] Predictably, this "proposal" was promptly implemented, with the result that in many cases "criticism-education" outside prison was substituted for the original sentence to prison. But it should be

[29] Mao, "On the Correct Handling of Contradictions among the People," *FKHP,* V (1957), 1, 13.

emphasized that the low value which the Chinese attach to the finality of criminal judgments is not an unmixed blessing for D, since postconviction review, like appeal, does not exist for him alone and can be used for the imposition of a harsher sentence as well as a lighter one. Newspapers contain many accounts of how, months after disposition of a case, angry letters and oral petitions from the dissatisfied masses stimulate the sentencing court to reconsider the matter and to double the original punishment.

8. *Release of a suspect.* At the major postdetention stages of the process thus far described—arrest, recommendation to prosecute, indictment, adjudication, appeal and postconviction review —there is a possibility that the case may be dropped and D released. This possibility diminishes as the process unfolds. Whatever the stage at which an innocent suspect must be released, such action is regarded as a sensitive matter by a totalitarian regime that seeks to preserve the criminal law's deterrent power and at the same time to minimize popular resentment and to maximize faith in the infallibility of its system. In these circumstances, if D is a member of a disfavored class or has a bad record or if there is some, albeit insufficient, evidence of his criminal behavior, he is told that he is being released because of the state's desire to be lenient to him rather than because the requisites of a criminal conviction are lacking. He is admonished to keep out of trouble in the future on pain of more substantial deprivations, and sometimes, as a reminder, the administrative sanction of supervised labor is imposed upon him. If D is a member of the masses with a pure history and is clearly innocent, usually a responsible law enforcement official privately apologizes to him for the inconvenience caused by his confinement and attempts to explain why it had been reasonable to suspect him. If, as sometimes happens, D has been languishing in jail for months or even years, the lengthy processing of the case is said to constitute evidence of the state's unremitting efforts never to convict the innocent. In cases of such severe hardship D may be granted a "living allowance," a euphemistic expression of the state's regret that compensates him for earnings he has lost during confinement. Necessary medical care is also provided, and, if D has been fired from his job as a result of his difficulties with the law, steps are taken to reinstate him or to place him in equivalent employment.

The regime's most delicate problem in handling cases of blatant wrongs is how to restore D's reputation without losing "face" before the masses. During the years 1952–57, when efforts were being made to "reform" the judiciary and then to educate all the law enforcement agencies and the masses in the conduct of formal criminal procedures, newspaper accounts of mistakes and abuses were fairly frequent. In early 1957 Mao Tse-tung, when calling for correction of abuses that occurred in the work of liquidating counterrevolution, proclaimed that corrective measures should be publicized as much as the original wrongs. But the anti-rightist movement magnified the regime's sensitivities on such matters, and published confessions of error have been rare in recent years.

9. *Sanctions against offending officials.* Some of the mistakes discovered in the operation of the criminal process are, of course, unavoidable. Others are the product of intentional or negligent violations of prescribed rules. Not infrequently violations are also discovered in cases in which D continues to be regarded as factually guilty. The regime recognizes the need to punish and correct law enforcement officers who fail to observe prescribed rules and to educate and deter them and their colleagues. But it strives to do so without diminishing the efficiency of the process. When a violation is discovered in a case in which the law enforcement agencies continue to regard D as factually guilty, sanctions are not imposed upon the violator or his unit in a manner that will benefit D. For example, to exclude damning evidence from consideration because it was illegally seized or to dismiss charges against a known criminal because of some other procedural irregularity would, according to current Chinese thinking, be the most misguided sentimentality. In the Chinese view, violations of prescribed rules should be dealt with exclusively by sanctions that are extrinsic to the processing of D's case. Even in imposing such sanctions upon law enforcement cadres, the regime remains alert to the danger that it may thereby dull their enthusiasm for their task. When Chairman Mao issued his call to re-examine the work of liquidating counterrevolution, he was careful to state that "we should not pour cold water on the broad cadres and activist elements but rather should help them."[30] Thus, in assessing responsibility for abuses, the balance to be maintained between assuring discipline and preserving morale is regarded as precarious.

[30] *Ibid.*

In D's case, for example, if a policeman had made a mistake that could not reasonably have been avoided, even though it had led to D's confinement for several months, the policeman's superiors would ordinarily impose no sanctions upon him. If the policeman had intentionally or negligently violated the rules, he would receive one or more of a number of government disciplinary sanctions ranging from criticism to loss of his job, as well as one or more of a similar range of sanctions relating to his Party or Youth League membership. If this violation is attributable to an excess of zeal, did not have serious consequences, and is the policeman's first transgression, he is generally required only to undergo criticism and make a self-examination before his governmental unit. Criminal sanctions are usually reserved for those whose unlawful acts arose from malice, retaliation, corruption, or other personal motives.

10. *Release based on reform.* If D is not vindicated at any stage of the screening process and is sentenced to reform through labor, his sentence may subsequently be modified on grounds that are unrelated to its original validity or propriety. If he consistently demonstrates those qualities that are associated with a thoroughly reformed offender—for example, fully confesses all past crimes, sincerely repents, enthusiastically labors, actively stimulates others to reform, and informs on others—he may be selected as one of the relatively small number of prisoners who are held out as models and granted early release, whether unconditionally or on parole. On the other hand, if D proves "backward" in his thinking or lazy in labor or actually engages in further antisocial behavior, he runs the risk of joining the relatively small number of prisoners at the other end of the spectrum who serve as negative examples and whose sentences are extended beyond their fixed term to allow them further opportunity to reform. Most prisoners are released at the expiration of their full sentence. But it is not unusual for some released prisoners genuinely to volunteer to stay on permanently in the status of civilian laborers at prison factories or labor camps. Moreover, if released prisoners have no family to which to return and no job to fill or if they have undergone reform through labor in a sparsely inhabited area and are needed for its continuing development, they may be "retained," as civilians, regardless of their own preferences.

CONCLUSION

So much for the skeleton of the criminal process. By concentrating on a few representative cases I have, of course, omitted all the variables that arise through different facts, differences in geographic location, and the Chinese Communist penchant for almost ceaseless experimentation and tinkering. I have also omitted altered procedures for particularly important cases, such as those involving major counterrevolutionary offenders or government or party officials, and for cases during one of the periodic mass movements. By focusing on an urban setting I have inevitably underemphasized the problems of assuring adherence to authorized procedures in China's vast rural areas, where cadres tend to be less educated and supervised than in the cities. Yet, despite all these caveats, enough has been said to prepare the ground for some general concluding remarks of comparison with the Soviet Union, a comparison that is made no easier by the fact that the criminal process in the Soviet Union has been more characterized by crosscurrents than has its recent Chinese counterpart.

Whether one sees primarily similarities or differences between the two systems of administering the criminal law depends in large part on the level of his point of view. From a high perch the contemporary Chinese and Soviet landscapes look basically alike. Both are marked by an authoritarian heritage. Both regimes purport to derive from Marxist-Leninist dogma an explicit commitment to authoritatively defined goals for transforming the social and economic order. Both apply that dogma to problems of crime and punishment, viewing the criminal law as a major instrument for crushing political dissent and for disciplining and educating their people to pursue those goals. Both allocate power among similar institutions for administering formal criminal punishment—police, procuracy, and courts—and rely on the ideology, policies, and apparatus of the party to unify and to guide their activities. Both employ informer-surveillance networks. Both subject the administration of justice to the impact of mass movements, periodically alternating pressure and relaxation, severity and leniency. Both operate according to rules that the party chooses to impose and that can be disregarded when required by expediency. Both recognize the limits of the formal criminal process; by means of "noncriminal" procedures not only do they inflict minor sanctions, such as warning and fine, for offenses too petty to warrant criminal punishment, but they also inflict major sanctions, such as the Soviet "resettlement" of parasites and the Chinese "rehabilitation through labor," for a variety of vaguely defined, antisocial acts. Both have also devised "popular" institutions, such as the Soviet people's guards and comrades' courts and the Chinese security defense committees, mediation committees, and struggle meetings, in an ostensible effort to substitute "persuasion" for coercion and to demonstrate the ever-broadening participation of the masses in the administration of social controls that is supposed to herald the approach of communism. Indeed, renewed Soviet interest in the progressive transfer to "social organizations" of the responsibility for imposing sanctions for violations of law and morality, which was prominently featured at the Twenty-first Party Congress in January 1959, may well have been spurred by an awareness of Chinese experimentation with such forms and of Peking's extravagant 1958 claims that "buds of Communism are sprouting everywhere."[31] Thus, at least one similarity between the two sanctioning systems may be attributable to China's having served as a goad, if not a model, for the Soviet Union in recent years.

Yet the view from so lofty a perch obscures important differences, some of which I have mentioned in describing China's post-1957 rejection of the Soviet model of the formal criminal process. These differences are not "merely technical" but are fundamental to the fair administration of justice. Space precludes reciting all of them, but it is worth noting that when the Soviet Union undertakes to rationalize its criminal law and to clarify some of its proscriptions, abolishes the doctrine of analogy, and requires publication of all national laws and decrees of general consequence, it is beginning to move its criminal law in a direction that is significantly different from that of a China that declines to take such actions. Similarly, when the Soviet regime establishes the procurator's supervision of investigation by the state security agencies, expands the scope of the pre-trial activities of defense counsel, enhances the role of public trial, and inveighs against party interference with the adjudication of individual cases, it is moving its criminal procedure in a direction that is significantly different from that of a China that shrivels the powers of the procurator, generally dispenses with both public trials and de-

[31] See *Jen-min jih-pao*, Aug. 6, 1958.

fense counsel, and preaches and practices party control over individual cases. It is true that legal rules imposed by the Soviet party are no less self-imposed than those imposed by the Chinese party. But what must not be overlooked is that the Soviet rules provide a criminal accused with substantial protections that the Chinese leaders have branded "rightist" and intolerable.

This trend in the Soviet Union toward increased formality, greater recognition of professional considerations, and a certain degree of autonomy for the legal system has even had a modest impact upon the "social organizations" that serve as reminders of the tasks that lie ahead for Soviet law reform. Recent RSFSR legislation on comrades' courts subjects that informal popular tribunal to a considerable degree of legal regulation.[32] And amendments to RSFSR legislation make approval of the procuracy and a court prerequisites to imposition of the most severe anti-parasite sanction of "resettlement."[33] In China, on the other hand, the trend in recent years has not been toward imposing legal safeguards upon informal and administrative modes of sanctioning but toward eliminating safeguards that were present in the formal criminal process.

Why should the administration of justice—one of the touchstones of the quality of any society—appear to be evolving along divergent lines in the two major Communist states? Western scholars have only begun to wrestle with this problem. Does the divergence reflect other factors than the relatively immediate political pressures that gave rise to de-Stalinization in Russia and to the anti-rightist movement in China? What, for example, is the bearing of history upon this problem? Are there revealing differences in the authoritarian traditions of the two countries? Both in basic assumptions and in institutions and practices the criminal process in contemporary China displays some striking resemblances to its Manchu predecessor. Indeed, Max Weber's characterization of the administration of justice in traditional China as

[32] See Berman and Spindler, "Soviet Comrades' Courts," *Washington Law Review*, XXXVIII (1963), 842, for a translation and analysis of the 1961 and 1963 legislation on the subject.

[33] Decree of Presidium of Russian Republic Supreme Soviet: On Amendments to the May 4, 1961, Decree of the Presidium of the Russian Republic Supreme Soviet 'On Intensifying the Struggle against Persons Who Avoid Socially Useful Work and Lead an Antisocial, Parasitic Way of Life.' *Vedomosti Verkhovnovo Soveta RSFSR*, No. 38(364), Sept. 23, 1965, pp. 737–39; English translation in *Current Digest of the Soviet Press*, Vol. XVII, No. 44, p. 13.

"a type of patriarchal obliteration of the line between justice and administration"[34] might also be applied to the contemporary system. What can be said on the Russian side? Did the efforts from 1864 to 1917 to westernize the Russian legal system and to build up a professional lawyer class leave a more indelible mark than comparable efforts to westernize Chinese justice during the half century prior to 1949?

Is an explanation to be found not so much in history as in contemporary political, economic, and social disparities between the two countries? Of what relevance is it, for example, that in China the revolution is younger, the economy less advanced, and the people more backward and far more numerous than in Russia? It is sometimes said that any regime that embarked upon the unprecedented task of not merely controlling but also mobilizing and modernizing 700 million Chinese could not be expected to demonstrate great sensitivity to Western legal values. But are Soviet conditions different enough to produce greater receptivity to those values?

Are there relevant distinctions between the Communist parties of the two countries? Can one account for differences in the criminal process by reference to the fact that the methods the Chinese party has employed to dominate the state apparatus have curbed professionalization in all spheres to a greater degree than have those employed by the Soviet party? What is the impact of the CCP's twenty-year experience—an experience that has no Soviet analogue—in applying primitive legal controls amid the rudimentary conditions of life in the "liberated areas" prior to 1949? Finally, are the Chinese leaders less sophisticated than the Soviet leaders in understanding the uses of law? Stalin's heirs have acted upon the assumption that essential to the successful functioning of a highly industrialized society is the enlistment of the creative energies and individual initiative of its people and that this requires a legal system that will minimize popular feelings of fear and hostility and will instill a sense of security in the social order. The Chinese leaders, on the other hand, have regarded the risks of implementing Soviet-style legality as far graver than the gains that might possibly be derived. It is unclear to what extent their judgment rests on the premise that, at least at the present stage of China's industrialization, economic ad-

[34] *Max Weber on Law in Economy and Society,* ed. Edward Shils and Max Rheinstein (Cambridge: Harvard University Press, 1954), p. 264.

vances are most likely to be achieved in an atmosphere of personal insecurity. Their distrust of fair criminal procedures may be predicated in part upon simplistic notions about the nature of law and the degree to which it frustrates political needs. This possibility occurred to me not long ago during an interview with Chang Kuo-t'ao, one of the founders of the CCP. I asked him why his former comrades seemed reluctant to improve the administration of justice in an effort to increase the enthusiasm of the masses for socialist construction. "Perhaps I can best explain it by giving you an example," he replied. "What if A kills a Communist on the order of B, and when B is caught he says, 'I didn't do it, A did.' Under the law, might not B go free?" Lawyers can only find such a remark pathetic in its underestimation of the resources of the criminal law. Is it an accurate index of the legal sophistication of Mao and his associates? If it is, we are unlikely to witness any fundamental change in Peking's version of "socialist legality" until the present generation of leaders has passed from the scene.

Law: The Function of Extra-Judicial Mechanisms

LEON LIPSON

AT THE outset we face a problem of scope that cannot be solved except by arbitrary exclusion and inclusion. In contemporary China and the Soviet Union, where society is organized tightly under direction and pressure from state organs and political leadership, many official bodies engage in investigation, fact-finding of a sort, and coercive decision; once the courts are abstracted, we are left with a wide variety of institutions including, in Soviet terms at least, party organs, state organs, and "civic," "public," or "lay" organs (*obshchestvennye*).

Some of the bodies that might fit such a definition have nothing directly to do with adjudication in the usual sense of the term. Take, for instance, the exposé essay or article in the newspaper, written by a special (and specialized) correspondent, reporting abuses of position or authority.[1] Often, according at least to the press reports themselves, a sort of adversary proceeding occurs in which the newspaper correspondent casts himself—or, especially in cases of education, youth or family morality, *her*self—in the role of judge and hears argument from accusers, the accused

---

The main stress of this paper is on the Soviet Union. A comparative description of extrajudicial mechanisms in China and the Soviet Union was provided for the Tahoe Conference by Mrs. Virginia Jones of New Haven, Connecticut, to whom the author expresses his thanks for research assistance.

[1] The resemblance to adjudication is enhanced by the arguments used in many exposés. Often the target is an official whose competence and conformity to rule are not only conceded but stressed; and the message in the exposé is that the official violated a policy deeper than that of fidelity to rule by failing to show humane sensitivity. At times the writer of the exposé seems to be appealing from law to equity.

official, party committees, local soviets, and witnesses. The follow-up report of "measures taken" continues the informal parallel, for in tone and context it bears some resemblance to a report of compliance with a judicial decree.

In a similar way, it would be possible to include under the head of extrajudicial mechanisms the work of the party-state control committees, which were set up in November 1962 for the primary purpose of helping to increase productivity by exposing slackness in administration of industrial and commercial establishments, by jacking up the procedures of quality control of production, and by uncovering incipient criminality in the management of production and distribution. It is still too early to say what place this new institution is likely to have in the era of Khrushchev's successors or what sanctions committees of party-state control may come to deploy.

A third institution that ought at least to be mentioned before it is banished to a marginal position in this study is that of the "political school" and its associated "circles," which appear to be used primarily for continuing adult indoctrination but also secondarily for verifying the doctrinal orthodoxy of those who perform in the system.[2] Similar tasks are performed for party members and Young Communist League members by special bodies. The institution of criticism and self-criticism, wherever it is practiced, can be thought of as a means toward officially induced correctness of behavior.

At the risk of misusing Western categories, however, it will be convenient here to focus on those bodies that have the most to do with a process most easily recognizable as law enforcement. The description may serve as a basis for discussion of the reason for the inadequacy of those institutions and possibly of the classification itself.[3]

[2] See unpublished Ph.D. dissertation by Ellen Mickiewicz, "Adult Political Education in the U.S.S.R.: The Political Enlightenment System of the Communist Party of the Soviet Union," Yale University, Department of Political Science, 1965.

[3] Some of the following text is drawn from my "Soviet Non-Courts," *New York County Lawyers Association Bar Bulletin*, XXI (1964), 222–29; "Hosts and Pests: The Fight against Parasites," *Problems of Communism*, Vol. XIV, No. 2 (Mar.–Apr., 1965), pp. 72–82; and "The Future Belongs to . . . Parasites?", *Problems of Communism*, Vol. XII, No. 3 (May–June, 1963), pp. 1–6.

COMRADES' COURTS

Until their revival in 1959, Soviet comrades' courts were limited chiefly to the hearing of cases of violation of labor discipline, though the decrees under which they were authorized would have enabled them to consider a broader group of cases. In their present form, first sketched in 1959 in obedience to the 21st Congress and adopted after some deliberation in the Russian Republic in July 1961 (in the Ukraine in August 1961), they are "elected organs of society, whose mission it is to assist actively in the inculcation of the spirit of a communist attitude to work and to socialist property, in the inculcation of a spirit of observance of the rules of socialist community life, and in the development among the Soviet people of feelings of collectivism and comradely mutual help." They were to accomplish these ends by deterring violations of the law and acts that caused harm to society, by education through suasion and social influence, by creating a setting in which all anti-social acts would be regarded as intolerable.

Comrades' courts are separate from the regular judicial system, though there is a large jurisdictional overlap. A comrades' court is not a court presided over by a professional judge, it is not a forum in which parties are represented by counsel, it is not governed by the regular judicial codes of procedure, and it is not in general subject to regular review by higher courts.

A Soviet comrades' court is set up either on a territorial or an occupational principle. Thus we cannot arrive at the average size of a comrades' court's constituency by dividing the 220 million inhabitants by the 230,000 courts, for many inhabitants come under the jurisdiction of both a territorial and an occupational comrades' court. If it is set up territorially it takes in an apartment building or a complex of them, or a collective farm, or some other residential unit. If it is set up occupationally, it takes in an industrial or commercial enterprise, or a subdivision of one, or an institution or organization such as an office or a government bureau, or a school. There seems to be no formal maximum number of persons in a collective to support one comrades' court; the minimum number is fifty. ("Comrades'" by the way is not used as a term of art; the court is not limited to party members.) The state does not in terms require such courts to be set up. The decision rests with a general meeting of the respective collective or residential unit; in the residential situation the agreement of the executive committee of the local soviet is required; in the occupational situation the initiative seems to be lodged in the local trade union committee. According to several recent complaints by legal officials and writers, the local trade union committees are frequently slack in forming, supplying, supporting, and superintending the occupational comrades' courts, which seem to work more crudely and irregularly than those at residential collectives.

The comrades' courts, unlike the anti-parasite tribunals, have a group of *members*, presumably smaller than the number of persons in the appropriate collective, who are elected by the general meeting of the collective and who serve for a term of one year. (The comrades' court thus has a bench; the anti-parasite toilers' collective has only pews; neither has a Bar.) The elected members in turn choose from among their number a chairman, vice-chairmen, and a secretary; if we take the grammar seriously, the number of members of the court must be at least four, unless a secretary doubles with a vice-chairman. A public hearing requires at least three members. The elected members need meet no formal qualifications except that they must qualify as members of the constituency by virtue of their place of residence or their occupational attachment. They need not, of course, have legal training; at each of the six comrades' courts I saw in Moscow in 1963, however, a member or the secretary had had some legal training and experience. It is said by Soviet authors that the great bulk of elected members are old enough to have sufficient "experience of life" and to be capable of deciding cases with patience and attention; but a plea has been made also for drawing into the elected membership some members of a younger generation, "all the more so because not seldom it falls to [the courts] to hear cases on the conduct of young men and young women whose psychology is not always understandable to the older generation."

The range of offenses which the comrades' court has jurisdiction to determine overlaps the offenses that fall within the cognizance of the anti-parasite tribunals (discussed below) or the regular courts when they hear cases of parasitism, and overlaps also the regular criminal code. Comrades' courts (in the RSFSR) hear cases on minor offenses against labor discipline or safety regulations, unworthy public conduct, minor damage to public property, violations of dwelling regulations, some property disputes, and—most important—various minor crimes. Judges of people's courts, prosecutors, and police may transfer cases of certain minor crimes to be heard by comrades' courts. Specific authority was given the comrades' courts in October 1963 to hear cases of petty theft of state or public property, petty hooliganism committed as a first offense, petty speculation, and first-time thefts of consumer goods from citizens belonging to the same collective as the offender.

So much for the targets of the proceedings. The court may (but according to the literature it too seldom does) move *sua sponte* or may be set in motion by a complaint from any citizen, by the transfer of a file by the organs of regular justice, by state agencies, or by various civic (non-state) organizations. The list includes trade union committees; volunteer people's police (public-order squads); street or block committees and other social organizations; gatherings of citizens; executive committees or standing committees of local soviets; state agencies, directors of enterprises, institutions, organizations, administrations of collective farms; a court (the Ukraine adds also "a [single] judge"); the public prosecutor; and the organs of inquiry (i.e., police, investigator) with permission of the public prosecutor.

When a case comes before the comrades' court, or when the comrades' court is convened in order to hear a case, the case may already have been investigated by the members or staff of the court in the fortnight that may intervene between the time the case is brought and the time it is heard. Attempts to compose differences and settle short of hearing have been receiving encouragement in the general press. Legal writers have apparently not resolved the question whether a comrades' court is most successful when it disposes of disputes by quiet mediation and reconciliation or when it stages a public hearing with rhetorical denunciation and the waving of ideological banners. The recent shift of commentators' emphasis toward the frequency with which comrades' courts are used for the prosecution of crimes may be expected to increase the relative weight of the public hearing as against the work behind the scenes.

The court may require witnesses and documentation in its own discretion or on the request of the respondent (*privlekaemyi*, the one brought up). It is not clear whether the court must grant that request; I have seen a case in which it was denied, for what appeared to be good reason. The court does not have the subpoena power, though witnesses are supposed to be obliged to respond to a summons.

The hearing takes place outside the working day (or between shifts), and is public. The respondent may challenge any member of the court for bias; this challenge is weighed, however, by the court itself, including the challenged member. The court hears the witnesses, the complainants, the respondent, and looks over the documentary material available. The audience may with the court's permission put questions and make comments on the case. Frequently the comments from the audience are dominated by party members, Young Communist League officials, and other activists, whose remarks appear to be preconcerted. The court secretary makes a minute of the session.

If the respondent does not respond—that is, if the person who is summoned fails to appear—the comrades' court must postpone the hearing once, but may later—how much later is not fixed by law—hear the case *ex parte* unless there are good reasons for continued absence; but if the case has come to the comrades' court on transfer from one of the regular organs of justice, the file is returned to the transferor for further action.

The court's decision is taken by a majority of the (elected) members participating, is expressed in signed writing with an account of the gist of the violation and the measure of "influence" or retaliation decided upon, and is announced publicly and further reported.

The measures of "civic influence" at the disposal of a comrades' court are limited. In order of roughly increasing seriousness, they include: letting the respondent off with a sincere repentance and the voluntary[4] compensation of damage he has done; requiring a public apology from the respondent to the injured person or to the collective; issuing a comradely warning; issuing a public reprimand (*poritsanie*); issuing a public censure (*vygovor*), with or without publication in the press; imposing a fine of up to ten rubles except in cases of theft or violation of labor discipline; suggesting to the management of the place of work a transfer to a lower-paid post or a demotion; suggesting the eviction of the respondent from his living quarters when he cannot get along with other tenants or takes a predatory attitude toward housing facilities or maliciously omits to pay his rent; and, along with the

---

[4] The term is used in the sense analyzed for the Chinese case by Ezra Vogel.

other measures, compelling the restitution of harm caused by the illegal actions in an amount up to fifty rubles.

In addition, the comrades' court may decide to transfer the case to a (regular) people's court if the case is too complicated for it, or may bring the case to the attention of the agencies in charge of preparing criminal charges or imposing "administrative" responsibility.

The decisions of a comrades' court may be reviewed, but not ordinarily by a court. Either a trade union committee or the executive committee of the local soviet—probably depending on whether the comrades' court has been set up respectively on an occupational or a residential basis—may, if the decision has been contrary to the evidence or to law, suggest to the comrades' court that it hear the case over again. If the decision has included an order for the payment of money as fine or compensation or some other property transfer, and the respondent refuses to comply with the order, a judge of the *people's* court may be applied to for a writ of execution, and in that event the people's court judge will in effect review the legality of the decision of the *comrades'* court. If his review indicates that the decision of the comrades' court was illegal, the people's court judge refuses to issue the writ and returns the case to the comrades' court and to the trade union committee or executive committee of the local soviet for a decision whether to rehear the case in the comrades' court.

The other sanctions at the disposal of the comrades' court are not apparently reviewable by the people's judge. The warning, censure, and reprimand remain in force for a twelvemonth and then lapse if no new offense has been committed; the court may also lift its sanction before that time, upon its own motion or upon application by the individual concerned or various public organizations vouching for him.

In some cities, including Moscow, the review that is exercisable by the executive committee of the local soviet is in effect done for it at the *raion* or borough by a formally advisory body: the lay council on comrades' courts. This is staffed mainly by pensioners, of whom some have legal training. It has recently been recommended that the lay councils be divided into sections, one of which would work on appeals and be staffed by jurists.

The accounts of cases brought before comrades' courts indicate that the principal object of the proceeding, in the eyes of the Soviet commentators, is not so much the disposition of disputes or the retribution of society upon an offender as it is the conversion of the offender, the setting him on the path of righteousness. The commentators dwell upon the wholesomeness of criticism and self-criticism, of revulsion and self-revulsion, and they stress the deterrent effect on others than the respondent.

Soviet commentaries, though lavish in recounting cases of catharsis and conversion, do mention some abuses. On one side some comrades' courts seem to have been used some of the time to settle private scores, to satisfy the hostility of the community to the non-conformist or its resentment of the "loner," or to prop the self-esteem of elderly busybodies: the pensioners who man the residential comrades' courts give full value to their roles. On the other side, there have been complaints in the lay and legal press of the practice whereby regular courts, public prosecutors, or police allegedly abuse the authority given them by statute to transfer petty crimes under certain conditions to the comrades' courts. There seem to be what one leading article called "profoundly mistaken and harmful views of comrades' courts as if they were organs supposed to 'unburden' the court, the public prosecutors, and the police of 'picayune' matters." Yet that seems to have been one of the motives behind the revival of the comrades' courts. Here, as with the other non-courts, it would be wrong to suppose a simple and consistent unity of motives on the part of the Soviet leadership simply because we have not been able to sort them all and label them with names of persons, parties, or factions.

Similarly, the frequent resort to the levying of fines has been criticized by legal writers as evidence that the comrades' courts have been shirking their social duty of mobilizing community pressure on offenders by the more "moral" sanctions available to them. Yet in January 1965 the Russian Republic increased the maximum fines that might be imposed for thefts coming within the jurisdiction of the comrades' court. Perhaps the conflict over the proper role of fines is symbolic of a difference of opinion over the proper role of the comrades' court itself. Some legal writers, trying to remain faithful to the "withering-away" ideal, look on the courts as a prism through which the moral indignation or exhortation of the local collective is focused upon an offender in the interest of his reform. The authorities are inclined rather to use the comrades' courts, whatever the ideological components in their origin and revival, as a mechanism to handle an administra-

tive problem by processing certain minor offenses and thus relieving the docket of the regular courts. Whether the new emphasis
on fines also reflects a theory of deterrence that lays more stress
upon economic deprivation than Soviet theory used to is not clear.

THE ANTI-PARASITE LAWS

The anti-parasite laws began their modern career before the
revival and reformation of the comrades' courts and the volunteer
people's guard. Draft statutes appeared in party newspapers
through the Union in early 1957. Under those drafts, "able-bodied
citizens leading an anti-social, parasitic way of life, deliberately
avoiding socially useful labor, and likewise those living on unearned income" could be tried at a public meeting of fellow
residents. In cities, the meeting would be convoked by a street
committee or apartment-house management's committee for cooperation in maintaining public order; in rural areas, by a village
soviet. Sentence could be passed by a majority of those attending,
who in turn had only to be a majority of the adult citizens of the
given local unit. Although the meeting could confine its action to
a warning for a period of probation, the primary sanction was
exile at forced labor for two to five years. The sentence would be
subject to no judicial review, but would go into effect on being
confirmed by the executive committee of the local soviet.

The drafts met opposition, some of which was made public in
articles and letters to the newspapers. A number of people asserted that the definition of living on unearned income was vague;
that sham workers should be included beside non-workers; that
the requirements for a quorum at the public meeting should be
tightened. Someone urged that the government prosecutor (*prokuror*) should be present at the trials to watch over legality; it
was suggested that the power of the general meeting should be
limited to the uncovering of facts to be brought to the attention of
the *prokuror* for further action in the course of regular criminal
prosecution; others urged that the public meeting be vested with a
wider range of possible sanctions than the choice between a
warning and two-to-five-year exile.

The anti-parasite measures were nonetheless enacted, mostly
in a form close to the drafts, in nine "outlying" republics between
1957 and 1960. In the Russian Republic and the Ukraine, no anti-
parasite law was enacted until 1961; opposition there may have
been even stronger though less visible.

There is reason to think that between 1957 and 1961 the opponents of an anti-parasite law sought to play off one non-court against another. The draft statute for the comrades' courts in the Russian Republic, published in 1959, included a provision that would have let a comrades' court hear parasite cases. As the sanctions available to the comrades' courts did not include anything so drastic as exile to forced labor for two to five years, the suggestion to bestow parasite jurisdiction on comrades' courts may have come from those who thereby desired to forestall the adoption of an anti-parasite law.

In late 1959 and 1960 the drive for more drastic punishment of parasites in the Russian Republic was renewed. A lead seems to have been taken by officials of the Young Communist League (*Komsomol*), whose institutional connection with the internal security apparatus has long been apparent. First, the Komsomol has administrative responsibility for many of the "welfare" activities aimed at combating the rise of juvenile delinquency. Second, it has special duties in organizing and controlling public demonstrations, both the carefully planned official demonstrations and the more carefully planned "spontaneous" demonstrations. Third, the Komsomol has played an active role in the establishment and staffing of local volunteer people's guards (*druzhiny*) and the units that the guards superseded. Fourth, the Komsomol, in its public pronouncements, has tended to uphold a stern, xenophobic, and maximalist standard on questions of ideological purity and public morality. Fifth, the leaders of the organization appear to form a pool from which the senior soviet security apparatus draws its staff.

Important, though still general, guidance came in September 1960, through a leading article in the official party theoretical organ *Kommunist*. The writers of this article acknowledged that "the struggle against parasites is being intensified at the present time"; attributed the persistence of parasitism to private-property psychology, which was nourished by contemporary influences from the bourgeois world; recommended stricter enforcement of existing laws and less emphasis in the press on speculators' ill-gotten gains; and ominously concluded with a word of praise for the anti-parasite law passed shortly before in Georgia and a call for new legislation making it possible to bring "administrative or criminal proceedings" against all parasites.

Jurists moved into the discussion in the latter part of 1960.

Two of them agreed that new penalties on parasites had to be set, but they advocated the use of sanctions adjusted to the offense.

Shortly thereafter a people's judge voiced two recommendations which found their way into an RSFSR decree six months later: one, that property acquired by means other than labor be forfeit; the other, that parasites should be not simply banished from the city where they happened to be offending but settled in definite areas and compelled to work there, on pain of criminal punishment.

The year 1961 was marked by the campaign against economic crimes and the expansion of the death penalty; it is not surprising that during that year public opposition to the stiffer form of anti-parasite law came to a halt. On May 4, 1961, the RSFSR at last enacted its decree, to which in the following months the legislation of almost all other union republics was substantially conformed. The opponents of anti-parasite legislation had lost. Comrades' courts, with their lighter sanctions, were not given authority over parasite cases as such; the new legislation retained the sentence of two to five years of exile to specially set-off regions, with compulsory labor at the place of settlement.

Opposition, however, had not proved altogether vain. The 1961 decree did contain one important change from the 1957 drafts, and thus also represented a departure from the legislation of the 1957–60 period. This was a change in the procedure for hearing cases. In the 1961 decree no role was left for the residential public meeting, and the lowest state court of general jurisdiction, the people's court, was assigned important duties. A procedural distinction was drawn between cases of parasites who did not work at all and cases of parasites who had been registered in a job but did not report for work. The parasite who held no job was placed under the exclusive jurisdiction of a people's court, which however was supposed to try the case non-criminally and thus without such safeguards as were contained in the Code of Criminal Procedure. The parasite who was enrolled in a sham job could be tried by a people's court or by a public meeting of workers; discretion to select the forum was not expressly lodged anywhere, but subsequent commentary has made it clear that it is the government prosecutor's office that makes the decisions.

According to the 1961 decree, cases heard by a people's court were not subject to review in ordinary appeal but might be protested by the prosecutor to higher courts. Cases heard by a public meeting were subject to no review in court, but the sentence did not take effect until it had been confirmed by the executive committee of the local soviet, which therefore was in a position to conduct an administrative review of the file; as the convocation of the public meeting might have come at the initiative, or at least with the approval, of the executive committee of the local soviet in the first place, the administrative review probably persuaded the reviewers in most cases that the sentence was right and should be confirmed.

Another change was that under the 1961 decree the warning became not one of the consequences but one of the prerequisites of the trial. An anti-parasite proceeding now was not to be instituted until after the offender had been warned by the authorities to mend his ways and had disregarded the warning. Some convictions have since been set aside, on protest, by appellate courts on the ground that the necessary warning had not been given; more have been set aside on the ground that too little time had been allowed for the warned offender to reform. The warning may be given by "civic organizations or state organs," including the police, the public prosecutor, a trade union, a comrades' court, and perhaps others. In most cases the way for a man to comply with a warning is to get a job, or, if he is already on the rolls, to work regularly at his job; however, sometimes it is hard to tell what the offender could have done after the warning to avert the subsequent proceedings. If the parasite had gone to work by the time his case came to trial or even by the time it came to the attention of a higher court (where that was possible), the exile was considered wrongful and must be set aside even though the offender took the job only after the expiration of a realistic term of warning; but he was to be supervised closely in his work lest the employment prove to have been a maneuver to circumvent the decree.

The role of the public meeting, reduced by the jurisdictional provisions of the 1961 decree, was reduced still further in operation. Most of the prosecutions under the law had to be brought before people's courts because the defendants were unemployed and thus not attached to any occupational collective. It has been said that the sham workers were too often protected by their fellows. Even the few sham workers who were tried were usually brought not to the workers' public meeting but to the people's court. The government prosecutors may have preferred this route because they regard the public meetings as too lenient, too different from ordinary criminal prosecutions, or too unfamiliar.

The compromise of 1961 lasted in its main outlines for four and a half years. In September 1965 a decree issued by the Presidium of the Supreme Soviet altered the procedure, and to some extent the grounds of proceeding, against parasites. The toilers' collective now does not figure at all, unless it counts as a "civic organization" that may issue the preliminary warning. The offender has a month's time, after he is warned by police or civic bodies, to avoid prosecution by getting a job. For offenders who do not heed the warning, further process depends on their place of residence. Those who live in Leningrad, in Moscow, or in Moscow Province around the metropolis may be brought before a (regular) people's court and there sentenced to exile to special locations, as under the 1961–65 version of the law, for two to five years of compulsory labor. Offenders who live elsewhere are liable to be sentenced by the executive committee of a local soviet to socially useful work at enterprises or construction sites located within their own province (*oblast'*), march (*krai*), or autonomous republic.

As before, a convicted parasite who refuses to work under sentence is liable to a term at "corrective labor" with partial docking of his wages, and if he still refuses to work he may be deprived of his liberty in an ordinary penal institution.

So much for a sketch of the way the anti-parasite laws work. Why were they passed?

The official accounts of the enactment of the anti-parasite laws stress the determination of the Soviet people to make every member of "socialist" society willing and eager to do his part, to work to bring a better life to pass in the higher phase of communism. This professed goal appears to have three aspects, which we may conveniently call the productional, the sanitary, and the salvational. Parasites are to be made to work in order that production can be increased, they are to be temporarily isolated from the law-abiding majority in order not to infect their betters with private-property views, and they are to be reformed because civic virtue is good in itself.

May one conclude, from the severity of the sanctions, that the Soviet leaders are alarmed by an increasing incidence of such "parasites"? The inference, though natural, is rejected in Soviet explanations, just as it is in the case of the recent broadening of the application of the death penalty. In both instances we are told that the reduction in crime and the rise in the moral level of the population have produced in the overwhelming law-abiding majority a growing determination to do away with the nuisance created by the ever smaller anti-social minority. Yet in the late 1950's when some criminal penalties were reduced and some criminal procedures were liberalized, one was informed that that change was occasioned by the reduction in crime and the rise in the moral level of the population. An explanation that accounts in the same way for contradictory trends is suspect, and we may be excused for continuing our search.

Until the revision of October 1965, the laws against parasites seemed to look two ways at once. One edge of the sword was turned against the violent drunkard, the wife-beater, the man who had never made it. Thus an American observer described the trial in Moscow of one Zbarski—drunk, loathsome, scandalous, without work—who was exiled under the decree for three years. Sometimes the decree was used to get rid of prostitutes, as appeared to be the case with one Maiseva, sentenced to five years after trial in the city of Chita. The woman who instead of working spent her time slandering her neighbors and complaining to the authorities about imaginary threats was also a fit subject for exile. Many of the offenders were young ne'er-do-wells who were depicted as living off their poor but industrious parents and spending their nights in drinking bouts.

The other edge of the sword was turned against the man who disrupted the economic order by turning an illegal profit, the overprivileged scion who sought shelter behind the broad backs of his rich and powerful relatives, the *stiliaga* in narrow trousers and duck-tail haircut lounging on the sidewalks of Gorky Street, the snob who liked to sport Western clothes and a Western nickname.

At this point the anti-parasite laws meet the problem of juvenile and young-adult delinquency. While the men who make today's Soviet laws are digging themselves out of their history, they are confronted by the perennial and universal revolt of the young, in the special variant of the nuclear era and the even more special subvariant of Soviet conditions. There must not be any admission that there is a conflict between Fathers and Sons. The ideology of Marxism-Leninism, which has paid so much attention to dynamics, which abounds in talk of stages and development and periodization, cannot recognize its own transitory character.

If the revolt of the young were only a political opposition, the regime could apply to it some of the lessons learned in sixty years of battle, before and after the October Revolution. But how shall the aging warriors combat the rebellious apathy of their own progeny? What if posterity simply ignores the victories bought at such a price? The anti-parasite laws show one way of trying to turn this tragedy into melodrama.

Yet it is also possible to speculate that the thrust of the sword is really all one, and that the weapon is being wielded in the interest of the values of a lower middle class rising to power. After all, many of the virtues celebrated in anti-parasite proceedings and in the literature about parasites are just those so often ascribed to a lower middle class: the glory of work in one's appointed calling; modesty in dress, toilet, deportment; adjusting to one's surroundings, making one's peace with the organization. In defense of these values the anti-parasite laws, like the comrades' courts and the volunteer people's guard, were used to repress "excesses" characteristic of either the lower or the upper class. On this view the self-appointed gravediggers of the bourgeoisie would be now busy making the land safe for the *petit bourgeois*.

This explanation of the anti-parasite laws has much in its favor besides irony; yet there are facts in the picture which it fails to fit. First, the men and women in the party establishment do not seem effectively subject to the anti-parasite laws or other non-courts in the public sector, though party discipline may be exerted from time to time for similar reasons on some "upper-class" cases. Second, the Soviet ideologists would deny that a social class structure in this sense exists in Soviet society; anyone in any station can be part of the *narod* (the people) just as anyone in any station can be an *obyvatel'* (Philistine, selfish vulgarian). Third, the procedures used to further these lower-middle-class values are derived from rather unlikely models, such as the village assembly and the pattern of peasant collective censure. Fourth, certain values usually associated with the lower middle class in European and American society are not only absent from Soviet ideology but attacked as unworthy: one thinks in particular of the value of personal thrift (or personal accumulation) and of the value of privacy or discretion in personal relations. The individual pioneer, the self-reliant Titan raising his edifice of thought or invention or production, has not been an approved model in collectivist society.

VOLUNTEER PEOPLE'S POLICE

The *druzhiny* (Volunteer People's Police, or Guard) grew out of a movement that seems to have started in late 1958 in factory committees in Leningrad, on the outskirts of Sverdlovsk, in Ena-kievo in the Donets basin, and a few other places. They took some of their tasks and forms from institutions that had operated sporadically before, the most recent having been the *brigadmily* (brigades of cooperation with the police) and the KAO (Young Communist League flying squads). They were set up to help keep public order; in many places the regular police had broken down in its efforts to cope with drunkenness and other breaches of the peace. The organizations were variously named people's police, workers' police, detachments for the preservation of order, etc. They had no common structure; some were set up on a military model, with three hundred to five hundred in a detachment, divided into brigades of fifteen to twenty. The detachment in these cases covered a borough (*raion*) and was headed by a council of five, six, or seven, including workers of the borough party committees, executive committees of the borough soviets, representatives of trade unions, the Young Communist League, and other social organizations. Their initial duties were to patrol the streets. In some places they went out on patrol at first on Saturdays, Sundays, and paydays, which suggests the importance of the drink problem. Later the patrols were made daily; the usual time is in the evening, six to ten or eight to eleven o'clock.

Now there are about 140,000 *druzhiny* in the RSFSR, probably over 200,000 in the whole Soviet Union. Most of the *druzhinniki* are enlisted at their place of work and, mustered in occupational detachments, serve on patrols in rotation. An ordinary *druzhinnik* may find himself on patrol one evening in every fortnight or so.

The offenses against which the *druzhiny* were to act, in aid and in the stead of the militia, were and are various, including besides general rowdyism (hooliganism) and drunkenness the theft of government and private property, violation of regulations of trade, speculation, moonshining, traffic violations, neglect of children, and others. They are also supposed to engage in preventive work, to suggest measures of civic influence to governmental and public organizations, to send materials regarding violations to the

comrades' courts or to the administrative agencies, to report
offenses where necessary to the procuracy for prosecution, or to
the press for exposure, and to conduct public education in the
maintenance of public order. The *druzhinniki* are authorized to
demand that a citizen stop violating public order and to demand
identification where necessary, to draw up statements on certain
violations and send them to the *druzhina* commander, to take
citizens to the commander (though it is not clear how far he may
act to overcome resistance), and to enter public places in order to
maintain order.

One of the more picturesque functions of the *druzhiny* is the
maintenance of Boards of Shame—the counterpart of the Honor
Rolls kept in factories and offices—on which miscreants detected
or detained by the *druzhiny* are named, depicted, and lampooned.
Some officials, especially in the larger cities, are trying to broaden
and refine the activities of the *druzhiny* so as to include social
welfare work: children's sport clubs, helping the retired and the
aged, marital counseling, coping with alcoholism apart from the
direct protection of public order, and organizing adult leisure
activities.

AUXILIARIES TO THE JUDICIAL PROCESS

Besides the marginal institutions mentioned briefly at the outset and the three institutions that have been most heavily stressed
in the past seven years (comrades' courts, anti-parasite laws,
volunteer people's police), the public has been associated in the
regular processes of justice by the establishment of certain auxiliary functions.

Under the Criminal Code an offender can be given a suspended
sentence (conditional conviction) and placed on probation to a
collective that takes responsibility for his good conduct; in some
cases, an offender can be released on surety to a collective without
conviction. The collective usually is an occupational unit (factory, workers, shop, trade union local, collective farm). Some
such device has long been employed in the Soviet Union.

In the last few years the public prosecutor's office (*prokura-
tura*) in some neighborhoods has had the assistance of groups of
lay helpers. So far as appears from the Soviet writing on the lay
helpers, they usually have no special training, are not used for
legal research or advocacy, but serve under instructions as unskilled or semi-skilled investigators, checking business documents

in economic fraud cases, searching neighborhoods for missing persons, weapons, or goods, and the like.

In the criminal trial, the Soviet judge may entertain argument from a lay defender or accuser, whose authority is decided by delegation from a collective interested in one or more of the parties, usually the accused or the victim. The collective, be it occupational or residential, is supposed to decide who shall represent it in court and whether the representative is to speak as accuser or as defender. Informal comments made by Soviet jurists suggest that lay defenders or accusers appear in as many as 10 to 15 per cent of all criminal cases tried in People's Courts and that defenders are heard more frequently than accusers; it has not been possible to check these statements.[5] The relationship between professional counsel and the lay representatives is unclear. Some writers have recommended that the prosecuting attorney work with the lay accuser, guiding his preparation and perhaps even, where time and the lay accuser's abilities will permit it, assigning certain parts of the case to him, and correspondingly for defense counsel and the lay defender. In practice, it seems, the lay speakers are not trained or qualified for such tasks, and professional counsel on both sides are reluctant to risk the fortunes of their side by relinquishing responsibility even in part. (If the lay accuser or defender were to take over a substantial part of the functions of his professional ally and do unexpectedly well at it, his professional ally might run still a different risk; but it is likely that the pressures of office routine and the traditions of single responsibility are more important than are the apprehensions of eclipse.) The content of the speeches in court is

[5] In Moscow in 1963 I saw no lay defender in about forty trials but three lay accusers: one in a shoplifting case where the accuser was an office-mate of the defendant; one in an anti-parasite trial held before a People's Court in circuit session in an apartment-house clubroom, where the accuser spoke as a neighbor of the defendant; and one in a comrades' court case involving a traffic accident, where the accuser spoke in the name of the defendant's residential collective but was not himself a resident and had performed as lay accuser for several different collectives as part of his extracurricular civic activity. A lay accuser took part in the 1966 trial of the writers Siniavsky and Daniel; his testimony is abridged in the *New York Times Magazine*, Apr. 17, 1966. There is opinion in the Soviet legal literature that disapproves the use of lay accusers or defenders in comrades' courts; the ground expressed is that lay accusers and defenders are supposed to represent the collective before a court but that a comrades' court, unlike a people's court, is the creature of the collective itself, or else of society directly, and needs no representative of the public to stand between the public and the court.

thus usually predictable and canned; the judges seldom interrogate the lay representative, the lay representative seldom interrogates parties or witnesses or offers evidence, the legal or factual merits of the case are seldom mentioned concretely.

If the institution of the civic accuser or defender is to be appraised by its effect upon the establishment of the relevant facts or the decision on relevant legal questions, it has to be written off as negligible. The extent to which the representations of the opinion of the collective affect sentencing is unknown, though judicial decrees will often mention favorable representations as an informal kind of extenuating circumstance and counsel in summing up will use those representations in argument if they are on his side. It would be wrong, however, to suppose that the main purpose of the civic accuser or defender is to contribute to a resolution of the issue before the court. It appears rather to be to help increase the solidarity of the collective by the activity of making the delegation and deciding which way to delegate; to give proof of the watchful concern of the appropriate collective, or its leadership, over the conduct of its members; and to provide yet one more outlet for the expression of certain moral values promulgated in the official culture.

It is worth guessing that the trend toward the transfer of functions from state bodies to nominally unofficial organs is being deflected if not arrested. What is happening is not usually that the lay bodies are being abolished or functions withdrawn from them; indeed, from time to time new groups are added, and new functions are entrusted to the most important of the existing ones. Instead the officials are reinforcing their connection with, and supervision over, the lay bodies. One example is found in the comrades' courts, where the augmented fining power may have the effect of making the people's judge the reviewing authority over a larger fraction of comrades' court decisions. A second concerns the anti-parasite laws; there, even before the amendment of October 1965, the combination of the formal division of jurisdictional authority and practical administration had put more and more of the cases into the line of the regular courts, partly by decision of the public prosecutor. A third is shown by the use made of the lay helpers of the prosecutors and investigators; though the lay helpers are indeed used for some tasks delegated to them by the officials, it now appears that this institution, far from prefiguring a transfer of function, is on the contrary being adapted as a screening and internship stage in the selection of cadres for the official staff.

If we attempt to sort the possible reasons for the prominence being assigned to the non-courts in the period since 1957, we may have provisionally to accept the relevance of a number of factors, among which we cannot be sure of identifying a dominant one.

(1) First we can mention the two explanations offered most often in the Soviet literature.

(a) *Down with Crime.* The argument here is that, thanks to the creation of socialism, the abolition of the exploitation of man by man, and the liquidation of antagonistic classes, all the objective conditions for the persistence of crime have been eliminated. There is no reason for crime to continue, except the survivals of the bourgeois past and infectious influences from the capitalist present.

(b) *"Withering."* As a result of the 21st and 22nd Congresses and the 1961 Party Program the classic Marxist vision of the withering away of the state was revived; its attainment was implicitly regarded as less remote than had once been thought, and the path to it was denominated the transition from socialist statehood to voluntary Communist self-government. One of the operating characteristics of the period upon which party dogma says the Soviet people are now embarked is the progressive transfer of some functions of government from the hands of the state into the hands of non-state, civic, societal organs. (The existence of the state is not immediately threatened by this doctrine; it is now admitted that it will continue, even for the exercise of coercion, well into the stage of communism.)

There is no reason to doubt the genuineness of the desire, on the part of at least some of the persons responsible, to draw in large masses of the people to the work of improving public order, deterring violators, and instilling the moral values of the regime. Sincerity does not guarantee effectiveness or justice. For one thing, the centrality of party control is not to be touched, and the multiplication of instruments is not to be considered an excuse for genuine pluralism of power. The excesses of the past are laid to personal whim, to arbitrary power, to insufficient vigilance, to breach of trust, to anything except systemic features of the Soviet state and party regime. In the field of law, those who have had to pick up the pieces after the breaking of the images are faced with a choice that has troubled them before. One avenue of reform lies through an improvement in procedural regularity and formality; another, through a broadening of the base of justice, bringing the law closer to the people. This conflict, from which no society is altogether free, has been intensified by the characteristics of the Soviet regime. It divides Soviet reformers—one may guess—not so much from one another as within themselves, and tends to make a confused zigzag of the course of reform.

(2) A second explanation would emphasize the economic aims of the regime. Attention has, thus, been drawn by observers abroad—accounting specifically for the 1961 wave of anti-parasite legislation—to the bad harvest of 1960; to the evidence of unexplainable wealth transpiring when old money was exchanged for new in early 1961; to the illegal combinations succeeding the abolished trade cooperatives; to the increasing wealth divertible to commercial use, to the interference with strict organization of distribution wrought by private trading; to the new taste for luxuries unsatisfied through official channels.

(3) A third explanation would account for the non-courts as a response, specifically Soviet to be sure, to problems of industrialization, urbanization, and post-adolescent rebellion that are encountered in not very dissimilar forms in Britain, in the United States, and in many other countries.

(4) To the doctrinal, the economic-determinist, and the sociological explanations we might oppose or add a fourth, which would stress the special need for institutions of control under Soviet conditions. Given the basic premises of the Soviet polity, which I suggest are changing but slowly, and chiefly under the surface, the Soviet state needs machinery of control in a degree not matched by societies that are—to use a reasonably dispassionate word—looser. Not only does it need powerful machinery of control, but it needs large numbers of engines and tends to produce many of them, playing one off against another.

One of the claims made for the non-courts in the Soviet Union is that they bring the processes of justice closer to the people and at the same time induce the people to take part in the processes of justice. In part, the claim is justified. When a lay accuser or defender speaks in a criminal trial, he does represent an organization or collective even though the collective decision authorizing his effort may have been inspired and guided from above. When a court holds sessions in the Little Red Corner of an apartment

house or the clubroom of a trade union local, many attend who
otherwise probably would not, and the responses of the audience
frequently interact (not always in the interest of justice) with the
proceedings "on stage." The speeches made by members of the
audience toward the end of a trial in a comrades' court, while
some of them appear to reflect the instructions of the local *aktiv*,
do convey a sense of popular morality—channeled into a state-
established, though nominally unofficial, sanction. The authorities go to considerable trouble before and during the trials of
accused parasites, both in people's courts and at public meetings
of workers, to mobilize the expression if not the reality of public
sentiment.

Nonetheless, it is clear that the "popularization" of justice
tends to bring an ever larger portion of life under the eye of a
watchful regime. The non-courts do not—as is sometimes asserted—merely relieve the official courts from that portion of
their case-load that can be handled with less formal procedures
and less drastic sanctions. A comparison between all the cases
handled by the regular courts in, say, 1956 and those handled by
the courts and non-courts today in 1964 would reveal that the
range of institutionally supervised conduct has markedly increased. So, probably, have the number of sanctionable offenses,
the total number of cases, the amount and perhaps even the
median severity of the penalties handed down. The comparison
would, very likely, hold good even if the 1956 figures were
augmented by the case-load handled by the predecessors of today's comrades' courts and of today's volunteer people's police.
The Soviet regime has become less repressive; but it does not
show many signs of becoming less comprehensive. The total
weight of the blankets is lighter than it was, but there are still
many blankets.

Procedures in Soviet non-courts fit into a pattern that has been
described more thoroughly in its application to small and limited
organizations than in relation to an entire polity. In many countries, certain types of institutions share an approach to the individual, an official ethic, and a mode of operation that have led
Erving Goffman to call them "total institutions." Examples may
be found in the work of many mental hospitals, insane asylums,
prisons, reformatories, army camps, concentration camps, some
preparatory schools, and the training programs of certain religious orders. Some of the features of these institutions closely

resemble ordinary life in the Soviet Union as a whole, and one of the most striking resemblances is the practice that Goffman has called "looping."

Looping takes place between institution and individual and appears most clearly when the institution is most nearly "total." In those cases, officials of the institution, doing their duty as they see it, have acted upon or against the individual (patient, inmate, prisoner, recruit, novice—or, in the Soviet Union, citizen). The subject responds by defensive reaction. Then—and here is the place where the loop is made—the officials of the institution treat the subject's defensive response as evidence confirming the rightness of their initial judgment or diagnosis or punitive measure, and inflict more of the same. Sometimes the loop is traveled through several circuits.

One instance of looping in Soviet non-courts is the counter-response to the Grin. In anti-parasite cases, as well as in comrades' courts and indeed regular trials, the defendant often reacts to his odd and unpleasant situation (no matter whether he deserves, by his or the regime's criteria, to be put in it) by a tight, fixed grin. Perhaps it is a mask behind which he comes to terms with this newest little defeat. The grin thereupon becomes an added offense; prosecutors, civic accusers, and judges comment on the grin, "which shows that this defendant has no respect for our Soviet laws, has a frivolous attitude toward his social obligations, and mocks the authority of this tribunal." The judgment itself, though it may not mention the grin specifically, will refer to the defendant's contemptuous attitude in court as one of the signs that he is in need of correction. The grin has its counterpart in the smaller "total institutions" when the subject is not permitted the luxury of an autonomous facial reaction (sneer, pout, disgust, frown) and must keep a blank face lest the severity of the sanction be increased.

Another example lies in the blurring of the lines between various parts of a subject's existence. In the mental hospital what the patient does or says in the ward where he sleeps or in the shop where he works is observed, perhaps by different officials, but it is part of the job of the institution to collate the observations, to relate them to a picture of the whole man. The freedom of ordinary civil life, where work, play, family, public service, social life can be kept in separate though not completely sealed compartments, is infringed in the total institution for the subject's own good as the institution views it. Correspondingly, in the Soviet Union it is not only permissible but obligatory for the authorities to collapse the separate structures of a subject's daily life by piecing together, especially in the non-courts, the observations recorded by his family, his colleagues, the housing committee, the union officials, the party representatives.

A third example lies in the use made by the official of information elicited from the subject himself in the interests of the program of the institution (again ostensibly for the good of the individual as well as society). A mild form of this can be seen in the use made of interviews and questionnaires in market research and political polling. A more intensive form is practiced in certain kinds of psychotherapy. In the Soviet Union, the authorities profess to encourage candor but in practice reserve the privilege of using the elicited material to justify further sanctions.

To a lawyer, the closest parallel in a looser society is the process by which a convicted defendant is sentenced. At the point of sentencing, the privacy and autonomy that have been preserved at least in the public forum are discarded; testimony, under safeguards of no great rigor, is taken from the district attorney, police officers, welfare workers, and others; the convict himself is heard, but what he says is likely to be used against or for him. Not only the Soviet non-court but also Soviet life as a whole is governed to some degree by similar rules. It is almost as if a Soviet citizen came into his society already convicted and ripe for the sentencing. The possibility that injustice will be tempered with mercy is real, and politically significant, but Soviet legal institutions are still at least as far as those in other lands from successfully adjusting the competing claims of ideology, public order, criminology, and due process.

Voluntarism and Social Control

EZRA F. VOGEL

A CRITICAL problem confronting the modern totalitarian regime is that of enlisting the active cooperation of its citizens. In an earlier age, states like China were content if their citizenry paid taxes and refrained from causing public disorder. But the demands of a modern industrializing state require active participation on the part of the citizenry; the state cannot be satisfied with mere passive compliance. The citizenry must be mobilized to take part in the productive work of the society. This shift in the citizen's role—from passive to active—is critical in a country starting on the road to modernization, and it is no accident that in Communist China the key expression used to describe a person sympathetic to the regime is "activist." Of the virtues extolled in Communist China none is greater than activism.

The change in role from passivity to activity demands a corresponding change in the sanctions exercised by the regime. The threat of force, while insufficient for maintaining order in any society, is nonetheless of significant value to a state whose interest in the citizenry is limited mainly to raising taxes and maintaining order. But the ingenuity of citizens in finding ways to obey the letter of the law while passively resisting and even sabotaging the spirit of the law is almost unbounded. A regime which aims at achieving the active cooperation of its citizens must rely on methods of rule more subtle, less terrifying, and more palatable than the threat of force.

The difficulties of developing sanctions less devastating to morale are compounded in a still underdeveloped nation such as Communist China. Because the state operates so close to the subsistence level, there is only a narrow margin of material incentives that it can afford to offer. In a year of poor harvests, when the food supply is exhausted in providing everyone with only minimal requirements, how can the regime offer positive inducements? When capital is in extremely short supply, how many advantages can the regime extend to the hard worker or the efficient manager?

Communist China has tried to cope with this problem by supplementing the limited material incentives with a consistent and sometimes ingenious use of non-material incentives. The regime has unleashed an almost infinite variety of propaganda campaigns, mobilizing small groups at work and in schools and neighborhoods everywhere, to encourage the hard working activist. Endless varieties of model cadres, model workers, model women, model students, model children are continually before the citizen's eyes and ears. Endless awards of red flags, collections of Mao's works, special holidays, and other commendations are ceremoniously presented to activists. Recently the regime has even resorted to promoting some workers in rank without offering corresponding increases in pay.

In this paper I shall not attempt to discuss the whole range of non-material incentives but only the method of dealing with one particularly delicate problem: How can the regime minimize dissatisfaction while making its people do what they do not wish to do? As Mao, following Lenin, has put it very clearly, there is a contradiction between the people and the rulers; the people think in short-range terms and are concerned with only their immediate part of society; leaders must think in long range terms for the benefit of the whole society. How can the leaders enforce their thinking on the masses without creating serious dissatisfaction? The answer to this problem was not developed by a rational decision-making process nor has it been formulated in a distinct and coherent doctrine. For obvious reasons the regime's strategy is never articulated to the common people, but the basic approach of the regime in dealing with this problem is perfectly understood by all cadres and citizens. For want of a better term, it may be described as "voluntarism." Citizens are not forced; they volunteer.

Volunteering is not a new approach. Although the Communist leadership has learned through bitter experience that older nativist approaches are not equal to complex industrial problems, the highly sophisticated Chinese tradition of rule has proved of great assistance in enlisting the cooperation of its modern citizenry. The practice of voluntarism, while consistent with some Communist policies, did not originate with the introduction of communism; it is an adaptation and expansion of a traditional concern for winning the cooperation of the population. In the villages of old China, for example, elder educated citizens lectured the others to explain the ethical concepts which underlay obedience to the state. Yet, while still viable as secondary approaches, the old formulas for obtaining voluntary cooperation lack the scope and intensity demanded of modern propaganda. With the new regime have come new techniques.

When Chinese leaders announce that there is a high tide of enthusiasm and that within a few months the proportion of the rural population in cooperatives or communes has jumped from less than 5 per cent to almost 99 per cent and that the people have taken this step voluntarily, the Western observer may suspect that the concept of voluntarism has lost any real meaning. Yet to dismiss the concept of voluntarism as mere sham is to leave the nature and use of this approach to rule uninvestigated and imperfectly understood.

In part, voluntarism is a matter of form, a social fiction in which a person who is about to do something he does not wish to do, says "I do it voluntarily." The youth taken from school and assigned to the country announces that he goes *voluntarily* from love for the party and for China. However, the question of sincerity is not entirely overlooked. Should the youth's zeal seem feigned, an official will question his true intentions. By his manner and rational arguments the youth will then give further evidence of his good faith and his overwhelming desire to serve the nation.

Voluntarism can also be a matter of staging. For example, to win volunteers for an undesirable assignment, a group of young activists and youth leaders may jump to volunteer, bringing others caught up in the wave of enthusiasm. Later, the young activists are told that because they are needed elsewhere, they unfortunately cannot participate in the projects for which they volunteered, while the others are graciously permitted to accept the assignment. If the activists too must endure the bad assignment, their chances of later reassignments to more desirable jobs are greatly enhanced.

But voluntarism is not merely a matter of form and staging. It is a complex concept encompassing at once situations in which everyone is expected to volunteer and situations in which people have the right not to volunteer.

When all are expected to volunteer, the essence of the concept lies in the attempt to maximize sympathy with the regime by postponing, disguising, diffusing, and minimizing the explicitness of the sanctions for refusal. Punishment is not designed to fit the crime nor is it administered immediately. If, for example, a student upon graduating from college is told that he is assigned to work in an isolated area and he does not volunteer to go there, it is quite possible that he will be permitted not to go. It is likely he will be told that his going would benefit the country, but that if he does not wish to go, he will not be compelled. Indeed, part of the form which the regime adheres to in its practice of voluntarism is that a small minority do not volunteer. In its statement on the formation of cooperatives, communes, and so forth, the regime always says that the vast majority volunteered to cooperate, but that a very small minority did not volunteer and were not forced to go along.

If a citizen is reluctant to volunteer, the regime first attempts to persuade. The citizen who does not respond to the appeal for volunteers is presented with rational arguments on why the regime needs volunteers. The arguments presented in a citizen's small group and the visits of numerous activists urging him to volunteer may arouse some anxiety, but in voluntarism, properly practiced, there is nothing to suggest the use of force. The citizen being persuaded understands perfectly that threats lie behind these rational arguments, but they remain implicit.

Nowhere in official public pronouncements are sanctions against non-volunteers specifically enunciated. Yet the regime's intention eventually to discipline those who do not respond to the call to volunteer is an open secret. The citizen besieged by persuaders does not expect specific sanctions but knows from the experience of others the myriad of difficulties he may encounter in the future. And he is well aware that in the meantime he will be continually harassed by comrades who "wish to help him."

The citizen being persuaded does not usually know when, where, or how he will be penalized. He is aware of the black mark on his record but does not know what it might later mean. In some cases the black mark is only a mental note made by his colleagues, his superiors, or some party officials he has encountered. In others, it is literally a black mark entered in his all-important personal dossier. All cadres, all intellectuals, all potential subversives, all students who have attended middle school, and all other people of importance have a permanent personal dossier which follows them everywhere they go. Not only does it follow, but it sometimes determines where they go, and how high. When eligibility for the Young Communist League or the Communist Party or liability to criticism in a rectification campaign is at issue, the dossier often provides the answer. In the event of a misdemeanor, a previous black mark may well determine the severity of a citizen's punishment.

Since a person never sees his own dossier, the slightest ill will from above—a refusal for admission to a school, a visit by an activist—raises the specter of a black mark on his record. The citizen who is hesitant to volunteer gradually builds up anxiety about what penalties he might some day face, and when the anxiety becomes too great, he takes the step and volunteers.

Thus, without overt force, the regime has brought the citizen to heel. The indefiniteness of the sanction system permits the authorities to maintain that the individual may freely choose. When voluntarism is practiced correctly, the activist may explicitly tell the non-volunteer that the decision is his. Finally, to the extent that the sanctions are vague and there is some chance that no sanctions will ever be imposed, the citizen being persuaded feels that he is really *volunteering* voluntarily. Since regime policies sometimes change so that volunteers are no longer needed, the decision not to volunteer may represent a hope or a calculated risk that the need for volunteers may end.

Desirable patterns of behavior are not only specified with great clarity, but the message is repeated in a variety of ways—at work and in the neighborhood group—so that there can be no question about what one should volunteer to do. Positive sanctions are usually sufficient to promote volunteering. The citizen who takes the lead in volunteering by his eagerness and enthusiasm is likely to be rewarded in some way; he may be promoted more quickly in his work or sent for special schooling, or he may be cultivated for membership in the Young Communist League or the Communist Party. And being slow to volunteer may be almost as serious in its consequences as not volunteering at all.

While the eventual negative sanctions may be difficult to assess exactly, the general range is quite clear. If the persuasion by a small group and the mobilization of activists are not effective, friends may be mobilized to help. Though the term "helping" can be a euphemism for subtle coercion, this is not necessarily the case. Indeed, the more activist citizen who persuades a friend to reconsider the situation and advises him to volunteer may really be acting in his best interest. For example, for any number of reasons a person may be so annoyed that he is emotionally unable to bring himself to volunteer even though he knows it is to his own best interests. A friend may be of help by calming his feelings and enabling him to volunteer without displaying any signs of annoyance with the regime. Furthermore, to use the regime's terms, the "advanced" friend tries to help his "backward" friend not only for the good of his "backward" friend but for his own good; otherwise, he would be implicated in his friend's refusal to volunteer.

More serious problems lead to criticism before large groups. In very serious cases, a person may be denounced in a large assembly, with all former friends and acquaintances invited to join in the denunciation (all the same kinds of consequences apply to refusal to join in the denunciation). Even in such denunciations, the individual is not criticized for his specific act of refusal to volunteer. Rather the attack is a diffuse assault on his character; and any kind of selfish, undesirable behavior, including personal, family, and work history may be included as part of the denunciation. Because the attack is general rather than specifically related to a single act, the result can be far more devastating personally. In line with the general pattern of postponement, these denunciations need not occur at the time of refusal to volunteer; they may be saved for the next rectification campaign when a refusal to volunteer will be taken as one important bit of evidence of rightist tendencies or bourgeois thought.

Beyond the immediate persuasion, group criticism, and harassment by activists lie more serious sanctions which may be imposed at unpredictable times. Welfare benefits for sickness, accidents, and old age, and loans in times of financial difficulty are not guaranteed by the regime, and the amount of help a citizen receives is often related to the degree to which he has responded to the appeals made by the regime. Special rations, sick pay, pharmaceutical needs, child care, and so forth, may all be determined by what the local census policeman has written in his little black book. Because the citizen depends so directly on the regime, the mere withholding or postponement of help operates as a very powerful sanction.

The regime may also send the citizen away for labor re-education or labor reform, or in some extreme cases he may be put to death. In the early days following the takeover, when the regime was still consolidating its power, the death penalty was often applied in such a way as to remove possible obstacles to political control as well as to punish severe cases of refusal to cooperate. In more recent times, the death punishment has been used more sparingly, but the large number of executions in the early years was sufficient to intimidate the population. It is still not uncommon for a person of some influence who consistently flaunts his refusal to volunteer to drop out of sight. His colleagues may not hear of him again and cannot be sure whether he is in further study, in labor camp, or whether he is dead. Whichever it is, the disappearance discourages his comrades from hesitating to volunteer in the future.

Not only is the nature of sanctions often vague, but the network by which information about refusal to cooperate is passed upward is highly diffused. By comparison with the Russian secret police, whose presence was obvious and frightening, the comparable officers in Communist China, the Public Security cadres, stand much more in the background. Most officers are plainclothesmen, and much of the information is not collected by them but by local activists who voluntarily pass on "little reports." The local census policeman, who is the only member of the Public Security apparatus with whom the average citizen has contact, has broad responsibilities. He not only keeps track of household population registers but handles small items such as the distribution of ration coupons or special allotments. He is usually friendly and properly polite, and his role in reporting is played down and kept in the background. Since much of the reporting work is done for him by members of the Lane Committee, he can assume a more friendly pose with the citizenry.

To a considerable extent, voluntarism, as outlined above, is not a specific doctrine but a pervasive and fundamental approach to rule. It involves attitudes and practices automatically invoked whenever the regime wishes the citizen to behave in a particular way. The conscious and deliberate practice of voluntarism with organized public declaration of willingness to perform a certain task is reserved for the more serious problems—when a large number of people are asked to do something they would rather not. When the regime decides to implement a new program, it is first introduced in certain test areas; once the patterns of refusal and persuasion have become clear, the citizenry is mobilized to volunteer. In accord with the concept of "democratic centralism" borrowed from Russia, Communist China has been sensitive to the wishes of the masses, but once a strong stand is decided upon, the masses are mobilized. It is instructive to examine some of the major instances in which the regime has mobilized the citizenry to do unpleasant tasks and to examine the variety of sanctions, formal and informal, which buttress the practice of voluntarism.

1. *Reduction in salary and housing space.* One of the problems in the period immediately after the takeover was rationalizing salaries and housing space. The critical problem, of course, was to win the acquiescence of those whose space or salary had been excessively reduced. The regime's approach was gradual but persistent. Since a person might have difficulty adjusting immediately to drastically lower standards, anyone with a very high salary was advised periodically to volunteer for salary reductions until his salary was gradually brought in line with those of others doing comparable work. Usually he was approached by an official at his place of work and told that the national economy was in difficulties because of the destruction caused by war, inflation, mismanagement, and foreign exploitation. Funds were badly needed for the development of the country. Didn't he think it would be only fair to accept a salary more in keeping with his actual contribution to society and with other people's salaries?

In the days shortly after the takeover it was not at all clear how the regime would treat members of the old power elite. Propaganda at the time indicated that the treatment of former entrepreneurs and landlords would depend greatly on their current attitudes and behavior. Most of these persons realized that they had little chance of resisting, and most felt it wise to be cooperative in the hope that they would receive favored treatment. The regime, within limits, accorded higher positions and more favorable status designations to those who took the initiative in volunteering, and the more "progressive" capitalists who were mobilized to help their more backward colleagues were rewarded. In most cases, the regime did not have to resort to force since the former bourgeois were anxious to prove that they were willing and ready to accept proletarian status. Since they expected reductions in any case, they commonly felt that the sooner and more enthusiastically they accepted them, the better.

Those reluctant to volunteer were visited more frequently by persuaders. If a person persisted in his refusal, he would be denounced at meetings by his colleagues and superiors as a bad example of the influence of capitalistic thought. Eventually, he might be told his salary was being reduced regardless, and that he was expected to make a statement accepting the cut. Further humiliations might ensue. Having announced his acceptance, he might be told that he sounded insincere and that to prove his sincerity he must humble himself in public statements, writing and rewriting until he had testified sufficiently to his own stupidity and to the party's wisdom.

The appropriation of housing space was often more subtle. Appraisals were made for tax purposes, and owners of large buildings or of smaller buildings with space their families did not personally occupy were taxed heavily. Many owners who to avoid taking in strangers urged relatives or friends to come and live in their homes and pay a small part of the upkeep, faced the risk that the relatives taken in would refuse to pay any rent. Sooner or later, as taxes became more and more unbearable, the owners voluntarily went to the local housing authorities to offer some of their space to potential renters. Eventually, to avoid the problems of renting and the expense of upkeep (which often took more money than they were allowed to charge for rent), many owners volunteered to turn over the management of their extra space to the housing authorities.

2. *Appropriation of businesses.* Before collectivization in 1955–56, private business was taxed and regulated by the government, with some firms (especially foreign and "undesirable" concerns) bearing the heaviest burden. Owners were required to buy goods from the government at specified prices, sell them at government-regulated levels, and then pay taxes on their profits, if any. Many owners, finding themselves constantly in the red, hastened to volunteer to sell or even donate their businesses to the government.

An offer of sale or donation by an owner did not necessarily bring about automatic acceptance by the government. In some cases, the government demanded that the owners pay additional back taxes before the regime would even accept the gift. Foreign-owned firms often had to request their home office to send additional funds to pay special taxes, assessments, and fines required for going out of business. Owners designated as undesirable quickly understood the hopelessness of their position, and quickly donated or sold *voluntarily*. Moreover, appraisals of businesses were often far below market value, but continuing losses during the negotiations of rates were sufficient to encourage most owners to accept the regime's evaluations. Many businessmen, anxious to escape the opprobrium of being classified as bourgeois, offered up their businesses long before their position became economically untenable.

3. *Collectivization.* In the countryside, not long after land reform, farmers were invited and later urged to turn their land, larger animals, and tools over to cooperatives. Officially, they were to receive compensation for any contributions above the group norms, and they were to be part owners in the cooperative. In practice, in the low-stage cooperatives, although cooperative profits were partly distributed on the basis of landownership, compensation was small and temporary. By the time the higher-stage cooperatives were established in 1956, peasants no longer received payments based on land contributed to the cooperative.

Before 1955 joining cooperatives was sometimes genuinely voluntary. In the rural areas, as elsewhere, activists (in this case the chiefs of the mutual aid teams) formed the vanguard and found rewards for their eagerness in volunteering their groups early. But when the system of compulsory buying and selling was instituted at the end of 1953 and certain goods became salable to the government, the regime applied increasing pressure to those outside the cooperatives. Members of cooperatives received favored treatment in commerce, and, with the decline of the free market in grain, opportunities for non-members were gradually eliminated. Furthermore, those who refused to enroll in cooperatives were forced to pay much higher taxes, making it clearly disadvantageous to stay out. Still, according to all official pronouncements, joining cooperatives was to be voluntary. Thus, the policy of the cooperativization period stressed that while 98 or 99 per cent of the people in a certain area wished to join the cooperatives, 1 or 2 per cent of the population had elected not to join.

Those who chose to remain outside the cooperatives were often the middle peasants who were loath to turn over their superior equipment and land. However, for all their determination, when economic pressures became unbearable, and their exclusion from welfare services, mutual protection, and other community privileges became too burdensome, they at long last "volunteered." To penalize them for their hesitation, authorities often charged that they lacked the proper attitudes required for membership. Only after a long waiting period of "showing proper behavior," "indicating a sincere desire to participate," and proving their "socialist spirit," were they finally permitted to join the cooperatives.

4. *Distasteful assignments*. Although Communist China has had since 1953 a highly differentiated wage structure which included incentives for hard work (at least in most fields during most periods), it has not relied on material incentives to recruit people for jobs which are inherently unpleasant or located in undesirable areas. In job assignments the critical problem has been to motivate people to leave their homes and assist in the development of more remote areas. This problem became much more acute after the failure of the Great Leap Forward, when the regime was confronted with the necessity of mobilizing millions or urban dwellers to relieve the burden of the underemployed city population and to assist in the raising of agricultural production. Moreover, the problem has been complicated by the enormous disparity in the standards of living of urban and rural areas. The contrast has been especially striking between the interior and those coastal cities which had benefited materially from their unique position as treaty ports and had acquired a high level of technological development and Western sophistication.

Again, unable to motivate with material incentives, the regime has come to rely on the well-tested approach of "voluntarism." Although the precise way in which assignments or reassignments are made varies according to place and level, the general approach is very much the same.

College students are assigned to jobs directly after graduation on the basis of a nationally integrated assignment system. Unavoidably, some graduates are assigned to rural areas. Before any assignments are made, a senior university official addresses the graduating class on the exigencies of national development which require educated people to be sent to remote new areas. He may begin by emphasizing the still underdeveloped state of the economy and explain how the assignments of graduates will serve the national good. He points out that there may be individual hardships in some assignments but invariably appeals to their sense of national pride, to their honor. The challenge of the opportunity will bring about enthusiastic acceptance of assignments. After this lecture, students discuss in smaller groups what their attitudes will be when assignments are made. Once assigned, students publicly declare their willingness to accept their jobs. They must support their announcement with statements hailing the challenge they face and declaring their resolve to meet it. Finally, there appears a press release to the effect that "[*number*] students volunteered enthusiastically to go to [undesirable place]."

While the Ministry of Education supplies the university with assignment quotas for certain undesirable areas, university officials still select the students who will meet them.

In the case of youths without university or special technical training, there is no national system of assignment, and individuals may find their own jobs through the Labor Bureau or Section in their local area. It is not easy for youths to find their own work, and most jobs are found only by going through the Labor office. Once they go to a Labor office, however, they will be expected to accept the assignment they are given. Those who refuse are not told explicitly what the sanction will be. The next time they apply for work, they will simply not be given assistance. If assistance is given, the assignment is less desirable than the assignment that the applicant previously rejected. Although the policy is never publicly stated, everyone knows, or at least suspects, it to be true. In any case, the official statements at the Labor Bureau are the familiar ones: the applicant need not take the assignment; he accepts voluntarily.

Another path to the rural areas is through the reassignment of people already working in the city. At times governmental offices, businesses, or schools receive orders requesting that they reduce the size of their staffs by a certain number and make available this excess personnel for "downward transfer," which most often means transfer to the rural areas. Work units are usually given some leeway in deciding how to recruit the volunteers, and since they are anxious to keep their most desirable workers, they are most likely to reassign their least motivated, least able, and most troublesome employees. Should these employees not volunteer for the assignments, they will be taken off the payroll and will not be able to find other jobs, at least to the extent that the bureaucracy is well coordinated and no other units are particularly in need of their skills.

Recognizing that rural assignments are almost universally despised, the regime supplements its recruiting of volunteers with a constant barrage of propaganda about the opportunities in the rural areas. Simultaneously, it attempts to minimize dissatisfaction in those already "volunteered" by reducing the disadvantages of a person being sent to the country. Thus, when a person is first assigned to the rural areas, he ordinarily starts at the same pay rate he received in the city. Furthermore, compared to the local population, he is given preferential treatment in housing and rations. After a time, however, discussion about the problem of rationalizing salaries, incomes, and living situations in the rural areas inevitably follows, and the person transferred from the urban area is asked to volunteer to accept a salary more in line with what the local people receive.

Refusing an assignment inevitably brings unpleasant consequences. For this reason, the major alternatives confronting a youth who has no college training and whose family can give him temporary financial support are not whether to accept or reject an assignment but whether or not to approach the Labor Bureau in the first place, thereby making himself liable to unfavorable assignment. Many young people take university entrance examinations repeatedly in the hope of passing or at least of postponing Labor Bureau registration until more promising job opportunities appear.

5. *Ration Reductions.* During the 1959–61 period when food shortages were especially acute, most people had to accept some reduction in their rations. Most citizens volunteered to accept formal reductions in their allotments and eventually even to give up some of the rations to which their already thinner coupon books entitled them.

For those who ate in dining rooms at work, the problem was generally handled in small work group discussions. For the most part, however, rationing was handled through the residential units, and thus the local Lane Committees were mobilized to hold ration meetings in which all might participate. It was explained that bad weather, the need to repay foreign loans by sending food abroad, and so forth made food shortages very serious; the regime was making a serious effort to see that the food available was distributed fairly; the citizens were urged to take the lead in tightening their belts. Individuals then discussed in small groups their own personal needs in terms of body size, physical condition, the nature of their tasks, and how much they would be willing to sacrifice. Group pressure generally forced the individual to accept the rations which the group considered reasonable for him. This aroused the other members of the group who were genuinely annoyed that despite their own sacrifices other members by their stubbornness and selfishness were receiving more than their fair share. Besides antagonizing his associates, a person who insisted on receiving more, risked being reported to higher authorities as being uncooperative.

Again, citizens who refused to volunteer for ration cuts ran afoul of the indirect sanctions implicit in the doctrine of voluntarism. The following example shows one way the doctrine of voluntarism was adapted to deal with this situation. The non-volunteer continued to receive his old allowance while his friends took the cuts for which they had volunteered. At the beginning of the following year, however, when the stubborn comrade attempted to turn in his expended ration booklet, the official could not locate the new one and could not understand what had happened. While the authorities searched for the new booklet, the recalcitrant comrade and his family were without any rations at all. After two or three repetitions of encounters with the officials, the message became abundantly clear, and the selfish citizen volunteered for the same cut in rations taken by his friends. The official at the local issuing station expressed appreciation for his desire to help the regime by doing without, but pointed out that they should consider the fact that others have already been sacrificing for some time. Did the comrade not think that it would be only fair for him now to volunteer to receive still less than his comrades were receiving? Feeling that he had little choice, the citizen volunteered for a further cut. Miraculously, the new ration book was found.

6. *Abridgment of Previous Assurances.* The previous examples refer to situations in which a citizen is asked to accept a new situation that he recognizes as highly undesirable. Voluntarism also applies to situations in which the regime finds itself unable to make good previously made guarantees.

The regime tries to avoid explicitly violating its word. An official may even recognize that the regime has made a certain promise; the government is not acting in bad faith; it merely asks understanding of the citizen and hopes that he will volunteer to do without because of the currently unfortunate national situation.

Perhaps the most striking instance of "redefinition" in lieu of specific contradiction, is the regime's attitude toward the rectification campaign following the period of the Hundred Flowers. During the early part of the Hundred Flowers, the masses were reluctant to speak openly, so leaders gave assurances that no one would suffer for his criticisms. Within a few weeks, the regime felt seriously threatened by the vehemence of the suggestions solicited and resolved that there could be no alternative to clamping down and discrediting those who had been most vocal in the opposition.

The rectification campaign which followed began not with outright denunciations of all those who had spoken out but with discussions to evaluate the truth of their criticisms. It was publicly announced that although most citizens expressed constructive criticisms as the government desired, some counterrevolutionaries, reactionaries, and others had taken advantage of the situation. Party and Young Communist League members hastened to urge that the regime take action, not against the masses for speaking out but against that dangerous minority. The regime obliged.

FUNCTIONS OF VOLUNTARISM

a. *Passing Downward the Responsibility for Enforcement.* Reference has been made several times to voluntarism "properly practiced." The techniques of voluntarism are not always perfectly implemented. Why? Because it is the bureaucratic middleman—the local cadre—responsible at once to the people and his superiors who must make them work. The low-level cadre is expected to maintain good working relationships with the masses, to have a working style that is not "bureaucratic" or "commandistic." He is supposed to avoid antagonizing the people and sowing the seeds of discontent. At the same time, however, he is expected to do the bidding of the regime, to see that the masses *do* volunteer.

The onus of authority for major reforms never falls directly on the higher levels of government. In no case does the government require that the citizens absolutely perform one kind of act or another. Official announcements state precisely the opposite. In decreeing agricultural cooperativization, for example, official statements did not specify that people must join cooperatives but that with an overwhelmingly "high tide of enthusiasm" the masses wished to join the cooperatives. Instead, it is the local cadre who must assume the responsibility for implementing policy. In reducing rations or transferring workers downward the cadre is confronted with a dilemma: he must fulfill the quotas handed him from above without explicit government support yet he must not arouse the animosity of the citizenry.

In pushing measures which are only mildly unpopular, an effective cadre can ease difficulties, effectively present the arguments in favor of the policy, and carefully mold local public opinion. When presented with an intensely unpopular policy, however, the cadre often has no choice but to coerce and so violate the canons of voluntarism.

He may, on the other hand, as many lower-level cadres did during the early commune period, try to remain close to the people by emphasizing his helplessness in the face of orders from higher cadres. Naturally, such a course is a serious breach of discipline and is not tolerated by his superiors. Confronted by pressures both from above and below, the local cadre who wishes to retain his position errs in favor of the regime.

Thus, one of the basic functions of the practice of voluntarism is that the public scapegoat for unpopular pressure is not the central government, which insists that measures should be taken only voluntarily. It is the lower-level cadre who is the immediate and only obvious source of coercion.

b. *Maintaining flexibility in administration.* Unlike Weber's ideal bureaucratic organization—a rational and integrated system of methods and regulations and a patterned distribution of activities in the form of assigned duties—Chinese communism provides considerable flexibility in its bureaucratic practice. Current policy announcements and directives take clear precedence over any usual procedures or rules. This complicates the problem of developing a rational system of administrative practices but aids in adapting organizational practices to meet the current situations. Voluntarism is an important component of this flexibility because once new policies are announced, even if they are clearly inconsistent with previous practice, the people can be mobilized to accept the current situation and to volunteer to do whatever is necessary.

Not only does voluntarism permit adaptability in time but also in space. The regime can adapt its current line to local conditions. Instead of having set requirements or fixed quotas, citizens can be encouraged to volunteer in accord with local needs. In fact, directives from above are usually in the form of guidelines rather than regulations. The controlling mechanisms are not rules but more diffuse expectations left, within limits, to the interpretation of local party committees.

Voluntarism exists to mobilize the people totally, to maximize the acceptability of unpopular measures and so neutralize negativism. It creates problems of order which organizations closer to the bureaucratic ideal can solve more efficiently. The confusions, the disorder, the irregularities have at times been very serious. But in a country such as China, undergoing vast changes in such brief periods of time, there is merit in sacrificing order for adaptability. The practice of voluntarism serves to enhance the adaptability because it provides a way of gaining a measure of public acceptance for policies regardless of how inconsistent they are with previous practices.

The effectiveness of voluntarism appears to rest on the peculiar relationship of the individual to the governmental and party apparatus. It rests upon a certain minimal degree of acceptance of the nation's goals by the citizenry. But it goes beyond this consensus to organize the citizenry by highlighting the importance of personal commitment. The citizen's own attitudes and commitment are always in the foreground. Volunteering, with its diffuse and delayed sanctions, creates anxieties that sooner or later bring about complete obedience. The surety of punishment coupled with the unpredictability of time, place, and method is a subtle and effective social pressure which makes resistance ineffective and undesirable. Current psychological research on compliant behavior indicates that individuals do tend to integrate their personal attitudes with their public commitment, that is, they begin to believe their public expressions and to bring their behavior into line with these expressions. There is ample evidence to indicate that the practice of voluntarism has not made unpopular measures popular but that it has served to mitigate the degree of negative reaction and to mobilize group pressure toward individual commitment that goes beyond mere passive acceptance of the regime's goals.

Soviet Society and Communist Party Controls:
A Case of "Constricted" Development

MARK G. FIELD

THERE is a Soviet story, apocryphal perhaps as most such stories usually are, and yet reflective of the realities of Soviet life, that a class of school children while studying Russian history, came to Napoleon's retreat from Moscow. One of the pupils raised his hand and asked: "Comrade teacher, how could we ever defeat the French when we did not have a [Communist] Party?" This naive question, coming from the mouth of a child, makes, however, perfect sense when viewed through the prism of Soviet culture, and particularly in the light of the critical importance officially attributed to the existence and the functions of the Communist Party of the Soviet Union. Indeed, according to the Soviet definition, the party is *the* keystone of Soviet society, the alpha and the omega, the cement that holds it together. Merle Fainsod in the first edition of his book *How Soviet Russia is Ruled* used the graphic expression "lynchpin" to characterize the role of terror in Soviet society; it may well be that at the present time the same could be applied to the Communist Party. At least the party would have no hesitancy to apply it to itself and to add that it was the supreme instrumentality in the Soviet Union's march toward communism. And it may well be that the party is, at least now, most of what it claims to be. It has become such an integral part of almost every aspect of Soviet society and is so interdigitated

I want to express my gratitude to Professors Jerry F. Hough and Robert C. Tucker, who critically read this manuscript and provided many important suggestions. The paper also owes more than I can say to Professor Talcott Parsons and to the ideas expressed in his course on Institutional Structure. Needless to say, I alone bear the responsibility for the contents of this essay.

185

with most social processes that its sudden elimination as a functioning organization would throw Soviet society, temporarily at least, into serious disarray, since there are few alternative forces or organizations that could take over the functions the party has arrogated to itself. For it is precisely part of the party's *modus operandi* that such forces should not be allowed to rise and in any way threaten its hegemony. If they arise, they are usually either incorporated into the structure of the party (as the intelligentsia was during the thirties) or placed under strict party controls and supervision, as the armed forces are. It is the military, incidentally, because of its organizational control of a large number of men and means of violence and its possession of a relatively autonomous communications network, that might be able to take over in the unlikely event that the party should cease functioning or falter. This potential power has, of course, been recognized by the party from the beginning of Soviet rule, and it has taken measures to reduce the likelihood of such an occurrence to a minimum.

It is the view taken in this paper that the existence and the functions of the party have critical implications for Soviet social structure, and that, contrary to the image it presents to the outside world, the party may well be, at the present time and on balance, more of a source of retardation and stagnation than of dynamism and progress. Indeed, the further "modernization" of Soviet society may hinge not so much on what the party will actively do to promote the process of modernization as on its ability (or inability) to let Soviet society become internally more "differentiated," and this independently of direct party control and management.

"CULT OF THE PERSONALITY" OR "CULT OF THE PARTY"?

The expression "cult of the personality" with which Khrushchev chose to stigmatize Stalin's rule was not entirely fortuitous. Neither was it quite accidental that Khrushchev, after his fall, has also been accused of having created a small cult of his own personality.[1] The word "cult" as used by Khrushchev and his

---

[1] For example, a movie entitled "The Chairman" has been held up because it portrays a Khrushchev type. The essence of that type was that the chairman knew it all and trusted no one: "Before us we have a chairman, a leader, who regards himself as a commander . . . in the sense that he knows only one way of dealing with subordinates, by command. It is no accident that he shouts so much. . . . This is an

successors has a distinct religious flavor and conveys the impression of a religious-like type of activity: in that context it denotes the uncritical worship of an individual leader who behaves as if he had divine wisdom and inspiration. Stalin was criticized, ostensibly, because he had cast himself in the role of an omnipotent and omniscient deity who could do no wrong. Implicit in that criticism, however, was another charge: that Stalin had arrogated to himself the role which rightfully belonged to the party, that he had reduced the party to a powerless instrument of his personal and unchecked rule, and that he had further degraded the party by undermining its hegemony through other organizational instrumentalities such as the secret police.[2] Khrushchev's aim, as expressed in his speech at the 20th Party Congress and in his subsequent statements, was to restore what he termed "Leninism," but what might better be called the "cult of the party," i.e., respect for and supreme worship of that mystic entity and collectivity constituted by the party which, for lack of a better term, might be called the Communist living church or the body of Marxism.

The resemblance of the party to a secular church and to the role played by an organized and established church may serve as a possible model for an examination of the systemic nature of contemporary Communist society, either of the Soviet or the Chinese type. The use of the "church" or "religious" model is not, of course, new or particularly original. What is proposed here is to attempt to follow some of the consequences attendant on this kind of structural model and to advance the hypothesis that Soviet society, although it is in many respects and trappings an industrialized, mechanized, and urbanized social system, may lack certain of the characteristics possessed by other societies of that type. Seen on an evolutionary scale, it may then fall somewhat short of being a fully modern social system in the terms that will be used and defined below. At this point we need only note that no value judgment is implied in the term "modern" or "advanced" any more than such a judgment is implied in saying

---

essential part of his style of leadership. He is the leader who decides everything for all, he does everything for himself, he entrusts nothing to anyone. If he consults with an experienced peasant, it is only as if he were an obedient 'apprentice,' nothing more." Cited in the *New York Times*, Dec. 15, 1964, p. 12.

[2] See, for example, Zbigniew Brzezinski, "The Nature of the Soviet System," *Slavic Review*, XX (1961), 351–68.

that a society is "primitive" or "pre-literate." These are classifica-
tory terms, and the criteria for their applicability, which will be
spelled out below, are those of internal differentiation, complexity,
and integration and not whether one society is "better" or more
conducive to "happiness" than another. The judgment, if any, is a
functional one, and the ultimate test is an appraisal of the
capacities of that social system to adapt to its environment.

SOCIETAL EVOLUTION AND DIFFERENTIATION

The recent (and somewhat hesitant) revival of interest among
sociologists in the process of societal evolution has been sparked
both by an increased interest in historical studies and by the
logical extension of the so-called "area studies" into comparative
sociological analysis. The hesitancy of this revival is perhaps due
to the inadequacy of earlier evolutionary models and the influence
of the radical cultural-relativists who regard all cultures and
societies as equally authentic and equally valuable in all respects.
Earlier evolutionary models had foundered, primarily on the
concept of "linearity" in evolutionary development as well as on
the "universality" of certain major "stages" through which all
societies must go in their unilinear progression from primitive to
advanced levels. As Eisenstadt has recently pointed out, these
studies had also failed "to specify fully the systemic characteristics of evolving societies or institutions, as well as the mechanisms and processes of change through which the transition from
one 'stage' to another was effected."[3]

Talcott Parsons, in his recent and as yet unpublished monograph on "Societies: Evolutionary and Comparative Perspectives,"
holds that it is possible to trace the evolution (and transformation) of different societies from the level of relative simplicity of
the so-called primitive society to the intermediate level (such as
Ancient Egypt, the Mesopotamian Empires, Israel and Greece,
India and China) to the modern societies, whose development
was made possible in part by the Renaissance and the Reformation. While Parsons uses a three-stage analysis, other writers use
more complicated schemes. The point at issue, however, is that it
is possible to order types of societies on a scale of increased

[3] See S. N. Eisenstadt, "Social Change, Differentiation and Evolution,"
American Sociological Review, XXIX (1964), 375–86; also Talcott Par-
sons, "Evolutionary Universal of Societies," *American Sociological Review*,
XXIX (1964), 339–57.

internal complexity and that "socio-cultural, like organic, evolution has proceeded by variation and differentiation from simple to progressively more complex forms." The most fundamental principle, as Parsons has outlined it, is that evolution consists in the improvement of the adaptive capacities of the relevant society or system, and that adaptation clearly implies the capacity to survive under conditions of the environment and in the ability to master that environment. This enables the system to cope with a range of different conditions and unexpected contingencies. The development of capacity to cope with and master the environment comes as a result of the internal differentiation and specialization of mechanisms of the organism, in essence a division of labor between specialized organs or structures. Thus, a relative undifferentiation between the kinship and the economic system (i.e., a system in which economic activities are all carried out within a kinship arrangement, as is the case in primitive agricultural societies or the "family firm") is not as efficient an arrangement as one in which kinship and economic activities are carried out in distinct contexts, and in which recruitment for the different economic tasks can proceed on the basis of ability or achievement rather than particularistic ties of descent or marriage. By the same token, the governing of men in today's large-scale society is carried out more efficiently by a separate and differentiated governmental structure made up of individuals who work in that structure on a full-time basis than would be the case if every citizen had to participate (on a part-time basis) in making every decision and in administering the state, as was the case in the Greek *polis*.

The key concept is thus that of differentiation. Eisenstadt has stated that it is like complexity and specialization. "It describes the way through which the main social functions or the major institutional spheres . . . become dissociated from one another, attached to specialized collectivities, and organized in relatively autonomous symbolic and organizational frameworks within the confines of the same institutionalized system."[4]

Thus, the process of differentiation, which may be described as the gradual liberation or emancipation of social processes from rigid kinship, tribal, or ascriptive bases, implies a fair amount of autonomy for the differentiated spheres and the development of

[4] "Social Change, Differentiation and Evolution," *American Sociological Review*, XXIX (1964), 375–86.

criteria of action specific to these spheres; it also raises the important question of the integration of these different areas through a system of exchange of outputs. If this integration is missing, the process then becomes one of segmentation rather than differentiation, and may lead to stagnation and breakdown. Differentiation, as Eisenstadt has also pointed out, opens up new possibilities for development and creativity—whether they be in the area of technological development, expansion of political, cultural, philosophical, religious, or personal powers and rights. It also poses the question of the delicate balance and interplay between social forces (such as interest groups) and the functional needs of the society. Indeed, differentiation, still according to Eisenstadt, may lead to what he describes as "constricted" development, a situation in which one of the differentiated spheres will attempt to dominate the others coercively by restricting and regimenting their tendencies toward autonomy. More precisely:

This probability is especially strong with respect to the political and religious (or value) spheres, because these spheres are especially prone to "totalistic" orientations that tend to negate the autonomy of other spheres. Religious and political elites may attempt to dominate other spheres, imposing rigid frameworks based on their own criteria. The aim of such policies is usually an effective de-differentiation of the social system, and they may result in rigidity and stagnation, or precipitate continual breakdowns of the system. These tendencies to de-differentiation are usually very closely related to the specific processes of change that may develop within any institutionalized system.[5]

To return to Soviet society:

The basic ethos of that society, its fundamental *Weltanschauung*, its normative base, is the body of ideas and theories generally known as Marxism or Marxism-Leninism. This theory constitutes an ideology and is not simply, as Marx would have claimed, an objective and scientific method of looking at, and understanding, man, society, and the historical process. It has reached the status of a faith, secular to be true (as Marx intended it to be) and yet endowed, by virtue of its position and role in the Communist world, with the characteristics of religious beliefs, doctrine,

[5] *Ibid.*, p. 381.

and often dogma. As Daniels has rightly pointed out,[6] the followers of the faith embrace the doctrine, not because it passes a
particular test of metaphysical or historical truth, but because it
conveys a sense of the exclusive possession of truth.

Durkheim had posited, a long time ago, that religion was not
merely a superstructure reflecting material interests (as Marx
did) but a fundamental matrix for the evolution of culture, from
which matrix, through a process of gradual differentiation other
elements of the culture had emerged. In primitive society, there
thus seems to exist no sharp break between what is sacred and
what is profane, nor is there a clear dichotomy between the
"natural" and the "super-natural." In this type of social order, the
society itself as a whole was the "church." It was only through a
long process of differentiation that boundaries were established
between the world of the sacred and the profane, and that there
arose a lay culture relatively independent of religious criteria,
injunctions, and sanctions. When it is possible, in the same
society and culture, to worship in church and to teach freely that
the earth is round or that man did not descend from Adam and
Eve, a process of differentiation has taken place. When, on the
other hand, persons are sent to jail or concentration camps for
holding certain scientific views (for example on heredity) which
are contrary to the "State or Party Truth," then the process of
differentiation is incomplete.

By the same token, at the societal level (by contrast with the
cultural level) the process of differentiation from the church-
society led, as in the case of Christianity, to the formation of a
specialized, separate, corporate entity, the church, staffed by full-
time religious functionaries, organizationally quite distinct from
other spheres, though its claim for competence has tended to be
"totalistic." In the Soviet Union, the analogue to that body is the
party.

It is contended here that Soviet culture and society have become differentiated but perhaps incompletely differentiated. At
least, as seen on a comparative and evolutionary scale, that
society falls short of other, more advanced, pluralistic social
systems. Furthermore, the process of differentiation is slowed
down by the "totalistic" nature of the value-system and the orien-

[6] Robert V. Daniels, *The Nature of Communism* (New York: Random
House, 1962), pp. 349–50.

tation of the Communist Party, the guardian of the Soviet *Welt-anschauung*.

Following this line of reasoning, it can be argued, for example, that in the Soviet Union *partiinost'* ("partyness") has often served as a criterion for the judgment of actions in most spheres of activities, i.e., as a test of Communist morality, as well of course as a device to bludgeon nonconformers, and that it has hindered the development of autonomous or independent criteria of thought or action so that "secular" culture has not yet completely emancipated itself (or differentiated from) "ideology."

Furthermore, if Marxism has become a faith, then the Communist Party is the guardian, the repository, a differentiated corporate embodiment of that faith; it has become a secular, or non-religious, but "established," official and unique church, and this regardless of whether party officials all believe "sincerely" in all its tenets or not. Indeed, there is no ground to assume *a priori* that the leaders of the Communist Party are cynical manipulators of the doctrine, interested solely in power and nothing else:

> . . . the evidence, by and large indicates that they were really persuaded of their true orthodoxy, and that the flexibility of policy on which they insisted was enhanced rather than restricted by the aura of orthodoxy which reinterpretation could confer on each new twist and turn.[7]

In addition, ideology and its symbolic linkage to the charismatic figure of Lenin provide the party with its claim to legitimacy, since this claim cannot be (to use Max Weber's terms) either of the *traditional* type, as in the case of monarchs and ruling houses, or of the *rational-legal* type, since it does not rest on the specific and limited mandate of an enfranchised electorate[8] and an effective constitution. The legitimacy of the party is thus of the "routinized charismatic" type. The party claims its right to exercise control and authority because it considers itself the only legitimate representative and interpreter of the ideology. If the party were to discover, or acknowledge, that its ideology is based on "false premises" (an improbable event, to be sure), it would logically have no choice but to dissolve itself. It is more likely, however, to assert time and again that the basic premises on which it rests are "true" in the sense that they rest on a

---

[7] *Ibid.*, pp. 32–33.
[8] Though the fiction is maintained, of course, that party congresses are means to convey the wishes of the membership to the party.

materialistic interpretation of man and society and that thus by implication they are also "eternal." Interpretation of the doctrine, however, makes it possible for the party and its leaders to claim that their doctrine is not "dogma," but that it is broad and universal enough to provide answers to a variety of changing situations, and that these answers, while fitting the situation of the moment, are nevertheless faithful in spirit to the original doctrine, i.e., to the "fundamental law" of Marxism. Furthermore, the party justifies its existence and its role in "functional" terms by claiming credit for all the achievements of the regime, i.e., as the "organizer of victories."

As *the* corporate body of the only *true* faith, the Communist Party therefore cannot admit the legitimacy or the existence (within the Soviet Union which it controls) of other faiths or parties, and therefore rejects any idea of ideological pluralism. The position of the party is that the doctrine on which it rests must (and will) become universal, i.e., embrace the whole of mankind, and its historical function is thus to help in the promotion of this inevitable march of history. The Soviet Union as such is the "resources' base" on which the movement depends, i.e., it provides the human and material underpinning for that movement, and the party is the agency responsible for the mobilization of these resources on Soviet soil. As such, the party as the proclaimed instrument of history has acquired a mystique of its own: its existence, its survival, and its perpetuation are the prerequisites and the guarantee for the actualization of the faith at home and in the world at large. This helps to explain the reluctance of such men as Trotsky to attack or split the party even though they opposed the leader of the party. In other words, there may be bad "popes" who temporarily seize control of the party machinery, but this does not in any way bring into question the justifiability of party supremacy.

We need not go, at this juncture, into the nature of the party as an organization of leadership within Soviet society, except to note its resemblance, once more, to that of an established church (it was more of a priesthood under Lenin), with a specific and differentiated membership, and to note (as others have on many occasions) that it does constitute, at least for its leading members, an interest group or, as Djilas puts it, a "new class." This class has at its disposal the major instruments of control, such as the use of political power, the control of the means of production (which is the equivalent, under Soviet conditions, to their ownership) and the honorific goods in terms of patterns of deference and prestige that are associated with a privileged caste, or indeed, an Establishment. Status within the party hierarchy is not, of course, hereditary in the traditional sense, though it could be argued that the children of highly placed and influential party members enjoy certain privileges in careers that other members of Soviet society (and particularly the non-party majority) do not. This is simply to state that many party members have an interest in the perpetuation of the *status quo,* i.e., the continuation of party controls over society, and therefore a vested interest in the maintenance of the system as now structured, and this again, regardless of whether they are sincere, believing Communists or not.

The party by being the only source of "Communist morality" attempts to maintain not only a totalistic hold on Soviet society but also a diffuse, undifferentiated power of control and review. Its sphere of influence and competence in theory admits of no limitations, constitutional checks, or boundaries; there are no "jurisdictions" over which it dares not trespass. The distinction, for example, between "private" and "public" interests does not hold. What a person is and what a person does for example at home, on the job, in public life, or in other areas is of legitimate concern to the party. The activity of a party secretary, according to Bialer,

is restricted only by the territorial limits of his jurisdiction and by the decisions of the next secretary up the line; he may exercise his authority in any sphere, imposing his will on the economic administration, the educational system, the local governmental apparatus, etc., professional interests and rights of interference are virtually absolute and all embracing.[9]

The party thus tends to operate in terms of a militant certainty and an absolutist outlook about objectively doubtful matters that is one, as Bertrand Russell pointed out a long time ago, "from which, since the Renaissance, the world has been gradually emerging into that temper of constructive and fruitful skepticism

[9] Seweryn Bialer, "But Some Are More Equal Than Others," in *Russia Under Khrushchev,* ed. Abraham Brumberg (New York: Praeger, 1962), p. 259.

which constitutes the scientific outlook."[10] And it is this certainty which permits the party (or the leader) to say to one man, or to a group, "You are right," or "You are wrong"; it gives rise to that simple and classic dichotomy offered by the party: "Either you are with us, or you are against us"; it makes the principle of a "loyal opposition" an absurdity (the opposition, by definition, is treasonable and should be either in jail or shot). In short, in its inability to recognize that there may be shades of gray in the world, in its not having gone through the painful and sobering emancipation embodied, for example, in the Reformation that reminds man he is fallible and that there are very few absolutes in this life,[11] the party has tended to assume the cloak of infallibility, without fully realizing, or realizing too late, that the cloak could also serve as a blinder. Bertram Wolfe once suggested that not only was knowledge power but that in the case of Stalin, Khrushchev, and the party in general, "power became knowledge," i.e., the position of the top leadership led to its being considered "infallible" in its pronouncements, whether they were on abstract art, genetics, the chemical industry, poetry, the frequency of the milking of cows, or the declaration of who was or was not an "enemy of the people." In some instances, this "infallibility" has not been one of Soviet society's greatest assets in solving the multitude of problems facing it.

In order to assess the role of the party more precisely, we now turn to a closer examination of the Soviet social system, and of the major forces which, at the cultural and societal level, and insofar as the party attempts to control them, provide us with a conception of contemporary Soviet society.

THE NATURE OF SOVIET SOCIETY

Baffling phenomena tend to be productive of "theories" that will make them more meaningful and understandable. Thus, with tongue slightly in cheek, Daniel Bell set out a few years ago to review, in a paper entitled "Ten Theories in Search of Soviet Reality,"[12] the major schemes proposed by various analysts to

[10] *Bolshevism: Practice and Theory* (New York: Harcourt, Brace and Howe, 1920), cited in Milovan Djilas, *The New Class* (New York: Praeger, 1957).

[11] On the importance of the religious tradition for this kind of perspective, see, for example, Harry and Bonaro Overstreet, *The Strange Tactics of Extremism* (New York: Norton, 1964), p. 120.

[12] In Alex Inkeles and Kent Geiger, *Soviet Society: A Book of Readings* (Boston: Houghton Mifflin, 1961), pp. 43–66.

"explain" Soviet society. These ranged from characteriological theories of the cultural-anthropological type in which Soviet behavior was explained in terms of national character and early personality formation (as in Gorer's now famous "diaperology"), to sociological theories (including the concept of the "social system" and its major operating characteristics) and Barrington Moore's "ideal types," to the political theories of the Marxist, Neo-Marxist and "totalitarian types" (Deutscher, Bruno, and Wolfe), to the historical theories including the importance of Slavic institutions (Berdyaev, Pares, and Maynard, among others) and geopolitical (Spykman, T. R. Fox, and Kennan).

It has been found convenient, for the sake of brevity, in surveying the plethora of theories of Soviet society, to regroup them into three main[13] (though by no means exhaustive) clusters, the first one defining in general terms the "culture" of Soviet society, and the next two the "structure" of that society in terms of its political and economic institutions.[13]

1. Soviet Culture: National-Communism

National-Communism may be described as the search, on the part of a nation that has recently emerged as a major power on the world scene, for a national and cultural identity and rests on the fusion of the doctrinal bases of the Communist movement and identification of the interests of that movement (which is, in essence, supra-national) with the interests of the Russian nation.[14] This fusion was born primarily out of the recognition, on the part of the Soviet leadership by the end of the twenties, that no proletarian revolution (except for the short-lived episodes in Bavaria and Hungary) was in sight and the resulting decision (primarily Stalin's) to build "socialism in one country." From that point on, according to Stalin, Russia was to be considered as the bastion of the Communist movement and, as a corollary, anything that added to the strength of Russia as a nation (industrialization, for example) was good for that movement. The kind of "reactive nationalism" (the expression is from Rostow) which

[13] I am, in essence, following and amplifying the analysis presented by Alex Inkeles and Raymond A. Bauer, *The Soviet Citizen* (Cambridge: Harvard University Press, 1959), and Barrington Moore, Jr., *Terror and Progress USSR* (Cambridge: Harvard University Press, 1954).

[14] Seymour Martin Lipset has described this process for the United States in his *The First New Nation* (New York: Basic Books, 1963), chap. 2, Part I, "Formulating a National Identity," pp. 61–98.

mobilized sentiments and emotions already established in the culture was clearly expressed by Stalin himself in his famous and almost masochistic recital in 1931 of the past exploitation of Russia by foreigners,[15] and the reason why industrialization must be pushed at all costs; it was intensified in the late thirties and reached a climax during the Second World War and the postwar period until the death of Stalin. A strong component of this cultural orientation has been, and still is to an important degree, its antagonism to the West, expressed both in terms of fear of Western intentions toward Russia and a feeling of inferiority toward the West, which comes out in the form of a compulsive assertion of the superiority of Russian culture and "priority" of the Russian inventive mind.

The regime, particularly under Stalin, has thus capitalized on these fears and insecurities by pursuing a policy of extreme cultural isolation and chauvinism and by applying strong pressures on the intellectual community; any attempt at "objectivity" toward the West was branded as potentially (if not actually) subversive. Although the campaign for cultural isolation has receded from its high-water mark of the Stalin years, the regime has continued to look with diffidence and suspicion at the West or at anything "foreign" to the Soviet spirit. In summary then, a very important component of contemporary Soviet society, a tone-giving element indeed, operating at the *cultural* level is that amalgam between the doctrinal bases of communism and Russian nationalism described here.

2. *Political Structure: Totalitarianism*

Totalitarianism, as a political phenomenon, has been well described in the literature. It may be defined as a commitment to the total mobilization of a society's resources to accomplish the goals and programs decided by the totalitarian leadership or by the dictator himself. In essence, some would define it as a new form of "oriental" despotism with a control over human beings, material resources, and commitments greater than any ever achieved before, thanks to developments in modern technology, the means of mass repression and mass communications. From his position in the Kremlin, the leadership (or leader) manipulates Soviet society (and until recently societies in which Com-

---

15 J. Stalin, *Problems of Leninism* (Moscow: Foreign Languages Publishing House, 1940), pp. 365–66.

munist regimes were subservient to the USSR) in any way it sees
fit. It destroys and creates social classes; it arrests, jails, tortures,
shoots, expels, exiles, or declares "unpersons" those it suspects of
disloyalty; it controls what is said over the radio, printed in the
press, seen on television, expressed in the classroom, depicted in
novels, or painted on canvas. It decides to invest in *sputniks* and
luniks rather than housing and flush toilets. It and it alone
determines what the correct party line is and decides who (or
what nation) is anti-party or un-Marxist. Absolute power and
control over the population is its first concern, and its unwillingness to compromise and to liberalize the system reflects its fear of
the dissatisfaction of the masses and its conviction that government from above by a small self-selected elite shall not perish
from the face of the earth. While the totalitarianism of the
contemporary Soviet leaders is different from that of Stalin, and
to some extent from that of Khrushchev, politically and quali-
tatively, the Soviet system may be characterized as totalitarian,
particularly when compared with other political systems of the
liberal and pluralistic type.

3. *Economic Structure: Industrialism*

Industrialism may be described as the form of the economic
structure of a society as it is affected by the use of a specific type
of production. This mode of production, the industrial firm, is an
important element of any modernization process and immeasurably increases the national product of a society; it is characterized
(regardless of its ownership form) by the concentrated employment of large armies of workers and employees. This mode of
production is usually operated by a professional management,
divorced from ownership in the legal sense (but not in the sense
of control and use) almost as much as the workers and employees, and in its operations it applies technology and scientific
advances. This is in sharp contrast to agricultural production or
the family firm of early capitalism with its fusion of ownership
and management, its more or less paternalistic attitude toward its
workers, and the limited scope of its operations because of limitations in available capital for expansion, managerial skill for
administration and supervision, and research.

In a society of this type, the individual's primary ties with his
family, church, village, and small community are weakened and
replaced by affiliations with larger reference groups, such as trade

unions, professional organizations, employee or worker groups, class, the firm, the party, and the nation itself as foci of personal loyalty and emotional commitment.

Industrialization brings, in addition, a whole spectrum of consequences resulting from large urban concentrations of population, the development of mass culture, and the gradual replacement of traditionalism, religious orientation, and family (or kinship) centered values and solidarities by new attitudes and commitments consisting of a sort of secular morality. This morality tends to emphasize the importance of occupation and to some extent the "consumption" ethics of the city rather than the "production" ethics of the countryside rooted in the soil and stressing physical toil.

Occupation, and particularly occupational achievement, tend to become the central determinants of an individual's life chances and of the society's pattern of social stratification. In this respect Soviet class structure resembles to a great degree that of other Western industrial societies. An increasingly important role is played by specialists, and particularly by professionals on whose activities the functioning of a modern society to a large extent depends. The rehabilitation of the intelligentsia in the Soviet Union during the thirties, in connection with the program of industrialization, provided dramatic notice that, in spite of ideological exaltation, manual laborers had become relatively unimportant when compared to specialists not engaged in physical labor. It also brought to light the uneasy relationship between specialists as a social force on whom the regime has to rely for the operations of the system but whom the regime also tends to distrust politically because of the power inherent in their activities.

With the development of classes and class-consciousness, Soviet society has not escaped such phenomena as the attempt on the part of the upper or middle classes to monopolize certain privileges and advantages and to pass these on to their children. This has been true for instance of the access to higher, university or professional education, i.e., the education that leads to high status and economic rewards. Conversely, the children of manual workers and peasants have found, in most instances, their careers channeled into the same occupations and low status as that of their parents, although the educational reforms sponsored by Khrushchev have been aimed at equalizing their opportunities. In the Soviet Union, as is often true in our own society, it does make a difference where one starts off in life.

Industrialism thus leads to important and largely irreversible structural changes in the society. Some commentators have argued, for example, that the excesses of the Stalin era were the results of the tremendous strains attendant on the rapid "take-off" (to use again Rostow's term) of a backward agricultural country into a mighty industrial power. These pressures, regrettable as they were, found their justification in the Soviet military actions against Germany during the Second World War and in the contribution they made to the Allied cause and freedom. Now that industrialization has been achieved and the wounds of the war have been healed, certain consequences are bound to occur, indeed according to some writers are happening under our very eyes.

For example, the increased rationality and education needed to operate an industrial and technological society, it is felt, cannot be limited to a narrow field but will eventually alter the entire nature of Soviet society, or expressed slightly differently, the economic system always places a constraint upon the political system. As the functions performed by the educated members of the middle classes (the intelligentsia) become more strategic, the regime will find it impossible to ignore their demands for greater freedom. Writers like Isaac Deutscher argue that Soviet society is now emerging from a period of primitive socialistic accumulation and is rapidly increasing its wealth. This will enable all classes to seek freedom of expression and association, "even if this should bring them into conflict with the ruling bureaucracy."[16] Thus, dialectically speaking, Stalin set in motion forces that spell out the end of Stalinism.

Industrialism may thus be said to characterize a force operating primarily at the *economic* level of society, though its consequences, as we have seen, extend beyond the confines of the economic structure, as do the consequences of totalitarianism.

In summary then, it may be said that it is the combination and the interpenetration of these three major elements (national-communism in the culture, totalitarianism in politics, and industrialism in economics) which may account for many aspects of

IT CAN be

16 "The Khrushchev Interregnum," in *The Great Contest* (New York and London: Oxford University Press, 1960), p. 21. Also see his *Russia in Transition* (New York: Coward McCann, 1957).

(This is primiarily what I'm TRYING EXPRESS IN THIS PAPER.

contemporary Soviet society. They permit us to judge, then, the impact that the party has on these forces, individually and in combination with each other.

THE QUESTION OF RELATIVE "UNDIFFERENTIATION"

The party has taken it upon itself to shape the culture, to govern the state, and to manage the economy. It has done so because its leadership, starting with Lenin, has been imbued with the conviction that nothing less than "total" controls in these spheres would permit it to remain in power and thus to accomplish its fore-ordained historical mission. Stalin combined the functions of archpriest, emperor (including military commander and supreme judge), manager of the economy, and minister of culture.

It may be argued, furthermore, that the party has played in the past a critical and "objectively" necessary role in the development of some aspects of Soviet society. It would be difficult, for example, to conceive of the *rapid* industrialization of Soviet society after 1928 without the existence of the party and of a Stalin (or some other similar organization or man) which would, through their control of the three spheres mentioned earlier, effect such a complete mobilization of human, material, financial, and emotional resources in the pursuit of that goal, particularly under conditions in which it was not felt desirable, nor perhaps possible, for the Soviet Union to borrow large amounts of capital from abroad. Indeed, it is as a result of the decision taken by the party to industrialize under forced draft and to engage in a process of primitive capital accumulation that the main contours of Stalin's Russia have emerged. It can also be suggested that because of the diffuse power with which the party is endowed, it can intervene like a flying squad or a benevolent monarch at almost any point in Soviet society and unravel knotty problems caused, for example, by bureaucratic conflicts or breakdowns in supplies. But these often tend to be particularistic interventions that need to be activated for the particular problem rather than universal regulative mechanisms of the type more available in pluralistic societies, such as an independent judiciary, the political franchise, or market mechanisms. There is no doubt, as Hough has recently pointed out, that the party plays a significant role in many aspects of Soviet political and economic life and has helped resolve "several important problems inherent in very large organizations."[17] In other words, Hough argues, and quite soundly, that the role of the party is functional, particularly at the lower administrative levels, in "getting things done," and that if there were no party, some other agency would have to perform these tasks. And yet, while the role of the party has been important and necessary in the past and remains so today, it is suggested that perhaps a continuation of party policies of control over the major spheres of Soviet society may be in the future not so much a source of success and strength as a cause of rigidity and weakness. According to Djilas, the party has become a parasite on society. While this is a politically inspired hyperbole, the party has become in many respects a conservative, if not a reactionary, force in Soviet society. Perhaps in the twenty-first century when the party will have passed into history, some schoolboy will query his teacher on how it was possible for Russia to win the war against Hitlerite Germany *in spite of* the existence of the Communist Party!

For the present, however, it is precisely the party's reluctance (and Stalin's earlier unwillingness) to relinquish controls that may slow down and retard further differentiation and modernization. This reluctance is based to some extent on a distrust of people not directly controlled by the party, a fear of their being "spontaneous" rather than "conscious," in the sense that Lenin used those terms in *What is to be Done?*. It leads to the kind of social structure which Kassof has called the "administered society,"[18] or what others have called "totalitarianism without terror" or "without coercion," in which one central authority plans and administers all social, cultural, political, and economic processes and in which mutual adjustments between the demands of these different spheres and the supply (conceived in a broad form) will continue to be "administered" rather than allowed to find their own level. This may lead to a situation in which "rational" planning and administering become irrational, uneconomical, and dysfunctional.

One imaginary illustration, from the realm of economic planning, but perhaps of broader significance, is the case of the pile of potatoes that must be fitted into a sack, so that the maximum

[17] Jerry F. Hough, "The Soviet Concept of the Relationship between the Lower Party Organs and the State Administration," *Slavic Review,* XXIV (1965), 215–40.
[18] Allen Kassof, "The Administered Society: Totalitarianism without Terror," *World Politics,* XVI (1964), 558–75.

amount of potatoes and the minimum amount of waste space occur. The "scientific," "rational," "planned," "administered" way to go about it would be to give each potato a different number; to draw profiles for each potato (let's say six to eight profiles per potato); to translate these profiles into codeable items, and with the use of a computer, to determine precisely how each potato is to fit with its neighbors so as to reduce the waste space to the least quantity. This is perfectly feasible; it may well entail the work of a team of mathematicians and may cost several hundreds or thousands of dollars, but it can be done. The other solution consists simply of dumping the potatoes into the sack and shaking hard, letting each potato adjust to its neighbor in a "spontaneous" manner. The difference between the two solutions, in terms of waste space, is not likely to be greater than 5 or 10 per cent, or perhaps a bit more. But the overall cost of the entire operation is likely to be considerably smaller.

It may be said, furthermore, that by comparison with the situation that obtained at the time of Stalin's death, there has been, relatively speaking, a substantial amount of "loosening" or "thawing" in Soviet society in the direction of decentralization and cautious attempts at some degree of differentiation, coupled with an increased awareness on the part of the party of the demands of different social groups for increased recognition and a larger share of economic production. One of these groups is undoubtedly the professionals, who need a fair amount of autonomy to pursue their activities at a high level of performance; since these activities are, in many instances, of critical importance to the regime in the pursuit of its domestic and foreign policies, it is perhaps in the cultural area that the process of differentiation has been carried furthest, though unevenly. It is now possible for scientists in the physical sciences to publicly espouse principles and theories that were placed on the ideological index only a few years ago for being of foreign, Western origins. In the so-called life sciences, in biology and genetics for example, the vicissitudes of Lysenko's career since 1954 indicate how gradual this process has been, and how deeply rooted was the idea that science must conform to ideological orthodoxy, rather than to scientific criteria of evidence. Lysenkoism is admittedly an extreme case, and yet it does illustrate the result of ideological controls over inquiry, the sanctions and punishments meted out to those who did not conform or recant their "mistakes," as well as the "price" paid by the discipline itself in lost time and advances. The position of Lysenko and his followers remained fairly strong, though under some attack throughout the Khrushchev regime. Indeed, Lysenko was removed from his position as director of the Institute of Genetics of the Academy of Sciences only toward the end of January 1965.[19]

In clinical medicine, to take but another example, the Central Committee of the Party refused, in 1962, to intervene in the case of a cancer cure that had been judged worthless by the Academy of Medical Sciences and prohibited by an order of the Health Ministry USSR. As the Central Committee declared:

> The Central Committee of the Communist Party of the Soviet Union does not consider it possible to take upon itself the role of arbiter in approving methods of medical treatment. Attempts to administer by injunction in science cannot be useful and, as is known, such attempts in the recent past led to the undeserved accusation and discrediting of some leading scholars and physicians of our country ("the doctors' case").[20]

A dozen years earlier the Central Committee and "Comrade Stalin personally" would not have been so diffident, nor would they have hesitated to take a stand.

There are, in the social sciences, some significant developments; one of these is the emergence of the discipline of sociology, a discipline which did not even exist a few years ago. It exhibits, however, as Fischer has pointed out, "a singular fusion of science with politics. On the level of theory this means the fusion of academic analysis of society with an official doctrine of society. On the level of research the fusion is between scholarship and all-out service to an omnipotent state."[21] Seen in the context of Soviet society, the mission of the social scientist officially stated, is to participate in, and contribute to, the "ideological struggle":

> The international obligation of Soviet scholars is to intensify the criticism of bourgeois ideology and first of all the reactionary conceptions of anti-communism. Criticism of bourgeois and reformist ideology must debunk not only the conclusions but also the arguments of anti-

[19] See announcement in the *New York Times*, Feb. 5, 1965. For a discussion of this question, see, for example, two articles by E. Delimars, "Nouvelle Eclipse de Lysenko," *Contrat Social*, Mar.–Apr., 1964, p. 87, and "La Biologie en Liberté Surveillée," *Contrat Social*, May–June, 1964, pp. 169–76.

[20] *Pravda*, Aug. 1, 1962, p. 2.

[21] George Fischer, *Science and Politics: The New Sociology in the Soviet Union* (Ithaca: Cornell University, 1961), p. 30.

communist ideologists. . . . The direct duty of scholars is to inform the world's public widely about the successes of the Soviet Union in all spheres of life, including the realm of the humanities.[22]

And yet Soviet sociologists are beginning to carry out some significant empirical research, particularly in the area of the sociology of work. The further differentiation of sociology and its autonomy from the political system, on the other hand, and hence its greater ability to contribute to sociological knowledge will undoubtedly be a long, and probably not unilinear, process.

The uneasy relationship between the regime and the intellectual community, particularly the artists and writers and more specifically the poets (with their Russian tradition of social protest), may also serve as an illustration of the congenital difficulty the party has in letting the muses sing without a party-appointed conductor. Although the demands and the strait jacket of "socialist realism" have been toned down, the artist still remains under some kind of surveillance, and those who exhibit too much independence are likely to find themselves invited to visit the hinterland to gather materials at the grass roots, or to engage in manual labor, as the recent case of Iosif Brodsky demonstrates.[23] Few, however, are likely to lose their lives or even their freedom, as was the case under Stalin. At one time, Khrushchev went so far as to tell the writers not to look to the party for guidance:

. . . you know that it is not easy to decide right off what to publish and what not to publish. The easiest thing would be to publish nothing—then there would be no mistakes. . . . But that would mean stupidity.

Therefore, comrades, do not burden the government with the solution of such questions—decide them yourselves in comradely fashion.[24]

The trouble, of course, is that such an attitude breeds, among the intellectual community, a kind of euphoria in which the works which had been written hitherto "for the drawer" (a

---

[22] *Ibid.*

[23] See, for example, the transcript of his trial in the *New Leader*, Aug. 31, 1964, pp. 6–17. As one of the witnesses for the prosecution said, ". . . if all the citizens of this country reacted toward the production of material wealth as Brodsky does, then it would take a long time to build Communism . . . he should be treated with forced labor. . . ." (p. 11).

[24] Third Congress of Soviet Writers (Moscow, 1959), cited in Harold Swayze, *Political Control of Literature in the USSR, 1946–1959* (Cambridge: Harvard University Press, 1962), p. 209.

euphemism meaning works that could not be presented publicly) clamor for publication: the regime has given one cautious inch and the intellectuals want to take a whole foot. The regime then finds it necessary to clamp down again, as it did toward the end of 1962 and the spring of 1963, when Khrushchev and Ilichev attacked abstract art and banned it from public exhibition.

"It is hardly to be expected," Swayze concludes, "that the party will renounce its claim to final authority in belles-lettres any more than in other spheres of Soviet life,"[25] though intellectuals (at least some of them) have been increasingly bold in clamoring for more freedom and in pointing to the ridiculous consequences of party directives in art. Thus Evtushenko did not shrink from disputing Khrushchev's views on aesthetics: "I find it difficult to admit, Nikita Sergeevich, that the insipid painting entitled 'Nikita Sergeevich Khrushchev among the Workers,' could please you,"[26] a question which, under Stalin, would have elicited a reply of the "Off with his head" variety. Though it is difficult to agree with Max Hayward that "the writers have in practice achieved a greater degree of independence from Party control than any other group in the population,"[27] the amount of progress and differentiation from the party must be judged in relative terms, i.e., compared with the situation under Stalin, and not in absolute terms. (It might at the same time be interesting to note that nowadays one of the ways in which the regime rids itself of particularly troublesome individuals who have committed no crimes is by arranging to have them committed to mental hospitals.)[28]

It might, finally, be interesting to speculate on what would take place if the party were to remove most or all of its strictures on cultural life. It may be conjectured on the basis of what has happened since Stalin's death that Soviet culture would only benefit through such a step. On balance, in cultural life, the party impoverishes rather than enriches, it constricts rather than promotes.

The same general considerations probably apply in the economic life of Soviet society. One might argue, for example, that

[25] *Ibid.*, p. 260. Also see Victor Erlich, "Two Stages of the Soviet Literary 'Thaw'," *Ventures*, Fall, 1964, pp. 15–22.
[26] *Contrat Social*, Mar.–Apr., 1964, pp. 83–84.
[27] *Soviet Literature in the Sixties,* ed. Max Hayward and Edward L. Crowley (New York: Praeger, 1964), p. 204.
[28] The case of Valery Tarsis is, of course, only one of many.

the Soviet economic system has reached a level of development and complexity that requires further differentiation from the party in order to acquire flexibility. This might mean, in addition to the relative decentralization of many economic decisions, the introduction of market types of mechanisms permitting an automatic or spontaneous adjustment of supply and demand, and rationality in terms of actual costs and customer demand, while keeping the economy still responsive to the needs and the interests of the nation as a whole. There are two elements that prevent, or at least slow down, such a development. One is the ideological impact of economic policy and decisions, and centers around the potential ideological erosion attendant on the introduction of devices that have been associated with "capitalism" or declared ideologically unacceptable. In other words, what the party ideologues are saying is "What does it matter if we become economically more efficient if this is purchased at the price of compromising our basic value commitments?" The other element is the loss of party functions and power that would follow the further differentiation of the economic life from party controls.

Ideological erosion: The cautiousness with which the Liberman plan was approached, discussed, and finally given some experimental sanction is a case in point. This cautiousness may have been due to a large extent to the fact that it involves the profit system, which implies in turn the "profit motive," and which smacks too much of capitalism and by implication of the "exploitation of man by man."[29] One should not underestimate the impact of such words and ritualistic formulae, and how seriously they are taken in Soviet society. The introduction of a profit system thus seriously tests the ideological system, and the problem it represents is one index of the relative lack of differentiation between party and ideological controls, and the economic sphere. Parsons has pointed out, for example, that the watershed between an intermediate and modern society is the differentiation of religious from secular culture "so that adherence to specific modes and patterns of secular action and organization [read: the rejection of the profit motive] as a test of religious 'sincerity' [read ideological sincerity] is no longer an imperative of religious [ideological] commitment."[30] In other words, as Liberman and others have argued, the introduction of profit as a device is *not* an

29 See Daniels, *Nature of Communism,* p. 330.
30 Parsons, *op. cit.,* p. 22.

ideological concession, it will in no way weaken Soviet socialism but will on the contrary strengthen it. They point out, in addition, that there is a fundamental difference between socialism and capitalism in the use of profit. "Denial of profit by socialism and recognition of profit by capitalism has never served as the feature distinguishing socialism from capitalism. . . . In the USSR profit belongs to the society as a whole."[31]

By the same token, the state of agriculture, which is perennially in a crisis situation, would improve if the peasants were given more latitude, particularly with respect to the private plots. But the private plots smell of private property, of the bourgeois spirit, of that "worm of private ownership" in the means of production which the party has sworn to extirpate from the consciousness of its people (and eventually of mankind). As Brzezinski has pointed out:

Although ample evidence has been cited by the Soviet leaders as well as by the recent statistical yearbook to show that productivity on private plots far outdistances the "socialist sector," all the solutions offered, both the conservative and neo-Stalinist, as well as the innovating Khrushchevist ones, specifically excluded any alternative which could increase agricultural production at the cost of ideology.[32]

Power Erosion: The other element that may hinder the economic system, as Nove has pointed out,[33] lies in the area of power held by the party and the vested interest of the party machine which . . . "by its decisions at all levels, replaces the operation of economic forces, i.e. the primacy of political decisions over economic rationality." Further, Nove points out, if the collective farms were really to make their own decisions by reference to objective criteria, "then most of the powers of the *raikom* secretary, and the bulk of its staff, would be lost . . ."

Thus, Djilas argues that the Soviet economy, although it is planned, is "perhaps the most wasteful economy in the history of human society."[34] On balance, the fusion of economic and party functions may, at the present level of maturation, constrict the further development of the Soviet economy.

[31] *Red Profits*, a letter to the editor of *Time* by Evsei Liberman, Mar. 5, 1965.
[32] "The Nature of the Soviet System," *Slavic Review*, XX (1961), 351–68.
[33] *Economic Rationality and Soviet Economics* (New York: Praeger, 1964).
[34] *New Class*, p. 118.

Perhaps, again according to Djilas, the moment is approaching when industrialization, which first made communism inevitable, will through further development make the Communist form of government and ownership superfluous.[35]

It is in the realm of politics and power that the least differentiation has taken place. The soviets have continued to remain the political instrument of the party, ruled, controlled, managed by the party, and have not been allowed to be what they claim: the representatives of the people; and neither has the concept of the polity, with citizens given an effective franchise and responsibility for the choice of those who govern them, been allowed to take root in Communist society. The unanimous elections are not expressions of popular suffrage but are contrived symbolic manifestations of the kind of organic (monolithic) unity which the party claims for the society it rules. By claiming to embody the "will of the people" the party has effectively deprived the people of this will. By claiming that it speaks for the interest of all groups in Soviet society, the party has deprived these groups of the ability to articulate, in public, these interests (they may be articulated, of course, within the bureaucratic structure of the party): it thus has eliminated and constricted public debates, and the possible enrichments, in terms of a variety of solutions, that might arise from such debates. It also remains to be seen how much such *regime-sponsored* devices as comrades' courts and other activities involving the population will become genuine expressions of popular will, or simply instruments for the clever manipulation of that will. Robert Conquest, without using the concept of differentiation, has expressed the state of Soviet society today and its dilemmas by likening it with certain trends that were current in the Western world in the nineteenth century:

The new social forces in Russia which make the Khrushchev regime look so old-fashioned have a great deal in common with the democratic moods of the last century. What the "revisionists", the writers and the students and all the others are asking for consciously . . . is basically just freedom of speech and a share in determining policy. . . . The Soviet Union is ruled by party officials who have certain fixed ideas about the nature of the desirable organization of society. Changes will not come about without considerable resistance from them . . . the regime will either evolve peacefully or it will perish.[36]

[35] *New Class*, p. 120.
[36] *Common Sense about Russia* (New York: Macmillan, 1960), pp. 174–75.

What Conquest probably meant by "peaceful evolution" was that process of differentiation we have attempted to describe here.

CONCLUSIONS

There is no indication that the party is prepared to "wither away" or to give up substantial portions of its power in controlling all aspects of the society it inhabits. There is evidence, however, that since the death of Stalin, some differentiation has taken place, although very cautiously and probably with mental reservations on the part of the party. It is possible that, with time, the professionals, the specialists, the managers, in short the members of the intelligentsia, will constitute an ever increasing and potentially more powerful pressure group in Soviet society, and that the party will have to grant them more autonomy.

It is also possible that the regime will grant more latitude to the operation of economic forces, particularly if it can convince itself that such a grant is a prerequisite for the maintenance of the Soviet posture in the world. There is no shred of evidence, of course, that the regime will ever allow a "loyal opposition" or a second party to develop, at least not publicly.

Thus the party which, in earlier phases of Soviet history was an element of strength in the mobilization of societal resources for specific goals, as it is in China today, may now (on balance) be a source of structural rigidity, and may account for the disappointment of those Westerners who had gone to the Soviet Union expecting to find there the "wave of the future." As one recent visitor to the USSR expressed it, paraphrasing the chestnut of the thirties: "I have seen the past and it failed." On second thought, and more soberly, he added: "Russia has not failed, far from it, but it has not succeeded either."[37] Thus the "archaic" nature of Soviet society may be due to the philosophy and the *modus operandi* of a party leadership which believes in the total centralization of control and which, in the process of enforcing this control, may well tend to stifle initiative and inventiveness that would immeasurably add to the power and efficiency of Soviet society. The party has done a fairly good job of surviving and keeping itself in power; it has been able, when necessary, to adjust its structure in order to admit into its ranks those members of society who were most important in reaching the goals defined

[37] Henry Anatole Grunwald, "The Quality of Life behind the Soviet Statistics," *Fortune*, Mar. 1964, pp. 146–47, 206–17.

by the party. It has been to some degree responsive to the demands of professionals, industrial workers, and (lately) the peasants. But these responses are necessarily in terms of party interests, party ideology, and party power. It may then be possible to entertain the hypothesis that the party may well contrive to retard and constrict the society it inhabits by keeping it relatively undifferentiated and at best unevenly developed, since further differentiation could be secured only at the cost of ideological erosion and power concession, a price it is extremely reluctant to pay. To echo in a radically altered form the classical statement of a latter-day American cultural hero, what is good for the Communist Party may not necessarily be good for Soviet society in the second half of the twentieth century.

* (T Refers to the erosion of that power which the party must assuredly possesses ; to the ellimination of their "ideological" enforcements.)

B FoLio

PART FOUR

Freedom and Control

Introduction

VICTOR ERLICH

THE TWO papers which follow approach their seemingly analogous topics in substantially different ways. S. H. Chen addresses himself primarily to matters of literary policy, to party directives, slogans, and campaigns. Sidney Monas focuses on the century-old "currents and impulses inherent in literature itself" which of late have sustained the dissident Soviet writer's resistance to totalitarian bureaucracy. To use the key terms of the session at which the papers were discussed, Monas's main theme is "freedom," Chen's "control."

It seems to me that these disparate emphases are eminently appropriate. Seen at closer range, the "Thaw" and the "Hundred Flowers" reveal, as Professor Chen has put it, "more contrasts than similarities." Even though, during the "tumultuous six weeks" of the officially sponsored pluralism, some dangerous thoughts did come to the fore in Mao's China, in retrospect the interlude appears primarily as an elaborate political maneuver, as a major phase in the process of streamlining Chinese culture. Conversely, though the recent succession of thaws and freezes in the Soviet Union has pointed up the limits of the party's tolerance of heterodoxy, the most significant aspect of the sequence lies in the spontaneity of the hemmed-in protest, in the resurgence "from below" of attitudes long discouraged or suppressed by the regime.

In the course of the lively and wide-ranging discussion, another apparent difference between the two situations came to light. In post-Stalin Russia, in the words of Max Hayward, "literature is the only field of . . . social and cultural activity in which overt differences of ideological nature are allowed to manifest themselves." Though this statement may be somewhat less true today than it was, say, five or six years ago, the role of the Soviet novelist, poet, or playwright in articulating the intelligentsia ferment has remained strategic. This, apparently, was not quite the case in China where, during the brief moment of quasi-truth, plain speaking and overt dissent bulked larger in some branches of scholarship than in imaginative literature. This discrepancy may be said to bolster S. Monas's thesis about the commitment to individual autonomy as a major theme in Russian literature of the last 150 years. When, in his closing remarks, S. H. Chen reminded the Conference of the role of literature as a repository and guardian of human values, he was urging a proposition of wide cultural resonance, yet one which has special applicability to the Russian intellectual tradition.

Whatever the differences between the "Thaw" and the "Hundred Flowers," these two episodes have at least one thing in common. Both helped reveal, in however muffled and distorted form, the residual conflict of interest between the intellectual, who has a natural stake in a measure of autonomy and integrity, and the Communist *apparatchik* bent on maximizing control and forging uniformity. This, however, is only one, and a relatively late, phase of the confrontation between the intelligentsia values and the Communist ethos. At the earlier stages, the clash was not always so apparent. In fact, it can be argued that some "pre-existing" attitudes of the Russian radical intellectual tended to increase his susceptibility to the Bolshevik appeal, or, to put it more negatively, to undermine his potential resistance to it.

Let me mention first what I would like to call the total negation syndrome, a repudiation of all traditions, all authorities, all established standards, a total commitment to a future thoroughly discontinuous with "everything that had gone before" (V. Mayakovsky). An exasperation over the oppressiveness of the Tsarist system and the "backwardness" of the traditional Russian society, often tinged with an upper-class sense of guilt vis-à-vis the long-suffering "people," gave rise to a sense of moral urgency, an eagerness for a purifying cataclysm, for a thoroughgoing social change, whatever the immediate human cost. This, to be sure, was not a uniquely Russian frame of mind. The unremitting hatred of the status quo was articulated with characteristic harshness by that ironic Communist, Bertolt Brecht:

> What meanness would you not commit, to
> Stamp our meanness?
> If, at last, you could change the world, what
> Would you think yourself too good for?
> Who are you?
> Sink into the mire
> Embrace the butcher, but
> Change the world: it needs it!

Some ten years earlier, a more fragile and esoteric poet, the leading Russian Symbolist Aleksandr Blok, pleaded with his recalcitrant fellow intellectuals to espouse the October Revolution because "it is necessary to change *everything!*" (my italics, V.E.). (As Sidney Monas recalls in his essay, it was the same A. Blok who, in 1921, on the eve of his untimely death, sounded a prophetic warning against the creeping bureaucratization of Russian literature.)

Blok's short-lived frenzy—characteristically followed by a profound disenchantment—was not widely shared. A somewhat more frequent attitude among the intelligentsia in the first years of the Soviet regime was one of vague sympathy, of hedged support. While the new system had not yet frozen into the totalitarian mold, while the Revolution was still young, it appeared to many a "freely responding and freely judging" artist, to use R. Mathewson's phrase, as an opportunity rather than a threat, as a release of hitherto untapped energies. The writer *qua* writer was more likely than not to be carried away by the sheer sweep of the events, to be vaguely buoyed up by the challenge to the routine, the fluidity and unpredictability of the new realities. Mikhail Zoshchenko, a gifted Soviet satirist, spoke for a number of his contemporaries when he declared in a whimsical credo published in 1922: "In their general swing the Bolsheviks are closer to me than anybody else. And so I'm willing to bolshevik around with them. But I'm not a Communist (or rather not a Marxist), and I think I shall never be one." Zoshchenko's semantics is rather symptomatic. "Communism" stands here for an alien doctrine, a total ideological commitment which is to be shunned; "Bolshevism" for the freewheeling, indigenous rebellion which holds considerable attraction to a venturesome and irreverent writer.

And finally, there is the dramatic and much-cited testimony on Boris Pasternak. Many of us will recall that the initial response of Jurij Andreevich Zhivago was one of an essentially esthetic admiration for the scope of Lenin's grand design, for the surgical decisiveness of his break with the old. As the revolutionary fervor became institutionalized, Zhivago's sense of wonder increasingly gave way to estrangement, indeed to boredom. We are back at our starting point—the clash between the poet and the bureaucrat or, more broadly, the plight of literature under totalitarianism.

Both as a focus for research and as a topic for journalistic reporting and speculation, the theme has been with us for quite a while. Yet, can we say that we know nearly as much as we should about this tug-of-war? I don't think so. To be sure, the best Western studies of Communist-controlled culture have explored much of the pertinent ground. The tortuous course of Communist literary policy has been traced with a great deal of care. The mechanisms of political control over literature and the arts have been reliably described. The crippling effects of these controls upon actual literary production have been chronicled in dismal detail. Yet we might be able to do a better job than we have done hitherto of conceptualizing the problem, of identifying those facets of Communist totalitarianism, especially in its extreme, "Stalinist" variety, which seem to make it inherently inimical to artistic creativity.

We often talk as if freedom were a necessary prerequisite for literature and art worthy of the name. Yet can we be reasonably sure of that? Art is known to have flourished under authoritarian regimes. Yes, one will interpose, but totalitarianism is different from mere authoritarianism. Precisely. That is why it is necessary to define more closely the characteristically *totalitarian* attitudes and techniques which inhibit, cripple, stultify a genuine creative achievement. Does the differentia lie in the *degree* of suppression, the sheer brutality and ubiquitousness of the regimentation? Or is it the nature of totalitarian censorship that is at issue here—the fact that in the Stalinist-type situation, the writer and artist are told not only *what* to write, what to paint or compose, but also *how* to do this? Or is it rather the stridently collectivist ethos, especially apparent in the avalanche of Chinese commune verse, which downgrades and thwarts the personal vision? All these factors have played their part, I believe. In addition, as the Lake Tahoe discussions have strongly suggested, there appears to be a fundamental incompatibility between the scope and the texture of the literary imagination and the inexorable demands of the totalitarian system, between the party propagandist's proclivity for seeing the world as a political melodrama and the modern writer's imaginative grip on the tragic complexity and intractability of human reality.

For a while, the ominously ambitious drive to simplify and streamline man rolled on virtually unimpeded. Yet the resiliency of the old Adam has proved greater than in our darker moments some of us feared it might. This, in fact, is the most significant moral of the post-Stalin ferment within the Communist bloc. Some overenthusiastic Western commentators notwithstanding, the "Thaw" has been neither a literary renaissance nor a profound intellectual crisis. It was rather a harking back to old-fashioned human values such as honesty, emotional privacy, integrity of the self, a partial recoil from the brink of 1984. Stalinist totalitarianism attempted nothing less than a rape of human nature. It is somewhat gratifying to be able to conclude that the effort has not been entirely successful.

The interplay between regimentation and spontaneity in Communist-controlled literatures is a vast and complex subject. Our discussions at Lake Tahoe have made an important dent in the problem, I feel, and, in doing so, have demonstrated that much still remains to be done by way of clarifying and redefining some of the most relevant concepts. I can only hope that at least some of the studies stimulated by these proceedings will have the finesse of Sidney Monas's wide-ranging essay as well as the wealth of documentation and the comparative range of S. H. Chen's illuminating inquiry.

Artificial "Flowers" during a Natural "Thaw"

S. H. CHEN

THE "Thaw" and the "Hundred Flowers," however facilely they can be linked as good natural imagery to symbolize conditions of cultural freedom, or the lack of it, in the Soviet Union and Communist China respectively, are in reality so different in their origin, manifestations, and effects that a study of them reveals more contrasts than similarities. The contrasts point to very different, even opposite, political climates during approximately the same period and despite what at the time seemed apparently the same general trend. It can now be said, if we borrow from Communist parlance, that the "Thaw" has been "an objectively extant fact," observable from both inside and outside Russia with respect to the realities of Soviet political and cultural life as well as her international relationships up to this day. But the "Hundred Flowers Blooming Together" has remained strictly a Chinese domestic slogan, strenuously interpreted and reinterpreted in verbal campaigns, as rhetoric with mercurial meanings rather than descriptions of real life under totalitarianism. Yet, in another sense, the "Hundred Flowers" movement is likely felt to be more forceful by the Chinese population as a conscious political endeavor on the part of the ruling regime to aggrandize its power, beset as it is with contradictions and immense problems of national culture and politics; whereas, the "Thaw," hardly ever officially acknowledged, and perhaps only involuntarily sensed by the Soviet and other East European governments, will likely remain atmospheric, widespreading, but variable and less definable by those living in it. Against it as a background, many changing national and international scenes have been set, and more will be. Here against it as a historical background, we shall focus on the Chinese "Hundred Flowers Campaign" as a garishly conspicuous scene.

There is a marked distinction between the origination of the "Hundred Flowers" and that of the "Thaw." For the interest of contrast, it may be well to begin by observing some parallels. We shall try to penetrate through the superficial resemblance of ideological jargon and reach for the actual content of the Chinese "movement," adumbrated, so to speak, by the Soviet phenomenon. But diverging from the latter, the Chinese movement soon uncovered specific cultural, socio-political, and historical problems to be dealt with, and produced its peculiar results that even betoken at least one aspect of the intellectual gap behind the Sino-Soviet political split.

It is symptomatic of the basic difference between the Chinese movement and the Soviet phenomenon that the name of the latter, the "Thaw," should have originated almost surreptitiously from a novel, giving expression, however covertly, to the latent Soviet popular sentiment against long-standing government authoritarianism; while the "Hundred Flowers Blooming Together," the "Hundred Schools Contending to Profess," were slogans drummed forth as a government policy generated by no less an arch-authoritarian than Chairman Mao himself. The "Thaw" has been customarily dated from May 1954, when the first part of Ehrenburg's novel bearing that name was published in *Znamya*. The "Hundred Flowers" campaign has been recognized as having unfolded its most dramatic scenes on April 30, 1957, with the publication of a directive of the Communist Party's Central Committee inviting, actually pressing for, public criticism and promising ideological education to be carried out like "a gentle breeze and mild rain." Some six brief weeks of freedom of speech lasted by party order until the reversal of that order in mid-June, when the party organ, the *People's Daily*, fired back the first shot against the "rightist" critics in an editorial of June 12 and published on June 18 the *amended* text of Chairman Mao's February speech, "On the Correct Handling of Contradictions among the People."[1] In the *amended* text the "Hundred Flowers Blooming

---

[1] About amendments of the text and parts of different versions, see Roderick MacFarquhar, *The Hundred Flowers Campaign* (New York: Praeger, 1960), pp. 262–84.

Together" was reiterated, but with very different implications. For then and there were added the six famous "criteria" to restrict criticism, which, in effect, were to be applied later in the anti-rightist campaigns as commandments of supreme authority to quash the erstwhile-abetted "free" critics.

For both the "Thaw" and the short free "Bloom of the Hundred Flowers" we can find earlier incidents signaling their advent but pointing to very dissimilar backgrounds and bearing very divergent significance, if we examine them on their native soil instead of generalizing about them from a distant viewpoint of international politics.

Scholars of Soviet literature look back and discern earlier portents of the "Thaw." Professor Gleb Struve noted as prominent among these the publication in 1953 of Ehrenburg's article "The Work of a Writer," of V. Pomerantsev's article on "Sincerity in Literature," of Abram Khachaturian's "On Creative Courage of Inspiration," and of F. Abramov's "People of the Kolkhoz Village in Postwar Prose" in April 1954, just a month before the novel with the symbolic title, *The Thaw*, came off the press.[2] All these appeared but a few short months after Stalin's death. Needless to say, many other voices of protest, especially those of new and less known authors, were raised and heard. The substance of the four articles that drew the special attention of Western observers may be summed up in two points: One is the rather sudden distinct change of attitude toward Western culture, the overt show of appreciation or generous tolerance by Ehrenburg and Khachaturian of some contemporary American and British novelists and of Western music; the other is the passionate plea for "personal feeling" as against "bureaucratic technique in literature" (Khachaturian), for "sincerity" defined as the feeling for "the directness of things" (Pomerantsev), for the writer "to tell the people something he personally feels, because he has begun to 'ache from his book'" (Ehrenburg), and for "unvarnished truth" about the *kolkhoz* among other things over against "an uninterrupted triumphal procession along the path strewn with roses" (Abramov).

The main point to recognize here is that in contrast to what preceded the "Hundred Flowers" drama in China, the Soviet warming toward Western culture and the impassioned pleas for

2 Gleb Struve, "Russia: Five Years after Stalin," *The New Leader,* Apr. 7, 1958, pp. 16–21.

personal feeling and unvarnished truth, which together ushered in the "Thaw," took their impetus from writers and critics who ardently cared for literary and artistic creativity as their primary concern. Theirs were the voices of individuals that rose from below as opposed to the dictates of the authoritarian bureaucracy from above. There was in these voices a degree of spontaneity, the force of genuine human longing, which, it seemed, could not help emanating after too long suppression, once the all-powerful dictator was dead. The main content of these protests—the wish to rejoin the international fraternity of artistic creation and the restoration of personal feeling and representation of individually experienced truth—seem to have found due articulation as harbingers and, through whatever tortuous course, somehow lasted to lend character to areas of the continual partial "Thaw" for quite a long time.

Not so motivated was the initiation of the "Hundred Flowers" campaign nor therefore could the campaign take the same course later. In fact, we can see precise opposites in its germination and progress, as well as in its results. Instead of the awesome dictator's demise that brought forth the Soviet phenomenon, it was the newly risen living presence of the towering figure of Chairman Mao to which the source of both the name and the power of this Chinese campaign must be traced. Instead of the articulations of individual artists and writers that heralded the "Thaw," it was the oracle from the Chair, first uttered in 1951,[3] followed by party harangues, meetings, and directives that ordered the "Hundred Flowers" to bloom together for a while. Instead of there being any degree of spontaneity, it was by persuasion, solicitude, cunning, cajolery, or stern command that the people, bewildered and unbelieving at first, were finally made to speak. Even before the six restrictive "criteria" added to the "amended text" of Mao's speech reversed the whole course, because the framework predetermined for the campaign was that of "how to solve the internal contradictions among the people" pronounced by Mao, the general attention of the whole country, even while it became vocal in its protestations for freedom, had been directed mainly inward, with a national self-consciousness rather than an international outlook. Whatever secret yearning for fraternization

[3] Reference made to the earliest source of this slogan of 1951 was by Lu Ting-yi, Vice-Chairman of the Ministry of Propaganda, in *Jen-min jih-pao* (hereafter cited as *JMJP*), June 13, 1956, p. 2.

with contemporary Western European and American art and
literature there could have been, it had been precluded by the
paramount political maxim of "leaning toward one side," namely
toward the Soviets as Mecca. But as to what was acquired from
the Soviets as we shall see, even the most caustic Chinese critic of
the party's cultural and literary policy, Hu Feng, who had to be
liquidated before the campaign but who was almost resurrected
during its most rebellious moment, could in 1954 do no better
than rehash Gorky, quote Fadeyev out of context, borrow some
suitable color from the chameleonic Simonov, and extol the
canonical wisdom and critical genius of Joseph Stalin, regardless
of the latter's contemporaneous disintegration under his native
"thawing" ground.[4]

The longing for free expression of personal feelings and for
sincere representations of truths individually felt and perceived
was no doubt latent in every mind, and was especially keen in
creative artists with individual experience and perception. But
Mao and the party's vociferous advocacy of spiritual as well as
institutional collectivism, their enforcement of organizational discipline to counter the proverbial Chinese "national shame" of lack
of organization, had been so effective that by the time of the 1957
campaign, human individuality had become virtual anathema,
and private personal values a social taboo. Therefore, if even the
Ehrenburgs and Pomerantsevs had to tread their ground cautiously as individuals,[5] when gathering their forces on their own
initiative and under more suitable "natural" conditions, it is small
wonder that no experienced Chinese writer, fully aware of the
artificial circumstances of the "Flowers," would openly assert
any individual value and speak out for "sincerity," "truth," and
"personal feelings," as his Soviet counterparts did. When the
campaign raged for a moment as if out of control, the only
genuine spark that flared, though all too briefly, alas, to light the
phantasmagoric path to intellectual freedom, was ignited by
young college students, with their innocent bravery, and with
more heated feelings in their blood than sophisticated arguments
in their heads. They were more prone, thanks to the party's
activist training, to rebellions, demonstrations of physical courage
ending sometimes in violence, than to waging intellectual battles

[4] See Hu Feng's *Opinions on Art and Literature,* parts published by the
Wen Yi Pao Editorial Office, 1955.
[5] See Harold Swayze, *Political Control of Soviet Literature in the USSR,*
1946–1959 (Cambridge: Harvard University Press, 1962).

for the mind. It could be expected, therefore, that the six most dramatic weeks of the "Hundred Flowers" campaign, which attracted world-wide attention and graphically revealed all the ills and agony under totalitarian rule, failed to leave a single intellectual monument worthy of the spirit of the freedom fighter.

From all the thousands of newspaper columns, articles, and recorded speeches, and for all the high caliber of the Chinese intellectuals engaged, we see more grievous complaints about material matters, hardships trivial or great, personnel problems, and administrative routine or formality, than any theoretical sophistication, not to say any creative work which could stand as worthy symbol. Expressions of intense hatred of communism, too, such as would have been uncharacteristic of the Soviet "Thaw," were uttered by the Chinese, but only spasmodically: ". . . the masses may knock you down, kill the Communists, overthrow you. This cannot be described as unpatriotic . . ."; "exterminate the Communist bandits"; "down with Communism."[6] These appeared amidst the declarations of university teachers and slogans on campus walls. But these and other violent words and actions only flashed the danger signal to the party, gave it good justification to reverse its policy and ruthlessly reap up the "weeds." From then on the "Hundred Flowers Blooming Together" has still continued to be panegyrized by the party leadership, but has entirely changed its meaning as it was once understood during this short spurt of the spirit of freedom.

The quick nip in the bud may be the immediate, obvious reason for the apparent lack of intellectual substance of the "Hundred Flowers" movement even during its heyday, as compared with the Soviet "Thaw." But a close look at the several antecedent intellectual movements guided and maneuvered by the Chinese Communist Party since it came to power reveals deeper causes. We shall examine both these antecedents that bear upon the peculiar character of this "Hundred Flowers" campaign, and the aftermath of the campaign which will show the present Chinese intellectual climate and the cultural problems being faced and dealt with by the regime.

The "Hundred Flowers" movement needs to be seen in larger contexts, historical and domestic as well as international. The death of Stalin in March, 1953, may be the single historic event

[6] Cf. texts quoted in MacFarquhar, *op. cit.*, pp. 87–89 and 142.

that marked the beginning of the cracks, in zigzag fashion, of the monolith of international communism. And no doubt the devastating post mortem on his rule and personal cult pronounced by Khrushchev at the 20th Soviet Party Congress in 1956, intensified the trend. The uprising of East German workers and its suppression in June 1953, the quelled revolt in Russia's own slave camps at Vorkuta in the Siberian wastes the same year, the Polish upheaval and the tragic Hungarian revolution in 1956, and lastly the short season of the Chinese spurious "Hundred Flowers" campaign have been viewed as a series of incidents to illustrate the same trend, set off, as it were, by the intermittent "Thaw." Valuable studies could be and have been made of them in general, either in terms of Communist international relations or to work out new themes on Marxism, communism, and freedom.[7] But not only do the dimensions, impacts, and results of each incident differ greatly; the actual content of each—the national, historical, human, and cultural factors involved—also yield very diverse pictures.

Of all these incidents, the "Hundred Flowers" campaign—at least in its most dramatic phase that caught the world's attention —appears to be for all its brevity perhaps the best controlled, like a juggler's show, devised, enacted, and called off at will. Even though there were occasional signs of consternation from the ruling party, on the whole it showed unfailing confidence of controlled manipulation. The confidence had been developed from a series of earlier domestic cultural campaigns through which the apparatus for manipulation had been neatly perfected. The "Hundred Flowers" may therefore obtain some new light if observed in the context of earlier campaigns as the realization of one facet of the party's grand political and cultural strategy for ruling China. Some explanations may also be found here for the fact that a real crisis seemed so easily warded off, on the one hand, with a minimum of physical violence as compared with the suppression in East Germany and Hungary, and on the other that the "Hundred Flowers" should have produced such intellectually lackluster results, despite its momentary emotional intensity, as compared with the Soviet "Thaw."

The two slogans "Let a Hundred Flowers Bloom Together" and "Let a Hundred Schools Contend to Profess" were combined into

[7] E.g., Raya Dunayevskaya, *Marxism and Freedom* (2nd ed.; New York: Twayne, 1964).

one and officially pronounced by the government spokesman, Vice-Minister of Propaganda Lu Ting-yi, in the summer of 1956. Both were cited, however, as cultural policy statements formulated and handed down by Chairman Mao himself at different times. The former was, as specified by the vice-minister, the directive for workers in art and literature, and the latter for workers in the sciences. The latter, "Let a Hundred Schools Contend to Profess," from all evidence was formulated as a policy by Mao at the National Supreme Council only some months before the decision to launch the whole dramatic campaign. It is obvious that if taken literally it would carry much more impact and give much more flare to the intellectual content of the campaign than the merely flashy, vaguely cheery "Hundred Flowers" slogan formulated earlier. For here "Hundred Schools" by classical allusion[8] meant a great variety of freely contending philosophical thoughts, and the sciences referred to might include social as well as natural sciences. A generous invitation to challenge the social philosophy of Marxism-Leninism would therefore seem to have been extended. But Mao's generous mood even as he spoke these words at the supreme council was very transitory indeed. Perceptive minds in the audience did not fail to notice his immediate modifications. For, as one of them later observed, the Chairman almost in the next breath declared, "Not only a hundred schools, there could be a thousand schools. Fundamentally, however, there are only two schools."[9] It became abundantly clear, right there and then, that one of these two schools was the sacrosanct Marxism-Leninism-Maoism, and all the rest, were there a thousand of them, if they "contended" would be foredoomed to be opposed as reactionary and antirevolutionary. No wonder, therefore, when the drama of the campaign was enacted for six summer weeks in 1957, the "Hundred Schools" slogan, nice parallel to the "Hundred Flowers" as it was, was for all practical purposes a mere foil to the latter in empty rhetoric. No school of thought arose to "contend to profess." For there was no school left, as we shall see, after the onslaughts upon all intellectual dissidents who were hounded out

[8] The term "Hundred Schools," or *pai chia*, in fact already implies heterodoxy in classical usage, understood as referring to other schools than Confucian orthodoxy, whether the CCP was conscious of this or not. E.g., Ssu-ma Ch'ien, *Shih-chi*, chap. 1, of the second century B.C.; or *Chuang Tzu*, chap. "T'ien Hsia," perhaps even earlier.

[9] Yü P'ing-po, "Casual Remarks on the 'Hundred Schools . . .'," in *Wen Yi Pao*, No. 1, Apr. 14, 1957, p. 9.

during the preceding years, especially in 1954 and 1955. Mao might have been sardonic but was nevertheless accurate in referring to "a thousand" of them as worth no more than one, and one of obviously negative value. For the thousand of them could now be no more than so many battered and splintered feelings and ideas, long since labelled antirevolutionary, anti-Marxian, capitalistic, and treasonable, therefore, utterly feeble and incapable of coherent articulation.

In discussing the "Hundred Flowers Blooming Together" and "Hundred Schools Contending to Profess" as a whole movement, we should therefore remember that one-half of it was stillborn, or paralyzed, even before it was set in motion. The "Hundred Flowers Blooming Together," the primary half of the slogan, initiated much earlier, with much wider connotations and different referents, however, remains in its variegated and mercurial manner, a fascinating symbol. It is through the initiation and manipulation of this contrivance that we can better trace the whole course of the Chinese Communist policy of cultural control since 1949, and observe the general direction, purpose, and effects of such a course thenceforth.

A traditional cliché, the phrase "Hundred Flowers Blooming Together" has a touch of vulgarism as contrasted with the classical flavor of "Hundred Schools Contending to Profess." The miraculous event of such a phrase suddenly rising to oracular solemnity, repeated worshipfully by myriads of cadres and activists after Mao adopted it in 1951, is a symbolic fact of the forcible elevation of traditional vulgarism, eclectically of course, to high cultural grandeur, signifying the general cultural and political strategy of the party. A series of domestic cultural campaigns since 1951, reaching different levels and assaulting different targets, bear the same hallmark of a peculiar kind of "populism," which was dictated from above and activated with Communist tactics to realize totalitarian Communist rule. Chinese Communist theorists and historians today have already had these campaigns chronicled in proud order,[10] in their tribute to the "Hundred Flowers." These campaigns were identified as a series of "Criticisms": "Criticism of the movie, *Life of Wu Hsün*" in 1951, "Criticism of the *Dream of Red Chamber Studies*," "Criticism of

[10] E.g., Chou Yang, "The Road of Socialist Literature and Art . . . ," *Wenxue Pinglun*, No. 4, 1960, p. 9; and Lin Mo-han, *Raising Higher the Banner of Mao Tse-tung's Thought in Literature and Art* (Shanghai wen-yi ch'u-pan she, 1960), pp. 18–19.

Hu Shih's Thought," "Criticism of Liang Su-ming's Thought," "Struggle against Hu Feng's Thought and His Anti-revolutionary Group," 1954 through 1955, leading to the crowning success of the exposure of the rightists in the crucial year of 1957.

It is significant that these campaigns since 1951, only one year after the party took power, should have started in the field of the most easily accessible forms of art, motion pictures and popular drama. It was in 1951, too, that Mao Tse-tung adopted the phrase "Hundred Flowers Blooming Together" in his speech to workers in dramatic art, and the slogan was consecrated in the years that followed. In enforcing Communist cultural policy in China, the party's attention as well as Mao's first turned to movies and drama, because these would be the most direct means of social and political propaganda to reach the broadest bases of the masses, who were for the most part as yet illiterate. Statistical figures cited for the year 1951 of the populations participating in the nationwide drama movement are astonishing. In the northern part of Kiangsu alone, not the whole province, there were 1,121 "countryside theatrical groups," with 20,893 members participating in stagecraft and acting. One county, Hsin-chang *hsien* in Southern Kiangsu, boasted of 136 theatrical groups, which in half a year gave 1,995 performances to audiences of 176,200. In one district, or *ch'ü*, of the Ta'i-hu county of Northern Anhwei province, every village had a theatrical group. A survey of the social backgrounds of the participating members of these village dramatic artists is very revealing: 70 per cent poor and middle peasants, 20 per cent grade school teachers, small merchants and peddlers, 10 per cent others.[11] That most of the applauded performances were crude improvisations directed by party cadres for the sake of indoctrination should be no surprise. But party indoctrination and ideology, whenever they seek to be realized in art, even in crude art, always have to face the dilemma of the boredom of didacticism and the delight of entertainment. In the Chinese villages as well as cities, colorful local operas of timeless tradition possessed of long-bred native talent began to revive, and sprouted alongside the dull "new plays" spawned by party ideology or those on older popular themes but adapted to meet with party approval. When Mao Tse-tung, as if in a festive mood, announced "Let a hundred flowers bloom together," he appeared

[11] See Tu Li-chün, "Raise the Quantity and Quality of Countryside Theatrical Groups," in *Wen Yi Pao,* Vol. IV, No. 10 (Sept. 10, 1951).

to be cheering this phenomenon of nationwide playgoing and play acting. Party critics of narrower minds and less dialectical cunning had been frowning upon the rivalry between the traditional operas and plays adapted from older familiar themes with great popular appeal on the one hand, and the ideologically "correct" proletarian stringent moral pieces on the other. Mao's utterance seemed to augur "gentle wind and light rains" for all the "flowers" of the theater to grow. As the well-known lover of traditional opera that he was, he perhaps meant it sincerely at the fleeting moment when he uttered the phrase, "Let a hundred flowers bloom together," *pai hua ch'i fang.* But as the master dialectician that he was, he did not neglect to add in the same breath, with typical oracular ambiguity, "Push along the old to derive the new," *t'ui ch'en ch'u hsin.* This could soon enough be interpreted at will by the party apparatus to mean that all the flowers might be let bloom, but some of them were to bloom only to show their true colors as "old" and "poisonous weeds"—and thereupon be removed. Thus 1951 foreshadowed 1957.

From 1951 to 1957 the series of culture campaigns may be seen as a whole spiral of a gigantic movement. None of them were spontaneous, but all were stirred up, fermented, guided and controlled by party directives and a host of tireless cadres. Creatures of the Chinese *partiinost,* they all bore the image stamped on them by the party, and, as cultural phenomena, they revealed that party's temperament and intellectual proclivity. The gigantic spiral started with the broadest basis of the grass roots in the most popular arts, as we have seen, rising to ever subtler and finer cultural and political issues until it reached the most sensitive areas of party ideology. But as the spiral rose and the targets became more concentrated and pinpointed, a kind of party-manipulated chiaroscuro became even more sharpened and widespread, until the Chinese mind was supposed to see only such vast contrasts of black and white as were willed by the party—or at least to say that it did.

The first of these campaigns, the devastating "Criticism of the *Life of Wu Hsün,*" a successful movie, was aimed at probing deep into the immense depths of traditional folk mentality and sense of values. And by "criticism" and "correction," the party could seize control of the mass imagination, and, furthermore, reshape it as the party saw fit. Wu Hsün lived in the mid-nineteenth century, during the T'ai-p'ing Rebellion. He became a legendary hero, who, as a beggar, dedicated his whole mendicant life to establishing schools for poor children in his native province of Shantung with the alms he received from his ingenious and persistent begging. His accomplishments were remembered as miracles. Tradition had it that he subsisted on insects, broken tiles, and bricks to save educational funds for others' children while he himself remained an illiterate beggar until death; and died without any private possessions or personal attachments. He broke with all relatives but gave his life like a martyr-saint to the cause of educating the poor. The motion picture producer, Sun Yü, must have thought that to elaborate on such a subject could certainly meet the standard of what Chairman Mao had preached at the Yenan Forum, to produce an art that "the common people are happy to hear and delighted to see." For it glorified the saintly virtues of which one of the commonest and poorest people, a beggar, could be capable. When the movie was first shown in late 1950, it was greeted with enthusiasm by the press, including some Communist papers, as well as the huge common audience. But higher up, the Central Committee of the party was watching, and carefully taking stock. The party knew well that the greatest appeal it had held for the vast number of poverty-stricken Chinese during the founding years of the Communist state was not its Marxist-Leninist proletarian revolutionary theories but its simple effective slogan, "the great turn of the tables for the poor" (*ch'iung-jen ta fan shen*). Now, in the founding years of the People's Republic, the tables having supposedly been turned, the party literary theoreticians, as well as the political leadership, must fit the immense poor population into revolutionary classes to carry on social struggle and reconstruction. What made this successful movie, the *Life of Wu Hsün,* so disturbing to the party was, as it turned out, that a mendicant, though the poorest member of the society, could not properly belong to either class, proletariat or peasantry. The very uniqueness of his "classlessness" made him unfit to be such a glorified subject as he was treated in the movie. But the movie was gaining greater popularity among huge popular audiences and increasing numbers of approving intellectuals. What aroused the party literary leadership most was the possible danger of the growth of heterodoxy that might stem from celebrating a dedicated strong individual as a social force, as opposed

to the orthodox collectivism that the party was vigorously instilling into the mass mind.

The measures that the party formally took against the *Life of
Wu Hsün* were most drastic. It not only attacked and stopped the
movie, but did everything imaginable to eradicate the traditional
image of Wu Hsün, and to recast it with thorough defamation.
He was assigned the role of what Marx in the *Communist Manifesto* called "the 'dangerous class,' the social scum" (without
reference, however, to the concessive part of the *Manifesto's*
whole sentence that this "social scum . . . may here and there
be swept into the movement by a proletarian revolution"). Sepa-
rated he must be from the now sacrosanct revolutionary classes
of the proletariat and the peasantry (conveniently unheeded, of
course, was the other part of the canon where the *Manifesto* calls
the peasants worse than conservative, "nay, more, they are reactionary, for they try to roll back the wheel of history.")[12] Not
only was "criticism" meted out against the movie producer and
"confessions" of crime exacted from him, but an "investigation"
was conducted against this beggar dead a hundred years. A host
of party activists were mobilized to "collect data" in Wu Hsün's
native district, and in a few months turned up with a handy volume of a report[13] in which Wu Hsün, the beggar, now appeared
to be "a big landlord, high-interest creditor, vagrant scoundrel
(*liu mang*) and cheat, . . . an exploiter of poor working people,
. . . a crystallization of feudalistic society."[14] Two large volumes
of *Criticisms of the Life of Wu Hsün* were quickly assembled,[15]
with a large force of "awakened" or "repentant" critics and journalists joining in unison to denounce both the movie and Wu
Hsün as "the foulest, most evil, most reactionary servitor."

How genuine the evidence was, and how fair its interpretation,
we do not pretend to judge. Iconoclasm against traditional celeb-
rities had frequently taken place in Chinese intellectual polemics
before, but never such complete, disproportionate reversal of
verdict against so helpless a defendant as a dead beggar of a

[12] Chou Yang, "Anti-People, Anti-Historical Thought, and Anti-Realistic
Art," in *Wen Yi Pao*, Vol. IV, No. 9 (Aug. 25, 1951); first published in
JMJP, Aug. 8, 1951.

[13] Entitled *Wu Hsün li-shih tiao-ch'a chi* (Peking: Jen-min ch'u-pan
she, 1951).

[14] Kuo Mo-jo, "Reading Wu Hsün li-shih tiao-ch'a chi," *Wen Yi Pao*,
Vol. IV, No. 9 (Aug. 25, 1951).

[15] *P'i-p'an Wu Hsün chuan*, Vols. I and II (Peking: Jen-min ch'u-pan
she, 1951).

hundred years before. But it would be too simplistic if this were laughed off as quixotic windmill fighting. On the contrary, its significance was calculated to be broad and far-reaching. On the broadest basis of mass culture, the anti-Wu Hsün movement ostensibly "corrected" the notion that the poor, oppressed people should ever humiliate themselves by "begging" to advance social reform. But, at the same time, by eradicating the traditional image of the paragon of virtues which each poor man might think himself capable of achieving by individual effort and strength of character, the leaders opened the way to substitute the image of the "positive hero," which the party willed to beget out of socialist collectivism under the star of *partiinost*. Humility, dedication, and self sacrifice are precisely the same virtues that the party would expect of the masses for the Communist purpose. But these virtues must be first divested of their old associations so as to serve the party totally. It was as if the party had to wrestle with the masses, lest these virtues should remain rooted in the personal moral sense and thus be independently hallowed when incarnated in such personages as Wu Hsün, without party guidance and therefore dangerous to the supremacy of the party's power. A sharp contrast between the party's attitude toward Wu Hsün and toward its most recently created positive hero is revealing. In the movie there is this dialogue between a young girl, Little Peach, and Wu Hsün:

LITTLE PEACH: Why do you always do those dirtiest, heaviest, and hardest jobs? . . . Others find you meek. They pile everything upon your shoulders."
WU HSÜN: Dirtiest, heaviest, hardest jobs! There must be someone to do them. . . . If I didn't do them, who else would?

This was singled out as an outstanding example to be attacked by the leading spokesman of Communist literary policy as "beautification of servile working attitudes and blind faithfulness toward feudalist landlords."[16] In the story of the most exalted "positive hero," of 1962, the young worker Lei Feng, on the other hand, when he volunteered to work in an iron ore factory, held a similar dialogue with another young worker:

YOUNG WORKER: To go there, one would be really a fool. Nothing good to eat, no good place to live in. There will be no increase of wages, nor any award. I won't do it!

16 Chou Yang, *op. cit.*

LEI FENG (*with moral indignation*): The party has taught and
  guided us: Wherever there is hard and painful work, we must
  go there; wherever we are needed we must go there. We want to
  be such 'fools.'[17]

This was extolled as one shining example of the positive hero's
"firm proletarian stand and noble Communist virtues." And people were exhorted to "emulate his self-sacrifice to the task of the
People's Revolution, and his indefatigable spirit of learning from
the books of Chairman Mao"[18]—even though he was, as his story
ended, physically so fatigued after ceaseless hard work that he
died stricken under a wooden post knocked down by a truck.

The movie *Life of Wu Hsün* must have been seen by millions
in 1951, and the book *Story of Lei Feng* was propagated at the
rate of 310,000 copies per printing in 1963, reaching an even
greater number. Wu Hsün was labeled "evil, hypocritical," or at
best a freak, while Lei Feng was hailed as "noble, progressive, and
typical" as a positive socialist hero. Wu Hsün and Lei Feng may
in fact have been the same drudge, subsisting and laboring in the
same conditions of material destitution. But so far as the party's
policy for art and literature is concerned, the ageless traditional
morals, personified and worshiped in one individual for his hu-
manitarianism, must be exterminated to clear the good earth for
"flowers" to be cultured or manufactured and therefore controlled
at the party's will, in the name of socialist collectivism, down at
the broadest mass level.

No wonder the desecration of the memory of the beggar-saint
Wu Hsün has been cited by the party leadership, speaking as
historians, as the first decisive step of their new cultural orientation, that of exterminating the deepest roots of the old values,
cherished by the world's largest population and perpetuated in its
most popular art forms. The vast movement of national cultural
campaigns, as we have noted, spiraled. And the next plane after
the popular drama and movies was the traditional novel, affecting
more sophisticated readers and the intelligentsia. The eighteenth-
century masterpiece, the *Dream of the Red Chamber*, had remained the greatest and most treasured legacy of fictional art to
the modern Chinese mind. To characterize the novel's complex
qualities and multiple effects, one would have to imagine a

---

[17] *In Lei Feng ti ku-shih*, or *Story of Lei Feng* (Peking: Chieh-fang
chün wen-yi she, 1963), p. 20.
[18] Prefatory Summary of Contents, *ibid.*

combination of Balzac-like comprehensiveness of scope and vivid meticulous documentation and Tolstoian sweep of panoramic pictures of profound humanism, with the subtle prismatic dimensions of meaning and the psychological dissection and symbolism of James or Proust. Moreover, it contains on the one hand profoundly religious and sublimated politico-erotic sentiments of Dantesque heights, and on the other a Wertherian appeal to sentimental youth. Yet its rich nuances and overtones are wrought with Buddhist-Taoistic and Confucian leitmotifs, all peculiarly Chinese.

The lore of *The Red Chamber* had for two centuries grown to immense proportions, occupying both the folk imagination and sedulous scholarly research. In 1954, Yü P'ing-po, a great authority on *Red Chamber* studies since the time of the May Fourth Movement, was encouraged by the party's slogan of "critically accepting national cultural heritage" to publish a "Simplified Discourse on the *Red Chamber*." It was called "simplified" ostensibly to suit the party's policy that erudite scholarship should emerge from the ivory tower to do popular service. Like the movie *Life of Wu Hsün*, the "Discourse" was first greeted with public acclaim. There Yü presented the realm of experience which the *Red Chamber* depicted as follows:

Although unreal, it is no mere castle in the air; although real, it cannot be read as *vitae* or chronicles. Although it praises, yet whenever has it actually sung homage? Although it criticizes, does it ever ruthlessly expose? About love and sex, it is quite positive, . . . yet at the same time it is extremely negative; . . . while it recaptures and retrieves vanishing human traces, it uses "fantastic talk," words that "don't really mean it," words "through the hat," so as to confound.

In Pao-yü, the hero of the novel, he saw the embodiment, unity, or reconciliation of the Buddhist concepts of *se-k'ung*, "color-nihility," or, in lay terms, "the vanity of all appearances." Of the two heroines Tai-yü and Pao-ch'ai, he said in the "Discourse":

They are like two peaks juxtaposed, twin rivers flowing separate courses: each is consummate in her own beauty; neither one is inferior. . . . If Pao-ch'ai were like trash, what then would remain of Tai-yü's stature to be worthy of any mention?

Yü thus maintained the ground that the *Red Chamber* was to be regarded as a rich repository of fascinating literary ambiguities, implying numerous possibilities of interpretation. So he, unwittingly perhaps, held open before the public, now under Communist rule, a vastly popular area for free literary inquiry, which had been characteristic of the neo-humanist spirit of the May Fourth period a generation before. But the party caught up with him soon enough. As had been the case with popular drama and movies, though only one work of art and one writer seemed apparently involved, it was as if the whole nervous system of the party were touched to the quick. It reacted in full force, and seized the opportunity to make out of a single issue a nationwide new cultural campaign, ranging from literary criticism on a most popular basis up to social, political, or more abstract philosophies, and indeed practically all branches of learning in the humanities. The campaign started by the party's wedging itself in, stirring up a tempest in a teacup, and then extending the battle. Two young students, cadre-inspired, had written virulent attacks on Yü's "Discourse." These were published and republished by important journals. Then, with the powerful party organ, the *People's Daily*, fanning the fire, more and more illustrious names were enlisted to join the onslaught. Branches of the Chinese Writers' Associations in Shanghai and Peking convened public meetings to denounce the erstwhile *Red Chamber* authority, and university presidents, professors, writers, and critics gathered to rant their condemnations in writing and in speeches, until the attention of people of all walks of life was turned on the target. For the *Red Chamber* had long been a household word, and many of its characters as real as anything in the nation's imaginative life.

Their arguments, even though laden with ponderous ideological jargon, may, at first glance, seem simple enough in essence to be summed up thus: In Communist literary criticism no ambiguity is tolerated, and, even less, allusions to its virtues; skepticism and agnosticism are as bad as, or even more insidious than, downright reactionary views; good and evil must be sharply distinguished, so that positive heroes and hateful villains are made clear-cut; the Buddhist concept of "vanity of all appearances" is the worst kind of nihilism.

Purely as literary doctrine, these dicta are stringent enough to be expected of a Communist regime. But applied in the year 1954 against Yü P'ing-po's *Red Chamber* studies, they represented only a part of a much larger strategy of a series of cultural campaigns leading to the short bloom of the "Hundred Flowers" in the spring of 1957. Yü's violation of these dicta were pointed out as only symptoms of much deeper ills, results of widespread inveterate capitalist thinking, feudalistic benightedness, compounded with imperialistic cultural dark plots which were carried through by treasonable cultural compradorism. The seriousness of these charges justified the mobilization of a host of leading intellectuals, many of high distinction, to cry in unison in denunciation of one man for his views expressed on one old popular novel.

Although the issue began with literary criticism, the polemics, or actually the unilateral condemnation of one by all, became so generalized yet so far-reaching that they were turned into an overwhelming mass movement. And the intellectuals enlisted were in their language and reasoning soon enough drunken with mass passion. Abuses were heaped up and repeated in a thousand variations on the same theme, with the same slogans which the masses and the intellectuals could shout alike. In the name of Marxist ideological revolution, for the good of the people and love of the country, with the masses at the basis and the party guiding from the top, the intellectuals were perhaps either convinced or compelled to do the only thing the party willed them to do. In any case, they were ready to move next to the kill, which the party aimed at in its grand design. And the party must be congratulated for having given them enough exercise to catch the bigger game, and still later to ensnare for it its more dangerous enemies within; the "criticisms" of Hu Shih and Liang Su-ming, and the purge of Hu Feng and Ting Ling, were a series of storm attacks by which the party took tight control of the Chinese intellect. All these, from 1954 to 1956, were successes of the party, before it could, in the next year, 1957, feel the national mentality malleable enough for it to let a "Hundred Flowers Bloom," even though for only a short while.

Even as the fires fanned up against Yü P'ing-po's *Red Chamber* studies were raging, Kuo Mo-jo, in his dual capacity as president of the Academy of Sciences and Chairman of the Enlarged Joint National Conference on Chinese Art and Literature, on December 8, 1954, announced at the conference, as if casually, to all the intellectual luminaries of the nation gathered there:

Incidentally, I want to report that the Academy of Sciences and the Association of Writers already have held a joint meeting last Thursday and passed a plan to call meetings to criticize the thoughts of Hu Shih. We have suggested nine topics to define the content so as to criticize separately Hu Shih's philosophical thoughts, political thoughts, historical viewpoint, literary thinking, and other related problems. Each problem will be written on by leading researchers to be publicly reported, and discussion will be carried on.

At this point, to the audience, who had by now already been conditioned to practice the Communist tactics of "Cultural Campaign," the menacing call of the pillory for Hu Shih was indicated clearly enough. But Kuo went on to say:

We want to employ this method to eradicate drastically the poisonous remnants of Hu Shih's reactionary thoughts in the literary and intellectual field. I appeal to every one of you, my friends, to do your utmost to cooperate and help, to enable us to fulfill our duties in this joint battle with victory.

Under the circumstances the victory was a foregone conclusion, won even before the battle was begun. But it was also a mock victory, for indeed it was a mock war. It was a totalitarian war on a nationwide scale, against the phantasm of an enemy who was nowhere thereabout. Hu Shih had, since 1949, been in the United States. Now he was watching, alternately in bewilderment and glee, the mock warfare against him far across the Pacific. He was only puzzled, as he told friends, including this author, what all this was for or about. But he could not—as few perhaps could—hide a deep sense of satisfaction and personal vanity, and of amusement too, that he should be such a focus of attention, a towering shadow of a target, set aflame in effigy. All his former friends, colleagues, students, admirers, intellectual beneficiaries, and associates of all callings, who vied with each other to enlarge the conflagration, could thus expiate themselves and be absolved of guilt.

Yet the whole affair was not merely a grand empty gesture. The names of these firebrand carriers read like a virtually complete roll call in the hall of fame, including most of the intellectuals who had earned a reputation since the May Fourth movement, and who had been left to live under Communist rule. All protesting and fulminating with apparently uniform indignation, the pageant was on parade, exhibiting philosophers and philologists, political scientists and poets, historians and grammarians, classical textual critics, and modern folklorists. They attacked Hu Shih from his Deweyite pragmatism to his research in traditional popular novels, from his political views to his literary theory, from his social reformism to his study of ancient pronouns in the first and second person. But despite the great range and variety of subjects, the conclusions of the "criticisms," in millions upon millions of words by scores of distinguished authors,[19] each known for his particular expertise, were all pointed to the same end. And they were no longer quite distinguishable as they were voiced, droning forth, as it were, in deafening unison. Even though there could be plenty in Dr. Hu's philosophy and scholarship that might be questioned as time had progressed, the sense of the arguments was now lost in scurrilous reflections, vituperative denunciations, and bombastic slogans, which would be worse than tedious to repeat.

The self-same tactics were applied to the "criticisms" of Liang Su-ming, under a slightly varied label. Both Hu and Liang were pilloried in the grand inquisition, of course, as anti-Marxist and anti-Communist. But as such they were charged with no mere ideological offense, but with treason. Hu, the incarnation of Western capitalist thinking, and Liang, that of native feudalism, were therefore both arch-enemies of the state and the people, so ran the general tenor of the "criticisms." And both were therefore dangerously saturated with "venom." Once the label was sealed upon each, it remained for every bit of the "criticism" by their peers to show by fine deductions their all-pervading poisonous effects. Even Hu Shih's errors in his study of pronouns in ancient Chinese grammar were pointed out as resulting "from a system of capitalist idealist viewpoints," in the words of linguist Pan Yün-chung, who proclaimed: "The poison of capitalist class thinking which Hu Shih . . . spread in our field of linguistics is serious. We are all more or less affected by its evil influence whether consciously or unconsciously. We absolutely cannot tolerate the venom of Hu Shih's school of thought which has for so long poisoned us."[20]

Liang Su-ming had been a leading intellectual force rivaling Hu Shih in prominence. A veteran philosopher and rural reformer, his appeal to the Chinese mind was on account of his strong faith in oriental cultural values, blending Confucian hu-

[19] A series of successive volumes of *Critiques of Hu Shih's Thoughts* was published by San lien shu-tien in 1955.

[20] Pan Yün-chung, "A Criticism of Hu Shih's Studies of the Ancient First Person (*wu, o*) and Second Person (*erh, ju*)," in *Critiques of Hu Shih's Thoughts*, No. 7, p. 408.

manism with Buddhist vision, and his personal sincerity and
fortitude, which had been tested in practice by both his criticism
of the Nationalist (KMT) rule and his opposition to the Communist insurrections to seize power in the 1930's and 40's. Liang,
under the Communist regime, in fact was once used as a lure to
win defection from Taiwan in 1952, when he was urged to, and
did, write an open letter "To My Compatriots in Taiwan," exhorting their allegiance to Peking. Now even that letter was under
severe attack in the mass movement of "criticisms" against him.
For there he dared to say that his own submission to the Communists was "not like the ordinary." This was singled out as a sign of
his "megalomaniac self-aggrandizement." It was linked with an
earlier statement he made when the Communists had just come
to power and sought his support as perhaps the most respected
leader of the Democratic League. In an article, "Establish Trust
and Seek Cooperation," he had said then: "There is obviously a
very great distance between the Communist Party and me. As for
theory and advocacy, they have a whole set of these, and I have
my own. This distance is not like the ordinary. But fundamentally
there is mutual accord: I have a heart, and they naturally have a
heart, too." The "criticism" says that he was aggrandizing himself
by making such a comparison: "He entirely fails to recognize that
his heart, stubbornly attached to landlordist standpoints, reactionary and anti-revolutionary, is different in basic essence from
that of the Communist Party members who raise aloft the revolutionary banner." And this was from Professor Ho Lin, an elderly
philosopher of thorough training and great erudition, in Ho's
article entitled "A Critique of Liang Su-ming's Intuitionism."[21]
From such a learned title treated by such a learned man, one
would expect some professional argument, scholarly logical debate, technical disquisition, or at least some more sophistication.
But in another article signed jointly by an equally elevated philosopher and his disciple, "On Liang Su-ming's Vitalist Philosophy,"[22] the main thesis was to expound a dictum of Chairman
Mao as the canonical truth: "In China both the landlord class and
the compradore class are vassals of the international capitalist
class. Their existence and development are dependent on im-

[21] In *Critiques of Liang Su-ming's Thoughts* (San lien shu-tien, 1955),
No. 1, p. 113.
[22] T'ang Yung-t'ung and Jen Chi-yü in *Critiques of Liang . . ,* No. 2,
pp. 11–13.

perialism." Liang's rural reformism having been labeled land-lordism, he therefore "perforce must prostrate himself before the feet of the imperialists, and serve as their lackey." The disciple in another article[23] called Liang even worse than Hu Shih, who was content enough with Deweyite pragmatism alone, while Liang "paid various kinds of homage to all imperialist-controlled philosophers, such as Driesch, Bergson, Dewey and others of the reactionary schools (including James and Russell)." But what Liang had mainly said, even as quoted in the article, was that he believed in Confucius' concept of *jen,* which he interpreted as "intuitive humaneness." And some Western philosophers, Liang observed, after a big detour, would inadvertently turn back to this direction, as Nietzsche, James, Dewey, Bergson, and Eucken did. But somehow in the logic of the article this made Liang an advocate of "Total Westernization." His faith in Confucianism and Buddhism somehow made him a champion of Western imperialism. A dominant note in the accusations of Liang and Hu was that they were both "anti-patriotic" (*fan ai-kuo,* or "against love of country"). Both were "malicious slanderers" of the Chinese national tradition, whenever they blamed their country's social, economic ills, political corruption, contemporary moral depravity, or cultural drawbacks on any reason other than those advanced by the Communist Party. Even Hu Shih's evaluation of the fourteenth-century novel *Shui Hu,* or *Water Margin,* was called a sign of his "extreme contempt for our people's creativity and our nation's superior tradition, a reckless smear on our classical literature and other cultural heritage."

These "criticisms," as can be easily seen, are in fact collective mass cries, and we must treat them as such to appreciate their purpose and the effects accomplished in the interests of the Communist rule of China in the past decade. We must avoid making stock responses to these materials or wearily dismissing them for their obvious crudity and monotony. We should feel the vehemence and understand the awesome collective power they represent. It is the mobilization and command of this power by the party that not only in 1957 brought on the dramatic bloom of the "Hundred Flowers" which were soon declared to be mostly "poisonous weeds," but later continued to manufacture and adver-

---

[23] Jen Chi-yü, "Expose the Compradorism in Liang Su-ming's Thoughts," in *Critiques of Liang . . . ,* No. 1, pp. 114–22.

tise those particular brands of "Flowers" designed for the cultural program in the Chinese Communist paradise.

Starting with the organized "criticisms" of the *Red Chamber* studies of Yü P'ing-po, and in the process of turning these "criticisms" into intellectual mass movements against the two most influential philosophers, Hu Shih and Liang Su-ming, as exposed targets outside the Communist camp, the party hierarchy also ensnared its enemies from within. These, most prominently, were Hu Feng and Ting Ling. Future history will probably record Hu Feng as a most courageous and talented maverick in the Chinese Communist fold. Having been during the twenties a member of the Communist Youth Corps, Hu Feng continuously served leftist causes later on, was jailed in Japan, and became most active in literary organizations which were Communist fronts. He therefore learned all the Communist underground tactics and politics. As a literary theorist, critic, poet, and essayist, he was regarded as the closest disciple and friend of the great Lu Hsün, who has been posthumously made Communist China's literary patron saint as Gorky was in the Soviet Union. He inherited Lu Hsün's mantle with his superb critical acumen, sharp and poignant style, and displayed the strong individual character and spirit of rebellion in his bones that his master had been famed for. He knew Marxism-Leninism and was well versed in dialectics. When the "criticism" of Yü P'ing-po's *Red Chamber* studies began, Hu Feng was among the first to speak up. In the general uproar, he saw an opportunity of gaining a forum. He not only denounced Yü P'ing-po, as the party directed, but made a sweeping attack on the upper echelon of the literary cadre and on the suffocating conditions of literary creation, of which he declared reform was overdue. He had been gathering forces among friends and associates of like mind by personal contacts and secret correspondence. Now, as the tide of "criticism" was rising, quite a few leading members of the literary cadre also made "confessions" of their own "negligence," "insufficient awareness," and other mistakes in need of correction. Hu Feng thought it was time for him to come into the open to criticize the party's literary policy and leading policy-makers as well. He should have been aware of the forces against him. His dissident views had been known and carefully watched. In the spring of 1953 he had been singled out for attack by two party literary ideologues of high authority. Lin Mo-han and Ho Ch'i-fang both repudiated him for his "subjectivism," his "failure to see the class nature of various kinds of realism," and his "denial of the *partiinost* principle in art and literature."[24]

These attacks, though seemingly in general terms, represented the stringent basic policy the party was to enforce on art and literature at all costs; and, as it turned out, when directed against Hu Feng, they were aimed at a specific target, a most potent force of internal opposition with a formidable following among the ranks of accomplished leftist writers. When these attacks were made in 1953, Hu Feng perhaps had been overconfident of his cause, or guided to action by quixotic illusions. At any rate, he had countered with a 200,000-word statement of "Opinions on Problems of Art and Literature,"[25] and presented it to the highest party authority, the Central Committee, in July 1954. There he not only severely criticized the strangling effects of the policy currently adopted by the leading literary cadre but proposed concrete measures of reformation. Invoking the Soviet dissolution of RAPP as a noble example to follow, he proposed that all the so-called organizations for literary and art creativity which were in effect "government administrative agencies," national or local, be dissolved, and all publications so vested with government authority eliminated;[26] the Association of Writers and Artists, equal in scope, power, and prestige to its Soviet counterpart, was to be reorganized along more democratic lines;[27] and a system of "cooperative units" for literary creativity was to be set up, each maintaining a fair degree of autonomy and headed by a writer of "leading influence" to "undertake voluntarily" literary enterprises, with the approval, of course, of the party's Ministry of Propaganda.[28] He cited Stalin's dictum, which Hu Feng claimed to have been directed against the RAPP spirit of the early thirties, such as was now plaguing Chinese literature in the early fifties. The guiding principle to remedy the situation should be—in Stalin's words, which Hu Feng gathered from various Japanese and Chinese versions to suit his purpose:[29] "Write about reality! Let the writer learn from life. If he can employ highly artistic

[24] See Ho Ch'i-fang, "Is It the Road to Realism or to Anti-Realism?," *Wen Yi Pao*, No. 3, 1953; and Lin Mo-han, "Hu Feng's Anti-Marxist Literary Thought," in *Wen Yi Pao*, No. 2, 1953. Both also appeared as appendices to Hu Feng, *Opinions . . . ;* see note 4.
[25] Hu Feng, *Opinions*. . . . See note 4.
[26] *Ibid.,* p. 149.
[27] *Ibid.,* p. 165.
[28] *Ibid.,* p. 152.
[29] *Ibid.,* p. 8.

forms to reflect the reality of life, he will arrive at Marxism."
Moreover, Hu Feng armed himself with statements of leading
Soviet authors of the "thawing" period of 1953. He enthusiastically, and of course again eclectically, quoted Simonov, Fadeyev,
and Ehrenburg of this period, and even referred to Malenkov,
presumably in relation to the latter's comment on "typicalness" in
his report to the Soviet 19th Party Congress, as advocates of
liberalization.[30] He obviously mistook the utterances of these
"greats" for sufficiently warm breezes from the "elder brother"
socialist nation across the Siberian border to help change the
cultural climate in China. But actually, under efficient tempera-
ture control in China, deep freeze was to set in upon him and his
like to sterilize the land before a brief "Hundred Flowers" season
was to open and close, and then to be followed by plans to
manufacture such artificial species at the party's will.

The party withheld action when Hu Feng submitted his "Opinions" in July 1954, until after the successful commencement of
the *Red Chamber* case in the winter, when Hu Feng emerged
among aroused crowds, which he thought would be drawn to
support his causes by his eloquent attacks on both the traditional
rightists and the doctrinaire bigotry of the party's literary leadership. But he ended with drawing enemies from both sides, and
exposing himself as a helpless target. The squelching of Hu Feng
marked the apex of the spiral of cultural campaigns, from the
liquidation of the dead beggar Wu Hsün, through the *Red Chamber* case, and the "criticisms" of Hu Shih and Liang Su-ming. Now
all these, seen tier by tier as it were, were integrated into a whole
movement, a full-fledged assault on the Chinese intellect, a whirl-
wind sweeping over the nation, to bend it to the party's will. The
attack on Hu Feng was much more vehement than the rest,
mobilizing all forces the party could muster, from the most
popular manuals for youths and the masses to the more sophisticated publications for experts. Not only did intellectuals from
practically all walks of life join in the outcry, but, for the first
time, the head of the Ministry of Security, i.e., the Chief of Secret
Police, General Lo Jui-ch'ing, uttered his strident words in a vastly
popular publication to pronounce the "Hu Feng Clique" a national
security menace to be stamped out.[31]

[30] *Ibid.*, p. 139.
[31] Lo Jui-ch'ing, "Increase Alertness; Avoid Benumbed Inertia," *Hsüeh-
hsi*, No. 7, July 2, 1955, pp. 14–16.

The indictments against Hu Feng were neatly summed up by Kuo Hsiao-ch'uan, a poet, in the same issue in which General Lo's criminological pronouncements appeared.[32] It is revealing to see how the assertion of such ordinary literary values and attitudes as can be taken for granted in a free society can be turned into treasonable crimes in the Chinese police state, or, conversely, how such values, when asserted persistently and eloquently enough by certain strong individuals, could so deeply disturb the party that it took every devious means and ruthless measure to eradicate them. Hu Feng's crimes in Kuo Hsiao-ch'uan's summation were as follows, each phrased and commented on in Kuo's own words and "proved" with quotations from Hu Feng himself:

1. *Theory of Darkness:* Hu Feng publicly declared, "As regards realism, precisely because it fights to obtain light, it must perforce exaggerate darkness." . . . This is not quite so strange . . . because they (his clique) are incarnations of darkness themselves. . . . Moreover, their . . . dark plot has been to invent darkness which absolutely does not exist among working people.

2. *Theory of Factionalism:* The Hu Feng clique has always called the Party and the literary fronts under Party leadership "factions." . . . Their "anti-factionalism" has as its mission the overthrow of the People's Republic and the restoration of the imperialist and Nationalist Party rule.

3. *Theory of Human Nature:* When Hu Feng speaks of the Typical in literary creation, he only says it is the living human being, the psychological conditions of the living human being, the spiritual struggles of the living human being, in absolute disregard of class content. In the writings of Hu Feng and his followers, regarded as starting points of human labor and struggle and sources of literary creation, are "sincerity," "kind and loving heart," "will and desires to seek life," "fortitude and honesty to undertake heavy tasks," and so forth, [and these prove that] while advocating human nature, he blows the bugle for individualism, . . . asserting "the principles of individualism are interrelated with collectivism; and those of collectivism can also be interrelated with individualism. . . ." Obviously, the purpose is only to use this "Theory of Human Nature" to oppose all our organizations, to oppose the solidarity among our people, to oppose collectivism and oppose thought reform.

4. *Anti-rationalism:* Hu Feng has always worshiped "spontaneity" . . . and praised "the people's primitive force". . . . Hu Feng's co-

[32] Kuo Hsiao-ch'uan, "Several Special Features of the Dark Plots and Activities of the Anti-Revolutionary Hu Feng Clique," *Hsüeh-hsi,* No. 7, 1955, pp. 20–25.

hort, Ah Lung, even publicly declared, "Poetry is fire," which "makes all the good and the beautiful shine in glorious flame and sends all the evil and the ugly through purgatory to perish as dead ashes"; and "a poetic line? . . . It is the cry 'to kill!' " This means in fact that they want to annihilate the world. . . . Their basic purpose is to oppose Marxism-Leninism, to oppose the foundation of the theory which guides our thought.

From the "evidence" demonstrated by such fragmentary quotations from the writings of Hu Feng and his "clique," Kuo Hsiao-ch'uan could, and did, conclude that Hu Feng was armed with weapons from "the arsenals of Trotskyite gangsters, Fascist bandits, the imperialists, and the KMT (Nationalist Party)." This last accusation was not intended to be metaphorical, but to be fatal and real. On account of such literary theories, ideas, and critical attitudes as Hu Feng and his group upheld and expressed, charges of espionage, sedition, and treason were brought against them, with the sanction of the party and the Security Police. In the meantime, Hu Feng had been made to write his "confessions" again and again, which were checked against, however, and published alongside "documents" supplied by a few of his former associates now pleading penitence and working for the party, to "expose" Hu Feng and others of his clique and to prove at every point that the verdicts on their crime were just and true.[33] The party organ, the *People's Daily*, for nearly a whole month, from May 15 to June 10, 1955, devoted itself to publishing these materials with biting editorial comments. The editorials exhorted the whole nation to "expose Hu Feng," as one of the captions put it, so as to "heighten alertness" against internal, infiltrating enemies. The whole nation, well-conditioned by earlier "criticism" campaigns, now responded with even more vigor. Reading the press of this period, one has the feeling that the intellectuals of the whole nation were shaking, outwardly with rage but inwardly with fear. The party's reigning literary ideologues now had gathered such overwhelming forces against any dissident that even such a well-established, distinguished novelist as Ting Ling, long celebrated as the best Communist woman writer and honored with a Stalin prize, could now, amidst well-controlled mass hysteria, be brought down from her pedestal. We shall not go into

[33] These were later published in book form, under the title *Materials Related to the Anti-Revolutionary Hu Feng Clique* (Peking: Jen-min ch'u-pan she, 1955).

detail about the Ting Ling case. Suffice it to say here that by 1956 the cultural control carried such sweeping force that the land was laid barren, so far as any deviating ideas about art and literary creation were concerned.

Thus we perceive a desolate landscape on the eve of the "Hundred Flowers" drama early in 1957, which was suddenly staged to the amazement of the outside world. In the space of six short weeks, the show of a "Hundred Flowers Blooming Together" was turned to that of the "extermination of poisonous weeds." And the amazement of the outside world was soon turned into a sense of wry-humored irony. Some serious and praiseworthy attempts, it is true, were made to collect the relics of the "poisonous weeds," in the form of whatever documents could be salvaged from what filtered through the "bamboo curtain." The most comprehensive collection to date in a well-arranged form available in English is, of course, Mr. Roderick MacFarquhar's *The Hundred Flowers Campaign and the Chinese Intellectuals*, published in 1960. And later there is *Communist China: The Politics of Student Opposition*, edited by Mr. Dennis Doolin. But these exhibitions, though notable as "a unique description of Communist totalitarianism from inside," in Mr. MacFarquhar's words, are for the most part, as we indicated earlier in this paper, no more than spasmodic expressions of long pent-up emotion and trivial, mundane personal grievances which, however poignant and genuine, were quickly and effectively suppressed. They were, because of the quick suppression and effective control, unable to show any intellectual depth. Less is it to be expected that there should be any literary or artistic monument to celebrate the quickly played tragedy, except desperate sounds of bawling and wailing, and perhaps spurts of blood, that vanished in a twinkling. Not comparable therefore is the "Hundred Flowers Campaign," viewed in the narrow sense of its brief dramatic moment, with the pervasive intermittent "Thaw" that has continually found expression in Soviet art and literature through the years and affected the climate of all eastern Europe.

The significance of the "Hundred Flowers" must therefore be viewed on a much broader plane. The very brevity of the dramatic moment of the tumultuous six weeks, the speedy action that brought the movement under control, should reveal the dire effects of the earlier series of cultural campaigns that spiraled in continuous circles from the time of the "dead beggar" case of the *Life of Wu Hsün* in 1951. Soon after this, indeed, the term "Hundred Flowers," with all its implications of dialectical skill and skulduggery, had already germinated. The wind that bore the tidings of the "Hundred Flowers" of the party's special brand had for more than six years been blowing and attacking with ever-renewed force. And after the "poisonous weeds" that during the six brief weeks burgeoned to the surface only to be eradicated, the party was ready to plant its garden with gigantic artificial blooms. Under its slogans of awesome intent to conquer nature and its powerful attacks on human nature,[34] the party will continue to develop its nationwide ideological horticulture, or more precisely, to manufacture its artificial blooms, and advertise them loudly with the patent name of "Hundred Flowers." We shall continue to hear of them and be strewn with them and feel their effects, which, although they may be only flashy strange colors and without natural odor, are nonetheless not to be ignored.

The formula to produce these new wonders can be summed up in one magic word, *Collectivism*. It is Collectivism as to both spirit of creation and method of production. It is this Collectivism that directs art and literature to serve the sacrosanct classes of "workers, peasants, and soldiers," among whom the artists and writers lose themselves and hence express only the mass spirit. And "collective creation," in the words of Chou Yang, the Chinese Zhdanov of today with unchallenged supremacy of power, "is already important as a form of our creative activities in literature and art, an important method that carries out the mass line in art and literary works."[35]

Overwhelming quantities of the collectively manufactured "flowers" have been spread all over the mainland, expecially since 1957. With the *hsia-fang*, or "downward transfer," movement of intellectuals and cadres since then, followed by the "Great Leap Forward," and then the stupendous social collectivization of the communes, actual new milieus were more than sufficiently provided to force the growth of an art and a literature to suit the ideal of collectivism which the party has willfully designed. An artificial quality devoid of individual feelings but contrived to

[34] As summed up in Chou Yang's "The Road of Our Country's Socialist Literature and Art: A Report to the Third Congress of Chinese Literary and Art Workers," *Wenxue Pinglun*, No. 4, pp. 6–31; and many articles attacking beliefs in human nature in *Wen Yi Pao* since 1957.

[35] Chou Yang, *op. cit.*

show the raw force of mass militancy or fanatic worship can be expected. A good instance to illustrate this successful mass production can be found in the "multi-million poem movement" of 1958, which this writer has treated in an article, "Multiplicity in Uniformity: Poetry and the Great Leap Forward":[36]

The Great Leap Forward has not only been measured by the claimed increases of grain and steel production by so many million tons. Peking boasts too that the Leap produced, in 1958 alone, millions and millions of poems and songs. These products, both in themselves as art and in their way and manner of accomplishment, should reveal a picture of how the mental life, or, more precisely, how the mental as well as physical energy of the nation is being vigorously mobilized, organized and directed. For, as much of the steel was, regardless of its quality, produced in "backyard furnaces," so are myriads of these poems and songs, regardless of their aesthetics, made by farm teams in the fields, workers in the factories, and laborers building roads or bridges. The people are goaded and urged, instructed and inspired by tireless party cadres who exhort all social and racial groups that, among other purposes, there has to be a new epoch of poetry production to celebrate the new era in Chinese history. There is enough evidence to show that the phenomenal, *quantitative* success is real. And the immediate effect of this success may be readily observed as therapeutic. It is as if the gasping, agonizing interjections of "ai-ya! ai-yo!" of men, and of women too, under the back-crushing weight of iron or earth were transformed into facilely rhythmic, and, more important, "ideologically correct" words, which they are told to recite or sing pridefully as their own invention. . . . One example out of myriads, from a song purportedly by peasants in Shensi Province, goes like this:

> Each year our farm production grows
> Grains and cotton pile up mountain high, Hurrah!
> Eat the grain, but don't forget the sower,
> The Communist Party's our Ma and Pa.

This song, like myriads of others of its kind, was supposed to have been derived from old jingles of folk poetry, through the advocated process of *t'ui ch'en ch'u hsin,* or "Push Along the Old to Derive the New," which was both a goal and a condition for the *pai hua ch'i fang,* or "Hundred Flowers Blooming Together," when the slogan was first issued by Mao around 1951, as we have earlier noted. Here we have an example of how, through this process, the artificial flowers were manufactured, with the party's

[36] In *The China Quarterly* No. 3, 1960.

machinations, the cadres' zeal, and the mass psychology thus manipulated. In 1960, when what could have been natural flowers had, since 1957, been nipped in the bud or exterminated as "poisonous weeds," Chou Yang was able to report the blooming of those artificial flowers on even a much grander scale. In his "Road of Our Country's Socialist Literature and Art," which is a long address to the Third Congress of Chinese Literary and Art Workers, he sings the most eloquent panegyric to the "Hundred Flowers" policy which has now produced what the party wished. Homage, of course, has to be paid first to Chairman Mao's infallible wisdom for initiating the policy. Then, he goes on, "This policy has promoted the development of multifarious varieties in all kinds of art and literature, and renovations of ancient tradition. . . . We have rejuvenated several hundreds of provincial dramatic forms which were dying out, brought anew to daylight myriads of librettos of folk plays, recorded, rearranged, and published every race's folk songs, folk epics, and folk tales in quantities as immense as the misty sea, supported and developed rich and colorful folk music, dances, and fine arts. We have opened one treasury after another of national folk art creation long since buried; we have cleaned and dusted all, so that, shining under the thought of Marxism, good flowers preserved and rid of weeds, each becomes brilliantly new and yields lights that dazzle the eye. Many superior traditional operas, musicals, vaudeville shows, puppet shows, and shadow-plays, after rearrangements and revisions have won the praise of vast audiences." Obviously, no simple restoration or revival, but, by rearrangements and revisions, "derivation of the new out of the old" was the party's overriding concern, with sometimes such extreme results as the new puerilely servile song from Shensi which we have quoted.

A predominant note in Chou Yang's address is strong nationalism. National form, national tradition, and national style are repeatedly emphasized, in conjunction with Collectivism among the national masses as a single criterion to guide literary values, which must furthermore be directed against internal and foreign enemies and for the conquest of nature, including human nature. "Nationalization and popularization," *min-tsu hua* and *ch'ün-chung hua*, seem to be inseparable slogans for art and literature. Even all foreign forms and other elements of foreign art and literature, including those from the "brotherly socialist countries," must undergo a manufacturing process of "reform, redigestion, and tincture of national colors"[37] to appeal to the broadest national masses.

As for the creativity of the individual artist or writer, according to the present "Hundred Flowers" policy and its vastly "successful" practice, his individuality is reduced to less than nil. It becomes a negative asset, when so much demand is made on him on the one hand to submerge himself under timeless national tradition and emerge with its renovation under strict party direction; and on the other he must lose and identify himself with an abstract class of several hundred millions of workers, peasants, and soldiers. The lives of these millions are supposed to be the only great reality that he must feel and must deal with. Yet still more is demanded of him as a non-individual. For there is the dictate of the "joining of Revolutionary Romanticism with Revolutionary Realism," credited again as "another great contribution of Comrade Mao to the Marxist theory of art and literature" in the all-powerful pundit Chou Yang's pronouncement.[38] This "Revolutionary Romanticism" is frankly defined by Chou Yang as "Revolutionary Idealism," as if philosophical idealism, anathema to dialectical materialism, as the writer must have sedulously learned in his schooling under Communist indoctrination, was now transformed by the magic epithet "revolutionary" into a holy concept. Under the new dictates, the writer or artist must now not only have "high regard for advanced thinking and scientific prophecy," but also "for the immense significance of revolutionary fantasy."[39] For him there is always a whole distant fantastic world of the brilliant future of communism on which he must fix his gaze and produce his art. But, failing this, if his work were to imply criticism of the present unwelcome reality such as tragic conflicts, suffering, starvation, and dark despair in a Communist society, it would be degeneration or treason. Anyone upholding nineteenth-century critical realism is again and again denounced as guilty of revisionism, degeneration, or treason. And as models for his characters, there is imposed on him a positive hero who does not quite belong to the present but to the future, who "always marches on, always marches foremost ahead of life."[40]

So not only have the ingeniously artificial "Hundred Flowers"

[37] Chou Yang, *op. cit.*, p. 14.
[38] *Ibid.*, p. 17.
[39] *Ibid.*, p. 18.
[40] *Ibid.*

continued to spread all over the mainland to glorify the present
but they are projected indefinitely into the visionary future. Chou
Yang's "Report to the Third Congress" is a remarkable document,
perhaps the most authoritative and revealing description, however hyperbolical in style, of the conditions of the cultural climate. A good contrast with conditions in the Soviet land of
intermittent "Thaw" is provided by the *Kommunist* (No. IX of
1964), in an article entitled "Against Dogmatism and Vulgarism
in Art and Literature," which is a piece of ruthless criticism of
Chou Yang's very "Report" itself. So much so that the Chinese
government organ, the *People's Daily*, has, in turn, reprinted this
article to "expose" Soviet "smear tactics." The Chinese have since
1964 been collecting "anti-Chinese propaganda" from the Soviet
Union, and counted "more than 1300 pieces of this in the months
of April, May, and June alone."[41] These were released by the
Chinese press with captions and running commentaries to warn
the people of foreign danger and to rouse their patriotism, and
perhaps also to forestall any uncontrollable response if these
criticisms should filter through from other sources.

The *Kommunist* article deserves special attention because it
might show how deep the Sino-Soviet split has gone, far beyond
mere political and economic conflicts of interest. There are indications of even two different world views, and different concepts
of human life in terms of literary values. The Soviets, of course,
first of all have to claim the authentic mantle of Marxism-Leninism, by calling the Chinese "dogmatist" and "factionalist" in their
art and literarature, as well as in their political ideology, to
counter the Chinese name-calling of the Soviets as "revisionist."
The *Kommunist* article takes to task the Chinese militant nationalism, "war fervor," as expressed in art and literature. The
"Hundred Flowers" slogan, as the *Kommunist* sees it, has been "a
notorious slogan to everyone's knowledge." It is, as it stands now,
in the opinion of the Soviet writer, "an ingenious piece of soph-
istry to justify persecution of the intellectuals in art creation," as
well as an apology for "Chinese nationalism and other erroneous
tendencies." The article attacks the personality cult whereby Mao,
as he is represented in art and literature, "is God and saviour of
all from distress and tribulations." The Soviets are offended by the
"extreme Chinese aversion toward the realistic representations in
art and literature of the Soviet people's life," whereas the Chinese

[41] *JMJP*, July 13, 1964.

"joining of Revolutionary Romanticism to Revolutionary Realism is a pretense, a sign of fear of reality, fear to stare squarely at truth."

What is especially noteworthy is the Soviet attack on the Chinese "anti-humanism" in their "ingenious policy" and their disregard for individuality and human happiness.

The Chinese leaders, to carry the slogans into absolute practice, in fact need individuality that is characterized by total lack of individuality. To the Chinese theorists, to depict anyone's individual personal fortune is revisionist. They want not to reveal the complex spiritual world of the individual, but are, in fact, exhorting the representation of the characterless masses.

The Soviet criticism is particularly severe on the present Chinese ideal positive hero, Lei Feng, who was exalted in a nationwide movement known as the "Learn from Lei Feng Movement," as we have earlier noted. "Lei Feng is not a human being," according to the Soviet observation. "He is just mechanically putting into practice the will of someone else, 'Mao Tse-tung's cog or screw.' "

Upon reflection, we can realize that a great deal of what *Kommunist,* and the Soviet literary press in general, say of Chinese art and literature now was thought or said of the Soviet not too long ago in the Western world. But today, on close examination, we can no longer regard this Soviet criticism of the Chinese as a case of the pot calling the kettle black. Actual cases can illustrate the sharp contrast, at least as regards the individual human personality. In his *A Precocious Autobiography,* Yevtushenko in the Soviet Union now can say:

Poetry is a vindictive woman who never forgives a lie . . . nor anything less than the truth. . . . What I have in mind is not only the substitution of the "we" for "I" preached by the Proletcult—the "we" that drummed and thundered from the printed page drowning out the music, subtle and unique, of the individual human personality. Long after the disintegration of the movement, many poems written in the first person singular still bore the hallmark of that gigantic stage prop "we." The poet's "I" was purely formal. Even the simple words "I love" were sometimes in so abstract, so oratorical a voice that they might have been "we love." . . . [But] when Mayakovsky says "we," he is still Mayakovsky. Pasternak's "I" is the "I" of Pasternak.[42]

[42] Y. Yevtushenko, *A Precocious Autobiography* (New York: Dutton, 1963), pp. 11–13.

. . . poets visited factories and construction sites but wrote more about machines than about the men who made them work. If machines could read, they might have found such poems interesting. Human beings did not.[43]

By contrast, Li Chi, one of the most successful Chinese poets today and, in a sense, a Chinese counterpart of Yevtushenko in stature, sees in the lighted towers in an oil field an artificial "Romantic" landscape, over which "a kind of tower-shaped constellation was added to the sky," and he declared:

> In the face of this exquisite, splendid night scene,
> How can your young heart not be aroused?
> Offer your youth that burns like flame,
> And jump forward, into the radiant Collectivity."[44]

Many more contrasts like these can surely still be found. And the *Kommunist* article is one instance to show how the land of intermittent "Thaw" and the country of the artificial "Hundred Flowers" are reacting to each other in the realm of art and culture. Artificial flowers, contrived against nature and human nature, may never manifest the true condition of the natural soil beneath, or how the human heart really feels in their midst. But their riotous colors at least for the present are impressive enough, or even intoxicating enough, to the Chinese leaders to make them think that their success that now crowns the whole gigantic spiral of their series of cultural campaigns is real. But at the same time, the Chinese leaders have to guard these "artificial" flowers more and more jealously against the "thawing" ground which might intermittently spread across the Siberian border. Also, however, would their specious colors, winterproof, become attractive to certain Soviet sectors where a new freeze is desired; or would such criticism of them as *Kommunist* has made become salutary warnings to the Soviets as well, and help the "Thaw" to continue more in earnest at home?

[43] *Ibid.*, pp. 75–76.
[44] Li Chi, *Nan-wang-ti ch'un-t'ien*, or *Unforgettable Spring* (Peking: Jen-min ch'u-pan she, 1959), p. 109.

The Revelation of St. Boris:
Russian Literature and Individual Autonomy

SIDNEY MONAS

ART AND SOCIETY

IN THIS paper I propose to discuss the extent and limits of the renewed concern for individual autonomy, privacy, and freedom in Russian literature, not in the light of official controls—these have been and are being widely discussed elsewhere—but rather in terms of certain currents and impulses I believe to be inherent in Russian literature itself. In some ways, these drive freedom on; in others, inhibit and limit it. I mean to suggest rather than to define the territory and the problems. I would like to begin by rehearsing some loose impressions of the relationship between art and society current in our own culture.

We do not regard art as altogether purposeless, but we do tend to regard its purpose as rather mysterious, and art and the artists as, to some degree, independent of moral claims that are exerted from elsewhere in the society. The relationship is an uneasy one, and the independence is at most never absolute. But art has shaken loose from the religious teleology of the Middle Ages and also from the moral didacticism of the eighteenth century. We no longer believe, like Alexander Pope, that the poet should be *representative*, should strive to represent the common opinions of his society, like a Congressman—"What oft was thought, but ne'er so well expressed"—yet we become a little restive, and eventually maybe even indifferent if he strays too far.

In the artist's commerce with his public, we expect a certain tension. Between them is the work of art. Implicit in the work of art is an *imaginary* audience different from the public as it actually exists. In the words of a contemporary American poet;

255

"The poem is creating the audience for the poem."[1] Sometimes the distance between the real, bourgeois public and the imaginary audience the poet is trying to create is so enormous the mind spins and standards collapse, because there is no way of reaching the intention or bridging the gap. Autonomy becomes unintelligibility, and communication breaks down.

Since the time of Napoleon, military metaphors have crept into talk about art. We speak of an *avant-garde* with which a "main body" will presumably someday catch up. We speak of the artist "conquering" new areas of experience. For Nietzsche, art, or at least tragedy, which he thought the highest form of art, is where "what is warlike in our soul celebrates its Saturnalia."[2] Sometimes it is experience that is conquered, sometimes the public, sometimes both audience and artist participate in a common conquest.

A number of metaphors are not directly military, but still imply struggle, tension, "wrestling with the angel." Some are passive and imply a kind of ravishment by, or self-sacrifice to, psychic forces. Keats spoke of "negative capability." Jung writes: "Art is a kind of innate drive that seizes a human being and makes him its instrument. The artist is not a person endowed with free will who seeks his own ends, but one who allows art to realize its purposes through him. . . . It is not Goethe who creates *Faust,* but *Faust* which creates Goethe."[3] Thus, in relation to society the artist may sometimes strut like a hero back from the wars; but in actual combat, he is helpless and merely endures the battle. In the crowd, Big Ego; home at his desk, he has between himself and the universe almost no skin at all.

Nietzsche and Jung are both very much part of what John Bayley has called in our literature "the romantic survival."[4] They do not altogether disregard society, but for them art is essentially something that takes place between the artist (the product of his culture and of his society, to be sure) and the dark forces of the unconscious. Not necessarily contradictory, but somewhat differ-

[1] Louis Simpson, "Confessions of an American Poet," *New York Times Magazine,* May 2, 1965, p. 110.
[2] Friedrich Nietzsche, "Twilight of the Idols," trans. W. Kaufman, *The Viking Portable Nietzsche* (New York: Viking Press, 1954), p. 530.
[3] Carl G. Jung, *Modern Man in Search of a Soul* (New York: Harvest Books, 1955), p. 169.
[4] John Bayley, *The Romantic Survival* (London: Constable, 1957).

ent emphases come from Marx and Engels on the one hand, Freud on the other.

Peter Demetz has recently written an extremely interesting book, *Marx, Engels und die Dichter*, in which he demonstrates at considerable length that Marxism does not necessarily lead to socialist realism. He points out also the vital connection between Marx and Engels and romantic literary figures like Gutzkow, Boerne, and Carlyle, whom Engels translated. Neither Marx nor Engels favored didacticism in literature; they did not advocate a positive hero or an insight into the unfolding of the rosy socialist future. In a number of works, both Marx and Engels, though they connected literature with the "superstructure" of society, took pains to give it a certain autonomy.[5] It is true, however, that both Marx and Engels logically and inevitably associate art with the division of labor, civilization, and civil society, so that in Marxist terms it has to be seen as an aspect of repression and alienation— a compensatory aspect perhaps but fatally connected. I quote from Engels' most profound, most poetic and touching work: "From its first day to this, sheer greed was the driving spirit of civilization; wealth and again wealth and once more wealth; wealth, not of society, but of the single scurvy individual—here was its one and final aim. If at the same time the progressive development of science and a repeated flowering of supreme art dropped into its lap, it was only because without them modern wealth could not have completely realized its achievements."[6] In the new society art will be replaced by the full flowering of the individual, whose very life will become a work of art, and who will therefore have no need of the estranged and alienated perspective of "civilized" art.

Freud's enormous respect for art is beyond dispute, as is the delicacy of his own artistic sensibility. While he shares their capacity for appreciation, he does not, as Marx and Engels do, consciously and deliberately, look forward to the future abolition or utter absorption of art. Nevertheless, like Marx and Engels, he tends to view art as a product of repression. Art is a form of sublimation, which is "successful" repression; yet it is inseparable from that "unsuccessful" repression which leads to neurosis,

[5] Peter Demetz, *Marx, Engels und die Dichter* (Stuttgart: Deutsche Verlags-Anstalt, 1959).

[6] Friedrich Engels, *The Origins of the Family, Private Property and the State* (New York: New World Paperback, 1964), p. 161.

aggression, and war. For about thirty years now, a number of writers on art and literature have tried to combine the insights of Marx and Freud—from Christopher Caudwell to Edmund Wilson. Only recently, however, two of them, Herbert Marcuse and Norman O. Brown, have drawn the logical conclusion that in a society without repression—*if* Marx and Freud are correct—art would wither away.[7]

Within the arts themselves, we have seen something like an anti-art movement, beginning with Dadaism and extending to the "happenings" of our own day. There have always been dissident "Bohemian" movements in the arts, at least since modern times, which, in assaulting the conventions of established schools, assault the conventions of the established classes of society as well, tend to associate themselves with democratic, radical political movements, to undermine "sacred cows," attack sacrosanct traditions, and in general make the atmosphere of art less stuffy, exclusive, aristocratic. As they succeed, they tend to become absorbed into the society they began by attacking. One generation's rebels are the academicians of the next. The Dadaists set out to be extremely destructive; they wished to destroy the very notion of "art" as something set apart and on a pedestal or in a frame. Yet before long they were considered "artists." The "happenings" are intended to lead art back into daily life, to inspire audiences to participate in and look upon the life around them with the kind of energy and attention they have been devoting to works of art. Yet the overall effect has been—or at least so it seems to me—not to make art more democratic, but rather less so; and Rauschenberg is in the museums.

The Russians, though they participate with us in a common culture, are less advanced in these matters than we are. Except for a relatively brief, wildly experimental period in the arts between 1909 and 1921, Russia has tended to be slightly archaic, somewhat of the past, especially in literature. This may turn out to be, as it once was, what saves it from exhaustion.

PUSHKIN'S TWO MUSES

In the last chapter of Pushkin's novel *The Captain's Daughter*, there is a scene in which Maria Ivanovna confronts the Empress,

[7] Norman O. Brown, *Life Against Death* (Middletown: Vintage Books, 1959); Herbert Marcuse, *Eros and Civilization* (Boston: Beacon Press, 1955).

Catherine II. She is on a self-imposed mission to plead for the life of her fiancé, unjustly condemned to lifetime exile in Siberia for his alleged participation in the Pugachev uprising, and she pretends not to know who the buxom lady is. Victor Shklovsky has pointed out that the Empress as she appears in this scene comes straight out of Utkin's engraving of one of her official portraits; her unseasonable attire emphasizes the artificiality of her pose and introduces a note of parody.[8] The entire scene and its sequel are highly stylized. They suggest the deliberately arranged pastoral dream of Arcadia in which Marie Antoinette (among others) used to play milkmaid.

Maria Ivanovna is no less stylized. If Catherine represents the muse of Empire playing at mercy and sentiment and spontaneity, at being a rococo shepherdess, Maria Ivanovna represents a real shepherdess—the daughter of a provincial garrison captain— playing at the same game. Behind her play, however, there is real earnestness of purpose: the life of her fiancé hangs in the balance.

In one of his very early poems, Pushkin writes of the private nature of his muse, his *tainaia devka,* and the rural place where she visits him secretly to give him lessons on "the seven-stopped flute" of pastoral. His most imposing heroines are associated with this muse, from the central figure of "Mistress into Maid" to Maria Ivanovna and Tatiana. In Stanza V, Canto VIII of *Onegin,* Pushkin tells of how he sought his muse literally among wild shepherd tribes only to find her on a provincial Russian landowner's estate, appearing as Tatiana: "She'd visited the quiet tents of nomad tribes in the depths of brooding Moldavia; among them, she grew wild, forgot godly speech, for those undeveloped, unfamiliar tongues, for the songs of the steppe dear to her. . . . Suddenly, everything around became transformed, and there she was in my garden, a provincial miss with a pensive look in her eye; a small paperbound French book in her hand." Just as the provincial estate of Tatiana's parents is a place halfway between the stylized Arcadia of European pastoral (as Nabokov has pointed out) and the fields Tolstoy's Levin watered with his sweat—so Tatiana, with her pale broodiness and her bookish melancholy is part of the process of transformation from the stylized shepherdess of conventional sentiment to the Natasha

[8] Viktor Shklovsky, *Zametki o proze russkikh klassikov* (Moscow, 1955), pp. 47–53.

who dominates the poetic atmosphere of the Rostov household and in whom, Tolstoy tells us, "body and soul are one."

For the moment, in the garden at Tsarskoe Selo, the "private muse" and the "muse of Empire" share a common convention, a common language. The real shepherdess, simple, faithful, modest, spontaneous, distinguished by her delicate but unobtrusive feelings, is nevertheless not without a touch of Machiavel. The Empress, for all of what Pushkin referred to elsewhere as "the cruel reality of her despotism," plays at delicacy of feeling, assumes the role of her own official portrait. She pardons the fiancé and spares him a life of Siberian exile. It should be pointed out that the fiancé is also the narrator, and hence the poet's surrogate; indeed, that is about the only character he has.[9]

Pushkin believed that good prose, unlike poetry, which he thought could afford to be somewhat more discursive, had to be "brief and precise" and loaded with "meanings" (*smysli*); and so I feel to some extent justified in expanding the meaning of this brief scene beyond the confines of the novel in which it occurs, in terms of Pushkin's associations, as expressed elsewhere.

Empire: for Pushkin, power and civilization together; Westernization, but on Russia's terms; *independent* civilization. All this is implied in the apostrophe to Petersburg that opens *The Bronze Horseman*, reminiscent, in its pomp and splendor, of the odes of Derzhavin. Poetry had been born at court, and the court poets sang full-throated praise of their Imperial mother. A brilliant Soviet ironist, Abram Tertz, and a scholar, Gukovsky, have called attention to the similarity between eighteenth-century patriotic and didactic verse and socialist realism.[10] Poetry praised Empire which had created the possibility of civilization in Russia. But civilization did not mean power alone: it meant also tradition, honor, welfare, privacy, family life, and a world of subtle and spontaneous human feelings.

This the world of lyric and pastoral, the world of the private muse. The worlds have different muses, but the common symbol

[9] It would seem evident, as Shklovsky suggests, that Pushkin, consciously or unconsciously, invested his real feelings about the Imperial order—which had at least a touch of restless, threatening, frustrated rebelliousness—not in the utterly conventional and merely convenient narrator but in the much more interesting "villain" of the piece, the turncoat nobleman, Shvabrin.

[10] Abram Tertz, *On Socialist Realism* (New York: Pantheon Books, 1960).

of their interdependence is Russian literature itself. Pushkin was the singer of Empire and freedom, as G. P. Fedotov once put it.[11] Yet as he grew older, Pushkin became aware of a tragic incompatibility between the two worlds. Evgenii of *The Bronze Horseman* aspired only to ". . . a table, two chairs, a pot of cabbage soup, and I my own master . . ." as did Pushkin himself. It is a dream that is denied Evgenii by the flood that drowns his sweetheart. He has a sudden insight into the cost of Empire and the arbitrariness of Imperial will. Yet he is himself so much the product of that will, his domestic dream and its poetry had been so utterly dependent on its benevolence, that his weak and momentary impulse to revolt dissolves in the very gesture and he goes mad. The statue of the horseman comes to life in his mind and seems to drive him into the Neva.

The private muse presided over Russian literature for decades to come, over prose as well as poetry; indeed, primarily over prose; over the greatest prose works of art produced in the nineteenth century. Her origins in pastoral should not be forgotten. The pastoral critique of urban ways is built into Russian literature at its very foundation.

The city is not only loud, gregarious, and corrupt; the specific quality of its corruption consists of a false rationality, based on the ego, the rationality of Economic Man and cost accounting, bourgeois rationality. The city is the place where careers are made and where military and police power are organized. Life is based on hard calculation, yet fundamentally it is irrational, divorced from the traditional, moral rationality of rural life. Those who try to bring to the world of the city the Edenic dream of the Russian countryside are defeated, disillusioned, and crushed as Pushkin's Evgenii was crushed by the monster within their own minds.

Oblomov cannot bring Oblomovka to St. Petersburg; in the upper reaches of the bureaucratic hierarchy, Kalinovich grows corrupt for all his good intentions; Raskolnikov, standing on a bridge over the waters of the Neva which are the waters of death, feels encroaching upon him the depressing melancholy of the beautiful, artificial city that has replaced the idyl of his childhood; with the energy and thought he has amassed in the country, Prince Andrei plays out to the point of disillusion the brilliant

11 G. P. Fedotov, "Pushkin, pevets Imperii i svobody," in *Novyi grad* (New York, 1952).

game of his career under Speransky; finally, in Biely's great hoax of a novel, *Peterburg*, the statue of the horseman pours itself in molten bronze down the throat of a double agent. The metropolitan city, symbol of power and civilization, paradigm of the intellectualized ego, the autonomous and alienated individual, paradoxically destroys the self that it asserts, breaks down the walls of individuality, undermines the authenticity of the individual, and drives him either to defeat, suicide, and destruction, or (literally or metaphorically) back to the Russian countryside, where, Antaeus-like, he may take fresh strength from the earth for a new beginning.

The Russian pastoral is not without its counterparts in Western Europe. There is a sense in which, for example, Flaubert's *Un coeur simple* might be considered a Russian novel. The pastoral critique of civil society is hardly limited to Russia! Even European sociology, let alone the novel, participated in this critique, as witness Engels' *Origins of the Family, etc.*, F. Toennies' *Gemeinschaft und Gesellschaft* and a number of other works. It is largely a question of emphasis and degree. The pastoral element is much stronger in Russian literature.

Unlike the American, the Russian literary landscape is essentially human. It is inhabited, settled, and its settlements have a close identity with the land itself, reaching far back into time. It is not "wild nature" from which man is alienated and to which he longs to return to be made whole. It is the landscape of poor villages, of Holy Russia.[12] When self-knowledge, self-fulfillment, self-revelation come to people in the European or the American novel, they come outside the scope of community, outside society, either in confrontation with wild nature, or with or against some other separate individual or individuals, in the teeth of a hostile society. In the Russian novel self-knowledge may come while separate from society, as to Prince Andrei under the sky at Austerlitz or to Ivan Il'ich on his deathbed, but self-fulfillment is always conceived in communal terms; in terms of the creation of a spontaneous human community, the model for which is the family, living in some kind of close connection with the landscape and the seasons. Even when family life (and life in the countryside, too) is depicted as horrible or terrifying—as it often is—the horror is seen against the implicit norm. I think this is true of

[12] On "Holy Russia," see Michael Cherniavsky, *Tsar and People* (New Haven: Yale University Press, 1960), pp. 101–27.

even so seemingly "detached" a story as Chekhov's "Peasants." In Dostoevsky, the ruin of the family as an institution means that its relationships must be recreated among all men—"All men are brothers," as in the late parable of Tolstoy.

Throughout Russian literature of the classic period runs an opposing set of images, two chains of association. On the one hand: the city, the state bureaucracy, calculated self-interest, power, self-aggrandizement, ratiocination, stagnant air, stifling rooms, artificiality, high society, rank, social prestige, aggression, vanity, self-will, intellectual pride. On the other hand: fresh air, trees, earth, water, the seasons, the "folk," family, tradition, kinship, community, a love for created beings, poetry, the acceptance of suffering, and the free and spontaneous play of the emotions.[13] Individual autonomy and integrity are seen to consist of detaching oneself from the first chain of associations and attaching oneself to the second. The poeticized family is potentially extendable to all of Russia, or even all humanity. Without this poetic potentiality the family remains the realm of *poshlost'*; without the familial strain, there can be no real poetry.

The realm least suitable for the private muse is the state, the chanceries of the state bureaucracy. Here men outwardly conform but are inwardly alone. The state is the opposite of the family, and hostile to it. It is the realm of ratiocination and self-will, illusion and death. Insofar as state figures appear in a sympathetic light (and there are few who do) they carry with them into the unfavorable atmosphere of the chanceries something of the Christian acceptingness of Platon Karataev, something at once priestlike, sacrificial, and familial, and rather foreign to the style of the world they inhabit. I refer primarily to Kutuzov in *War and Peace* and Porfiry Petrovich in *Crime and Punishment*. Kutuzov is almost a complete counterpart of Karataev, and is reviled and mocked by those around him. Porfiry is respected, but has nevertheless about him something monkish and awkward. His relation with Raskolnikov goes beyond the official and assumes something of the paternal. Above all, he keeps his role a modest and a secondary one, in spite of temptations to self-assertion.

In *War and Peace*, the opposition between state and family appears most starkly, most articulately and extensively. Curi-

[13] See the highly suggestive article by George Gibian, "Traditional Symbolism in *Crime and Punishment*," PMLA, LXX (1955), 979–96.

ously, the novel was conceived and written over a decade (1857–67) during which the power-state seemed to be demonstrating in the most drastic and spectacular manner that it was the determining historical force of the era. I refer not only to the cult of Napoleon in France, but to Bismarck and Cavour, the American Civil War, the Second Reform Act in England, the independence of Canada, the creation of the Hapsburg dual monarchy, and last but far from least, the whole complex of Russian legislative reforms that followed from the Emancipation of the serfs. To crown this decade, Tolstoy wrote a book that attempted to demonstrate the utter futility and illusoriness of acts of state and the intentions of statesmen. In the clearest, most commonsensical prose, Tolstoy tells us that history is unknowable.

History is unknowable, not because God chooses to obscure the functions of great men and state institutions, but because neither great men nor state institutions have anything to do with the course of events. God expresses himself not in affairs of state, with their difficulties, complications, and technicalities, but in the most ordinary, familiar, and commonplace events and patterns of everyday life. God's expression is by no means obscure—merely vast and far-reaching in space and time, orchestrated with such extraordinary nuances that no man can hope to understand it in its totality, though its fragments are the most ordinary yet most marvelous stuff of which our lives are made. What the discursive passages do for the narrative passages in *War and Peace* therefore is indirectly to imbue them with the force and magic of destiny. They show, as Hegel said it was the task of philosophy to show: "Here is the rose; dance here."

With its emphasis on community, the family, nature, acceptance of the world as God created it, yet with continually fresh and renewed responses, Russian prose literature could be characterized by its comprehensiveness of form and spontaneity of style. Common colloquial speech is always the standard referred to and played upon, even by such baroque stylists as Gogol and Leskov. As Eric Auerbach has put it, the Russian novel on the whole represents a world view that is essentially Christian in its sense of creatural realism—that magic sense of the miraculous and the eternal about to burst into epiphany in the most ordinary and everyday circumstances: shepherds tending their flocks, or the birth of a child; the fateful junction of the divine with the commonplace—and hence all the more impressive for seeming, when it became known in Europe late in the nineteenth century, a little archaic, a little behind the times.[14]

If the didactic, civilization-affirming, power-sponsored muse of Empire tends to disappear as an important concern and inspiring presence in Russian literature, she bobs up again in a curious and unexpected place: in literary criticism. Of course, the politically radical critics, from Belinsky to Mikhailovsky, opposed the state-order, and in more cases than not were as "populist" in their attitude to the peasant and the village commune as the writers. Their hopes, however, were more rationalist, more affirmative of science and civilization and even of "civil society," though not of the particular form of civil society they perceived in Russia. They were less overtly religious in their outlook, though not in their tone or temper. For them, from Belinsky on, literature was primarily an occasion, an opportunity to speak out on what really mattered, which was not literature but morality. Moralizing critics in the century of Taine and Arnold, Sainte-Beuve and Ruskin, were plentiful elsewhere, too. Belinsky and his heirs were certainly not the only critics to tell writers how they should go about their business or who, like Belinsky in his letter to Gogol, bullied and threatened them with moral excommunication. But in Russia such critics had a special claim on the conscience of both public and writers. In the struggle against the repressive aspects of autocracy, the critics occupied a far more exposed and danger-ous position, and they wielded the power of their impending martyrdom with a holy, self-righteous, and zealous flair. Of course, the radical critics were essentially partisan, and the great writers only incidentally and peripherally so. Both, however, addressed themselves to the *narod*—the vital audience they felt themselves in the process of creating out of the Russian reading public. It was Belinsky who first announced that Russian litera-ture had created the possibilities for human self-awareness for free and meaningful and honest and spontaneous human inter-course that power politics in Russia had failed to create, that the private muse had created a nation, or was on its way to creating a nation where the Imperial muse had failed. The fact that litera-ture was a tiny island of privileged freedom, where the values of individual autonomy, spontaneous and honest expression, and the sincere pursuit of a meaningful morality could enjoy a haven

[14] Erich Auerbach, *Mimesis* (Princeton: Princeton University Press, 1953), pp. 520–24.

amidst the icy blasts of autocracy, the critics insisted, imposed a kind of *littérature oblige,* which writers found extremely difficult to resist, especially within themselves. The critics turned Oblomov into Oblomovism, superfluous men into *the* superfluous man, Yaroslavna and Tatiana and Natasha and Grushenka into *the* strong woman, Bazarov into nihilism, and the writers protested, sometimes vigorously, but in some corner of their souls they capitulated, as even Gogol, I suspect, capitulated to Belinsky. In his youth, Tolstoy ridiculed Chernyshevsky and the critics of the *Contemporary* who tried to lionize him. In his sixties, the guilt-ridden nobleman wrote a long, brilliant essay on art that went far beyond Chernyshevsky in the extent to which it insisted on lacing art into a moral-utilitarian strait jacket. Art was community—a work was art to the degree it could "infect" others, could communicate the expression of a common experience; but it was "good" art only to the extent that it was moral, and it could hardly be moral, as some had it, "in spite of itself"; the artist's intentions must be clear as well as beneficent, and the moral folk tale became the standard for all written art. Not only Shakespeare and the earlier Tolstoy were tried and found wanting by this standard but even large parts of the Bible. Not long after Tolstoy finished *What is Art?* he began the task of clearing the Bible of its "priestly" excrescences, clearing away its obscurities so that "the people" could for the first time understand it in its "true," i.e. purely moral, sense.

By 1897, the year in which *What is Art?* appeared, Pushkin's two muses had inspired a long, complex, and extraordinarily brilliant development. The Imperial muse had left the court for the thick journals, and the private muse seemed affected and cliquish and showed circles of fashionable European weariness under the eyes. One could hardly imagine them sitting on a bench in the same garden. . . .

APOCALYPSE

"All great art," writes Boris Pasternak in *Doctor Zhivago,* "resembles and continues the Revelation of St. John."[15]

St. John of Patmos wrote the Revelation in the second century, when Christian apocalyptic expectations were beginning to fade.

---

[15] This line began to reverberate in my mind and memory after I heard N. O. Brown one evening take off from it into a possible chapter of his forthcoming book. Of course, his use of the line was very different from my own.

The end had not come. In order to stave off disillusion and desiccation of the faith, John translated Christian expectations into a *symbolic* quest for the meaning of the end whenever it might come. In a prolonged and intense meditation on death, he dredged up Christian and pagan symbols, red and green dragons, beasts from the abyss, trumpets and seals, arranged them into the patterns of an esoteric number-symbolism, hoping to replace the expectation that certain events would take place in the external world with the notion that the expectation was its own meaning and bore a sign from God, though the actual "when" and "how" of the events might be a dark matter indeed. I think, at least, that this is what "St. Boris" had in mind: that literature is "a meditation on death in the hope of overcoming death."[16]

Most Russian writers, like the intelligentsia of which they were a part, opposed the Bolshevik revolution. A number, however, tried to come to terms with it, tried to see it in the perspective of a broader vision in which the specifically Bolshevik and Marxist features were assimilated to Russian destiny or to an unknown but dimly perceived human and cultural revolution which was not necessarily the revolution the Bolsheviks carried through, but of which the Bolshevik revolution might be the historic agency. There is something of this in Eurasianism, in the Scythian movement, in the Living Church, in Blok's *The Twelve*, Pilniak's *Naked Year*, and many years later in *Doctor Zhivago*. One of the most eloquent and elegant discussions of the apocalyptic cultural revolution occurs in the "Correspondence Between Two Corners," between M. O. Gershenzon and Viacheslav Ivanov in the summer of 1920.[17]

Both Ivanov and Gershenzon see as "the authentic vessel of reality" the individual. Both believe in some form of personal immortality, though both insist that the "immortal part" has nothing to do with what is conventionally known as "the self," which is a merely contingent social mask, a persona. Both try to find some relationship between culture and the "new rebellion that is shaking the earth . . . striving to free itself from age-old

---

[16] For an interesting recent interpretation of the Book of Revelation, see Austin M. Farrer, *A Rebirth of Images: The Making of St. John's Apocalypse* (London: Dacre Press, 1949); see also D. H. Lawrence, *Apocalypse* (New York: Viking Press, 1932).

[17] M. O. Gershenzon and V. Ivanov, *Perepiska iz dvukh uglov* (Petrograd, 1921); English translation, "A Correspondence Between Two Corners," *Partisan Review*, XV (1948), pp. 951–65, 1028–48.

complications, from the monstrous fetters of social and abstract ideas. . . ." Ivanov affirms cultural continuity, "Memory, mother of the muses," insisting that a revolution which attempts to abolish inherited cultural forms and start anew will produce not something new but merely a deformed and monstrous version of the old. What prevents cultural forms from becoming stifling and deadening is the ever-present possibility of vertical transcendence, the individual's access to the godhead. His argument resembles at points that of T. S. Eliot in "Tradition and the Individual Talent," where Eliot argues that any tradition "to be inherited, must be made new"; freshness comes from the continuity of culture, not from its disruption.

Gershenzon starts from a personal experience of spiritual weariness and exhaustion. He feels trammeled by the enormous cultural apparatus he carries with him, trapped by the tyranny of logic, ensnared by hollow metaphysical systems. "For me," he writes, "there is prospect of happiness in a Lethean bath that would wash away the memory of all religious and philosophical systems; all scientific knowledge, arts, and poetry could be washed away from the soul without a trace; and then, to re-emerge on the shore, naked as the first man, naked, light, and joyful, stretching freely and lifting to the sky my naked arms, recalling from the past only one thing—how burdensome and stifling were those clothes, how light and free one is without them." Ivanov accuses him of Rousseauistic primitivism; he replies that, like Rousseau, he wants to unburden himself of a dead culture in the hope of being able to create a living one. What Ivanov fails to grasp, he argues, is that the "vertical transcendence" Ivanov relies on as an escape from culture is itself inhibited and actually debilitated and defeated by the desiccation of the religious forms through which, presumably, this transcendence takes place—religious forms which suffer the same creeping death as culture in general.

The further course of the revolution did little to nourish the hopes of either man. It is curious that Gershenzon, who wished to throw off the burden of the past, was a historian by profession; and Ivanov, who defended cultural continuity, had previously played an important role in bringing the cult of Nietzsche (with its anti-historicism) to Russia, and was best known as a difficult, experimental *avant-garde* poet.

In 1918, Alexander Blok urged the Russian intelligentsia to "listen to the music of the Revolution," which he interpreted as an elemental upsurge from the depths of the people and which he, like Gershenzon, hoped would re-energize a "weary, stale, and bookish literature." The revolution, like a storm, teemed with "the new and the unexpected." The intelligentsia, unlike the bourgeoisie, was hindered by no worldly chattels or vested interests from affirming this new and unknown force. Blok urged it to "tune in" on the Revolution.

Three years later he struck a somewhat different note. Speaking on the anniversary of Pushkin's death and not long before his own death, Blok denounced those who were trying to harness the poet to tasks that were external to poetry. The poet's role, he insisted, was not to "instruct his brethren" but to bring rhythms from "primal chaos" and embody them in language. Those who tried to make out of the institutions of the state "one organ alone, the censorship," had been called by Pushkin "the high-society mob," Blok said. Then he went on, and he was no longer speaking of Pushkin: "Let them beware of a worse epithet, those officials who are trying to direct poetry into channels of their own, infringing on her inner freedom and preventing her from fulfilling her mysterious calling." The aims of art could not be known, and to attempt to interfere with the poet's "fancy" (*prikhot'*), his imagination, his *private* freedom, was worse than censorship.[18]

Gershenzon and Ivanov had been entirely private figures. Blok was a very influential poet but still essentially a private man. The literary concern that the apocalyptic mood seemed to foster was shared, however, by so prominent a public figure as Trotsky. In a book published three years after Blok's death, *Literature and Revolution,* Trotsky anticipated the official position on literature of the Central Committee of the Party, a position that would hold from 1925 to 1930, and the predominance of RAPP.

It is a remarkable book, brilliantly written, witty, self-assured (perhaps too much so), full of insights any literary critic or social historian might well envy. Deriding the notion that a socialist revolution should strive to produce a proletarian art, it seems anti-doctrinaire. Proletarian art Trotsky views as an interesting and instructive but relatively weak sister beside older traditions. He

---

[18] The two pieces referred to may be found in Alexander Blok, *Sobranie Sochinenii* (Moscow-Leningrad, 1960–62), Vol. VI.

sees the production of a great culture and a great art as the purpose of history, the purpose and hope of the October Revolution. Ultimately, he says, every society will be judged by the culture it creates. "Communist man . . . will develop all the vital elements of contemporary art to the highest point. . . . The forms of life will become dynamically dramatic. The average human type will rise to the heights of an Aristotle, a Goethe, or a Marx. And above this ridge new peaks will rise." One may criticize this as Marxism, but its messianic splendor is genuine and clear.

There were some more ominous notes. Although Trotsky mentions casually in passing that Freud and psychoanalysis might ultimately be reconcilable with Marxism, it is the party that "will have to look into it," and it is the party that will decide. Throughout, he celebrates consciousness at the expense of "blind, elemental forces," at the expense of the unconscious. He sees progress in history not in terms of the achievement of harmony between the conscious and unconscious in man, but rather in terms of the conquest of the unconscious, step by step, by reason and the will; he seeks not coexistence with the unconscious but total domination, the triumph of the will, a *fully* conscious and completely transparent art. If such a thing can be imagined, it is difficult to see how it would differ from socialist realism, or why it should. "The art of this epoch will be entirely under the influence of the revolution," he says. It requires "a new self-consciousness" and is incompatible with obscurity of any kind, mystical or romantic; "collective man must become sole master, and the limits of his power are determined only by his knowledge of natural forces and his capacity to use them."

What Trotsky most wholeheartedly admires in art belongs either to the past or the future, especially the latter. Of the present he is extremely skeptical. Many of his critical remarks on his contemporaries are shrewd and true, yet behind them lurks the assumption that the true poets of the time are the Bolsheviks, poets in revolution rather than verse, but much more creative than the literary variety and far more to be admired. A society must, according to Trotsky, ultimately be judged by the art it produces, yet society itself is the ultimate art form. The Bolsheviks are better poets than the poets, and the function of the latter must therefore be subordinate, a secondary one, "to haul away the rubbish and police the streets," as Blok would have put it. Trotsky's artistic insights and his own poetic flair went far beyond that of any "culture commissar" who was to succeed him; yet even he found little room for any conception of creative freedom that ran counter to his own.

THE CONSPIRACY OF FEELINGS

Andrei Babichev, "the great sausage-maker," mutters over the sleeping figure of his foster son Volodia, the absolute technocrat and true man of the future. "If everyone were a technician, wickedness, vanity and other petty feelings would disappear. . . ." Kavalerov, whom Andrei has tossed out, has taken refuge with Andrei's brother, Ivan, and hears him talk in turn of "shaking the heart of a burned-out era." Ivan Babichev wants to muster "the representatives of what you call the old world. I mean feelings like jealousy, love for a woman, vanity. I want to find a blockhead so I can show you: look, comrades, here's an instance of that human state called stupidity. . . . To me has fallen the honor of conducting the last parade of the ancient human passions. . . ."

These are passages from Olesha's great forlorn novella of the twenties, *Envy*, the story of the futile and absurd "conspiracy of feelings" against the gleaming, entwining, sterile, collectively euphoric utopia that is leaping up about and around Kavalerov and Ivan Babichev, and against which they have no chance. The sausage-maker is obviously right. He has everything but language on his side. Kavalerov and Ivan Babichev have nothing but language: wonderful, spinning, burning, gleaming words, out of which they make a secret weapon of malice and revenge— "Ophelia." But even Ophelia turns against them in the end and they lapse into indifference. The reader, however, is indifferent only to the other pair, for it remains painfully clear that the shining Volodia is nobody anyone would ever like to be.

So it was with the other great revolutionary writers of this time; with Mayakovsky and Babel, and even the grand old man, Gorky. They wanted wholeheartedly to affirm the revolution and the wholly rational world the revolution seemed to promise. They tried to kill the Kavalerov and the Ivan Babichev in themselves. It wasn't easy.

Mayakovsky didn't want to foster his private feelings, which were anyway, like his ego, "too big for him." He wanted to "turn himself inside out," make himself "all mouth." Not only did he write placards and posters and advertisements; he wanted to make poetry itself into a placard and a poster for the new world in which the torture of privacy would become definitively outmoded. He not only wanted to abolish those domestic parlors where stale, trite thoughts sat like lackeys on overstuffed couches; he wanted to abolish the privacy that had produced these monsters. The idea of poetry on a pedestal tormented him. Forgetting what happened to indiscreet poets who addressed monuments, he asked Pushkin to come off his pedestal but did not really know how to entertain the stone guest. He made his life into a public spectacle. The primping and pampering and rococo posturing of the Bayans and the Elsevera Renaissances of this world fascinated and revolted him. He did not want to be like that. He wanted above all to be ordinary, to be human, to be part of everyone else. His apotheosis to Lenin was based on the consideration that Lenin was "the most ordinary man." He wanted poetry to be a social, sociable task. "My job's like any other," he told his imaginary tax collecter. Even his suicide note turned into a poem and began with self-mocking irony: "She loves me? She loves me not?" Identifying with Prisypkin-Skripkin, he wanted to eliminate this bedbug-self and turn into mankind. Yet in the end it was the future that became unreal, a never-never land of cold, sterile chrome and glass against which echoed a human bedbug's genuine cry of pain.

Gorky belonged to an older generation, but in his work too the conspiracy of feelings mustered arms against a self-willed and self-imposed utopianism. As Erik Erikson has pointed out, Gorky's autobiography is an account of how he liberated himself from that great-souled temptress, his grandmother, whose universal compassion and acceptance of her own suffering were so much in the tradition of the Russian heroine.[19] She was beautiful and attractive; but she accepted all the brutalities of her environment and seemed to call on him to accept them, too. It was not to be accepted, but overcome. Later, Tolstoy assumed for Gorky when he thought back on him the guise his grandmother had assumed in *Childhood*. From both he had learned beauty; both urged upon him a passivity he wanted to break. Gorky could not stomach the doctrine of Christian acceptance, yet whenever he is not thinking

[19] Erik Erikson, *Childhood and Society* (New York: Norton, 1963), pp. 359–402.

about it, he slips naturally into an attitude of passive receptivity, alert but unassertive.

For Gorky, liberation came through book learning, and book learning so strenuously acquired that it almost *had* to seem useful to justify itself. Book learning that merely accentuated or deepened or framed suffering, or added to the bewilderment, could be a terrible and pathetic thing, as with Lyuba in *Foma Gordeev*. Gorky drew back instinctively from an aesthetic view of literature. If he could not *do* anything for people, he wanted to be able to inspire them to do something for themselves. At the turn of the century, when almost all important literature was a literature of despair, he tried to sound optimistic. Chekhov accused him of being "literary" and highfalutin. It was true, and he tried to become simpler; but the one thing he really could not stand was the notion he might be useless. Once during his youth when he had suspected this might be the case, he had tried to kill himself. Gorky regarded this as shameful, and mentions it only in passing in his autobiography.[20] Yet of all his literary creations the only ones that live and have resonance in the imagination are the "useless" ones, who suffer and are defeated by suffering and who struggle to be able to accept life as it is rather than to make life good. The grandmother, all those magnificent tormented women in *Foma Gordeev*, that other tormented woman, the Volga, Piotr Artamanov, or that surface-cold but deeply introspective *intelligent*, Klim Samgin, who in pursuit of an authentic personality finds himself unable to make a deep commitment to any of the significant historical movements of his time and whose failure to find integrity and autonomy is expressed in a nightmare in which he sees himself split into a wild number of disparate personalities.[21]

They did not approve of such characters, these writers. But as Olesha identified himself with Kavalerov, Mayakovsky with Prisypkin, so Gorky, too, identified himself with Klim Samgin and was unable to finish the long, fascinating "chronicle" of which

[20] For a luminous understanding of this episode in Gorky's life, see Helen Muchnic, *From Gorky to Pasternak* (New York: Random House, 1961), pp. 79–90.

[21] For an interesting interpretation of *Klim Samgin*, which (outside the Soviet Union) is generally regarded as the most elephantine of Gorky's white elephants, see Juergen Ruehle, *Literatur und Revolution* (Cologne: Kiepenheuer & Witsch, 1960), pp. 38–44; this book also contains chapters on the Chinese left-wing writers and those of other Asian countries.

Klim was the central figure. The case of Isaac Babel is somewhat different.

In his masterpiece, *Red Cavalry*, Babel, or rather his narrator, has a threefold range of identities. First, the Jews of the Pale in their long-suffering and helpless pathos. Both sides in the war ride roughshod over them. It is to root out such human misery that the bespectacled narrator has joined the Cheka and the Red Cavalry. The Jews are his people; he feels a tender irony for them, but steels himself against solicitude. Their pathetic helplessness is almost more than he can bear. The starry-eyed, bookish idealism of Gedali, the rag-and-bone man who longs for an "international of good people" speaks to him, but he must guard against the Gedali within himself. To break the subtle bonds of passive suffering the narrator has committed himself to the present international with all its violence and imperfections.

His second identification is incomplete, but he strives to perfect it. He wants to make himself like the men of power and courage who are fighting the revolution, the Cossacks and the Red commanders. They are crude, savage, violent; but they are doing what needs to be done, and in an epic manner. The narrator tries to make himself as they are, against the intellectual he still is. He tries to be violent and savage in a situation in which violence is more merciful than mercy.

There is yet a third identification. "The wise and beautiful life of Pan Apolek went to my head like an old wine," the narrator writes. Pan Apolek, the drunken artist of the Novograd-Volynsk churches, who sees the poor miserable sinners of these Polish towns and villages as eternal archetypes of good and evil and in his paintings and frescoes creates a powerful and disturbing relationship between the living inhabitants and the long dead of the Bible. He paints people as they are, with recognizable and living features, yet at the same time as archetypes. A local Jewish whore is seen as Mary Magdalene. In the Novograd church, his miraculous virgins break out in sexual sweat at the sight of the men of Savitsky's squadron. Pan Robacki assures the narrator that Pan Apolek will come to no good end. Surely, the Church—or *some* Church—will have him inquisitioned for heresy. Meanwhile, he is Apollo himself, and all that is left of the life of these poor towns is in his pictures.[22]

[22] If not Apollo, at least Orpheus, through whom Apollo spoke.

THE SAUSAGE-MAKER CAPITULATES

The sausage-maker had his wish and the reign of Volodia, the man of steel, settled on the land. Everyone became a technician. First, the production and publication of literature were organized; then, by means of socialist realism literature was inwardly organized. The private muse, like Pasternak's Larissa, became a number and disappeared in one of the innumerable "mixed or women's concentration camps in the far north." Love could be made only to tractors. The emblems, the signs, the symbols, the metaphors, the referents of love, and of nature, too, culled from the classics, combed "systematically" out of old songs and folklore, proverbs, expressions that had soaked in the air around the peasant stove—vernalized, Lysenkoized, rendered purely emblematic—were worked into poetry and prose and produced on a mass basis. All the muses wore a solemn mustache, at which it was death to laugh.

"The growing strength of the positive hero," writes Abram Tertz, "is shown not only in his incredible multiplication—he has far surpassed other kinds of literary character in quantity, put them into the shade and sometimes replaced them altogether. . . . He . . . becomes more and more persuaded of his own dignity, especially when he compares himself to contemporary Western man and realizes his immeasurable superiority. 'But our Soviet man has left them far behind. He is close to the peak while they are still wandering in the foothills'—this is the way simple peasants talk in our novels."[23]

Then Stalin died. "Ah," wrote Tertz, "if only we had been intelligent enough to surround his death with miracles! We could have announced on the radio that he did not die but had risen to Heaven, from which he continued to watch us, in silence, no words emerging from beneath the mystic mustache. His relics would have cured men struck by paralysis or possessed by demons. And children, before going to bed, would have kneeled by the window and addressed their prayers to the cold and shining stars of the Celestial Kremlin."

The undermining had actually set in before Stalin died. Perhaps the first "new" writer was the inobtrusive, unspectacular, but quietly private Vera Panova. Controls remained; but after 1956,

[23] Abram Tertz, *op. cit.,* pp. 53–54.

conviction drained from them. There was unease and bad conscience in the party hierarchy, before the popular disquiet on the one hand, and the disquiet of its own intellectual children on the other. The children were eager to break away from the stereotyped pseudo-culture of their fathers. Literature seemed to offer once again the warmth of a true community, and in spite of many and frequent setbacks, everything seemed to conspire to increase its range.

Even the Sino-Soviet conflict helps loosen the literary bonds. Attacked in August, 1964, in the Chinese press, Voznesensky, Evtushenko, and Akhmadulina were defended in *Izvestia* in the same terms they had used themselves the previous spring against their present defenders.[24] Kochetov, praised by the Chinese as the one genuinely revolutionary writer in Russia, thereupon shook hands with Dudintsev and invited him to contribute his new novel to *Oktiabr'* rather than *Novy mir*.

From Pomerantsev's famous article in December, 1953, to Tvardovsky's recent editorials in *Novy mir*, the persistent concern with sincerity, honesty, authenticity in literature has set up as its all too vulnerable targets the *lakirovanie* (varnishing) and *retushirovanie* (retouching) of Stalinist rhetoric. Indeed, Georg Lukacs to the contrary notwithstanding, there is little left of socialist realism but its title. There are many bad books, as everywhere; but one does not judge the course or nature of a literature by them.

It is one thing to demolish a rhetoric, another to create a new literary language or even to revive an old one. Suddenly, the few grand old men (and one woman) who had survived the Stalin era emerged from obscurity. Voznesensky brought his poems to Pasternak at Peredelkino. Vinokurov visited Zabolotsky. Akhmadulina gave Akhmatova an absolutely symbolic "lift" in her *Pobeda*. Memoirs began to appear.

"History," Ilia Ehrenburg writes in *People, Years, Life*, "is full of gorges and abysses, and men have need of bridges, however fragile, to link one epoch with another." In spite of the great bulk of these memoirs, which he is still writing, Ehrenburg's style is terse and dramatic. He has obviously made some effort to pare away the fatty clichés he had cynically learned to manipulate

[24] M. Mikhailov, "Moskovskoe leto," *Novoe russkoe slovo*, March 27, 1965; in somewhat the same manner, I suppose, the visiting American businessman finds himself defending, when in Moscow, abstract art.

over the years. He is talking, now, to the younger generation. In large measure, the memoirs are an apologia. "Many of my contemporaries have found themselves under the wheels of time. I have survived—not because I was stronger or more far-seeing, but because there are times when the fate of a man is not like a game of chess dependent on skill, but like a lottery." This is almost too modest. Throughout the memoirs, Ehrenburg attempts subtly to extricate himself from any close knowledge of or participation in what went on in the high places. It comes as a surprise to most of his readers that, as he notes in a recent installment, he never saw Stalin till late in his life, and then only at some distance. Extricating himself from the Kremlin *collective*, Ehrenburg takes great pains and makes vivid prose to identify himself with the *community* of art. Suddenly it means something positive to be a cosmopolitan. Ehrenburg's memoirs are peopled with exotic, fabulous figures, the denizens of the Cafe Rotonde and the lost Russian writers of three decades. Art as a way of life is, in places, marvelously dramatized. This may perhaps be an instance of an audience—those intense young men in the turtleneck sweaters, the shy, eager girls with the knit brows—creating a writer. Certainly the memoirs contain the best prose Ehrenburg has written.

Paustovsky's memoirs are different. They come in two sets. One is called *A Story About Life*. The other, *The Golden Rose*, might easily bear the subtitle, "A Story About Art." The first contains hardly a single famous person except the author. It is full of sights, sounds, smells, colors, tones, remembered with a precision of detail and a power of evocation that is truly astonishing, from the Ukrainian farm of his childhood to his life as a streetcar conductor in Moscow. It consists perhaps too exclusively of minutely wrought and knitted together sensual details. The second seems more spontaneous and more varied, containing notes on books, on the craft of writing, as well as reminiscences of writers, and the places and the very particular and peculiar landscapes and environments associated with particular writers —Odessa with Babel, Tarusa with Bunin and Blok and Prishvin. Paustovsky is also building bridges. "The grandsons do not understand," he writes, "and do not want to understand the poverty wept over in songs, adorned with legends and fairy tales, with the eyes of timid mute children, and with the lowered eyelashes of girls, and agitated by the tales of wanderers and cripples, by the constant feeling of an unbearable mystery living alongside one in the forests, in the lakes, in rotten logs, and in boarded-up peasants' houses, and the always present sense of a miracle. 'I slumber and behind my slumber is a mystery, and in the mystery you sleep, Russia.' "[25]

Even Evtushenko, when he was only thirty, felt compelled to write (he was later reprimanded) what he rightly called *A Precocious Autobiography*. It was written abroad and never published in the Soviet Union. Much of it is hasty, carelessly put together; much of it is hollow, and there is some false posturing. His "imaginary audience" is with him in places, though, and there are passages that have the ring of authentic statement. He is not so much concerned, like Ehrenburg and Paustovsky, with the gap between generations (on the contrary, he makes himself at home, though not altogether at ease, with the language, the poses, the attitudes, of writers as diverse as Mayakovsky, Pasternak, Hemingway) as with what he calls "that most dreadful menace in the history of any people—a split between their external and their inner lives."

In the first long poem that made him famous, "Winter Junction" (later, he wrote a sequel, "Again at Winter Junction," and he has made numerous references both to the poem and to the trip), Evtushenko described an Antaeus-like return to his Siberian home, where the strength of an integral family tradition of nonconformity and stubborn idealism refreshed his confidence that had suffered such a staggering blow from the first awareness of the "split" mentioned in the Autobiography. Evtushenko is lyrically most at home in the presence of someone of an older generation, preferably someone who isn't famous. His best poems are about old women and an old man. The sense of encroaching death, the pain and pathos of fading away, the sense of pain of personal loss make poems like "Our Mothers Are Leaving Us" (an emotion all but impossible to convey in English, in spite of the excellence and authenticity of the Russian original) and "The Windows Look Out on the Trees" (which Evtushenko reads aloud with such simple and astonishing drama) among the best now written. His father, with whom, one gathers, his relations are sometimes touchy, comes alive in a casually and incidentally inserted anecdote in the Autobiography, in which, as Evtushenko

[25] Quoted from *Pages from Tarusa,* ed. Andrew Field (Boston: Little, Brown, 1964), p. 361.

tells it, he and his father are refused admittance to a Moscow restaurant one evening for not wearing neckties, and his father tells him how at his age he was thrown out of the university because he wore a tie.

Evtushenko denounces the "lyrical hero" of Stalinist days. He wants to be his own lyrical hero, the "I" of his poems to be his own "I." "Even the simple words, 'I love' were sometimes spoken in so abstract, so oratorical a voice that they might have been 'we love.'" Yet in his attempt to speak for himself, to speak for his friends the young writers, to speak for the Jews, to speak for Cuba, and for Hemingway, to speak for communism, he defeats his own integrity. It is possible, as Pushkin did, to invoke the Imperial as well as the private muse. It is possible, like Mayakovsky and Gorky, to feel torn between them. But one cannot pretend they are one and remain the poet Evtushenko wants to be. Evtushenko is the prime victim of what, in a brilliantly perceptive article, Vera Dunham has called "spokesmanship."[26] A hollow, bragging sound slips into the "I." Without wishing to belittle the courage or the generosity that went into the famous poem "Baby Yar" one has only to compare it with Auden's "The Diaspora" to see at once how affected it is, how short of its subject. And if the following modest disclaimer did not sound just a little bit false there would be something pathetic in it: "My poetry is only the expression of moods and ideas already present in Soviet society but which had not so far been expressed in verse. Had I not been there, someone else would have expressed them."

The new Soviet literature has been much underrated in this country. It is fresh and vigorous, if not altogether new. Akhmadulina's long poem "The Rain" has a marvelous frisky animism; I know of nothing fresher, more alert, more personal. Voznesensky's poems range from the gay satire of "Fire in the Architectural" through the wistful nostalgia of "Moonlit Nerl" to the somber, dark-syllabled play of "I Am Goya." Kazakov writes little, but his short stories are among the best anywhere of the past ten years. True, he is not as good as Chekhov or Bunin, whom he resembles, but neither is anyone else. Nagibin and Aksionov are uneven, but vital and interesting. Nevertheless, for all the awakened interest in the private muse, in style and honesty, in the exploration of personal relations, private moods, in the prob-

26 Vera S. Dunham, "Poems about Poems," *Slavic Review*, XXIV (1965), 57–76.

lematics of everyday life, in the nuances of personal psychology, something is deeply lacking.

Here is a passage from a proletarian novel of the RAPP period around 1930, Libedinsky's *Birth of a Hero*. The central figure, a Bolshevik, finds himself torn between his assistant, a formalistic bureaucrat, and his wife, whose narrow domestic concerns have their counterpart in his own soul. ". . . a quiet new meat grinder glistening in the corner, and her comfortable worn slippers under the bed. And he looked upon all this, which had before been so sweet to him, as a new manifestation of the old enemy, as the elemental repetition of immemorial and hateful forms of life. He had fought with them all his life, all his life he had exposed them, tearing the hypocritical masks from them; and now he had even discovered them inside himself."[27]

Not great literature, certainly; but it has a certain dignity, an impressive thematic weight. Here is a parallel passage from a recent novel, Granin's *After the Wedding*. True, the household items are seen from the point of view of the bride, but she is meant to be altogether sympathetic. " 'All this is ours, mine. My window sill, my window. I'll wash it myself, and I'll seal it with paper, and between the frames I'll put heather. . . .' From work, she ran straight to the department store. . . . Tonia could look at the dinner sets for hours, price the vases, turn the meat grinders. She hadn't suspected there were so many wonderful things in the world and that they were all absolutely necessary. Mentally, she decorated her room with them, disposed them about her kitchen. The number of things that were necessary depressed her. There was no chance of acquiring all this, even in the next few months. She railed at herself for her greediness, called herself a *meshchanka*, a bourgeois housewife; she and Igor didn't really need a thing. And she was really quite happy in their empty, unfinished room. She even exulted in her contempt for all 'trappings.' Yet when she dropped into the store, surrounded by things that flashed their newness, she forgot about everything, roused by the desire to possess all these pretty things. Not for herself—for the home. She was ready to deny herself food and clothes, to economize on everything. The enticement was too great; she could not restrain herself, and every single time, she bought some petty

27 Quoted from Edward J. Brown, "The Year of Acquiescence," in *Literature and Revolution in Soviet Russia*, ed. Max Hayward and Leopold Labedz (London and New York: Oxford University Press, 1963), p. 54.

item. These unforeseen acquisitions ruined all her accounts and plans, but in return she experienced incomparable pleasure walking home along the streets with her heaps of parcels and most important, when she got home, unloading all this noisily on the table. 'Guess what I bought!' "[28]

The second passage is pleasant and humorous, if a little long. It hints at greater if less passionate complexities than the first, affirms domesticity, and is gay about privacy. But it has a touch of soap opera. It has a touch of *poshlost'*. One is tempted to ask: "So what?" It lacks dignity. It is bourgeois.

The very best stories and poems have been written about children, about love affairs, about old people, social outcasts, *otshchepentsy*, about nature. These are the themes that are furthest removed from the compromising rhetoric of Stalinism, and at the same time closest to the tradition of the private muse. They concern present experience as opposed to the corrosive joy of the Happy Future, which is, however, a difficult monster to exclude.

But something is missing. Something is being avoided. It is not just the false genuflections to the Imperial muse, not just the incapacity to woo her with real flair. Even in the realm of privacy and private feelings, the ultimate concerns are being avoided, the strenuous attempt to break through beyond privacy into the world of Molly Bloom's night thoughts, some major effort to come to grips with, to discover, whether man is after all "the sum of his social relations" as Marx in one of his more extreme moments said, or whether, past all the entanglements, there is indeed something there that is more.

ST. BORIS

"A voice from the grave," Isaac Deutscher called Pasternak's *Doctor Zhivago*.[29] Superstitious, he seems afraid to listen.

True, the novel reaches back into the past. Pasternak invokes Pushkin's private muse, the family theme, the traditional association of poetry-family-landscape, the Tolstoyan sense of the freshness of ordinary things, seen as though for the first time, as over and against abstract ideas and metaphysical systems which blear in retrospect. He invokes Chekhov's self-effacing inwardness. As

[28] Daniil Granin, *Posle svad'by* (Moscow-Leningrad, 1964), p. 8.
[29] Isaac Deutscher, "Pasternak and the Calendar of the Revolution," *Partisan Review*, XXVI (1959), 248–65; see also the reply by Irving Howe in the same issue.

in many of his poems, he attempts to build into the novel itself discussions, hints, suggestions of his *ars poetica*. He uses not only the tradition of the private muse but the creatural realism of the New Testament, in which the sense of miraculous destiny is transferred from the realm of enormous and public events like the plagues of Egypt or the opening of the Red Sea to the ordinary, the private, and the everyday—the vigil of shepherds, or the birth of a child. He refers to Flemish paintings of the nativity, in which the creatures of nature group themselves around a crib and the darkness organizes itself around the light.

As to its thrust into the future, it is still a difficult book for anyone to come to terms with. I believe that Edmund Wilson's allegorical exegesis, though valuable in many of its details, has done the book scant service, for what we need most to take in hand are not the book's (on the whole not very formidable) obscurities of reference but our own feelings about its major themes.

I have noticed that my very best students when they write about *Zhivago* tend to write badly; they become sentimental, vague and lax, and feel unduly called upon to make some great but amorphous gesture of affirmation. If great books create their own audiences, one can say that *Zhivago* has not yet created the one it needs. It has been treated not as a novel or a poem (and it is both) but as a moral treatise or an early Christian commentary, which in some sense at least it really does resemble. In the Soviet Union it will remain unpublished even with the forthcoming Collected Works of Pasternak. Yet it is unmistakably, uncomfortably, ineluctably *there*. Pasternak regarded it not only as the climax, but as the summing up of his entire poetic career, and as a Summa, a gloss, a commentary, a clarification of all his previous work in poetry and prose. There is no mind, inside or outside the Soviet Union, at all concerned with Russian literature in a serious way, within which this bear does not cast a great shadow.

The Christian symbolism that runs throughout the book strikes me as token of a poet's Christianity, a poet so strong and sure in his sensibility that the religion seems rightly to derive from the poetry, not the other way round, yet without sacrilege. Uncle Nikolai Vedeniapin tells us that the meaning of Christianity consists on the one hand of "the mystery of the individual," and on the other of "the idea of life as sacrifice." Around these two seemingly contradictory but actually dialectical notions, the novel is built. The central figure, who bears the name of life itself, is a poet; in the course of the novel his life is used up and exhausted by his poetry, which, after his death, organizes a human community around itself in much the way Belinsky once described Russian literature as organizing a genuine Russian community based on freedom and a fresh conception of life. The novel is about the life of the poet, his personal death, and his resurrection in the species.

"The novel gives no real picture of the country or the people," the editors of *Novy mir*, rejecting Zhivago, wrote to Pasternak. "Nor consequently does it explain why revolution became inevitable in Russia. . . . Theoretically speaking, it would be hard to imagine a novel in which the scene was set to a large extent in 1917 that would not, in one way or another, give definitive appraisal of the difference between the February and the October revolutions."[30] Indeed, there is barely any mention of the most important historical events in Russia between 1917 and 1921; the Civil War is seen from the point of view of a minor backwater in Siberia, and the NEP summed up by Zhivago's heart attack in a stalled trolley. Deutscher joins the editors of *Novy mir* in emphasizing Pasternak's lack of concern for the major events and major issues of the time.

It is not, however, Pasternak who is unconcerned, but Zhivago who *makes* himself "unconcerned" at enormous effort and paying a great price—his family, his friends, his career, much of his own more active quality as a human being. During a partisan battle in the Siberian forest, he pities both sides and concentrates his attention on the tree of life. All the important events of his life are internal events. They are affected—indeed, the arena is prepared—by time and place and circumstances, yet they are in touch with a larger cosmic order in the grip of which time, place, and circumstances are also seen to play. "Art," writes Camus, "teaches us that man cannot be explained by history alone and that he also finds a reason for his existence in the order of nature."[31] On that reason, Zhivago concentrates. He is first and foremost a poet, and it is as a poet that he maintains his integrity. Late in the novel, he bewails his earlier commitment to the Revolution, not because he feels he did anything wrong (it would

[30] The letter is translated in full in Robert Conquest, *The Pasternak Affair* (Philadelphia: Lippincott, 1962), pp. 139–63.

[31] Albert Camus, *The Rebel* (New York: Vintage Books, 1958), p. 276.

be difficult to discover that he did anything political at all) but because he has come to realize that such a commitment *if made inwardly* precludes, or at least infects, all others.

The book is not meant to justify an ivory-tower attitude or indifference to human beings who do, after all, take part in history; but rather to exalt intensity of purpose, the "safe-conduct" of destiny, the role of poet, a moral burden of the kind that Zhivago's "Hamlet" assumes in the first poem of his cycle—especially when "the time is out of joint" or "a play not to the taste" is actually on the boards. The poet must be an individual, not like those dominated by the "herd-instinct" (*stadnost'*) no matter whether the group they flock to bears the banner "of Kant or Solovev or Marx." It is by the quality of his perceptions, not by what he does, that the inner Zhivago is made known to us.

Zhivago is extremely sensitive to light, which he sees in the whiteness of it; that is, not in the political significance of "white" but in the sense of wholeness, that which contains within itself the possibility of all colors. He is an expert medical diagnostician and an authority on sight. The way in which Zhivago "sees the light" characterizes him. He notices Lara's candle shining from behind a frozen window as he passes by on a Moscow street. "Consciousness," he says, "is like a locomotive headlight. Turned outward it lights up the track for miles; directed inwardly, it blinds." He is not, therefore, introspective, *self*-conscious, but, if one may switch metaphors, in *tune*, alert to the world around him. In contrast, Strelnikov (who on occasion suggests the lonely pathos of Mayakovsky) is all self-consciousness. On his wedding night, the light he is most acutely and uncomfortably aware of is the street light shining *in*. He always feels the streets observing him instead of observing the streets. The quality of his sight is defined by the color "red"—only partly intended in its political sense, much more so as the color of blood, the color confronted when straining to stare at the world through closed eyelids.

Zhivago's perceptions are always his own and his opinions are related to his perceptions. Throughout the book there is a constant denigration of groupiness and "playing at people." Social relations are not altogether ignored, but downgraded, seen as somewhat incidental and secondary, if often mysterious and interesting and compelling. "National" or "folk" character is also seen as an interesting side effect, something already receding into the background. Lara, for all her associations with Mother Russia, has a Greek name and is of Belgian extraction. Evgraf has "narrow Kirghiz eyes." Russians, Jews, Europeans, and Orientals mingle among and amidst and within each other. Social position and material affluence are unimportant to Zhivago and most of his friends, nor do such matters seem to have much to do with which side of the revolutionary struggle the characters choose. Zhivago is certainly not a bourgeois individualist like Komarovsky; he is, indeed, starkly contrasted with him. Komarovsky's individuality depends on his property, on the things he owns and the routine he establishes around them: his apartment, landlady, friends, his English bulldog. Although he is moved by Lara, he cannot accommodate her into his routine, for she, classless and without property, will not be made into a fetish. Zhivago, on the contrary, sees her as life itself: "You cannot communicate directly with life, but she was its representative." He lives with her in a kind of perpetual present, devoid of routine, where there is neither time nor money. But it is Komarovsky who comes out on the right side of the revolution.

As a doctor, Zhivago resembles Chekhov in his modest urge to be useful. Chekhov also figures in Pasternak's *ars poetica*, along with Pushkin, as the unassuming kind of writer—unlike Dostoevsky or Tolstoy who thundered big panaceas at the world—minding his own business, and almost as if by accident, so to speak, allowing the world to discover that his business was also everybody's business: the artist who maintains the integrity of his sensibility in the face of loud moral imperatives. T. S. Eliot's mysterious remark about Henry James, that he had "a mind so fine, no idea could violate it," seems much more aptly applied to Chekhov or Pushkin or Zhivago.[32] In his work as a doctor, Zhivago displays the same qualities that he displays as a poet: perceptiveness, skill at diagnosis, imaginative contact with the world of organic nature. He has no sweeping theories and makes no grandiose self-assertions.

He is also a husband and a family man, not a very good one as it turns out. At first, Zhivago affirms the traditional Russian identification of poetry with domestic life: "This was what art aimed at—homecoming, return to one's family, to oneself, to true existence." And Zhivago often thinks, in connection with his family, of Nikolai's observation that "Christ speaks in parables

[32] And yet, it cannot be denied that, through Zhivago, Pasternak commits himself to "spokesmanship" of a kind.

taken from life, that He explains the truth in terms of everyday reality." Under the stress of cataclysmic events, however, as "the landscape assumed the form of modern art," distaccato, fragmented, wrenched awry from its normal positioning, poetry loses its old connection with the family and has to fall back on a more intimate relationship with life itself.

If Zhivago has, therefore, no unmitigated commitment to private property, the family, or the state, wherein (since, as the editors of *Novy mir* rightly point out, Pasternak's tone of irritation is unmistakable) lies his quarrel with Marxism?

In spite of the irritation, neither Zhivago's nor Pasternak's quarrel with Marxism implies a complete or absolute rejection. The first objection is that Marxism claims too much for itself. It is not a science, and in advancing the claim to be one, it tramples whatever may be left of a disinterested regard for the truth. Secondly, in exalting human consciousness and will not only above all else but literally without limits, it destroys man's connection with the source of his own energies. " 'Transformation of life' . . . can only be talked of by people who don't know life. . . . In them, existence is a lump of coarse material which has not been ennobled by their touch and which requires fashioning. But life has never been a material, a substance. . . . It is constantly refashioning and realizing itself and it is far beyond our boneheaded theories about it." Thirdly, Marxism is life-denying by its enormous emphasis on the future, which tends to displace a sense of the importance of experience in the present. "A man is born to live, not to prepare to live. And life as such—the phenomenon of life—the gift of life—is so thrilling and serious! Why then substitute for this a puerile farce of adolescent contrivances, these Chekhovian children's flights to America?" (The reference is to a story by Chekhov in which children, beguiled by the gadgetry of America, decide to run off there but get no further than the next town.) This seems to be the full extent of Pasternak's quarrel with Marxism.

Zhivago's individualism, then, is mainly a certain power of resistance to the grand encroachments of his time, his capacity to be himself under all circumstances, not to be violated by ideas, no matter how tempting, to keep his consciousness and his sensibility intact. It is not self-aggrandizement. At the highest point of his life, when he is living with Lara at Varykino and writing his best poems, the closest to Eden he ever comes, it is as though not he himself is writing but rather "the force of poetry in his time." This richly rewarding, almost selfless piety towards life also has, eventually, its price. It makes him perhaps too passive and yielding to circumstances, and in the end Zhivago deteriorates unnecessarily rapidly, to live again only in his poems.

Pasternak's novel sits like a great beast in the center of the new period of Soviet liberalization. The editors of *Novy mir* made no bones about rejecting it on ideological, not on aesthetic, grounds. Actually, their discussion of these ideological grounds, which was entirely serious and which included numerous quotations from the book (later published) revealed also a colossal aesthetic and philosophical misunderstanding of the book, a misunderstanding by no means based on lack of generosity but rather on the blighting principles of socialist realism, which, though no writer follows them, are the only official criticism there is. It is curious and striking that today, when asked why *Zhivago* has not been published, official Russians, if they are also clever, fall back on the diversion that it was "a bad novel." During the last year of his life, Pasternak exercised, and he still exercises, an overwhelming influence, both personal and poetic, on all the younger Soviet poets with any talent at all. "People," Evtushenko writes, "react to Pasternak not as to a man but as to a color, a smell, or a sound." He is a force. With that force Soviet literature will yet have to reckon.

PART FIVE

Strategies and Tactics of Economic Development

Introduction

GREGORY GROSSMAN

THE TWO papers in this section compare the Soviet and Chinese economies from two distinctly different standpoints. Dr. Yeh's is a quantitative comparative analysis of the strategies of development in terms of statistically ascertainable patterns of resource mobilization and resource use. Professor Schurmann weaves an intricate account of organization and reorganization in the two countries as they traveled the hard road of early industrialization. Nonetheless, the two papers have much in common, for strategy and organization are intimately intertwined, and both are linked to the regimes' goals and to the ideological spectacles with which they perceive reality and envision their future.

What do the Soviet and Chinese economies have in common? Why compare them at all? Do they have more in common than, say, the American and the West German economies, or even the American and the Soviet?

Perhaps the readiest answer is that both economies, the Soviet and the Chinese, are lodged in similar doctrinal-political matrices. They are both integral aspects of totalitarian societies and one-party states that officially designate themselves as Marxist-Leninist by ideological commitment, Communist by party label, and socialist by politico-economic order. The Chinese regime today, like the Soviet at a comparable epoch following its own revolution, regards itself as almost friendless among the powerful of this world and under an actual state of siege.

Further, both are acutely aware of, if not obsessed by, the fact that their countries are economically and technically backward in comparison to their chief actual or potential adversaries. And, of course, Russia in the twenties and thirties was by this yardstick a poor country, predominantly agrarian, as was China in the fifties and sixties to an even greater extent. Their large unschooled and underskilled peasant populations bear promise for the future but pose great problems for the present.

It is therefore quite natural that the basic economic goals of the two countries have been broadly similar: very rapid economic growth, steep technological advance, maximum acquisition of economic power for the state's ends, rapid build-up of defense potential, autarky (for both security and prestige reasons), and speedy completion of their domestic social revolutions.

But there were also major differences, of course, both in the circumstances in which the two Communist economies found themselves from the start and, naturally enough, in their responses to the different circumstances. Dr. Yeh's and Professor Schurmann's papers, in a sense, deal respectively with just these differences in responses in the realms of resource allocation and organization.

A few words about these differences in circumstances. One might mention first—at the risk of abysmal banality—the very different historical heritages of the two Communist giants. Having thus reminded ourselves that Russia is Russia and China is China, we may proceed to more specific things. Of these, we should like to list three. All three have been repeatedly discussed in the relevant Western literature. First, there is a striking difference in the way the two Communist regimes came to power. The Bolsheviks seized power in a quick military action in the capital and had to fight a prolonged, extremely difficult civil war to retain power. They had no experience of either governing men or administering things before October 1917. They lost much of the peasants' good will in the course of pursuing economic emergency measures in order to survive and win in the civil war. By contrast, their Chinese counterparts governed territorial and military enclaves for decades before overrunning the whole country in the late forties; were peasant-based and obtained much experience with peasants before assuming national responsibilities; and won their civil war before assuming state power.[1]   Second, China

[1] On these and other comparisons and contrasts of China and the USSR on the eve of their first five-year plans, see especially Alexander Eckstein, *Communist China's Economic Growth and Foreign Trade* (New York: McGraw-Hill, 1966), chap. 2.

was on a much lower economic level, say, on the eve of her First Five-Year Plan than Russia was at the beginning of hers. As Dr. Yeh vividly shows in summary fashion in his Table 2,[2] China produced and consumed, per capita, less of almost everything. Equally significantly, she had been in the habit of saving a much smaller fraction of her national product than Russia had already been doing decades before 1928. China's stocks of modern plant, scientists, engineers, and technicians—the tangible ingredients for a take-off into rapid modernization and industrialization— were much thinner.

Third, from the very outset, the Chinese People's Republic had the advantage of the existence of the Union of Soviet Socialist Republics. Thus, unlike the USSR in 1917 or 1928 or 1937, the CPR had a powerful source of aid and counsel, as well as a compelling politico-economic model to emulate—or to be misled by. We leave it to future generations of Sinologists and economic historians to debate whether in the long run China's economic fortunes were enhanced or hampered by the existence of this friend.

It was no doubt this last factor, the existence of the friend-adviser-model, that explains the many remarkable parallels between China's development strategy and economic institutions during its First FYP (1953–57) and Russia's during its first two plans. By dint of what was undoubtedly a great feat in mobilization and organization, China raised its gross investment rate to about 20 per cent (by Dr. Yeh's own estimate), or rather close to the Soviet average level during 1928–37. The sectoral distribution of this investment was also very similar to the USSR's with industry receiving an even higher proportion of the total. (See Dr. Yeh's Table 1. As Professor Abram Bergson argued at the conference, if the omission of private investment were allowed for in the Chinese figures, they would come even closer to the Soviet figures both in the rate of investment and in the sectoral distribution.)

The borrowing of Soviet developmental strategy was accompanied by a massive borrowing of institutions and procedures in the organization, planning, and management of the economy— and especially of industry. With a few notable exceptions, some to be mentioned in the next paragraph, the Chinese took over almost the complete structure of the Soviet command economy and the complete methodology (or lack of it) of Soviet planning on all

[2] For more detailed data see Eckstein, *op. cit.*, p. 20.

levels. While Professor Schurmann's paper offers some fascinating pages on the organization changes and issues during the pre-1957 period in China, the fact remains that this movement was within a framework that is strikingly familiar to the Sovietologist.

Of course, there are notable deviations from the Soviet paradigm to be noted even in the Chinese First FYP period. Perhaps the most striking of these is that collectivization was carried out in China much more smoothly and with apparently very little of the painful and disruptive consequences that were characteristic of Soviet collectivization. Surely, the Chinese Party's incomparably greater presence and stronger position in the countryside, as well as the structural differences between the two agricultures, had much to do with this contrast. (As was stressed in the conference discussion, it is the *communization* of 1958 rather than the Chinese collectivization of 1955–56 that provides the more meaningful parallel with Soviet collectivization.) Another major contrast to be noted is that in general the Chinese Party exerts a greater manipulative control than the Soviet Party within the respective societies. It was probably largely for this reason that the Chinese showed much greater tolerance than the Russians toward the survival of small-scale enterprise and privately operated handicrafts, and toward the use of market-like controls in this sector.[3] And lastly, another contrast must be at least mentioned: substantial Soviet economic and technical assistance in that period.

One of the more remarkable features of Soviet history is how long Stalin's developmental strategy and institutional system have persisted. For over three decades they suffered only relatively minor adjustment (apart from concentration on military production rather than investment during the war) despite the enormous changes in the country's productive capacity and socio-economic structure, and in the international environment. Even Khrushchev's replacement of industrial ministries by regional *sovnarkhozy* and his largely successful rescue operations in agriculture amounted to rather minor secondary tinkering with the Stalinist system. It remains to be seen whether the economic reform decreed in October 1965 (part of which was a return to industrial ministries!) will result in major systemic changes.

Not so in China. A significant deviation from the Soviet road to

[3] Cf. Dwight H. Perkins, *Market Controls and Planning in Communist China* (Cambridge: Harvard University Press, 1966), *passim*.

socialism began even before the end of the First FYP, in 1957, and the Great Leap of 1958 was not so much forward into material abundance as away from the Soviet model. Only in one sense did the events of 1958 and, especially, the closely connected political conflict between the two Communist giants, which was about to come into the open, carry China closer to the early Russian experience: China was now to enter upon a defiant isolation from the rest of the world that greatly resembles that of the USSR in the twenties and thirties.

Both of our authors have much to say on the post-1957 period in China. Dr. Yeh finds that the Great Leap Forward was much more damaging to China's economy than collectivization was to the USSR's. (Perhaps one ought to add: in the short run. We cannot yet say about the long run.) Where the progress of Soviet economic development was "only" seriously dampened—though not without profound social and political effects on the country—China's economy went into an absolute decline from which it only now is slowly emerging. The collectivization disaster in the USSR caused neither a major change in priorities (at least not until Khrushchev's rescue of Soviet agriculture a quarter of a century later) nor any major institutional reform. In China it precipitated both. Dr. Yeh explains this fundamental difference by the much lower capacity of the Chinese economy to absorb the shock, a much lower margin of "fat" above bare subsistence. When the damage struck, all attention had to be diverted to mere survival, i.e., to agriculture, light industry, and the massive importation of food. To be sure, in the USSR in the early thirties millions of persons failed to survive because of shortage of food; but the system survived and fed on itself.

It is not surprising that there was a drastic reaction in China on the institutional plane as well, of which Professor Schurmann presents an extensive account. Also not surprising, the issues that are always endemic in such a formal organization—centralization versus decentralization, the coastal areas versus the hinterland, the center versus the regions, town as against country, party cadre versus expert, the Party machine versus the governmental apparatus, indoctrination and political control as against material incentives, market versus command—were fought over, whether in the open or behind closed doors. What emerged by about 1961 was a new strategy ("agriculture first") and a distinctively Chinese organization with a high degree of decentralization to intermediate levels, apparently very little central planning, and a peculiarly active role of the party. Whether this new strategy and organization will bring the Chinese economy to the point where it can undertake a new rapid advance remains to be seen. But in any case it is difficult to believe that the distinctive Chinese model of the first half of the sixties is anything but transitional. Both success and failure, not to mention the early departure of the present leaders from the scene, are likely to render it obsolete. Will Soviet and East European experience by that time offer to the Chinese a wider menu of economic models to select from, or will they again be forced—by economic logic or national pride—to cook up something distinctively their own?

Politics and Economics in Russia and China

FRANZ SCHURMANN

In BOTH Russia and China, the main business of the state bureaucracy is the administration of the economy. In both countries,
the policy-makers determine the major goals of economic activity
under conditions of chronic and severe shortage of resources. The
policy-makers regard the state bureaucracy as their instrument
for gathering information on the country's economic capabilities
and performance, formulating plans which mesh policy goals
with economic realities, and put them into operation through
administrative command. Unfortunately Friedrich Engels' dream
of administration by things and leadership by productive processes is yet far from being realized.[1] Perhaps some day, aggregate
economic data will perfectly reflect economic reality and be fed
into elegant computers, which will formulate optimal decisions in
terms of goals and capabilities, which will then be automatically
transmitted to the computers of the production units. The goods
and services are produced; output is immediately translated into
data and fed back up. Thus we have rule by productive processes.
However, as long as we have "administration by men," we have
politics. Politics may be seen as the struggle of men, individually
or collectively, to achieve aims under conditions of scarcity; in
other words, gain for one will mean loss for the other. Since the
economies of Russia and China still depend largely on command,
politics pervades the administration of the economy. Different
segments of the state bureaucracy compete with each other for
scarce resources, and put pressure on the policy-makers to set

[1] Karl Marx and Friedrich Engels, *Selected Works* (Moscow, 1958), II,
151.

297

goals which favor themselves. The main aim of every organization of the state bureaucracy is the maximization of its own interests. What both the Russians and Chinese denounce as a major defect of bureaucracy, namely, departmentalism (*vedomstvennost'*) or localism (*mestnichestvo*)—*pen-wei chu-yi* for both in Chinese—we see as an action pattern in the pursuit of these interests.[2]

Seen as an arena of politics, economic administration in Russia and China is difficult to regard as the implementation of plans designed according to ideas of optimal development and based on accurate information. The long-term plans are general programs which sketch out the goals of the policy-makers, but the short-term plans are continuing compromises that somehow reconcile the clashing demands of the different actors in the political drama.[3] Yet beneath the ebb and flow of politics, there are deeper currents which have grown over the years. Human relationships tend invariably to become institutionalized, and so patterns of structure and function develop which cannot easily be changed. Politics becomes increasingly governed by ingrained practices, a phenomenon which Max Weber called routinization. As a result of routinization, a kind of economic politics arises in which the actors remain generally the same, but the play changes as they assume different roles. In the following essay, we should like to identify the main actors in the drama of economic politics and indicate how at different periods of Russian and Chinese development they have put on different performances.

Let us first introduce three functional concepts: policy, operations, and coordination. Policy may be defined as a statement of goals with prescribed means of action. *Policy* assumes such importance in Communist countries because of (1) the ideological commitment to change and development, and (2) the organizational character of Communist societies. Ideology and organization are closely linked, for the very nature of modern organization, a conscious construct designed to achieve goals, makes policy a necessary aspect of organizational function. Although clearly the highest agencies of government have supreme policy-

[2] Barry M. Richman, *Soviet Management* (Englewood Cliffs, N.J.: Prentice-Hall, 1965), pp. 27–28; Harry Schwartz, *The Soviet Economy Since Stalin* (Philadelphia: Lippincott, 1965), pp. 91–92.

[3] Naum Jasny, *Essays on the Soviet Economy* (New York: Praeger, 1962), pp. 159 ff.

making powers, this does not mean that lower echelons cannot, at times, initiate policy. The Chinese, for example, distinguish between general and specific policy, that is, general goals for the country as a whole, and specific goals for each concrete situation. If a lower echelon agency has the power to initiate specific policy, albeit within the framework of general policy, this often greatly modifies the general goals.[4] This distinction between general and specific policy was of considerable importance during the Chinese Great Leap Forward.

By *operations* we mean the implementation of policy. Once policy goals have been set, they must be translated into operational directives. This can only be done by organizations which have command over resources and men. Operational control therefore is a source of political power.

By *coordination* we mean linking discrete operations together in such a way that the over-all goals are achieved, that serious bottlenecks are avoided, and that inter-unit conflicts do not lead to disruption. The compiling of national material balances is coordination.

In Communist countries, policy-making powers are usually lodged in an agency of the party, be it the Politburo, a fraction in a ministry, or a party committee in a unit of production. However, as all students of organization know, policy is not always made at the top. Sometimes, impulses come from the middle and lower levels of organization, and are only legitimated by the executives at the top.

Communist countries are all characterized by immense state bureaucracies. These usually take the form of ministries and special agencies which control sectors and branches of organized society. These bodies usually consist of a nationwide hierarchy of administrative and production units which form a kind of small bureaucratic empire. Since the ministries are responsible for performance and output, operations is one of their main functions.

The state bureaucracy and the party contain a number of committees (councils, commissions, etc.), whose members belong to different branch organizations and whose main function is political and economic coordination. Since the main business of the state bureaucracy is running the economy, the chief coordina-

---

[4] P. J. D. Wiles, *The Political Economy of Communism* (Cambridge: Harvard University Press, 1962), pp. 145–46.

tive agencies are the state planning and the state economic commissions.[5]

In Communist countries, politics is essentially bureaucratic politics, that is, various segments of government and party struggle with each other to maximize their own interests in a context of perpetual scarcity of resources. In this paper we suggest that the successive patterns of economic administration can be seen in terms of bureaucratic politics, and, indeed, we believe that further research might indicate that the successive economic plans themselves can be seen in the same way. We shall discuss the well-known issues of centralization and decentralization to try to show the link between politics and economics.

The issue of centralization/decentralization implies an hierarchical organizational structure. For analytical purposes, let us suggest that each of the two main organizational hierarchies, government and party, may be seen in three levels. There are central party and government agencies, regional party and government agencies, and lastly the units of production with their attached party committees.[6] If the powers of policy-making, formulation of operational commands and procedures, and the making and implementation of coordination are concentrated at the central level, we may regard this as extreme centralization. The opposite case would be one in which all three powers were widely distributed at the bottom, and lodged in the units of production. Extreme centralization was characteristic of Soviet economic administration during the Stalinist period, particularly after the great purges. The only instance of far-reaching decentralization was that which occurred in Yugoslavia shortly after the break with the Cominform.[7] It appears today, however, that Communist countries shift between these extremes, with the particular state of centralization or decentralization never remaining constant. Since we have isolated three main functions and six major structures, one can envisage a considerable variety of different patterns of power distribution.

[5] Abram Bergson's distinction between general organs of government, agencies for operational control, and functional agencies corresponds to our own distinction between policy-making, operational, and coordinative agencies. *The Economics of Soviet Planning* (New Haven: Yale University Press, 1964), pp. 26–40.

[6] Franz Schurmann, *Ideology and Organization in Communist China* (Berkeley: University of California Press, 1966), pp. 139 ff.

[7] Fred Warner Neal, *Titoism in Action* (Berkeley: University of California Press, 1958), pp. 50–53, 234 ff.

Let us begin with a brief examination of the centralization/ decentralization problem in Communist China. We know this story better than that of the Soviet Union, and our observations on China might help in making some comparative judgments on the Russian developments.

When the Chinese Communists came to power, they nationalized a large segment of the modern economic sector. By 1956 they completed nationalization by bringing remaining private business under state control. Also by 1956 agriculture became almost completely collectivized. The Chinese refer to the state-owned and the collective sector as planned and non-planned respectively. This means that state-owned enterprises are subject to policy, operations, and coordination controls and that the state can therefore determine future performance. On the other hand, though the collective farms have to meet state-determined procurement targets, the state does not have the instrumentalities to impose full planning controls. In view of the heavy dependence of Chinese industry on farm output, this means that central planning is dependent on a sector over which it has incomplete control. That annual economic plans are set only at the year's end, when farm output figures are known, has been repeatedly admitted by the Chinese themselves.[8]

There are two types of state-owned enterprise in China: central state-owned and regional state-owned. The former are directly attached to central ministries, whereas the latter are attached to some body of regional or local government (province or city). Although in the early years after 1949 only minor industries were left in regional hands, in the mid-1950's the distinction became much more important.

In 1949 the Chinese Communists inherited an economy that was about as "decentralized" as it could be: business and industry were disorganized and whatever enterprises were still working had to fend for themselves; a disastrous inflation gripped the country. The Chinese Communists, emulating the Soviet model, followed a course of centralization of policy, operations, and coordination. The entire Stalinist system of economic administration was introduced and implemented. The new government was determined to gain central control as rapidly as possible over money, supplies, and production. Aside from using drastic meas-

[8] Dwight H. Perkins, *Market Control and Planning in Communist China* (Cambridge: Harvard University Press, 1966), p. 204.

ures to curb inflation, Peking quickly set up a nationwide banking system with branch banks in every part of the country. Every enterprise was required to establish an account with a branch bank, and all financial transactions had to be cleared through the bank. Control over the supply system was achieved by forcing every unit of production to deliver its output to state-owned purchase and procurement agencies. Supplies could only be allocated according to state decisions. Production controls were more difficult to impose. However, through the use of state-set control figures, enterprises were generally impelled to produce what the state wanted. By late 1952 the Chinese felt that they had achieved sufficient control over their economy to begin central planning and start their First Five-Year Plan.[9]

In discussing the beginnings of central planning, one cannot overlook a significant political fact—the autonomy of Manchuria. In 1949 China was divided into six Large Administrative Regions, each of which was allowed a certain degree of administrative autonomy. In fact, because of a political history which is still not fully clear, only Manchuria enjoyed an autonomy of a sort that Communist leaders themselves later described, at the time the Manchurian party chief Kao Kang was purged, as an "independent kingdom." What, one may ask, was the significance of this "independence" in relation to the administration of the economy? If the resource allocation conflict is one of the permanent issues of bureaucratic politics in Communist China, then "independence" meant the power to command its own resources. However, Manchuria's power and influence extended beyond its administrative borders. Kao Kang was chairman of China's first State Planning Commission, constituted on the eve of the formal beginning of the First Five-Year Plan. That commission, among others, included his deputy, Ma Hung, and Jao Shu-shih, party boss of the Eastern region of China (centered on Shanghai)—all three of whom were purged early in 1955. We know that one of the specific manifestations of the resource allocation conflict related to the location of new industrial construction. In general, the question was whether new investment should go to coastal areas (essentially Manchuria, North China, and East China) or to inland areas (the remaining regions). The detailed draft of the

[9] Cheng Chu-yuan, *Communist China's Economy 1949–1962* (South Orange, N.J.: Seton Hall University Press, 1963), pp. 84–105.

First Five-Year Plan, published in the summer of 1955, proposed heavy investment in inland areas for industry and construction. However, judging from the actual regional development, which indicated that the coastal areas remained in the lead, and from the fact that the Soviet-sponsored projects, which formed the core of the first plan's industrial development, were centered mainly on Manchuria, one can conclude that the original plans drafted in 1951 showed a strong bias in favor of the coastal regions. Since Kao Kang and Jao Shu-shih were linked in the 1955 purge, it would appear warranted to suggest that the political power and influence of these two men constituted a major factor in the making of economic decisions which favored their regions of control.[10]

Effective central planning demands nationwide administrative unification, namely, that the powers of policy, operations, and coordination be concentrated at the political apex. Such a condition was not achieved until the summer of 1954, when the Large Administrative Regions were formally abolished and Peking assumed full control of the entire nation. It expressed this newly acquired control by promulgating the new constitution of September 1954. Thus central planning became possible only at that time. Significantly, the drafting of the final version of the First Five-Year Plan began only in February 1955, a month before the expulsion of Kao Kang and Jao Shu-shih was announced. The sharp drop in Manchurian representation in the Central Committee of the Eighth Party Congress (September 1956) reflects the diminished political power of Manchuria in the political scene of the mid-1950's.[11]

The Chinese Communists, from the beginning, had decided to set up a state administrative structure closely modeled on that of the Russians, and, ergo, on that of Manchuria. In their struggle

[10] Choh-ming Li, *Economic Development of Communist China* (Berkeley: University of California Press, 1959), pp. 49–52; Yuan-li Wu, *The Economy of Communist China* (New York: Praeger, 1965), p. 119. The importance of industrial location in the resource allocation conflict is indicated by the fact that section 2 of the chapter on industry of the First Five-Year Plan strongly voices the determination of the government to shift industry to inland regions for economic and national defense reasons.

[11] Donald Klein, in a personal communication, has pointed out that whereas 25 per cent of party leaders in five of the old Large Administrative Regions were elected to the Central Committee of the Eighth Party Congress, only 11 per cent from Manchuria were elected.

with Manchuria, the Peking leaders greatly expanded the power of the ministries. When the Large Administrative Regions were abolished, the Peking ministries acquired control over the vast network of production units which earlier had been subject to regional rather than national power. This can be seen, for example, in the greatly expanded powers of the Ministry of Railroads which, only in 1954, acquired complete power over the country's railroad system.[12] Freight-car space was a scarcity item over which the resource allocation conflict raged, and the achievement of centralization meant that whoever made policy in Peking could decide who was to get what freight-car space. Ministerial centralization was also reflected in the so-called "above-norm construction projects" announced in the revised version of the First Five-Year Plan. These were integrated projects (planning and budget under single control), the great majority of which (573 out of 694) were under the jurisdiction of central industrial ministries. Since these "above-norm construction projects" explicitly included all of the 145 Russian-sponsored projects then under way, they may be seen as a device to exercise centralized control over regional industrial development.[13]

Thus, by the end of 1954, Peking had managed to concentrate all policy-making powers in its hands, specifically, in the Politburo of a newly unified party. Operational powers, particularly over the modern sector, passed into the hands of the central ministries. Coordinative power was assumed by a reconstituted State Planning Commission, headed by Li Fu-ch'un. An ideal condition for the implementation of central planning appeared to exist: the top party leaders set the goals of economic development, the State Planning Commission, using its statistical data and national balances, formulated the plan, and the ministries were ordered to implement them.

However, in early 1956, voices began to be raised demanding a modification of the system of central planning. By the time of the Eighth Party Congress, the call for decentralization had become a major theme of the Congress, as expressed by Li Fu-ch'un. Coincident with this came a call for greater stress on the development of inland industries, an expansion of light industry, and

[12] See Schurmann, *op. cit.*, pp. 208–9.
[13] Li, *op. cit.*, p. 11, note 28. See section 1 of the chapter on industry of the First Five-Year Plan.

more directed development of agriculture. Although talk about decentralization in Russia undoubtedly influenced the Chinese,[14] more fundamental political and economic factors also were involved. In the spring of 1956, the Politburo decided to slow down the pace of collectivization, launched the previous year, and begin a period of economic consolidation. This became evident in the reduced growth rate for 1957 and in a decline of trade with the Soviet Union.[15] That the slowdown was politically motivated is indicated by the suddenness with which Mao Tse-tung's ambitious plan for the uninterrupted development of agriculture disappeared from public consideration.[16] Political motivation is also indicated by the fact that economic plans are generally set in the fall when the harvest figures are finally in, and not in the spring.

If the redrafting of the so-called First Five-Year Plan was only begun in February 1955, then it is surprising that already in the spring of the following year, an economic philosophy should have begun to emerge which appeared to contradict some of the basic premises of the plan. The targets of the First Five-Year Plan were mainly achieved during the great production and collectivization drive of 1955–56. However, even before the final results of the drive were in, the new economic thinking called for greater attention to agriculture and light industry and to the need for creating an integrated national economy. The conflicts within the new thinking will be discussed below.

In the course of these economic discussions, three approaches to further economic development were revealed. The first favored a continuation of the economic strategy which dominated the First Five-Year Plan period. That involved a continuing stress on the development of a heavy industrial base in a few select locations with the remaining sectors of the economy providing the bulk of the savings. The second favored a more integrated development of the economy with a slower rate of growth in heavy industry but greater output of consumer goods. The third favored a crash program to revolutionize agriculture while at the same time maintaining high growth rates in the heavy industrial sector. The second approach was advocated by Ch'en Yün, one of the top

14 Gregory Grossman, "The Soviet Economy," *Problems of Communism,* Vol. XII, No. 2 (Mar.–Apr., 1963), p. 36.

15 Li, *op cit.*, p. 40; Wu, *op. cit.*, p. 176.

16 Schurmann, *op. cit.*, p. 200, note 24.

members of the Politburo and then Minister of Commerce, and the third by Mao Tse-tung.[17]

What is significant in the economic and political discussions of this period is the absence of any serious advocacy of the first program, in effect a continuation of the Stalinist model of development. That approach was clearly rejected at the Eighth Party Congress. Moreover, no member of the Politburo, with the possible exception of Marshal P'eng Te-huai, a leading member of the first State Planning Commission, is known to have advocated such a policy. Moreover, the drop in Manchurian representation on the Central Committee of the Eighth Party Congress reflects a considerably lessened role for the natural advocates of a continuing program of primacy for heavy industrialization. Thus when China had finally acquired the political and institutional mechanisms to make possible a centrally directed command economy suited for the further implementation of the Stalinist developmental model, China's leaders began to talk of embarking on a different developmental path. Whatever their disagreements, the two wings of the new economic thinking both advocated some degree of decentralization.

In brief terms, let us state the agreements and disagreements of these two groups on economic strategy. Both agreed that the "planful proportionate" development of the national economy had to be modified in favor of a more balanced and integrated development. This meant devoting increased resources to light industry and agriculture, while continuing high investment in heavy industry. If we accept the interpretation that Stalin's crash program for heavy industrialization was basically motivated by his fear of "capitalist encirclement," then it is significant that neither group in the dispute appeared to advocate the deployment of maximal efforts to create, as rapidly as possible, an independent heavy industrial base for China. This suggests that both groups assumed the presence of a Russian defense "shield" for China for an indefinite period. Thus freed from a military-industrial burden that weighed heavily on Russia in the 1930's, the two groups espoused programs for the all-sided development of the Chinese economy. Where they differed was in the methods to be used and the rate of growth envisaged. As far as the rate of growth is concerned, the disagreement can be summed up in the following simple way: Mao advocated a strategy of fast but risky,

[17] Wiles, *op. cit.*, pp. 173–75.

and Ch'en Yün advocated a strategy of slow but safe. As far as methods were concerned, Mao advocated a continuation of the social mobilization policies that had first been tried with agricultural collectivization in the fall of 1955, whereas Ch'en Yün advocated a policy of material incentives. These disagreements clearly had direct consequences for the kind of decentralization that was to be pursued.

The Ch'en Yün approach to decentralization, which appears to have been in favor until October 1957, when it was suddenly dropped, is indicated in an article by Hsüeh Mu-ch'iao, then director of the State Statistical Bureau. Hsüeh, in effect, came out for decreasing the powers of the central policy-making economic agencies (notably the State Council) and transferring them to (1) ministries, (2) regional governments, and (3) the enterprises. What this meant concretely was that the State Council was to surrender its powers to determine the supply, production, and distribution of a broad range of products.[18] The State Council retained full control over major industrial and agricultural products. The ministries and regional governments were allowed to have supply, production, and distribution controls over a range of products not covered by the first category. Lastly, all other products could be freely produced, procured, and distributed according to demand-supply conditions determined by the market. This three-category supply system was not adopted in 1957, but

[18] Hsüeh Mu-ch'iao, "Preliminary Opinions on the Current System of Plan Management," *Chi-hua ching-chi*, No. 9, Sept., 1957, pp. 20–24. Hsüeh states: ". . . At present there are only a few hundred items of planned products which we control; this is a very small number in view of the thousands and thousands of products which there are. Some comrades think that this is too little, making it impossible to balance production and sales. Yet on the other hand, it is also not easy to make the production and sales conditions of so many hundreds of products clear. In fact, what can be made clear are the production and sales conditions of a few score or a few hundred of the most important products. For the rest, there is no way of calculating them precisely. If we now demand that they be produced according to plan but do not allow people to make adjustments if they find out that they are not needed, then we lose a lot by this. . . . The State Council should just retain control over the most important products affecting the state plan and the people's livelihood. Relatively secondary products should be controlled by the branch agencies and by the provinces and cities. . . . As far as even more secondary products are concerned, one does not need to nor can one fit them into the state plan. It is best to allow enterprises to fix their own production plans in accordance with market demand. The state commerce agencies can make adjustments by supply and sales through the medium of manufacturing and ordering [contracts]." Pp. 23–24.

was promulgated in April 1959, in the wake of the confusion of the 1958 Great Leap Forward.[19]

Obviously, this far-reaching transfer of economic power would greatly affect the planning system. Hsüeh suggested that plans be divided into two kinds. One, which he called the "small circle," would be plans with exact target specifications for the most important products as determined by the State Council. The other, which he called the "large circle," would be plans based essentially on estimates. Annual statistical reports would indicate what the real output was for the preceding year, and these figures would be used as bases for making projective estimates, and so worked into the plan for the following year. It is likely that this is what the planning agencies were doing anyway, and so Hsüeh was just calling for legitimation of what was *de facto* practice. Hsüeh's proposals would reduce the burdens of the State Economic Commission, of which he was a member. Its task would therefore be to draft annual plans which would be based on the "little circle" impulses (little, because they included relatively few items) coming from higher policy-making echelons, and "big circle" impulses coming from below, that is, ministries, regional governments, and the enterprises.

As far as the State Planning Commission was concerned, Hsüeh does not go into detail on what it should do, but Li Fu-ch'un, in his report to the Eighth Party Congress, already outlined their tasks: work out long-range programs (*kuei-hua*) of economic development and, especially, concentrate on the task of comprehensive balances.

Hsüeh also does not go into the delicate problems of price policy for reasons that one can easily understand. Nevertheless, his suggestion that enterprise profit be regarded as the chief success indicator of enterprise economic activity makes correct price policy an extremely important matter. Hsüeh states:

Although in the past profit targets were controlled by the Finance Ministry, they were never worked into the plan tables. But in reality from the very beginning they have been used to check on enterprise production success and have been a very important index for determining enterprise rewards and [profit] shares. Since we have changed the enterprise profit-sharing system, the importance of the

19 *Ta-kung pao* (Peking), Apr. 4, 1959. Under the Czech economic reforms, a similar pricing system has been proposed; Michael Gamarnikow, "The Reforms: A Survey," *East Europe*, Vol. XV, No. 1 (Jan., 1966), p. 16.

profit target will become even greater rather than decrease; the "secondary" effects which this might give rise to must be prevented by all kinds of means.

After the economic crisis of 1960, when Peking finally implemented the approaches suggested by the Ch'en Yün group, it adopted a flexible pricing policy called "qualitative pricing." Under this policy, price ranges were set for (1) heavy industrial products, (2) light industrial products, and (3) other products. The better the quality of the product, the higher the ex-factory price the enterprise could set, within the given limits. Qualitative pricing was regarded as a way of rewarding efficient producers and stimulating less efficient producers to improve their output. Price ranges for heavy industrial products were set by the state and the ministries concerned. Price ranges for light industrial products were set by regional governments. Price ranges for "other products" were not set, but the enterprise itself could set its own price with reference to the price of a "standard product." Presumably, in the latter case, prices fluctuated according to the market, with the "standard product" functioning as an administrative device which local administrative agencies could use if prices got out of hand.[20]

In general, one might say that the price policy finally adopted after January 1961 corresponded to the three-category supply system. There were (1) centrally determined prices, (2) prices "elastically" determined by the political and economic units involved, and (3) free prices.[21] The second category, as can easily be imagined, created the most problems. In 1958, regional authorities acquired a powerful voice in fixing prices of commodities within their jurisdiction. After January 1961, much of that power was once again withdrawn, and the ministries and enterprises were given a greater voice in the matter of price determination.

Let us try to reinterpret Hsüeh Mu-ch'iao's decentralization proposals in terms of bureaucratic politics. We have stated above that in the game of bureaucratic politics, all players strive to maximize their self-interest. By this we mean that they will try to increase their political decision-making powers and their control over economic resources. Political power in the economic realm, for example, means the power to make and implement invest-

[20] Yang Fang-hsün, "Base Prices on Quality—The Better the Quality, the Better the Price," *Ta-kung pao* (Peking), July 16, 1962.
[21] Cheng, *op. cit.*, p. 95.

ment plans and to create favorable conditions for realizing such plans (e.g., pricing powers). Control over economic resources means having command over supplies, productive plants, and distribution channels, Hsüeh Mu-ch'iao proposed, in effect, that increased powers be given (1) ministries, (2) regional governments, and (3) the enterprises. What he means by (1) and (3) is clear. If we read how he qualifies (2), it is also clear what he means: "regional *party* and *governmental* leadership agencies." In other words, Hsüeh implicitly admits that the provincial party committees were the main wielders of power at the regional level.

When the first State Planning Commission was formed late in 1952, it was an extremely powerful body, commanding ministries, regional government, and enterprises. As it lost its power, that of the ministries grew greater. At the same time, party committees were asserting themselves at the regional level, in accordance with a policy, pursued since the early 1950's, called "regionalization of the party." But enterprises also began to assert themselves, in the face of the obvious inability of centralized direction to work. What Hsüeh therefore proposed was to legitimate a *de facto* situation. Let the ministries have their hierarchical economic empires. Let regional government get greater powers over economic activities in the provinces. Let enterprises enjoy the "independent operational autonomy" which they already have. To make this possible, one must reduce the scope of control by the central policy-making agencies, notably the State Council, and by clear-cut implication, the Politburo. Planning would now consist largely of long-range programming, flexible annual plans, and economy-wide balances.

Although in general Hsüeh Mu-ch'iao's proposal advocated some form of decentralization, it would be misleading to see it only in such terms. When Western scholars speak of decentralization in Soviet-type countries, they generally mean that greater decision-making powers are given to the production units, in the manner advocated by Evsei Liberman in the Soviet Union or Ota Šik in Czechoslovakia. Since there is another kind of decentralization, we shall refer to this as decentralization I. Hsüeh Mu-ch'iao proposed decentralization I, for example, by urging that enterprise profit be made a major success criterion to replace the old "gross output value" indicator. In this way, the manager would be freed from item-by-item dependence on the ministries, could determine his own product mixes, make autonomous supply and sales contracts, and be responsible largely for a given profit target. On the other hand, Hsüeh Mu-ch'iao also advocated increasing the powers of the intermediate administrative level, namely that of the party-dominated regions. Students of Soviet-type economies have often doubted that this type of change could be considered "decentralization," inasmuch as it appears to be simply a transfer of administrative authority to a point farther down in the administrative hierarchy. Indeed, the Chinese (and the Russians) have never referred to this as decentralization, but as "the downward transfer of authority." Nevertheless, as we have indicated, provincial government is a very important level of administration in China, and not only a regional branch of the state administration. Transfer of power to their hands is far from being an insignificant change, as the Great Leap Forward indicates. Therefore, we shall refer to this as decentralization II. Hsüeh thus advocated both types of decentralization.

At the same time, Hsüeh also proposed increasing the powers of the central ministries. Judging from the three-category supply and price system, this presumably meant giving the ministries a tighter grip on the modern strategic sector, principally heavy industry. Thus we can say that, while advocating decentralization moves of different types, he also proposed that the modern strategic sector remain under strict central control.

Hsüeh Mu-ch'iao thus simultaneously advocated centralization, decentralization I, and decentralization II. If it had been implemented, this would have created a highly competitive situation, or, more likely, legitimated one which in fact already existed. One might remember that one of the main accusations leveled against Soviet-style planning during the Eighth Party Congress (September 1956) was, as Li Fu-ch'un put it, "We watch everything too much and too closely." What was needed was more "liveliness, flexibility, creativity, initiative." Under Hsüeh Mu-ch'iao's proposal, ministries would fight with provincial government, enterprises with both, and all with the State Council. It is noteworthy that Hsüeh Mu-ch'iao, like most others in the Ch'en Yün group, comes from Eastern China, which had long experience in the competitive business world. For them, economic struggles were not something to be feared.

Nevertheless, if Hsüeh, following the rules of bureaucratic struggle, represented his own interests, then what he proposed would have made the coordination factor exceedingly important, notably the role of the State Economic and State Planning Commissions, and his own State Statistical Bureau. If different rather than uniform rules of the game prevail in the system of economic administration, then the balancing and planning agencies have to act as powerful arbiters in the game of economic politics.

Competitiveness makes sense only if something comes out of it. What the Ch'en Yün group undoubtedly had in mind was that the greater power and autonomy granted the different organizational sectors would spur them on to maximize their own spheres of activity. The ministries largely controlled the modern strategic sector. Thus the ministries would be impelled to improve their performance in that sector. Regional governments largely controlled light industry, and thus would be impelled to improve performance there. Enterprises, and by implication agricultural production units, would similarly be impelled to improve their own performance.

It was around this time that the idea of an integrated economy and balanced growth through the development of a triangle of relationships between heavy industry, light industry, and agriculture began to arise. Mao Tse-tung himself espoused this idea in the concluding section of his February 1957 speech on internal contradictions within the people. What was at the basis of this conception of development was the growing realization that China could not depend on the Soviet Union for basic support, as it had in the past. This finally took form in the slogan of self-reliance (*tzu-li keng-sheng*), which was originally proposed by the Ch'en Yün group rather than by Mao. One can reinterpret this approach to economic reorganization in terms of this triangle of relationships. Centralization would assure an administrative situation allowing for continuing emphasis on heavy industry. However, the gradual substitution of the profit for the output-value principle of enterprise success, as well as the reduction of state controls over enterprises, would allow even heavy-industry enterprises to produce, to some extent, for demand. Thus heavy industry could be partially reoriented to supply the needs of other economic sectors. Giving provincial governments control over light industry (which was in fact what happened according to the late 1957 decentralization regulations) would give them greater incentive to raise light-industry output, making more producer and consumer goods available from that sector. Extending enterprise autonomy and also that of the rural collectives, along with the introduction of the free market, would create conditions for material incentives to spur output and performance.

Above we have outlined what may be called the moderate approach to the problem of economic reorganization. From all indications, this is essentially the path that Peking decided to follow after early 1961. Early that year, Peking greatly expanded the power and autonomy of production units in both industry and agriculture. At the same time, it undertook a program of re-centralizing the ministries. This was particularly marked in the fields of finance, trade, communications, and certain strategic industries. The recentralization of the banking system was particularly remarkable after the debacle of the Great Leap Forward. Thus in 1961, Peking implemented centralization and decentralization I at the same time. The excesses of decentralization II, which will be described below, were greatly modified. It was also at that time that Peking instituted a policy of self-reliance, such as had been proposed in 1957, for the country as a whole, based on a triangle of relationships between heavy industry, light industry, and agriculture.

Above we have discussed the Ch'en Yün approach to economic reorganization. That approach was not implemented in 1958. What was implemented may be called Mao Tse-tung's dialectical vision for the total transformation of Chinese society. It involved a decentralization of a completely different type. This second approach need not be stated in the abstract. It suffices simply to describe what actually happened.

In essence, what was implemented late in 1957 was an extreme version of decentralization II. The three decentralization regulations on industry, commerce, and finance make it unequivocally clear that great power and resources were to be put into the hands of provincial government. Almost all of China's light industry passed into provincial hands. Except for certain key commodities, all other commodities came under provincial control. There was no mention of a free market for "third category" goods. The Ministry of Commerce was virtually dismantled. Its so-called specialized trading corporations were abolished. Provincial governments were allowed to set up their own procurement and distribution networks. Provincial governments acquired broad price-fixing powers. Although the regulations on industry broadened the scope of managerial power, it was made absolutely clear that this concerned only internal enterprise matters. Moreover, even though enterprises were allowed to retain a bigger share of above-target profit, provincial governments, according to the regulations on finance, could tap their profits to make up budgetary deficits. Provincial governments acquired far-reaching powers to hire, fire, and transfer personnel. But that was by no means the end of their powers. Provincial governments, through dual rule, acquired a powerful voice over central state-owned enterprises located in their territory. This meant that they were able to place orders with them and so work them into their provincial plans. This prerogative was fully exercised, as became clear in 1958. Provincial governments were even given foreign currency quotas to make purchases abroad.

No mention was made of broadening the powers of the ministries. On the contrary, the ministries lost large chunks of their empires, either through direct transfer to provincial governments or through dual rule. The blow which the ministries sustained became clear in February 1958, when a large-scale ministerial reorganization was promulgated. The powerful Ministry of Commerce, headed by Ch'en Yün, was split in two. The various machine-building ministries were amalgamated. The State Construction Committee was abolished. The Materials Supply Bureau, which formerly had broad controls over supply allocation, was made into a part of the State Economic Commission.[22] In a sense, the Chinese, without actually abolishing the ministries, did just about what the Russians tried to do in May 1957 when they abolished most of the economic ministries and set up their regional economic councils (*sovnarkhozy*).

The extreme way decentralization II was carried out made both centralization at the top and decentralization I at the bottom impossible. Moreover, it meant a triumph of the territorial principle over the production principle of organization. The provinces emerged as quasi-autarkic economic regions. With their newly-acquired power and resources, they began to engage in ambitious production and construction programs. Provinces began to act like underdeveloped countries, each trying to set up a modern industrial sector. The state economic plan, which was supposed to be binding on the whole economy, became meaningless. Long-range planning was in effect replaced by what were called provincial developmental programs. Provincial governments set forth

[22] *Chung-kung shih-nien* [*Communist China, Ten Years*] (Hong Kong: Union Research Institute, 1960), p. 46.

long-term developmental goals, and based their annual plans on them. Under these conditions, the idea of comprehensive balance was shattered. In May 1958, Liu Shao-ch'i attacked the idea of balance, and, as a result, the planning agencies were virtually dismantled. It was not till December 1958 that an attempt was made to put a halt to these centrifugal tendencies.

Until October 1957, all signs indicated that Peking was going to implement a program of administrative change similar to that outlined by Hsüeh Mu-ch'iao. Yet when the final decentralization decisions were officially promulgated in November, it was revealed to be a decisive decision in favor of decentralization II. There can be no doubt that this was due to a sudden shift in the power constellation of the game of bureaucratic politics. The Mao-Liu program of economic development had won out. The Ch'en Yün decentralization proposals reflected political compromise: all major actors in the game got something. The return in 1961 to the Ch'en Yün program and Peking's adherence since then to a flexible and pragmatic approach to economic administration indicates that bureaucratic compromise continues to characterize China's economic politics. However, in late 1957, normal politics were upset by the clear-cut triumph of the Mao-Liu group.[23]

The main political change was the attack on bureaucratic professionals, particularly in the central ministries, during the anti-rightist movement, and the emergence of provincial party figures loyal to the Mao-Liu line. Late in 1957 a series of political purges of leading provincial party officials began, lasting well into 1958. In contrast to the Russian purges of the mid-1930's, the Chinese purges of 1957–58 involved no bloodshed. Moreover, instead of destroying regional party machines, they helped build them up to such an extent that they were able to launch the great provincial development programs of the Great Leap Forward. The provincial party committees became so powerful that they were able to mobilize the resources of almost every regional economic sector, without interference either from national or local branch agencies.[24] In the enterprises, party committees took over from management, thus creating an uninterrupted span of control from the provincial capital downward. Thus while decentralization took place at the national level, a centralization occurred at

[23] See my discussion of the 1957 decentralization in Schurmann, *op. cit.*, pp. 195 ff.
[24] *Ibid.*, pp. 215–16.

the provincial level. The communes were an example of this apparently contradictory process. While given a certain autonomy from state administrative control, the communes themselves were highly centralized. The absence of decentralization I meant that there were no counter-tendencies to check the centralizing tendencies radiating out from the regional and local levels.

These political changes were a direct result of major policy changes at the top. Mao Tse-tung demanded a program of social mobilization which could guarantee a rapid increase in farm output. His instrument for realizing this program was the party, as it was Stalin's instrument in the collectivization of the late 1920's and the early 1930's. However, the transfer of power to the party meant that the provincial and local party organizations gained significant command over men and resources. Thus, the provinces began to engage in ambitious construction and production programs of their own. The new developmental model was the medium- and small-scale plant utilizing heavy labor inputs and traditional methods, and dependent on an ever-increasing supply of agricultural raw materials. Peking could not have envisaged the strain on the economy which the Great Leap Forward of 1958 created. It had set certain wheels in motion to achieve its particular goals, but once the wheels were turning, it was difficult to stop them.

From the foregoing discussion, it is clear that the issue of centralization and decentralization involves a transfer of power among the various policy-making, operational, and coordinative agencies in terms of the three levels of organization: central, regional, and production unit. Moreover, except in dramatic instances, such as the 1957 decentralization decisions of late 1957, centralization and decentralization are not necessarily mutually exclusive.

If we look at the history of Chinese economic administration over the last decade and a half, there is no doubt that there is a general trend toward decentralization, not so different from what has been happening in the rest of the Communist world. However, from a political viewpoint, it is more meaningful to see this development as one going from concentration to distribution of power. "Structural differentiation," as the sociologists put it, seems to be one of the consequences of system institutionalization over time, and in this sense power distribution can be said to signify institutionalization. One can also view the developments in Eastern Europe and Russia in the same way. While there too the over-all trend has been from centralization to decentralization, the strong resistance to making a final move towards "market socialism" indicates that what we call decentralization I, or large-scale transfer of economic powers to the production units, is not the basic political-economic aim of the changes. Rather it is one of distributing powers more broadly, so that the production units gain some new powers, but the other bureaucratic units, central and regional, retain their share.

One of the conclusions which emerge from the Chinese case, and for which there is evidence from other Communist countries, is that the party as organization appears to exercise particular power at regional levels. The simplest explanation may be that at the regional level the party faces less competition from state administrative organizations than at the central level. Since the administrative apparatus is smaller, the party secretary knows most people in power and can deal with them personally. However, there may be another reason. Regional governments, in contrast to the state ministries, have control over a wide range of different administrative and managerial units. The kaleidoscopic nature of regional administration is partly due to the fact that light industry and agriculture constitute one of their major economic domains. Factories are small and very different, and the farms each have their local peculiarities. Thus one of the major functions of the party is coordination. Since the party machine has contacts with every segment of organization, the party committee or secretary is the logical person to turn to if some one needs help in a business deal. For example, during the last years, provincial party committees have organized "materials exchange meetings" (*wu-tzu chiao-liu-hui*) which bring buyers and sellers together and result in the conclusion of economic contracts.

If the party does tend to develop particular power at the regional levels, then one can envisage a continuing power conflict between the central state ministries, regional party organizations, and the production units. Each of these organizational units tries to maximize its own interests in the resource allocation conflict, but each needs the support of the top policy-making body (Politburo or State Council) in order to gain maximum advantage.

In late 1957 the Politburo threw its full weight behind the regional party machines. There can be no doubt that this political move had a decisive influence on the nature of economic development in 1958. However, decentralization did not affect the heavy industrial sector, where the central ministries retained tight control. Here we enter an even more obscure realm of economic politics, for heavy industry in China, as in the Soviet Union, is bound up with military and strategic interests. The trade agreements concluded with the Soviet Union in 1958 and 1959 guaranteed the Chinese a stepped-up inflow of needed capital goods. However, heavy industry was still dependent on local resources. With the increased power of local party committees and their ambitious development programs, a resource allocation conflict between the party and the military may have developed. This may have been a factor in the significant political changes that occurred in October 1958 in the highly industrialized Liaoning province of Manchuria. The exacerbation of the Sino-Soviet dispute and the ouster of Marshal P'eng Te-huai in September 1959 may have marked the full victory of the party in the power political game.

Given the patterns of economic politics we have discerned in China, let us now see if they are of use in understanding the history of economic politics in Russia. Since the Soviet 20th Party Congress (February 1956), economic reform has been the subject of continuing discussion in official and academic circles in Russia and Eastern Europe. Yugoslavia, of course, was the first Communist nation to implement far-reaching economic reform, but not until the 20th Party Congress was it possible openly to advocate similar reforms in Eastern Europe and Russia. Decollectivization in Poland started the process of economic reform in Eastern Europe. In 1957, Khrushchev introduced a series of administrative changes which appeared to indicate a move toward decentralization. At the present time, several East European countries are beginning to implement programs of economic reform moving in the direction of decentralization, notably East Germany, Czechoslovakia, and Hungary. Yet, while it has become generally accepted that economic controls have to be loosened and production units given greater freedom to determine their own economic programs and operations, in every country of Eastern Europe and in Russia, there has been continuing resistance against the full implementation of reform programs. Though in part this is due to Stalinist and conservative opposition to change, it can also be seen as resistance by vested interests in the game of bureaucratic politics. To see whether there are similarities to the Chinese situation, let us first briefly examine the history of economic administration in Russia.

The Soviet Union of Stalin has been regarded as the typical model of a Communist country seeking to industrialize rapidly through central planning. When the Chinese, in the early 1950's, followed the Soviet model, it was essentially the one developed under Stalin. However, Soviet centralization was of a particular type. As a result of the great purges of the mid-1930's, the great central ministries in Moscow acquired almost total control over the country's resources and productive capacity. The ministries developed great economic empires, much like the gigantic corporations of the West. Regional government had control over what was left, largely small consumer goods industries, which were of secondary economic importance. Overarching this ministerial structure was *Gosplan*, a powerful body which collected information on the entire economy, worked out national balances, and drew up plans on the basis of policy decisions. Economic policy was made by a small circle of advisers around Stalin. Policy, operations, and coordination were all concentrated in Moscow. To get something, local officials and managers had to go on *komandirovki* to Moscow.

However, without the great purges of the mid-1930's, it is doubtful whether Stalin would have been able to implement fully such a program of extreme centralization. The NEP policy, in effect until 1928, had given the production units considerable autonomy, even though it was subject to constant encroachment by the growing central ministries. However, the termination of the NEP in 1928 saw a transfer of power to another segment of the structure. Collectivization of agriculture was carried out, not by the ministries but by regional and local party organizations. Similarly, the enforcement of the norms set down by the First Five-Year Plan was also implemented by the regional party organizations. Thus, whatever the opposition to collectivization in certain central party circles, the adoption by Stalin of what was essentially Trotsky's program led to a remarkable growth in party power. That this had economic consequences is indicated by Professor Merle Fainsod's findings, in his Smolensk study, that the *oblast'* had "a degree of initiative on the part of the *oblast'* authorities which is in some contradiction to the usual emphasis on the centralized processes of Soviet planning." In fact, the *oblasti* had regional developmental plans of their own.[25]

Despite a continuing purge, central party factions and regional party machines succeeded in increasing their power sufficiently to enable them to mount serious resistance to Stalin's programs. The clear signs of compromise during the 17th Party Congress of 1934 indicated that Stalin was not yet able to enforce his single will over the party. There are so many personalities involved in the politics and purges of the first half of the 1930's that it is difficult to discern any clear-cut patterns. However, the fact that major opposition came from the so-called Leningrad circle and that the subsequent purges hit particularly hard at the regional party machines suggests that these regional machines, which had become strong as a result of the collectivization program, were making their power felt in the Central Committee. One of the charges leveled against Stalin in the early 1930's was that he was creating a bureaucratic despotism. The truth of those charges is indicated by the triumph of ministerial centralization as a result of Stalin's victory over the party. Stalin's victory of 1935 had the exact opposite effect of Mao's victory in 1957. In the former case, the ministries triumphed over the party, and in the latter case the party triumphed over the ministries.[26]

Though it is difficult to interpret the politics of the early 1930's in terms of the resource allocation conflict, here too we may hazard a guess regarding the patterns. The investment targets of the First Five-Year Plan were the most ambitious of any period of Russian economic history. These targets greatly exceeded growth possibilities. If the Second Five-Year Plan was drafted under the "compromise" conditions prevailing in 1932 and 1933, then one can understand the reason for the scaled-down targets. After the trauma of collectivization, considerable pressure came from different areas of the political scene to allow the country a period of respite. The high investment targets of the First Five-Year Plan required a massive mobilization of resources, for which the party and the central ministries functioned as two main instrumentalities. Since the goals of collectivization and of industrialization went far beyond reasonable possibilities, one can only see them as

[25] Merle Fainsod, *Smolensk under Soviet Rule* (Cambridge: Harvard University Press, 1958), p. 103.

[26] Merle Fainsod, *How Russia Is Ruled* (Cambridge: Harvard University Press, 1958), pp. 171–72.

political devices serving the aim of power concentration. Thus collectivization and rapid industrialization had major political as well as economic aims. However, the simultaneous growth of party and ministerial power brought about conflicting claims on the country's resources. We may note that per-capita consumption rose during the Second Five-Year Plan, but fell again under the Third Five-Year Plan.[27] It is not inconceivable that pressure from the party, which was in closer contact with the needs and demands of society than the ministries, was responsible for the scaled-down targets of the Second Plan and the improvement in the consumption picture for the country as a whole. Thus to implement fully his crash program of rapid heavy industrialization, Stalin opted for the one instrument of rule which was best designed for this purpose: ministerial centralization. Thus Stalin had to destroy the bases of party power, and make what was left of the party a bureaucratized apparatus completely loyal to the center. The irony is that Stalin destroyed the very agency through which he rose to power.[28]

De-Stalinization, led by N. S. Khrushchev, reversed the political developments of the great purges. Basing his strength on a revived party, Khrushchev began his campaign against the great ministries. In May 1957, when he abolished twenty-five major ministries and made them into offices of the *Gosplan*, the struggle with the proponents of ministerial rule, presumably the "anti-party" group, boiled into the open. Convening the Central Committee with its regional party bosses, Khrushchev reversed the Politburo's adverse decision against him and so finally consolidated his power.[29]

Most significant, in regard to economic administration, was the formation of *oblast'*-level *sovnarkhozy*, that is, regional economic councils which were given broad powers to initiate, operate, and coordinate economic activity. In form, Khrushchev's decentralization was quite similar to that carried out under Mao Tse-tung's initiative in China. The difference is that the greater power of the

---

[27] Bergson, *op. cit.*, p. 315. Investment targets also declined during the period of the Second Five-Year Plan (p. 311, note 6).

[28] The sharply increased recruitment of new party members from the intelligentsia, the rising young technicians of the country, may also be interpreted as a shift from party to bureaucratic rule; see Leonard B. Schapiro, *The Communist Party of the Soviet Union* (London: Eyre and Spottiswoode, 1960), p. 438.

[29] Schwartz, *op. cit.*, pp. 88–92.

party and the lesser power of the ministries led to an effective decentralization in China's case, whereas in Russia "creeping recentralization" began almost at once. The ministries, albeit under a different cloak, were able to sustain the branch empires they had built up over the years.[30]

As regards the economic plans, there is a further similarity between the Russian and Chinese developments of 1958. In both cases, sustained growth in heavy industry was seen as compatible with a leap forward in light industrial production and in agricultural growth. In both cases, economic development programs were launched in regions earlier disfavored by the commitment to select development. Similarly, the 1958 decentralization in both the Soviet Union and China did little to increase the autonomy of factory managers or kolkhoz directors. The main beneficiary of the decentralization policy was the party.

While Khrushchev, like Mao, was intent on cutting down the powers of the ministries, he also strove to create more effective coordination at national as well as regional levels. The establishment of the State Economic Commission in 1956 was designed to broaden the coordinative powers of central government and counteract the departmentalism of the powerful ministries. The encouragment given new planning techniques, such as input-output, can be interpreted politically as a device to increase the coordinative powers of the central government. Khrushchev's program can be described as one which retained top policy-making functions in central hands, but decentralized operational controls farther down the system, notably at the strong points of party rule, the republics and the *oblasti,* but tried to counteract this by increasing the coordinative mechanisms of government.

Like the Chinese Great Leap Forward, Khrushchev's decentralization was of short duration. Since the late 1950's, there have been continuing administrative changes, reflecting both a groping toward a new system and the struggle of competing bureaucracies to defend and expand their interests. Perhaps the most significant change has been the recognition that production units must be given a share of economic power, as indicated in the cautious moves to implement the Liberman program. Thus, despite the sharp ideological differences between the Russians and the Chinese, both economies exhibit similar administrative tendencies: the autonomy of production units (enterprises and farms) has

[30] Grossman, *op. cit.,* pp. 37–39.

been expanded, intermediate administrative levels, i.e., regional and local, have retained a considerable degree of economic power, and the central ministries have reasserted themselves in the wake of the loss of power experienced in 1957 and 1958.

In Russia, China, and Eastern Europe, the obvious failings of central planning have strengthened the voices of factory directors who wish to broaden their autonomy. The iron lesson of economic failure thus gave strength to the politically least influential group within the nexus of bureaucratic politics, namely the factory managers. However, the counter-forces are strong. Not only do the ministries resist decentralization, but the party resists it too. Thus, in many countries we find decentralization down to the production unit level (decentralization I) frustrated by policies aimed at creating intermediate units to make decisions on enterprises. This happened, for example, in Eastern Germany, where trusts (*Vereinigungen VEB*) were set up which have control over a number of similar product enterprises;[31] earlier in the Soviet Union, a similar device, the *firm,* was set up for the same purpose.[32] In Yugoslavia too, the extreme decentralization of the early 1950's has been followed by the growth of such intermediate levels. From what we know of the politics of Communist countries, it is precisely at this level that the party is able to exercise its strongest control. If the top policy-makers are afraid of such regional *mestnichestvo,* then they can counteract it by expanding the powers of the managers, but also by reaffirming the ministerial branch system. However, every concession to the latter tendency means a return to the road of centralization.

What our analysis suggests is that the history of economic administration of Communist countries from Asia to Europe indicates that, after a number of single-shot administrative approaches, economic power has become more broadly distributed. A kind of bureaucratic pluralism has arisen, making it difficult for any particular economic interest to establish its primacy. Thus if the ministries reacquire power, the policy-planners will seek to offset this by strengthening some other segment of the economic administration, for example, the central coordinative agencies, the intermediate structures, or the production units. Conversely, any move toward excessive decentralization will soon knock against resistance from other interests. This is apparently what

[31] Gamarnikow, *op. cit.,* p. 16.
[32] *New York Times,* Aug. 29, 1962.

has been happening to the ambitious reform program of the Czechs.

Some observers have envisaged a solution to the economic dilemma where far-reaching powers are granted the production units but central planning is preserved through powerful state planning and state economic commissions which make use of modern information-gathering and -processing devices to come up with optimal plans. However, such a solution appears unlikely in view of the entrenched nature of two basic administrative and political structures: the state bureaucracy and the party. Neither would consent to its own withering away. Thus, politically, market socialism appears to be an unlikely future for the Communist countries. Nevertheless, the development of a true bureaucratic pluralism, while not doing away with waste and inefficiency, tends to preclude radical programs and to assure reasonable economic growth within the given system. One cannot fail to note the growing appearance of realism in the economic plans of both Russia and China. Such realism is the result of compromise. To set unrealistic goals would encourage certain bureaucracies to think that they had gained a decisive victory in the resource allocation struggle and would upset the webs of balance that have been developing.

Earlier we suggested that not only the patterns of economic administration but the economic plans themselves may be seen as expressions of bureaucratic politics. This is much easier to conceive if we see the plans as essentially political rather than economic documents. Both the Russian and Chinese five-year plans have exhibited such irrationalities that real economic performance has rarely met the specifications of the plan. But we must remember that the main effect of a plan, as in a Western budget, is to grant agencies and enterprises a certain measure of economic power, that is, command over men and resources. What they do with that power is another matter, usually determined by economic realities rather than by the objectives of the policy-makers. In this respect, we should like to suggest one basic political-economic pattern.

If the party indeed tends to develop its power mainly at the regional level, then we must remember that a large part of the men and resources it commands are in the agricultural and light industrial sectors. This means also that agriculture and light industry tend to become major concerns of the party. In 1958, both the Russian and Chinese parties launched a vast program to bring about a leap forward in these two sectors. Because of the particular constellation of power at the center, in both countries regional party organizations were able to command men and resources to try out their programs. We should like to suggest that an increase in party political power at this intermediate level of organization, that is, the regions (whether republic or *oblast'* in Russia, or province and *hsien* in China), creates pressure to divert resources into these sectors. It is significant that when Malenkov sought to strengthen his position within the party in 1953, he unexpectedly espoused a program of increasing consumer goods output. The Russian and Chinese programs of 1958 failed largely because decentralization II could not arouse true initiative and creativity on the part of the production units. Thus opponents of party-led decentralization have argued for production-unit autonomy as the best way to increase consumer goods, ideas that are being implemented in a limited way both in Russia and China at the present time. Local party leaders in Communist countries tend to have commitments to their region and develop a kind of paternalistic pride in the welfare of their constituents. To mark his administration, a local party leader may build a big swimming pool, establish a new clinic, or do something else to please his people. Macropolitically, such attitudes create pressures for the country to move in a welfare direction, pressures which conflict with the growth maximizers of the central ministries. In this sense, the strong local party organizations can be seen as the main proponents of a "Great Society" for their own countries.

The strongest argument which the ministerial centralizers make to perpetuate and expand their control is that of *la patrie en danger*. Whether Stalin really believed in 1928 that a capitalist attack was inevitable is immaterial. That was the argument he used to justify both heavy industrialization and ministerial centralization. The present growth of ministerial power in the USSR again may not be directly related to the worsening international situation, but a linkage cannot be dismissed out of hand. Khrushchev made peaceful coexistence and raising of consumer goods his two major policies. His talks with President Eisenhower at Camp David in September 1959 appeared to result in firm Soviet-American agreement that the United States too adhered to this policy. We have evidence that the U-2 incident of May 1960 badly shook Khrushchev's position in the face of his opposition which demanded continued adherence to a strong defense and heavy industry policy. It is not difficult to guess at the link between these two policies. If there be true peaceful coexistence, then the hard-liners have fewer arguments to justify their claim to scarce resources, and more can be diverted to peaceful uses.[33]

In the Chinese case, the link between domestic and inter-national policies is more difficult to establish. However, a starting point is the fact that in 1958, both Russia and China were pursuing similar domestic policies—both had their "leaps for-ward." Since peaceful coexistence is predicated on the assumption that attack from the other side is not to be feared in the immedi-ate future, it is noteworthy that in 1958 the Chinese dismissed the leading advocate of the idea of threatening American attack, Su Yü, chief of staff of the P.L.A. There is evidence to suggest that the Chinese Communists in 1958 believed that the balance of forces in the world had so shifted that general war was unlikely and that national defense could be subordinated to the immediate needs of economic development. Such a view, of course, implied continuing reliance on the Soviet deterrent and on Soviet military aid, a position espoused by Marshal P'eng Te-huai. The latter's dismissal in September 1959, after the Camp David meeting, and the reappointment of Su Yü to the Ministry of National Defense in 1959, mirrored the growing Sino-Soviet conflict.[34]

Recentralization in China occurred after the economic crisis, partly as a reaction to the breakdown of central control and perhaps also as a reaction to the growing sense of *la patrie en danger*. However, both decentralization and regional party power continue to characterize economic administration in China. Thus we would say there remains a strong commitment to the primacy of economic development, and of agriculture and light industry in particular. However, with the dangers of war growing, the calls for mobilization have been increasing and undoubtedly also the pressures for centralization.

[33] On the resource allocation conflict in the Soviet Union, see Carl Linden, "How Strong is Khrushchev?" *Problems of Communism*, Vol. XII, No. 5 (Sept.–Oct., 1963), pp. 27–35.

[34] Alice Langley Hsieh, *Communist China's Strategy in the Nuclear Era* (Englewood Cliffs, N.J.: Prentice-Hall, 1962), pp. 65–66, 117.

Soviet and Communist Chinese
Industrialization Strategies

K. C. YEH

I. INTRODUCTION

THIS paper compares the Soviet and Communist Chinese strategies of industrialization during the period of their respective first
two Five-Year Plans (FYP), that is, 1928–37 for the Soviet Union
and 1953–62 for Communist China. The discussion is limited
mainly to three broad problems of development policy: the allocation of resources to investment, the priority of industry in the
allocation of capital investment, and the choice of techniques and
scale in industrial production. To be sure, the question of choosing among alternative patterns of resource use has more facets
than those mentioned here,[1] and industrialization is certainly
more than an economic problem. The delimitation is intended in
part to focus attention on certain major issues, and in part to

The author is a member of the Economics Department of The RAND
Corporation, Santa Monica, California. Any views expressed in this
paper are those of the author, and should not be interpreted as reflecting the views of The RAND Corporation or the official opinion or policy of
any of its governmental or private research sponsors. The author is indebted to Abraham S. Becker, Oleg Hoeffding, Richard Moorsteen, Richard
R. Nelson, Egon Neuberger, Nancy Nimitz, and Richard and Helen Yin for
helpful comments. He is also grateful to Richard Moorsteen and Raymond
P. Powell for permission to use the results of their forthcoming monograph, *The Soviet Capital Stock, 1928–1962,* and to Norman M. Kaplan for
permission to use the results of his forthcoming monograph on Soviet
capital formation. In revising this paper the author has greatly benefited
from discussions with Abram Bergson and Gregory Grossman. Of course,
the author alone is responsible for any error that may occur.

[1] For example, interesting issues such as investment in human versus
physical capital and the extent of participation in world trade will not be
discussed here.

avoid infringing upon the domains of other speakers of this conference. Within this narrow scope, the treatment of the topics included in this paper is uneven. Greater emphasis is placed upon Communist China's development policies, since these have been little explored. Two particular areas are relatively neglected: the Soviet Second FYP, primarily because its essential features were fairly similar to those of the First, and China's post-1959 policies on which only limited information is available.

A word on the choice of periods for the comparison is in order. In the forty-some years of Soviet economic development since 1917, at least four phases can be broadly distinguished: the periods of War Communism, the New Economic Policy, industrialization under the first two FYP's, and the post-1953 development including the recent slowdown after 1958. I selected the period 1928–37 in the Soviet Union for comparison with the similar Chinese period 1953–62 primarily because Communist China patterned her industrialization drive after the Russian experience with the Stalinist model in mind. Clearly, the choice of period here has its limitations. The Soviet Union was already on her way to industrialization long before 1928, and certain interesting parallels between the Soviet economic policy in the other periods and the Chinese case will be neglected.

Section II compares the industrialization strategies during the respective Soviet and Chinese First FYP periods (1928/29–1932 and 1953–1957). Section III contrasts the broad economic background against which the Soviet and Chinese policy decisions were made. Section IV discusses China's development policies during the Great Leap Forward in 1958–59 and the aftermath of the Leap in 1960–62. Section V draws some tentative conclusions on the Sino-Soviet experience.

II. SOVIET AND CHINESE INDUSTRIALIZATION STRATEGIES DURING THEIR FIRST FYP PERIODS

The Soviet strategy designed to achieve rapid industrial growth is well known. Its main features include: a steep rate of capital formation, overwhelming emphasis on industrial development above everything else, high priority of heavy industry in investment allocation among the various branches of industry, and preference for large plants and capital-intensive techniques. On the eve of her First FYP, Communist China (hereafter, China for short) declared that "the Soviet path to industrialization was the very road that China should and must follow."[2] I shall try to pinpoint the specific areas where the Soviet model has left its direct imprint and where the Chinese have departed from the Soviet experience during this period.

The Rate of Investment

To compare the policies of the two countries with respect to the share of output devoted to investment, the relevant measure is the rate of investment in current factor cost. Unfortunately, statistical information is incomplete. For the Soviet Union, estimates of the ratio of gross investment to gross national product in current factor cost are available only for 1928 and 1937. They range from 20 to 25 per cent for 1928, and from 21 to 26 per cent for 1937.[3] For the intervening years, the share of investment in income probably rose and then declined.[4]

For Communist China, the ratio of gross investment to gross domestic product in terms of prevailing prices in 1952 was about 20 per cent.[5] It probably rose somewhat during 1952–60 and then declined after 1960.

The comparison of these estimates is subject to many qualifications. Three should be mentioned here. First, the Soviet data are based on the adjusted factor cost standard, which operationally means that both gross investment and gross national product are net of turnover taxes and gross of subsidies. For lack of information in the Chinese case, no such adjustments have been made.[6] Second, the concept underlying the Soviet data refers to the ratio of national capital formation to national product, whereas that for China refers to the ratio of domestic capital formation to

2 Editorial of *Jen-min jih-pao* (People's Daily) (hereafter cited as *JMJP*), Peking, Dec. 26, 1952.

3 Estimates by A. Bergson for 1928 and 1937 are 25.0 and 25.9 per cent respectively. A. Bergson, *The Real National Income of Soviet Russia since 1928* (Cambridge: Harvard University Press, 1961; hereafter cited as *Real SNIP*), p. 237. The estimates by Moorsteen and Powell are 20.3 and 21.1 per cent. Richard Moorsteen and Raymond P. Powell, *The Soviet Capital Stock, 1928–1962* (forthcoming), Table T-50.

4 A. Bergson, *The Economics of Soviet Planning* (New Haven and London: Yale University Press, 1964; hereafter cited as *Soviet Planning*), p. 311.

5 K. C. Yeh, "Capital Formation in Mainland China, 1931–36 and 1952–57" (unpublished).

6 As pointed out by Professor Bergson, the use of factor cost weights would yield a rate of investment somewhat higher than that in prevailing prices because of the inclusion of indirect taxes in the prices of consumers goods.

domestic product.[7] A third problem arises because of possible differences in the price structure. By and large, the Soviet Union in 1928 was industrially more advanced than China in 1952. The prices of capital goods relative to those of the rest of the national product were likely to be lower in the USSR than in China. This disparity was probably further widened by the acute shortage of capital goods in China due to the Western blockade of China during the Korean War. Thus the use of 1952 price weights for China is likely to show a higher investment share than would have been the case if the Soviet price weights of 1928 were used.[8] Nonetheless, in my judgment, the errors introduced by these complications are not serious enough to change the broad observations suggested by the comparison: during their respective First FYP periods, both countries adopted the big push policy of devoting a relatively large share, some 20 to 25 per cent of their total output, to investment.[9]

The distinctive feature of the Soviet investment share as compared to those of Western countries and Japan, however, is not so much the high investment ratio as the rapidity with which the

[7] The difference is simply that the "national" concept includes, while the "domestic" concept excludes, net changes in claims against foreign countries. If China's net change in claims against foreign countries is positive (i.e., domestic savings invested abroad exceed investment from abroad), then national capital formation would be larger than domestic capital formation, and the investment share would be higher than the 20 per cent given above. This is because adding a positive amount to both the numerator and denominator of a ratio less than unity will raise the ratio. According to China's claims, there had been a net outflow of external assistance during 1953–57. United Nations, *Economic Survey of Asia and the Far East, 1957* (Bangkok, 1958), p. 103. To the extent this is true, the "national" ratio should be somewhat higher than 20 per cent. In any case, the net change in claims is not likely to be large relative to total domestic capital formation so that for the present purpose the "domestic" ratio would not be significantly different from the "national" ratio.

[8] According to the State Statistical Bureau, an accumulation rate of 25 per cent based on the Chinese prices would amount to about 20 per cent when computed on the basis of Soviet prices. Chang Chu-chung, "A Critique of the Theory of Fixed Accumulation Proportions," *Chi-hua ching-chi* (Planned Economy) (hereafter cited as *CHCC*), Peking, No. 8, 1958, p. 24. It is not clear which Soviet prices the Bureau was using. Presumably the Soviet prices refer to 1925/26 prices.

[9] The similarity in the two investment shares conforms to Kuznets' findings about the uniformity of investment shares among Communist countries with widely different per capita income. Simon Kuznets, "Quantitative Aspects of Economic Growth of Nations," *Economic Development and Cultural Change*, VIII:4, Part II (July, 1960), pp. 20–21, 27–32. In the present case, the similarity should not be overdrawn, for the estimates for China are rather crude.

high level was attained.[10] As noted by Professor Bergson, the Soviet high level in 1928 probably had been achieved in the course of a few preceding years.[11] In the case of China, no estimate for the immediate pre-1952 years is available. But what little we know suggests that a sharp upturn in the investment share also occurred in the few years prior to 1952. The rise was probably even steeper than in the Soviet case. For the USSR by 1913 was already on her way, albeit slowly, from being a 5 per cent saver to becoming a 12 per cent saver,[12] whereas China's rather low investment share in the 1930's (about 6 per cent) shows no marked upward trend. The Sino-Japanese War during 1937–45 and the civil war thereafter were hardly conducive to economic progress and even less to increasing savings. According to a tentative estimate, output in 1946 was below the prewar level.[13] During the immediate postwar period, the pent-up consumer demand, the acute shortage of capital goods, and the increase in military expenditures following the gradual spread of civil strife might well have brought the rate of investment in those years considerably below that of the 1930's.

The steep rise in the investment share of the two countries seems all the more remarkable if one recalls that the upward trend occurred in a period of rising military expenditures.[14] Moreover, the high rate of investment was achieved with little external financial aid. In the Soviet case, while some short-term and long-term credits were received from abroad during 1928–32, they were miniscule compared to total investment.[15] In China

---

[10] Simon Kuznets, "A Comparative Appraisal," in A. Bergson and S. Kuznets (eds.), *Economic Trends in the Soviet Union* (Cambridge: Harvard University Press, 1963; hereafter cited as *Economic Trends*), pp. 353–56.

[11] *Soviet Planning*, pp. 312–13.

[12] Oleg Hoeffding, *Soviet State Planning and Forced Industrialization as a Model for Asia* (The RAND Corporation, P-1450, Aug. 5, 1958).

[13] Ou Pao-san, *National Income of China, 1933, 1936 and 1946* (Nanking: Institute of Social Sciences, Academia Sinica, 1947).

[14] *Soviet Planning*, p. 317; Liu Shao-ch'i, "Political Report," *Hsin-hua pan-yüeh-k'an* (New China Semi-monthly) (hereafter cited as *HHPYK*), Peking, No. 20, 1956, p. 9.

[15] According to Holzman's estimates, the Soviet Union in 1928 incurred a trade deficit of 198 million rubles, or 2.9 per cent of gross investment. The importance of capital inflow in the subsequent years was declining. This is supported by the Soviet official estimate which shows that foreign credits (i.e., trade deficit plus deficit in the invisible account) in the First FYP period amount to only 2.7 per cent of capital investment. Franklyn D. Holzman, "Foreign Trade," *Economic Trends*, p. 320.

during 1953–57, there was actually a net outflow of external economic assistance.[16]

It seems reasonable to interpret the rapid rise of the investment share in both countries as the result of deliberate decisions of the leaders.[17] What were their underlying theories concerning the size of the investment share? It appears that, in the Soviet Union, the directors' "concern is to realize the highest possible rate of growth of the country's income, or the highest possible level at some future time. The volume of investment is determined accordingly."[18] In actual planning, the division of income into investment and consumption is made on the basis of the projected growth rates of the "means of production" and the "means of consumption."[19]

During a larger part of the First FYP period, the Chinese leaders apparently adopted the same policy. According to the chairman of the State Planning Commission, the volume of investment was determined by pushing the scale of the investment program toward the level corresponding to the highest possible growth rate, until it hit the ceiling of one or a combination of the three major constraints: "financial resources," technical manpower, and equipment supply.[20] In the present case it was the second and third constraint that limited the volume of investment in the First FYP. Only after resource requirements for

[16] United Nations, *op. cit.* An unknown amount of Soviet military aid was extended to China. This, however, was probably offset to some extent by China's military aid to North Korea.

[17] This statement implies that the leaders exercise considerable control over the size of the investment share. Of course, their control cannot be complete. But by and large, their influence was probably decisive. In general, the influence was probably much stronger over longer than shorter periods and in specific sectors and types of investment than in the aggregate. In the case of China, centralized control was probably less direct and less effective during this period, partly because there was still a large private sector prior to 1956 and partly because of the dominant influence of the harvest conditions on savings.

[18] *Soviet Planning,* pp. 303–26. A possible alternative hypothesis may be suggested: the directors seek to minimize consumption for any period, allowing for "necessary" increases due to such factors as population growth, and then allocate the rest of the output to investment. This may be termed the maximum saving capability approach as distinguished from the former hypothesis, which may be called the optimum investment requirement approach.

[19] *Soviet Planning,* p. 325; Robert W. Campbell, *Soviet Economic Power* (Cambridge: Riverside Press, 1960), p. 148.

[20] Li Fu-chun, "Report on the First Five Year Plan to Develop the National Economy," *Hsin-hua yüeh-pao* (New China Monthly) (hereafter cited as *HHYP*), Peking, No. 8, 1955, p. 8.

the construction of the investment projects were met would the consumers get their share.[21] Toward the end of the period there were indications of a shift away from this policy.

The Pattern of Capital Investment Allocation

A comparison of the distribution of capital investment by four economic sectors in the USSR and China is presented in Table 1.[22] The four sectors are (1) "industry," which includes mining, manufacturing, electric power stations, construction, and surveying; (2) "agriculture," which includes state farms, collective farms, machine tractor stations, and such activities as irrigation, flood control, prevention of soil erosion, and afforestation; (3) "transport and communications," which include railroad, water, land and air transportation, mail, telephone, telegraph, and radio; and (4) "other," which includes all sectors other than those in the first three categories. A sub-item in the "other" category, housing construction, is also separately listed.

Total capital investment here includes state investment (both centralized and non-centralized) and collective farm investment, but excludes private investment and labor participation in road-building.[23] For the Soviet Union, investment in each of the first three sectors does not include "non-productive" investment. This is presumably true also of the Chinese figures.[24] The Soviet figures also include capital repairs but the Chinese figures do not.

[21] Hsüeh Mu-ch'iao, "The Problem of Balancing Purchasing Power and Commodity Supply," *T'ung-chi kung-tso* (Statistical Work) (hereafter cited as *TCKT*), Peking, No. 13, 1957, p. 1.

[22] The term "capital investment" in the Soviet and Chinese usage roughly corresponds to gross fixed investment in the Western terminology. For the Soviet definition, see Norman Kaplan, *Capital Investments in the Soviet Union, 1924–1951* (Santa Monica: The RAND Corporation, 1951; hereafter cited as *Capital Investments*), p. 1. For the Chinese definition see T. C. Liu and K. C. Yeh, *The Economy of the Chinese Mainland* (Princeton: Princeton University Press, 1965), pp. 702–4.

[23] The reason for excluding private investment is that I am concerned here with the problem of decision-making of the planners. Hence only the investment under the direct control of the state or its agencies is relevant. However, it is important to note that this exclusion probably understates agriculture's share in total investment in China.

[24] Although the Chinese data are not fully annotated in the source to indicate clearly the scope of the figures, the distribution is said to be based on "functional classification." State Statistical Bureau, *Ten Great Years* (Peking: Foreign Languages Press, 1960; hereafter cited as *Ten Great Years*), p. 59. The sizable gap between the "functional" and "administrative" distributions for the first three categories suggests that the "functional" distribution excludes nonproductive investment.

TABLE 1

<small>DISTRIBUTION OF PUBLIC CAPITAL INVESTMENT BY ECONOMIC
SECTORS, USSR, 1928/29–1937, AND COMMUNIST CHINA,
1953–59* (PER CENT)</small>

	USSR		Communist China	
	1928/29–32	1933–37	1953–57	1958–59
Industry	40.9	39.3	47.9 (52.0)	(65.1)
Agriculture	19.2	15.5	14.9 (7.6)	(8.7)
Transportation and communications	18.4	16.7	15.1 (16.4)	(14.3)
Other	21.5	28.6	22.1 (24.0)	(11.9)
housing	9.0	8.7	7.3 –	–
Total	100.0	100.0	100.0 (100.0)	(100.0)

*The underlying data are in current prices. Figures in parentheses do not include investment by collective farms.

— Not available.

Source: Data for the USSR are taken from a forthcoming study by Norman Kaplan on capital formation in the Soviet Union. Those for Communist China, 1953–57, are derived from: state investment given in State Statistical Bureau, *Ten Great Years,* pp. 57–58; collective farm investment based on an estimate in current prices (K. C. Yeh, "Capital Formation in Mainland China," unpublished manuscript), the price index for capital investment for 1952–57 (T. C. Liu and K. C. Yeh, *The Economy of the Chinese Mainland,* p. 235), and the percentage of farm households collectivized (*Ten Great Years,* p. 35); and investment in residential housing construction given in Tso Yen-hsing, "Arrange Urban Construction Work according to the Guiding Principle of Building Our Country Industriously and Thriftily," *Chi-hua ching-chi,* No. 12, 1957, p. 4. Those for 1958–59 are computed from data given in *Ten Great Years,* pp. 57–58, and Li Fu-chun, "Report on the Economic Plan for 1960," *Jen-min jih-pao,* March 31, 1960.

For later discussion, data for the Soviet Second FYP and for Communist China in 1958-59 are also presented in Table 1.

The results of the comparison may be summarized as follows: (1) China followed very closely the Soviet investment policy of concentrating the bulk of her resources on industry. But while the predominant emphasis on industry is conspicuous in both countries, it is even more so in China. Her capital investment in industry amounts to 48 per cent of the total, considerably larger than the Soviet share over the comparable planning period. The comparison, however, is complicated by the inclusion of capital repairs in the Soviet data.[25] On the basis of scattered data, Professor Kaplan suggests that the exclusion of capital repairs will increase the Soviet investment share in industry.[26] Thus proper adjustment would narrow the gap somewhat, but it seems unlikely that capital repairs alone could alter the distribution appreciably.[27]

In the Soviet Union, industry's share of capital investment rose in the first part, and declined somewhat in the later part of the Second FYP period.[28] Apparently a similar tendency occurred in Communist China. Industry's share of total investment (excluding collective farm investment) shows a marked increase during 1958–59. Thereafter the ratio most probably declined.

(2) The share of agricultural investment shows a rather sharp contrast. It was considerably larger in the USSR than in China during the First FYP period. In the Second FYP period it declined slightly in the USSR but probably increased somewhat in China.

(3) Investment in transport and communications has constituted a slightly larger proportion of capital investment in the USSR than in China. The exclusion of labor participation in road-building probably understates the percentage share for this sector in both countries, but perhaps more so for China than for the USSR. If this item were included, the difference might well be smaller. Over time, the percentage exhibited little change in the Second FYP period in the USSR. The trend in China is not clear.

(4) The share of "other" investment has been roughly the same in the two countries, about one-fifth of the total. As is well known, the low priority assigned to housing construction was a

[25] The inclusion will distort the comparison if the distribution of capital repairs among the sectors is not the same as that of investment excluding capital repairs.

[26] Norman Kaplan in his forthcoming study on Soviet capital formation. Kaplan's observation implies that the share for the other three sectors as a whole would be lower. However, the effect on the individual sectors is not clear.

[27] If we compare the distributions of capital investment including capital repairs in both sets of figures, there might well be a wider difference in industry's share than that shown in Table 1, for in the Chinese case, industry's share of total capital repairs probably is larger than its share of total capital investment (excluding capital repairs).

[28] Norman Kaplan, "Capital Formation and Allocation," *Soviet Economic Growth*, ed. A. Bergson (Evanston, Ill. and White Plains, N.Y.: Row, Peterson, and Co., 1953; hereafter cited as *Soviet Economic Growth*), p. 52.

distinctive feature of Soviet investment policy. China adopted the same policy and channeled even a smaller share of resources into housing construction.

In sum, the over-all investment patterns in the two countries are very similar. The only notable difference is the larger share of agricultural investment in the USSR, mainly in farm machines, compared to China's smaller share, mainly in irrigation and flood control projects. Possibly the difference was due to the following factors. First, there was probably more private farm investment in China than in Russia. Second, China was able to avoid the Soviet misfortune of heavy loss of draft animals in the process of collectivization. Furthermore, for the Soviet Union, the agricultural problem was essentially one of extracting both the "farm surplus" and labor. The sizable share of investment in agriculture together with collectivization was necessary to make the transfers possible. For China, the crucial problem was the production and collection of farm products but not the release of farm labor. Because of rural overcrowding, at no time was there any real danger of overdrawing labor from the farms during the First FYP period, and hence there was no need to pour in capital to substitute for labor withdrawn. As the leaders saw it, the key to the farm problem was reorganization rather than more material aid. Collectivization was to precede mechanization. Finally investment in water conservation or land reclamation projects in China could not be carried out on a large scale at the present stage because of the shortage of technical information and engineers.[29]

The difference should by no means obscure the fact that the purpose in both countries was to hold back investment in agriculture (and for that matter, investment in transport and "other" sectors) as far as possible in order to permit a maximum flow of resources into industry. The similarity actually went even further. Not only did both follow the rather special development strategy of emphasizing industry above everything else; they also adopted the same extreme form of industrialization centering around the development of heavy industry. Thus above 85 per cent of total capital investment in industry was allocated to heavy industry in both countries during their First FYP periods.[30] Of the total

[29] Li Fu-chun, *op. cit.*, p. 4; Shih Wei, "The Problem of Investment Allocation in the First FYP," *Hsüeh-hsi* (Study) (hereafter cited as *HH*), Peking, No. 9, 1955, p. 21.

[30] Heavy industry refers to the extractive industries, electric power generation, timbering and that part of manufacturing producing muni-

investment in heavy industry, the largest share, some 20 per cent, went to machine building and metalworking.[31]

I shall not examine the familiar precepts underlying this allocation policy.[32] Instead I would like to draw attention to another aspect of this policy. It seems fair to say that in both countries the heavy industry was oriented almost exclusively to the needs of defense and its own growth. The Chinese were perhaps more radical than the Soviet leaders. Apparently they assigned even lower priorities to those heavy industries producing for agricultural needs. Since agriculture provided a major share of total savings,[33] the essence of this industrialization policy was simply a continuous net outflow of resources from agriculture to heavy

tions and producers' goods. Soviet investment in "Group A" industry in 1929–32 amounted to 86 per cent of industrial investment. Norman Kaplan, *Capital Investments*, Table 9, p. 60. The proportion of industrial investment devoted to heavy industry in China in 1953–57 was 85 per cent. *Ten Great Years*, p. 61. Conceptually, heavy industry is not the same as producers' goods industry or "Group A" industry. But in Communist usage, the three terms are often defined loosely to mean more or less the same thing. For our purpose here, the ambiguity is not serious. For a discussion of these ambiguities, see P. J. D. Wiles, *The Political Economy of Communism* (Cambridge, Mass.: Harvard University Press, 1962), pp. 272–83.

[31] Norman Kaplan in his forthcoming study on the USSR; *Ten Great Years*, p. 57, and Chao Yi-wen, *Hsin-chung-kuo ti kung-yeh* (New China's Industry) (Peking: T'ung-chi ch'u-pan-she, 1957), p. 42. The figure of investment in China's machine industry given in Chao is said to refer to actual investment. It seems more likely to be actual investment in 1953–56 plus planned investment in 1957.

[32] For a discussion of the origin and nature of this policy, see: Evsey D. Domar, "A Soviet Model of Growth," *Essays in the Theory of Economic Growth* (New York: Oxford University Press, 1957), pp. 223–61; A. Erlich, *The Soviet Industrialization Debate, 1924–1928* (Cambridge: Harvard University Press, 1960); and "Stalin's Views on Economic Development," in Franklyn D. Holzman (ed.), *Readings on the Soviet Economy* (Chicago: Rand McNally, 1962); G. Grossman, "Suggestions for a Theory of Soviet Investment Planning," *Investment Criteria and Economic Growth* (Cambridge: Center for International Studies, Massachusetts Institute of Technology, 1955), pp. 91–115; Nicholas Spulber, *Soviet Strategy of Economic Growth* (Bloomington: Indiana University Press, 1964).

[33] To my knowledge no independent estimate of this share has been made. According to Joan Robinson and Sol Adler, "The real as distinct from the financial share of agriculture in accumulation has been estimated (officially) at roughly 40 per cent." Apparently this figure does not include such items as the differential between the procurement price and market price of agricultural products. Joan Robinson and Sol Adler, *China: An Economic Perspective* (London: The Fabian Society, 1958), p. 6. In any case, as Mao himself pointed out, a "substantial" portion of the accumulation came from agriculture. Mao Tse-tung, "The Problem of Agricultural Cooperativization," *HHYP*, No. 11, 1955, p. 5. Presumably this is also true of the USSR in the comparable stage of development.

industry. The crucial assumption underlying this policy is that agriculture could sustain its own expansion more or less independently of any resource feedback, or alternatively, that rapid industrial growth could be maintained for a prolonged period even though agriculture stagnated.

Choice of Technique and Scale

The Soviet choice was to invest in relatively large, capital-intensive projects.[34] Apparently this policy was the combined result of the leaders' complete neglect or understatement of interest charges in choosing between alternative projects, their obsession with technical rather than economic efficiency, and their "gigantomania" that identified bigness of size with economies of scale.[35] However, the choice was not without some economic justifications. First, to adapt the modern technology to the local conditions would require research, experimentation, and above all, engineering design talent, which was acutely short. The necessary research and development might not be of the advanced type, but it was research and development in a very real sense. The direct borrowing of modern technology might be a sensible way of substituting scarce capital for the equally scarce or scarcer technical manpower. Similarly the shortage of managerial skills might have been a major consideration for having a small number of large production units. Second, the modern plants were carriers of technological advance, and thus offered the facilities for training skilled labor and perhaps even technical manpower to design similar plants. Third, the choice of an uneconomic technique or scale might be justified over a longer time horizon in anticipation of a labor shortage or rising demand. In practice the highly mechanized operations were often supplemented with labor-intensive operations, and the capital-labor ratio for a modern plant was generally lowered by putting more labor to work in multiple shifts. But to say that the policy is not without sense is not to say that from the standpoint of efficiency the Soviet choice was optimal. Western studies have come to the conclusion

[34] Conceptually, the choices between techniques and between scales are two different problems. I lump them together since more or less the same considerations governed the choice of both.

[35] Gregory Grossman, "Scarce Capital and Soviet Doctrine," *Quarterly Journal of Economics*, LXVII (1953), 311–43; Franklyn D. Holzman, "The Soviet Ural-Kuznetsk Combine," same journal, LXXXI (1957), 368–405; Leon Smolinski, "The Scale of Soviet Industrial Establishments," *American Economic Review*, LII (1962), pp. 138–48.

that, by and large, capital intensities in the nonfarm projects have tended to be too high, and their sizes too large.[36]

China's technological choice was little different from the Soviet policy. The backbone of her First FYP was the 156 large, modern projects designed and built with the aid of the Russians. Investments in the below-limit projects were trifling by comparison.[37] If the Soviet choice was economically irrational, it would clearly be even more so for China. Why did the Chinese adopt such a policy? It might be that the same considerations governing the Soviet decisions were also important to the Chinese. But there was an additional constraint. Given the limited capability of the Chinese to design and build new plants themselves and the fact that the Soviet designs and equipment were about the only ones available, the range of choice was rather narrow.

In any case, the implication of this policy was clear. Because the gestation periods generally were three to five years, these projects would absorb enormous amounts of resources but contribute little to output or employment for a long while. As in Russia, there was an enormous variation in labor intensity of different operations within a plant or within an industry.[38] Furthermore, investments in non-productive sections of the project were cut to the bone.[39] But the most significant adaptation was their policy towards handicrafts. Instead of deliberately undermining the handicrafts as the Soviet planners did, the Chinese tried to preserve the handicraft industries and to encourage them to expand.[40] To be sure, these industries were not the

[36] *Soviet Planning*, pp. 241–74; L. Smolinski, *op. cit.*

[37] Below-limit projects are those the investment costs of which are less than the specific amounts established by the State Planning Commission. In general, the large projects are above-limit ones. According to one estimate, less than 15 per cent of capital investments in industry was allocated to the below-norm projects. Yang Ying-chieh, "Coordinated Development of Newly Constructed and Existing Enterprises, Large and Medium or Small Enterprises," *HH*, No. 8, 1955, p. 8.

[38] J. Robinson and S. Adler, *op. cit.*, pp. 11–12; Felix Greene, *Awakened China* (Garden City, N.Y.: Doubleday & Co., 1961), p. 80.

[39] Li Fu-chun, "Exercise Thrift and Struggle for the Fulfillment of Socialist Construction," *HHYP*, No. 7, 1955, pp. 166–68.

[40] According to one study, employment in small-scale industry in the USSR fell from 2,408 thousand in 1927/28 to 861 thousand in 1933. Adam Kaufman, *Small-Scale Industry in the Soviet Union* (New York: National Bureau of Economic Research, 1962), pp. 19–45. By contrast, handicraft employment showed a slight increase during 1952–57 in China, and the First FYP anticipated a 60 per cent increase in handicraft output over the same period. Liu and Yeh, *op. cit.*, p. 196; *HHYP*, No. 9, 1955, p. 133.

stars of the show, but they had their proper place in the over-all strategy. This policy makes economic sense, for the handicrafts not only provided an outlet for employment, but their output also could fill part of the gap (between the rising income and the limited supply of consumers' goods) created by the construction of the large, capital-intensive projects.

To sum up, there were strong parallels in the Chinese and the Soviet industrialization policies during their first FYP periods. The similarities are most profound in the scale and the direction of the big push and in the choice of techniques and size of industrial establishments. That this was so should hardly be surprising. Their overriding goals were the same. The success of the Soviet Union must have had its demonstration effect on the Chinese. Moreover, the latter's lack of experience in economic planning forced them to turn for guidance to the Russians, who naturally offered their one and only Stalinist model since they had tried and believed in little else. The Soviet influence was particularly dominant in the earlier part of the period, so much so that in some respects Soviet precedent was mechanically copied.[41] But the Chinese strategy was not an exact duplicate of the Soviet counterpart. In some respects, the Chinese were more radical. The increase in the rate of investment before the big push was probably more abrupt. The emphasis on industry was more pronounced. Public investment in agriculture was considerably less. However, in one respect the Chinese were more pragmatic. They had preserved their handicraft and small-scale industries.

III. CONTRASTS IN SOVIET AND CHINESE ECONOMIC AND DEMOGRAPHIC CONDITIONS

For both countries, the over-all record of the First FYP was one of impressive achievement, particularly when measured in terms of the official statistics.[42] Not surprisingly, the Soviet strategy underlying the Second FYP remained essentially the same as that

[41] For example, during the Hundred Flowers period, an official in the Ministry of Communications asserted that "since Russia during their First FYP allocated 1 per cent of their investment to communications, we doctrinally and subjectively did the same. Later developments showed that this proportion was inadequate." *Ta-kung pao* (hereafter cited as *TKP*), Peking, June 1, 1957, p. 1.

[42] Maurice Dobb, *Soviet Economic Development since 1917* (London: Routledge and Kegan Paul, 1948); N. Jasny, *Soviet Industrialization* (Chicago: University of Chicago Press, 1961); Choh-ming Li, *Economic Development of Communist China* (Berkeley and Los Angeles: University of California Press, 1959); T. C. Liu and K. C. Yeh, *op. cit.*

of the First.[43] The story of China's Second FYP, however, was more complicated. In September 1956 the party adopted a preliminary proposal for the Second FYP. The broad outline of this proposal was similar to that of the First FYP. Its main features included: (a) The rate of investment was to be somewhat higher than during the First FYP. Total capital investment was to double. (b) The share of capital investment allocated to industry was to increase. So was the share of agricultural investment, but the planned increase was modest, from 7 to 10 per cent of the total. The central task of the Plan remained the same—top priority development of heavy industry. (c) The emphasis was again on modern capital-intensive techniques. Thus no more than 6 to 7 million new workers and employees were to be absorbed during 1958–62. There was, however, greater emphasis on small-scale enterprises.[44] About two months after its adoption by the party, it was reported that the proposal had been abandoned. The exact causes of the abrupt shift in policy are not clear. But the radical change in the leaders' appreciation of the Soviet experience during this period was apparently one of the major factors.

Prior to 1956, the applicability of the Soviet model to China was rarely questioned, and rarer still were instances in which the model was actually modified. In September 1956, in an opening address to the Eighth Party Congress, Mao pointed out that the task confronting China was similar to that of the USSR in her early stage, but "one must know how to learn from the Russians."[45] By the latter, he obviously meant that learning should no longer be the indiscriminatory transplant of almost everything from Russia. This point was made clear in a major document put out by the party in December 1956: "All the experience of the Soviet Union, including its fundamental experience, is bound up with definite national characteristics, and no other country should copy it mechanically."[46] In another address in early 1957, Mao's emphasis on selective borrowing was more explicit: "Learn those

[43] Dobb, *op. cit.*, pp. 268–89; *Su-lien kuo-min ching-chi chien-she chi-hua wen-chien hui-pien: ti erh ko wu-nien chi-hua* (Collection of Documents Relating to the Soviet Plans for National Economic Construction: the Second FYP) (Peking: Jen-min ch'u-pan-she, 1957).

[44] Chinese Communist Party (CCP), "Proposals for the Second Five Year Plan for Development of the National Economy (1958–1962)," *HHPYK*, No. 20, 1956, pp. 164–70.

[45] *HHPYK*, No. 20, 1956, p. 2.

[46] Editorial Department of the *JMJP*, "More on the Historical Experience of the Dictatorship of the Proletariat," *HHPYK*, No. 2, 1957, p. 6.

things that are suitable to China's conditions."[47] Although all these statements were made in a rather broad context, there can be little doubt that they applied to problems of development strategy. The time had arrived for a careful examination of the crucial questions: What were China's national characteristics in contrast to Russia's? Were there any inherent conflicts between these characteristics and the Soviet strategy which China had been following so closely up to now?

The major documents of the early 1957 period indicate that the leaders were aware of at least three basic characteristics that stood in marked contrast to those of the Soviet economy: China's population was much larger, but its per capita output and capital stock were much smaller.[48] Some indicators of these characteristics in the two countries are presented in Table 2. The figures are official figures and therefore are subject to varying degrees of biases. Furthermore, the definitions of labor force and of urban and rural population are not exactly the same for both countries. However, the contrasts are so striking that the defects of the data are not likely to change the picture appreciably. Let me take up these differences in turn.

(1) China's demographic setting differed sharply from Russia's in size and rate of growth. China's population in 1952 was 570 million, almost four times that of Russia in 1928, and was growing from its huge base at the rate of over 2 per cent per annum. The absolute annual increase was about 13 million during 1952–57, compared to less than 3 million in the USSR during 1928–32.

The implications of these differences for resource allocation are profound. In the first place, to maintain a high saving-income ratio would be a far more exacting problem in China than in the USSR because of greater pressure to increase both household and communal consumption in China. The pressure to increase household consumption would be greater, for the number of mouths to feed increased faster. In addition, real wages of non-farm workers in China increased, albeit moderately, in contrast to

[47] Mao Tse-tung, "On the Correct Handling of Contradictions among the People," *HHPYK*, No. 13, 1957 (hereafter cited as Mao, *Contradictions*), p. 14.
[48] For example, Mao, *Contradictions;* Li Fu-chun, "Report before the National Conference on Design Work," *Chien-she yüeh-k'an* (Construction Monthly), Peking, No. 8, 1957, pp. 1–8.

TABLE 2

COMPARATIVE LEVELS OF ECONOMIC DEVELOPMENT IN THE
USSR AND COMMUNIST CHINA, SELECTED YEARS

	USSR		Communist China	
	1928	1932	1952	1957
Population (millions)	150	161	567	637
Urban (millions)	28	36	67	91
Rural (millions)	122	124	500	546
Labor force (millions)	86	90	338	380
Nonagricultural workers (millions)	10	19	19	25
Per capita output of:				
grain (kg per person)	566	458	311	290
Sugar (kg per person)	8.5	5.2	0.8	1.4
Vegetable oils (kg per person)	3.0	3.1	1.7	1.7
Cotton cloth (m per person)	17.7	17.0	7.3	8.0
Electric power generating capacity (kw per thousand nonagricultural workers)	190	250	100	180
Length of railroad (km per thousand nonagricultural workers)	7.8	4.4	1.3	1.2
Crop area per head of rural population (acre per person)	2.3	2.7	0.7	0.7

Source: For the USSR: Warren W. Eason, "Labor Force," in *Economic Trends,* pp. 72, 77, 86; D. Gale Johnson and Arcadius Kahan, "Soviet Agriculture: Structure and Growth," in Joint Economic Committee, 86th Congress, *Comparisons of the U.S. and Soviet Economies,* Part I (Washington, D.C.: U.S. Government Printing Office, 1960), p. 231; Yang Chienpai, "A Comparative Analysis of China's and the Soviet First Five Year Plans," *HHYP,* No. 9, 1955, p. 195; Janet G. Chapman, "Consumption," in *Economic Trends,* p. 237; *Su-lien kuo-min ching-chi chien-she chi-hua wenchien hui-pien: ti erh ko wu-nien chi-hua* (Collection of Documents Relating to the Soviet Plans for National Economic Construction: The Second Five-Year Plan) (Peking: Jen-min ch'u-pan-she, 1957), pp. 792, 809, 818; Central Statistical Board of the USSR Council of Ministers, *Forty Years of Soviet Power* (Moscow: Foreign Languages Publishing House, 1958), pp. 76, 159, 206. For Communist China: T. C. Liu and K. C. Yeh, *The Economy of the Chinese Mainland,* pp. 132, 181–212, 458; (labor force

a decline in Russia.[49] Since farm consumption in China probably did not deteriorate, the rise in real wages tended to raise the average consumption level. The rise in real wages also tended to perpetuate or even widen the sharp difference between the urban and rural living standards in China, and the gap in turn provided strong inducements for the peasants to migrate to the cities or to consume more than before as a result of the demonstration effect of the city folks' higher living standard.[50]

China's higher rate of population growth had another unfavorable impact on savings. A population with high fertility and mortality rates generally has a higher ratio of dependent children to population of working age than populations with low mortality and fertility.[51] The abrupt reduction in infant mortality rates, claimed to have occurred in China, would raise this ratio further.[52] This in turn would call for more communal consumption such as education, child care, and health services.

Another major problem very much intensified by China's enormous population size and its rapid growth was that of underemployment of labor. To begin with, the number of unemployed in the cities was sizable even before the First FYP was launched.[53]

---

includes population of age 15 to 64 years; nonagricultural workers include those in: industry, construction, modern transportation and communications, trade and restaurants, civilian government employees, and finance); Yang Chien-pai, *op. cit.*, p. 194; State Statistical Bureau, "Communiqué on the Results of the First Five-Year Plan," *Hsin-hua pan-yüeh-k'an*, No. 8, 1959, p. 49; *Ten Great Years*, pp. 100, 128, 144.

[49] Richard Moorsteen, "Economic Prospects for Communist China," *World Politics*, XI (1959), 208–9; A. Eckstein, "The Strategy of Economic Development in Communist China," *American Economic Review*, LI (1961), 512.

[50] According to the official statistics, per capita consumption of the workers was twice that of the peasants. Po I-po, "Report before the National Conference of Model Agricultural Workers," *HHPYK*, No. 6, 1957, p. 58. See also J. Robinson and S. Adler, *op. cit.*, p. 14. This is not to say that the difference in living standards in the USSR was negligible, nor that the Russians faced no problem of unplanned peasant migration into the cities. Presumably their problems were perhaps less formidable than those of the Chinese.

[51] J. D. Durand, "Population Structure as a Factor in Manpower and Dependency Problems of Underdeveloped Countries," *United Nations Population Bulletin*, No. 3, Oct., 1953, pp. 1–16.

[52] Tai Shih-kuang, *1953 Population Census of China* (Calcutta: Indian Statistical Institute, 1956).

[53] According to the official estimate, unemployed in the cities totaled more than 3 million in 1952. State Council, "Decision on the Problem of Employment," *HH*, No. 6, 1952, p. 35. This is probably a gross underestimate. Liu and Yeh, *op. cit.*, pp. 101–5.

In the villages there was undoubtedly a huge reservoir of underemployed farm labor.[54] The problem became more acute because of the large annual additions to the labor supply on the one hand, and the rather limited absorption by the nonfarm sector on the other. The annual increase in nonagricultural employment in China during 1952–57 was about 1 million, while the total labor force increased by about 8 million per year.[55] By contrast, the average increase in Soviet nonagricultural employment during 1928–32 was 2 million per year, compared to an annual increase of 1 million in the total labor force. Clearly there was a sharper conflict in China than in the USSR between the preference for capital-intensive techniques and the supply of labor.

(2) Exactly how poor China was, compared to the USSR, is difficult to determine. But it is almost certain that the Soviet per capita income in 1928 was much higher than that of China in 1952.[56] This impression is confirmed by the rather wide differences in the per capita output of four major consumers' goods (grain, sugar, vegetable oils, and cotton fabrics) shown in Table 2.[57] Moreover, the living standard in China might well be close to the subsistence level. This appears so at least in the case of grain consumption, the most important single item in the consumers' budget. Grain consumption per capita in 1952 was only about 240 kg,[58] slightly lower than the traditional Chinese

[54] That rural underemployment existed was clearly recognized by the Communists themselves. *JMJP*, Apr. 17, 1953. According to their estimate, 10 to 20 per cent of the rural labor force in some localities was surplus labor. *CHCC*, No. 3, 1958, p. 3. Presumably surplus labor refers to labor idle all the year around. If one includes seasonal unemployment, the percentage would undoubtedly be much higher. J. L. Buck, *Land Utilization in China* (Chicago: University of Chicago Press, 1937), p. 294.

[55] Employment here refers to wage and salary workers only and does not include those in handicraft, peddling, or old-fashioned transportation.

[56] According to A. Eckstein, Soviet national income in 1928 was about 17 per cent above that of China in 1952, but per capita income was four times as much. W. W. Rostow, *The Prospects for Communist China* (New York: Technology Press and John Wiley and Son, 1954), pp. 258–59. Another estimate shows that Soviet per capita income was about eight times that of China. Alfred Zauberman, "Soviet and Chinese Strategy for Economic Growth," *International Affairs*, XXXVIII (1962), 341.

[57] Admittedly per capita output is not a satisfactory measure of the standard of living. Differences in non-consumption uses, e.g., exports, would affect the comparison. However, it is believed that the distortion is not serious.

[58] Liu and Yeh, *op. cit.*, p. 132. The official figure is even lower.

"no hunger no gorging" standard of 250 kg,[59] and about the same as what the Communists themselves consider the minimum requirement for the urban population.[60]

The implication of these contrasts is clear. In general, a higher income and consumption per capita means a larger proportion of expenditures on "non-essential" items and therefore more room for reduction in the standard of living. Thus, poor as the USSR was in 1928, it was still possible to increase the rate of saving substantially by lowering consumption per capita. China, however, enjoyed no such advantage in 1952. The scope for further reduction in the standard of living was much narrower. This meant that any sizable increase in the rate of savings must come primarily from an increase rather than redistribution of output.

An important case in point is the abject poverty of the Chinese peasants and its relation to grain marketings.[61] The size of the grain marketings is of crucial significance because it represented a major component of the total savings of the still predominantly agricultural Soviet and Chinese economies, and because it was the most important wage good for the nonfarm population. The Soviet Union in 1928 collected or purchased about 9 million tons of grain,[62] slightly lower than the Chinese figure of about 10 million tons in 1952.[63] However, there were two rather striking contrasts in the grain situation. First, that part of grain output

[59] The traditional standard is 400 catties of husked grain a year. Fei Hsiao-t'ung and Chang Chih-i, *Earthbound China* (Chicago: University of Chicago Press, 1945), p. 158. This comes to about 500 catties, or 250 kg of unhusked grain.

[60] Sun Wai-tsu, "Principles of Drawing Up the Grain Circulation Plan," *CHCC*, No. 2, 1958, p. 25.

[61] Unless otherwise specified, grain refers to unhusked grain and includes potatoes at one-fourth of their actual weight.

[62] Bergson, *Real SNIP*, p. 327.

[63] Total amount collected or purchased in 1952/53 was 27.8 million tons of "commercial grain" (partly husked grain), including soybeans. Sha Ch'ien-li, "Glorious Achievements on the Grain Front," *TKP*, Oct. 25, 1959, p. 3. This figure also includes a sizable amount sold back to the peasants. No estimate of this portion is given. I assume it to be the same as that for 1953/54, 17.1 million tons given in State Statistical Bureau, "Basic Conditions of China's Unified Purchase and Sale of Grain," *TCKT*, No. 19, 1957, p. 32. This leaves 10.7 million tons. The ratio of commercial grain to unprocessed grain is about 0.86:1. Chen Yün, "On the Problem of Unified Purchase and Sale of Grain," *HHYP*, No. 8, 1955, p. 51. Converted to unprocessed grain, total marketings were 12 million tons including soybeans. Output of soybeans in 1952 was 9.5 million tons. *Ten Great Years*, p. 124. The percentage of output marketed is assumed to be 30 per cent, the same as the average for the prewar period. J. L. Buck, *op. cit.*, p. 236. Unprocessed grain marketings thus come to about 10 million tons.

left in the hands of the rural population was about 620 kg in the USSR, very much higher than the corresponding figure of 330 kg for China.[64] Other things being equal, this would imply that there was much more room for increasing the marketings in the USSR than in China.[65] Second, the marketed total of 9 million tons was used for exports and feeding an urban population of 28 million in the USSR, whereas a slightly higher amount had to provide for exports and food for 67 million Chinese, 2.5 times the urban population of the Soviet Union. In short, there was far more leverage in the USSR with respect to grain collection and its use because of the relatively large supply of grain on a per capita basis in both the rural and urban areas.

China's relatively unfavorable position in 1952 probably worsened during 1953–57. Grain output expanded only moderately, some 3.7 per cent per annum according to official statistics, which are probably on the high side. About two-thirds of this claimed increase was absorbed by the increase in population. Within the rural areas, there was additional demand originating from more intensive use of the peasant labor following collectivization and the reported increase in the number of farm animals.[66] In the nonfarm sector, real wages of the workers rose,[67] and probably because of the extremely low living standard to start with, the additional income was spent primarily on grain.[68] In the face of rising nonfarm demand, the state stepped up its collection. The obligatory delivery system was introduced in 1953, and the annual volume of marketings rose sharply from about 11

[64] For data on grain output and rural population used in calculating these figures see Bergson, *Real SNIP*, p. 327; Liu and Yeh, *op. cit.*, p. 132; Table 2 above. If the Chinese official figure for grain output is used, the difference would be even more striking.

[65] To be sure, other things are not exactly equal. At least three complications should be noted. First, because of a colder climate in Russia, the per capita caloric intake derived from grain was probably higher. Second, the major grain crops in the USSR were wheat, rye, and oats, whereas in China they were rice, wheat, and kaoliang. Hence, the percentage of Soviet grain output used for seed is likely to be higher than in China. Third, according to the official statistics, the number of livestock (except hogs) in the USSR was larger than in China in 1952 and probably required more feed grain. There was however a marked decline in the Soviet livestock population during 1928–32, whereas the Chinese claimed a slight increase in population (except for hogs) during 1952–57. But all these differences are not likely to be large enough to invalidate the argument here.

[66] *Ten Great Years*, p. 132.

[67] *Ibid.*, pp. 173, 216.

[68] See, for example, *HHPYK*, No. 1, 1957, p. 60.

million tons in 1952/53 to 18–20 million tons in the four succeeding years.[69] But the drastic redistribution of grain provided
no solution to the problem of grain supply. On the one hand,
there are indications that, with output unchanged, 20 million tons
was about the maximum that could be squeezed out of the
villages. In 1954/55, the marketing reached 18 million tons,
leaving 230 kg per capita in the villages.[70] The result was an
acute shortage of grain in the spring of 1955.[71] Peasants demanded an increase in supply by the state.[72] Even the leaders
admitted that they had overpurchased from the peasants.[73] On
the other hand, the total volume of marketings was apparently
inadequate to meet the demand of the nonfarm sector. In 1956/
57, when the supply of grain to the urban population (including
military servicemen) reportedly reached the peak of 19.5 million
tons,[74] grain supply per head of urban population was barely 220
kg.[75] The state had to cut grain exports and dip into its stockpile
to meet the deficit in grain consumption.[76]

Turning to the Soviet Union, one sees a somewhat different
situation. During 1928–32, grain output fluctuated between 74
and 96 million tons, averaging about 83 million tons.[77] But the
total population increased only moderately. Thus even in 1932,
the poorest crop year of the First FYP period, grain output per
capita was about 460 kg, still considerably higher than the 290 kg

[69] For the estimate for 1952–53, see note 63. For those in the succeeding years, see State Statistical Bureau, *op. cit.*, p. 32. Grain in this particular context refers to commercial grain and includes soybeans.

[70] Total amount of grain output left to the peasants in 1953/54 given in
State Statistical Bureau, *op. cit.*, p. 31, divided by rural population of 510
million at the end of 1953 given in *TCKT*, No. 11, 1957, p. 24.

[71] Li Hsien-nien, "Financial and Economic Work and Agricultural
Cooperativization," *HHYP*, No. 21, 1955, p. 165; Liao Lu-yen, "Report on
the Conditions of Agricultural Production in 1954 and Current Measures to
Increase Output," *HHYP*, No. 4, 1955, p. 116.

[72] Chen Yün, *op. cit.*, p. 50.

[73] Chen Yün, *op. cit.*, p. 51; State Statistical Bureau, *op. cit.*, p. 31.

[74] State Statistical Bureau, *op. cit.*, p. 32.

[75] Total marketings divided by total urban population of 89 million at
the end of 1956, given in *TCKT*, No. 11, 1957, p. 24.

[76] Yeh Chi-chuang, "On Foreign Trade," *HHPYK*, No. 16, 1957, p. 91;
U.S. Department of Agriculture, *Trends and Developments in Communist
China's World Trade in Farm Products, 1955–60* (Washington, D.C.: U.S.
Government Printing Office, 1962), p. 26; Sun Wai-tsu, *op. cit.*, p. 25.

[77] D. Gale Johnson and Arcadius Kahan, "Soviet Agriculture: Structure
and Growth," in Joint Economic Committee, 86th Congress, *Comparisons
of the U.S. and Soviet Economies*, Part I (Washington, D.C.: U.S. Government Printing Office, 1960), p. 231.

for China in 1957. This, however, does not mean that the Soviet economy was immune to the adverse effects of a reduction in grain output. The decline in 1931–32 undoubtedly depressed the standard of living. In 1932–34, a famine developed largely as a result of overprocurement.[78] In each of the two years following a poor harvest (1933 and 1937), capital investment in the socialist sector declined. But by and large, the Soviet economy was less vulnerable to setbacks in grain production than the Chinese economy. In a sense the Soviet leaders had a trade-off between stagnation in grain output (in fact in total agricultural output) and rapid industrial growth in the early phase of Soviet industrialization. The trade-off was feasible within limits because of a relatively favorable resource base to begin with and because of a slow population growth. For China, where no "grain surplus" of comparable scale existed and where population growth was much faster, a rapid increase in per capita agricultural output was clearly a prerequisite for industrialization.

(3) No comparable estimates of capital stock in the two countries are available. Table 2 shows the differences in electric power generating capacity and length of railroad per worker, and crop area per head of rural population. The first two are rough indicators of capital per worker in nonagricultural production and in modern transportation. Both measures show that the Chinese workers had relatively less "capital" to work with. It is interesting to note that the length of railroad per worker declined in both countries, as a result of their deliberate policy not to invest heavily in transportation. However, Russia again was in a much better position, so far as living off the past investment is concerned.

The weakest link in China's economic base was perhaps its small crop area per head of rural population. In 1952, on the average, each Chinese peasant had only 0.7 acres of cropped land, compared to 2.3 acres in the Soviet Union.[79] The ratio for China hardly improved during the First FYP period, in contrast to an increase in the USSR. Thus toward the end of the period, the competition for the use of farm land among different crops, particularly between grain and cotton, became more severe. The agricultural problem, as the Chinese leaders saw it, was to in-

[78] Dana G. Dalrymple, "The Soviet Famine of 1932–34," *Soviet Studies,* XV (1964), 250–84.

[79] The difference in arable land per head would be even wider since the multiple cropping index was higher in China than in the USSR.

crease the yield per acre. But here the Soviet experience could provide no useful guidance. Since the pressure for increasing yields was much lower, the USSR could afford to and actually did ignore the problem at least for a long period.[80]

The implication of these contrasts for China is clear. The Soviet strategy required a continual diversion of resources from agriculture to heavy industry for a prolonged period with virtually no counterflows. This was feasible for the USSR largely because she had started from a relatively strong resource base, particularly a sizable grain surplus, and had a slow rate of population growth. Yet these feasibility conditions hardly existed in China. Compared with the Soviet Union, China had abundant labor but little capital inherited from the past and a much smaller agricultural surplus to live on during the early phase of the industrialization. The crucial problem was not just to collect and to convert the agricultural surplus into industrial capital as in the USSR, but to create a large surplus in the first place. Thus to allow agricultural output to stagnate for a long period as the Soviet Union did while population increased rapidly would surely reduce the rate of savings. Nor could the urgent demands of the non-industrial sectors for capital be ignored for long, as they had been in the USSR. Furthermore, to adopt the Soviet pattern of technological choice would intensify China's chronic underemployment problem. In the light of these considerations, it is hardly surprising that the original proposal for the Second FYP, which bore a close resemblance to the Soviet plan, was eventually abandoned. In its place a policy for a new industrial upsurge, the Great Leap Forward, was adopted in 1958.

IV. CHINA'S DEVELOPMENT POLICY, 1958–62

The Great Leap Forward, 1958–59

To China's leaders, a "great leap forward" meant annual rates of industrial growth on the order of 25 per cent or more.[81] This

---

[80] The crop yields in the USSR declined markedly during 1925–34. D. Gale Johnson and A. Kahan, *op. cit.*, p. 211.

[81] Chou En-lai defined a "great leap" as follows: "Taking into consideration the rate of economic growth in the socialist countries and our own experience during the First FYP, one should say that an annual increase of 20 per cent or more in industrial output is a leap forward, an increase above 25 per cent is a great leap forward, and an increase of 30 per cent or more, an exceptionally great leap forward." Chou En-lai, "Report on the Adjustment of Major Targets in the National Economic Plan for 1959 and Further Development of the Campaign for Increasing Production and Practicing Economy," *HHPYK*, No. 17, 1959, p. 22.

breakneck speed was to be maintained for three years.[82] Over the longer period, the task was to catch up with or overtake, first Britain in the main branches of industry in fifteen years, and then the United States economically in another twenty to thirty years.[83] The general notion behind the Leap was to accelerate simultaneously the growth of both the modern and the traditional sectors, the former with savings largely supplied by the traditional sector, and the latter primarily by massive use of China's abundant manpower. The following three aspects of this policy are discussed in turn: (1) a return to the high investment rate policy, (2) the simultaneous development of the modern and the traditional sectors of the economy, or "walking on two legs" as the Communists called it, and (3) the abandonment of the birth control campaign.

In the report that formally launched the Great Leap, Liu Shao-ch'i issued a call to raise the savings ratio (presumably above the 1957 level).[84] The concern over accumulation was natural, for the pace of the Leap, particularly in the modern sector, was largely determined by the volume of savings. To the accumulation-conscious leaders, such a policy was not new. What was new was a more optimistic outlook on savings than was prevalent in early 1957. The basic premise underlying the 1957 retrenchment was that, with consumption more or less determined by the size of population, the volume of savings must depend on output. Since output could not be expanded rapidly because of lagging agricultural production, investment had to be cut. In 1958, this sober view was replaced by a much more optimistic attitude, based on two simple concepts. The first was that investment need not be a residual depending on output and consumption. It could be increased automatically with output in the form of investment in kind.[85] The source of saving was idle labor which China had in superabundance. The second concept was that output, not consumption, was the key to the problem.[86] To increase savings, one

[82] Liu Shao-ch'i, "Report on the Work of the Central Committee," *HHPYK*, No. 11, 1958 (hereafter cited as *Work Report*), p. 4.

[83] *Ibid.;* editorial in *JMJP*, Jan. 1, 1958.

[84] *Work Report*, p. 10.

[85] See the editorial in *CHCC*, No. 3, 1958, p. 6. This is of course the familiar disguised unemployment thesis. Mao himself had long been thinking along such lines. See his comments in *Socialist Upsurge*.

[86] Ch'en Po-ta, "Under the Banner of Mao Tse-tung," *Hung-ch'i* (Red Flag) (hereafter cited as *HC*), No. 4, 1958, p. 5.

should raise output instead of cutting consumption, by developing the modern and the traditional sectors simultaneously.

The simultaneous development policy called for the use of both the modern and indigenous techniques of production and parallel expansion in industry and agriculture, heavy and light industries, centrally managed and local enterprises, large and medium or small enterprises. However, from the standpoint of allocating resources mobilized within the state investment plan, this did not mean equal priority for all the sectors. Take the case of industry versus agriculture. As Table 1 shows, the share of state investment in industry was actually much larger in 1958–59 than ever before, whereas that in agriculture had increased only slightly. This was mainly because the very purpose of simultaneously developing agriculture and industry was to supplement and reinforce rather than replace the Soviet-type industrialization policy of concentrating on modern heavy industry.[87] During the First FYP period China had pursued this extreme form of industrialization policy with little regard to agricultural production and met with disastrous results in late 1956. But now the Chinese believed that they had found a solution to the problem: to reorganize and to indoctrinate the rural population intensively and thereby to make full use of labor in farming, small construction projects, local industries, local transportation, and other productive activities.[88] By so doing, not only agriculture but also the entire rural, traditional sector was to generate self-sustaining growth within and by itself, and simultaneously provide sufficient resources to support rapid growth in the urban, modern sector.

The rationale for developing heavy and light industry together is similar to that for developing both industry and agriculture. First, profits and taxes from light industries were a major source of savings.[89] Thus, in discussing the road for China's industriali-

[87] "An Interview with Government Officials on the Problem of Simultaneously Developing Industry and Agriculture," *TKP*, Nov. 15, 1957.

[88] The Vice Chairman of the State Planning Commission stated: "Peasants whose political ideas have been liberated can increase agricultural output very rapidly even without the supply of large quantities of tractors and chemical fertilizers." Sung Ping, "Recognize and Utilize the Law of Planned, Proportionate Development of the National Economy," *CHCC*, No. 12, 1958, p. 2.

[89] According to the official statistics, taxes and profits of the state-owned light industries in 1952–55 exceeded the total state expenditures on these industries by 10.8 billion yuan, or more than 40 per cent of the total state capital investment over the same period. State Statistical Bureau, "Several Problems in China's Socialist Industrialization," *HHPYK*, No. 1,

zation, Mao pointed out that as agriculture and light industry develop, there will be a market for heavy industrial products and capital for heavy industry to grow, and heavy industry will expand faster than if agriculture and light industry did not develop.[90] Second, the expansion of heavy industry has a dual effect. It creates additional income, a substantial part of which flows into the hands of the wage earners. It also increases output, but the output of heavy industry generally cannot be used to absorb the increase in wage income. An increase in income does not necessarily increase the effective demand for consumers' goods, for such additional income can be disposed of in other ways such as by being saved voluntarily by the workers, taxes, or borrowed by the state. But in the present case, the newly created income usually increased consumption expenditures, perhaps even more than proportionately, probably owing to the rather strong desire of the people to raise their standard of living from their current low level.[91] If the increase in the demand for consumers' goods is not matched by an increase in supply, inflation will ensue.[92] The inflation in 1956 indicated that such a sequence of events probably occurred. If inflation is to be avoided, light industry generally will have to expand.[93]

Whether or not there should be an increase in investment in light industry, however, would depend on a number of factors, including the rate of utilization of the existing capacity. The preliminary economic plan for 1958 did not provide for an increase in state investment in modern light industry.[94] As the Great Leap unfolded, the number of small-scale industries pro-

---

1957, p. 69; *Ten Great Years*, p. 56. Of course, a considerable part of the profit in the light industry originated in the differential between the market price and compulsory procurement price of agricultural products and was actually a concealed tax on the agricultural population.

[90] Mao, *Contradictions*, p. 14.

[91] Chen Yün, "The Problem of Increase-Production and Practice-Economy," *HHPYK*, No. 7, 1957, p. 16.

[92] Hsü Li-chun, "On the Policy of Walking on Two Legs," *HC*, No. 6, 1959, pp. 9–11. The reasoning comes close to a two-sector growth model developed by S. C. Tsiang, "Rehabilitation of Time Dimension of Investment in Macrodynamic Analysis," *Economica*, N.S., XVI (Aug., 1949), 204–17.

[93] This argument assumes that the proportion of total consumption expenditures spent on manufactured consumers' goods was constant or rising, and that supply of these goods cannot be augmented by reducing inventories or through foreign trade.

[94] *CHCC*, No. 2, 1958, p. 5.

ducing consumers' goods multiplied. Total investment in light industry as a whole in 1958 doubled over 1957, but its proportion in total industrial investment declined because investment in heavy industry increased even more sharply.[95]

The most dramatic aspect of the simultaneous development policy in 1958 was the mushrooming of small, indigenous plants all over the country. These plants were said to offer many benefits. The capital-output and capital-labor ratios of the small enterprises were much lower, and the gestation period was shorter, than those of the large ones.[96] These arguments were not new; actually there had been a shift of emphasis towards the small plants in 1957. What distinguished the 1958 policy from the earlier experience was the unprecedented scale of the development.[97] During the first nine months of 1958, 7.5 million small industrial plants, including handicraft workshops, were established, of which 6 million units operated within the communes.[98] They included iron and steel foundries, fertilizer factories, oil extraction, machine shops, cement manufacture, coal and iron ore mines, and food processing. Why the sudden expansion on such a colossal scale? In part, the massive program was characteristic of the Communist way of organizing activities. This campaign type of approach—directing highly concentrated effort and publicity towards a single purpose—was designed "to stimulate not only the executants but also the controllers" of the centralized system to promote growth.[99] In Communist China, the need for a big push was perhaps greater than in the USSR, if only because

[95] Ten Great Years, p. 61.

[96] Fan Jo-yi, "On the Profit Rate of Capital and the Faster, Better, and More Economic Policy of Reconstruction," CHCC, No. 8, 1958, p. 22. Capital-output ratio of small enterprises was claimed to be one-fourteenth of that of large ones. The ratio refers to that of fixed capital to gross value of output in state industries in 1953–55. Apparently it is an average concept. Because of the Communist "factory method" of computing gross value of output, and because the large enterprises are generally more integrated vertically than small ones, the ratios given in this source are biased against the large enterprises.

[97] Even here the principle of developing small industrial plants in rural areas on a large scale was anticipated by the anthropologist Fei Hsiao-t'ung, Hsiang-tu chung-chien (Reconstruction of the Rural Society) (Shanghai: Kuan-ch'a she, 1948), pp. 99–133, 163–68. See also his earlier ideas in Shih Kuo-heng, China Enters the Machine Age (Cambridge: Harvard University Press, 1944), pp. 151–77.

[98] HHPYK, No. 20, 1958, p. 59.

[99] Alex Nove, The Soviet Economy (New York: Praeger, 1961), pp. 289–95.

the shortage of decision-makers was relatively more acute and the traditional inertia and aversion to change more difficult to break through.

Apart from the question of policy implementation, other reasons for the large-scale development were also given. Supposedly, the mass participation in industrial production would help to spread the industrial technology among a large section of the population who hitherto had never or seldom been exposed to mechanization. Also, the dispersal of industry probably had strategic advantages. But the primary purpose of the campaign appeared to be economic. The intent was to utilize the local resources fully in order to provide for the needs of the local communities.[100] Thus the capital used to build the small plants was to come mostly from the local communities themselves. Natural resources—scattered all over the country and otherwise idle—were to be exploited. And, most important of all, the abundant manpower in the local communities was to be utilized to the fullest extent.

The employment-generating effect of the small plant campaign is especially noteworthy. China's unemployment problem was of such a magnitude that the demand for labor in the modern sector was not likely to expand fast enough to absorb all the available manpower in the foreseeable future. As noted earlier, the proposal for the Second FYP anticipated an increase of nonagricultural employment of only 7 million within a five-year period, whereas the total labor force would increase by that number every year. The development of rural industries on a large scale would provide a possible solution to this problem. Moreover, the rural unemployment was largely seasonal. There were labor shortages during the busy farming seasons, but an enormous amount of labor usually remained idle during the slack seasons.[101] Permanently removing the labor from the farms would adversely affect agricultural output. Thus it seemed sensible to set up industries in the villages instead of in the urban centers. This policy had the additional advantage of avoiding some of the urbanization costs

[100] Yu Yü, "Simultaneous Development of Centralized and Local Industries," *CHCC*, No. 6, 1958, p. 4; editorial in *HC*, No. 12, 1958, p. 5; Chen Ta-lun, "The Principle of Developing Simultaneously the Industries under the Central and the Local Authorities, and Large, Medium and Small Plants," *Ching-chi yen-chiu* (Economic Research), Peking, No. 6, 1958, pp. 51–52.
[101] J. L. Buck, *op. cit.*, pp. 294–301.

that generally accompanied industrialization. The economizing was important because by the end of the First FYP period, urban facilities such as housing, transportation, and power supply in the established industrial centers were already taxed to the limit, and costs of expansion or developing new centers were rather high.[102]

With the new emphasis on mass utilization of labor, there was a corresponding change in the leaders' notion of the relation between population growth and economic development. Actually the change began while the 1957 birth control campaign was still on. In early 1957, Mao enunciated: "In drawing up plans, handling affairs or thinking over problems, we must proceed from the fact that China has a population of six hundred million people. . . . This is our asset. A large population is a good thing."[103] In 1958 Liu Shao-ch'i expounded this thesis further: "All they [the Malthusians] see is that men are consumers and that the bigger the population size, the larger the volume of consumption. They fail to see that men are first of all producers and that as the population gets larger there is also the possibility of greater production and more accumulation."[104] Liu's concept of the dual role of population growth parallels the reasoning of the Harrod-Domar models. An increase in population increases: (a) the demand for output on the one hand, and (b) the size of labor force, and hence the supply of output on the other, and conceivably there is a warranted rate of growth of output that balances

[102] Chen Yün, "Several Major Problems in Current Basic Construction Work," *HC*, No. 5, 1959, p. 5; Fan Jo-yi, *op. cit.*, p. 22.

[103] Mao, *Contradictions*, p. 9. Why did Mao make a statement which apparently contradicted the official birth control policy? Three possible explanations may be suggested. First, the statement might represent a disagreement on population policy between Mao and the more pragmatic group whose ideas were dominant in policy-making during the brief period between late 1956 and mid-1957. Thus far, for simplicity of exposition I have been talking about the Chinese leaders as if they were a unanimous group so far as development policies were concerned. This is somewhat misleading. There were clearly sharp disagreements, although differences of opinion had not been openly aired. See Roderick MacFarquhar, "Communist China's Intra-Party Dispute," *Pacific Affairs*, XXXI (1958), 323–35. Promotion of birth control might well be a controversial issue among the leaders. Second, there might be a time lag between Mao's decision in early 1957 and the suspension of the birth control campaign a year later. Third, the contradiction between Mao's statement and the birth control campaign may be apparent rather than real. Mao was concerned with the benefits that might be derived from the existing large population, whereas the campaign attempted to curb further growth of population.

[104] *Work Report*, p. 8.

the aggregate demand and supply of labor. There is, of course, a limit to which an increase in labor alone can increase output. Apparently the Chinese believed that the current rate of population had not exceeded this limit. For even though the State Planning Commission anticipated a total population of 700 million or more by 1962,[105] the birth-control campaign was abruptly called off at about the time the Second Session of the Eighth Party Congress convened in May 1958.

To sum up, the program underlying the Great Leap in 1958–59 was truly a unique Communist Chinese design. Its basic precept was simply to transform peasant labor into industrial labor, and labor in general into capital. However, this policy was not intended to replace the Soviet strategy adopted for the First FYP but to make it workable in the Chinese demographic setting.

Aftermath of the Great Leap

The outcome of the Great Leap is well known.[106] In 1958 both industrial and agricultural output rose sharply, but from then on the upsurge lost its momentum. In 1959, industrial output continued to expand but at a lower rate of increase, and agriculture probably suffered a marked decline despite official claims to the contrary. When the harvest failed repeatedly in 1960–61, the economy went into a slump. A severe food crisis developed. Short of raw materials, light industry stagnated. Exports fell precipitously. For the first time since it came to power, the regime had to import grain on a sizable scale. In short, instead of moving the economy forward in great strides, the Great Leap brought it to the brink of ruin. What went wrong? The causes of the crisis are many, and cannot be fully explored here.[107] I shall suggest only

[105] *CHCC*, No. 3, 1958, p. 1.

[106] For discussions of what happened to the Great Leap, see H. F. Schurmann, "Peking's Recognition of Crisis," *Problems of Communism*, Vol. X, No. 5 (Sept.–Oct., 1961), pp. 5–14. Cheng Chu-yüan, *Communist China's Economy, 1949–1962* (South Orange, N.J.: Seton Hall University Press, 1963); Yuan-li Wu, Francis P. Hoeber, and Mabel M. Rockwell, *The Economic Potential of Communist China* (Menlo Park, Calif.: Stanford Research Institute, Vols. I–II, 1963; Vol. III, 1964); A. Eckstein, "On the Economic Crisis in Communist China," *Foreign Affairs*, July, 1964, pp. 655–68; Choh-ming Li, "China's Industrial Development," in C. M. Li (ed.), *Industrial Development in Communist China* (New York: Praeger, 1964), pp. 3–38.

[107] The Communists' explanation of the crisis was simple enough. It was largely the result of three consecutive years of natural disasters. In 1961 the leaders attributed the difficulties also to shortcomings of the cadres and to sabotage by bad elements. Later, when the Sino-Soviet

some of the factors that account for the collapse of the agricultural program and the small plant campaign, the two cornerstones of the development policy for 1958–59.

Apart from natural disasters, at least three other factors contributed to the decline in agricultural output: a planning error in 1958, an ineffectual remuneration system in the early stage of the communes, and the almost complete disregard of technical expertise in the agricultural program.

Misled by false reports of fantastically high yields in 1958, the leaders believed for a while that they had solved the agricultural problem once and for all. A new policy of "plant less and reap more" was adopted.[108] Accordingly, they cut down the sown acreage for 1959 and planned to reduce the cultivated area eventually to one-third of the total arable land, leaving the rest to lie fallow or to be afforested. The illusion was quickly dispelled by the discovery in mid-1959 that the harvest of 1958 was grossly exaggerated. The leaders hurriedly reversed their policy.[109] But the damage to the summer harvest of 1959 was already done.

A second and more fundamental cause of the agricultural crisis was a remuneration system that dampened the peasants' incentive to exert their effort. In an important sense the agricultural crisis was a failure of the leaders' attempt to increase output by organizational and ideological means alone. The institutional framework to implement the latter policy was the commune system. Under the communes, the political consciousness of the peasants was to provide the drive behind the peasants' effort. Individual interests were therefore de-emphasized. Private lots were confiscated, rural free markets abolished, and most significant of all, output was distributed on a more or less egalitarian basis. However, to the peasants, ideology was apparently not a satisfactory substitute for material reward. When the intensive effort necessary for the type of garden farming in China was not forthcoming, agricultural output fell. Subsequently, the decline in output set in motion a vicious circle with food shortage on one side and the peasants' disillusionment, resentment, and hunger on the other.

---

discord was brought into the open, they put part of the blame on the Soviet withdrawal of specialists in 1960. At most, these factors provide only part of the explanation.

[108] CCP, "Resolution on Certain Problems of the People's Communes," *HHPYK*, No. 24, 1958, p. 7.

[109] *JMJP*, June 11, 1959.

Two additional factors also aggravated the situation. Many farm techniques (such as deep plowing and close planting) that were extensively applied during this period required relatively large quantities of labor. Furthermore, one of the advantages claimed for the commune was that rural labor could be rationally utilized by redeploying labor to nonfarm activities. Although the idea was sound, it apparently had been carried too far. Despite a much higher labor participation rate than ever before, labor was reportedly short on the farms in 1958–59.[110] Although probably exaggerated, there might well be some truth in the official claim that the labor shortage in the harvest season of 1958 had adverse effects on output.

The agricultural problem was not one of dampened personal incentive alone. The program to increase output was pushed so rashly that the technological constraints were almost entirely ignored. Under such guiding principles as "amateurs can lead experts" and "break through regulations," untested farming techniques were often applied uniformly over large areas, irrespective of differences in local conditions and without proper technical guidance. In water conservation, the traditional irrigation systems were partly destroyed to make way for the new. Yet the new systems were often defective in design or in construction. The result was an enormous expansion of income but no corresponding increase in physical output. In fact, there might well be a net loss, for the alternative cost of these labor participation programs was by no means negligible. More food was needed. Large quantities of construction materials and some capital were used in the process. Sometimes the reckless digging caused alkalization of the soil with damaging effects on output.

The collapse of the small plant campaign was essentially a failure in the attempt to industrialize the rural area by unplanned, uncoordinated mass movements. The tremendous political pressure from above and the decentralization of control over finance since late 1957 provided the local cadres the initiative, the authority, and the necessary means to push the campaign in a guerrilla-warfare manner and at breakneck speed. In this fanatic drive to develop local industries, three problems arose that eventually brought the campaign to a collapse. First, the products of many small plants were of such poor quality that most of them

[110] CCP, "Communiqué of the Eighth Plenum of the Eighth Central Committee, *HHPYK*, No. 17, 1959, p. 1.

had to be scrapped. The "native iron" was a striking example. As in the labor-intensive projects in agriculture, the basic cause of this blunder was the gross neglect of technology in the campaign. In general, a fair amount of technical knowledge was required to build and operate a small plant. But the available technical skills were hardly adequate for the ambitious task in 1958–59. The big push regardless of the technological constraint inevitably resulted in the mass production of useless products.

Although some plants encountered no technical difficulty, their production costs were high relative to those of the large plants. In part the high production cost was the result of the indiscriminatory development of small plants in almost all industries. Some plants were physically inefficient at relatively small scales of operation, requiring more input per unit of output than the large plant. The small petroleum refinery was a case in point.

The disregard of cost considerations at the local management level was another reason why many of the small plants were uneconomical. Since the most important success indicator for the local cadre was the degree to which he could fulfill or overfulfill his output quota, he concentrated his effort to increase production even at the expense of quality and cost. The cadres' attempts to maximize output regardless of cost were not only uneconomical from the standpoint of the firm but also wasteful for the economy as a whole. The local cadres tended to ignore such questions as whether or not their output would be needed, whether or not the neglect of repairs and maintenance would be costly in the long run, and whether or not the input consumed could have been more productively used elsewhere.

A third problem that forced many small plants to close down was the acute shortage of fuels or raw materials. The shortage was largely the result of the agricultural crisis, but the transportation bottlenecks, the exhaustion of fuel supply or the limited mineral deposits in many localities, and the lack of coordination between different industries during this period also contributed to the downfall of many local industries.

Policy Changes During 1960–62

As the crisis deepened in 1960–62, the basic tenets of the Great Leap development policy were quietly abandoned one by one, and out of the struggle for economic revival a new policy evolved. Its main features included: (1) Agriculture was to be the foundation of the economy rather than simultaneous development of industry and agriculture. The scale of priority development was to be agriculture, light industry, and heavy industry, in descending order.[111] This change of emphasis marked a shift farther away from the Soviet model than ever before. (2) In basic construction and industry, "readjustment [of the pace of development], consolidation [of existing plants], reinforcement [of the weak links], and improvement [of quality]" was adopted, and the scale of the investment program was to be reduced.[112] (3) Greater emphasis was now placed on the use and spread of existing technical skills, training, and research, and on borrowing advanced techniques from abroad through the importation of equipment and whole plants from the West. The change reflected the recognition of the importance of technology following the failure of many small plants and labor-intensive projects and the abrupt withdrawal of Soviet experts in 1960. In 1963, Mao reaffirmed this policy when he singled out scientific experiment along with class struggle and production struggle as the three overriding goals that the party must strive to accomplish.[113] (4) Since 1962, the regime put forth a renewed effort to control population growth with primary emphasis on late marriage.

Beyond these bare outlines, little is known about the new policy. Nor is it clear whether this is the road China will continue to take for the coming Third FYP.

V. CONCLUDING REMARKS

The intent of this study has been to delineate certain development problems and policies during the first decade of the respective Soviet and Chinese industrialization drives. It is seen that both began their First FYP with the same goal and more or less the same big push, heavy-industry-first strategy. But although the Soviet Union held on to Stalin's formula steadfastly throughout the decade, China modified it before her first Plan came to a close, and since then has experimented with three alternative policies: the retrenchment in 1957, the Great Leap in 1958–59, and the readjustment in 1960–62. Judging from the limited knowledge we have of the economic performance during this period, one could perhaps say that, by and large, Russia fared much better

[111] *JMJP*, Apr. 17, 1962.
[112] CCP, "Communiqué of the Ninth Plenum of the Eighth Central Committee," *HC*, No. 3–4, 1961, p. 2.
[113] *HC*, No. 19, 1964, p. 5.

than China. It would be presumptuous to suppose that the contrasting patterns of development could be explained in terms of their policy decisions alone. But surely the particular choice of strategy had a major part to play. What broad implications may be drawn from the foregoing discussions?

First, the Soviet and Chinese experiences suggest that the problem of capital formation has two distinct aspects. To raise the investment rate in the initial period is one thing, and to sustain it at high levels from then on is quite another. Both nations succeeded in raising the investment rate very rapidly at the initial phase of the drive. But as their plans unfolded, the investment rate remained high despite some fluctuations in the Soviet Union, whereas it dropped probably quite sharply in China in the post-1958 period. One plausible explanation of this is that the problem at the initial stage was essentially one of mobilizing the investable resources, and that, where resources existed as they apparently did in both countries, effective organizational controls could bring about a steep rise in the investment rate. But in the second stage, the tasks facing the two countries differed sharply. For the USSR, it remained largely a redistribution problem. Having started from a relatively strong economic base and a favorable ratio of population to natural resources, Russia could continue for some time to amass large quantities of the unconsumed output and direct it towards industrial development without having to worry too much over the major source of supply. It was not until 1953–64 that the USSR had to confront the problem of agricultural underdevelopment. For China, the problem had a different dimension. Because of extreme poverty and the enormous, growing population, there had to be a production breakthrough in the agricultural sector to provide the bulk of the savings. It was largely the failure to bring about the crucial breakthrough that led to the retrenchment in the later part of the period.

Closely related to this problem was the question of "balance" between agriculture and industry. It is clear that agricultural development need not be a necessary precondition or even a concomitant requirement in the early phase of industrialization. The decisive factor was the "agricultural surplus" rather than agricultural output. As the Soviet experience shows, industrialization was possible with a stagnant agriculture. But the Soviet case, after all, is an extreme case. Its permanent agricultural crisis was tolerable for a long while since population growth exerted little pressure upon its resources. By comparison, China's permanent population crisis was real and formidable, for the whole economy could not move forward with a modest rise, let alone a decline, of agricultural output. The first decade of China's industrialization witnessed the gradual awakening, first, to the Malthusian ghost which never haunted Russia, and second, to the fact that institutional and organizational means alone could not solve her basic problem of industrialization.

In highly simplified terms, one can describe the Soviet industrialization strategy as an attempt to convert the agricultural surplus into industrial capital, and the Chinese strategy as one to convert labor into industrial capital. For other countries where the absorption of manpower into nonfarm activities is a fundamental problem, the Chinese case provides both positive and negative lessons. The positive elements are that real opportunities generally exist for substituting labor for capital (such as better road maintenance to reduce wear and tear of trucks, and construction of irrigation projects), and that to a large extent rural labor could be used productively in nonfarm activities, thus lowering the urbanization costs. But although the Chinese policy was strategically correct, it was a tactical blunder. The leaders overlooked the fact that, in general, some new technology is indispensable in utilizing manpower and that selection of projects and the scale of the program must depend on the technological capability constraint. In the characteristic Communist fashion of identifying the maximum with the optimum, the labor utilization scheme was pushed in all directions and clearly beyond its rational limit.

Finally, one may note that for poorer countries like China, the range of choice in the use of resources is much more limited than in the case of Russia, for there are boundaries beyond which the Soviet pattern of choice would be infeasible or undesirable. Moreover, the very fact that a country is poor makes it imperative to choose the strategy of development carefully. As the economic aftermath of China's Great Leap clearly shows, an economy advancing from a subsistence level can ill afford waste and errors.

PART SIX

Russia and China in International Affairs

Introduction

ALEXANDER DALLIN

THE AIM of this section was to compare the views of the outside world held by the Soviet and Chinese leaderships. What we meant by world views, in this connection, was neither the formal system of doctrine subscribed to by the respective regimes, nor the sum total of transient foreign policies pursued by them at any given moment. We hoped to compare, in other words, what our jargon-happy colleagues would call the "operationally-relevant" perceptions of the world—both the Communist and the non-Communist —by each of the two major Communist powers.

By definition, this world view could not be lifted from the pages of official texts, nor from a compendium of diplomatic moves. And, beyond the valuable papers presented in this section, there remains a cluster of serious problems of methodology which deserve earnest attention: How does one identify the "world view" of each power? How does one compare the two? How does one test the findings? Of these questions, the first is the most elusive and bothersome. And, as in other sections, the difficulty in resolving some of the disagreements which arose in the course of the ensuing discussion stemmed not so much from the problems of comparison *per se* as from failure to agree on what it was we were comparing.

Logic might have led us to seek agreement on (*a*) What is the Soviet world view? and (*b*) What is the Chinese world view? before (*c*) attempting to compare the answers to *a* and *b*.[1] But

[1] Admittedly, there is here (as in other areas of comparative government) something of a vicious circle, for the uniqueness of either *a* or *b* cannot be established until each is compared with the world view of other powers.

this could not be done in this context. Hence there remains some disagreement about the underlying characteristics of each.

Since it is hard, therefore, to build on a common denominator, I propose to restrict the universe of possible inquiry and hypothesis by pointing to certain approaches which, in my judgment, lead into intellectual blind alleys divorced from the factual evidence. In particular, we may usefully raise warning signals against

—the danger of ignoring Communist "ideology" as allegedly irrelevant to motives, world views, or policies;

—the danger of interpreting Soviet or Chinese conduct as a rigid pursuit (or implementation) of doctrine;

—the danger of viewing the Russian and Chinese world views and values as necessarily constant or consistent.

Despite the healthy instinct which makes many of us shy away from the interminable wrangles over the role which "ideology" plays in Soviet or Chinese conduct, the problem cannot really be avoided. What perhaps deserves reiteration is the fact that in the Communist mind "ideology" does not consist of a set of philosophical abstractions but rather, at the level of which we speak, amounts to generalizations of political and revolutionary assessments and strategies. In this light, it would be impossible to understand the development of either Russian or Chinese communism—for instance, their bitter internal debates of the 1920's as well as of the 1960's—without a sophisticated reading of "Marxism-Leninism" in its different variants.

It should be equally clear, on the other hand, that "ideology" is not an unequivocal "guide to action" in specific cases. It cannot be; and no decision-maker would let it be. Moreover, both the Soviet and the Chinese elites have frequently used "theory" to legitimize their policies—including foreign policies—even where these could scarcely be justified in orthodox terms. Nor does the record of ideologically-couched debates reflect the full range of disagreements; while later evidence has fully validated, for instance, Professor Zagoria's reading of the Sino-Soviet dispute, the body of documents from which he worked did not convey the importance of such issues as the Chinese Communist demand for a nuclear weapon—and the ultimate Soviet refusal to provide it.

Furthermore, in the opinion of many observers, there has occurred a gradual decrease in the specifically Communist elements of Soviet conduct, whatever the formal professions of faith; while the Chinese Communists' world view, according to many specialists, has always had certain ingredients not adequately explicable in strictly Communist terms. And the recent conflict between the two powers has further crystallized the differences in outlook. As one of the discussants astutely pointed out:

The Chinese world outlook emphasizes anarchism, populism, nationalism, racialism, and even developmental pessimism, while the Soviet world outlook emphasizes technocratic optimism, increasingly stressing the positive role of the state, and tempered by the growing realization that industrialization and urbanization create new social and cultural problems. In terms of both outlook and appeal, neither viewpoint is adequately subsumed by traditional Marxism-Leninism.

Still, it would be thoroughly fallacious to regard the Soviet and Chinese world views (and hence, presumably, their long-range policies) as "mere" continuations of the traditional prerevolutionary outlooks dominant in the two countries. Thus, the fact that, both before and after the Revolution, Russia has sought to extend its influence or control to the same neighboring areas (e.g., Poland, Finland, Northern Iran, Manchuria) and that Communist China has been similarly mindful of the special relationships which once existed between the Middle Kingdom and the areas of Southeast Asia, really tells us nothing about the motives and perceptions of the present leaders. Given the unchanging nature of geography, the continuity or identity of the loci of (potential or real, political or military) expansion is hardly an indicator of the constancy of political goals.

Nor can the Sino-Soviet dispute be reduced to a clash over territorial issues. The contested areas between the two states and along their borders (e.g., Sinkiang, Mongolia, and the Maritime Province) have been there all along, both when Sino-Soviet relations were good and when they deteriorated.

Indeed, attempts to dismiss all "ideological" elements are probably more indicative of American attitudes than of Soviet or Chinese world views. They are further contradicted by an analysis of the public pronouncements of the respective leaders. In both Moscow and Peking the rulers have been trained to see the world in terms of categories which, over a lifetime of reiteration, become so deeply engrained as to be virtually—though not quite —ineradicable. Yet some room for individual variations in perception and in ability to change one's outlook does remain. And a close examination of the writings and statements of a Mao or Khrushchev permits the reconstruction of the individual's value system and objectives in a fashion validated by the congruent evidence of their actual conduct.

Now it is true that in both instances an awareness of national traditions, self-interest, and priorities has reasserted itself. By an easy and perhaps unwitting mutation, the Soviet elite shifted from seeking power as a means to an end—communism—to the view that anything that strengthens one's own state and society redounds to the ultimate benefit of the larger objective. In the Chinese case, the (temporarily suppressed or repressed) consciousness of quasi-colonial inferiority and animus against foreign encroachments—Western, Japanese, and Soviet—helps explain the Communists' reaction and paves the way for their appeals to national "self-reliance" as well as their charges of Soviet "great-power chauvinism."

In more general terms, it is safe to predict that the emergence of a Communist multiple-power system (as of a non-Communist one) was bound to lead to competition and conflict among the component powers. And, given the fact that they operate in a system of nation-states, national rivalry was bound to be one way in which the tension between them expressed itself.

Professor Lowenthal, in the following paper, relates the different Soviet and Chinese outlooks and assessments to differing national experiences. Thus, for example, the protracted civil war led by the Chinese Communists from the countryside against the hostile cities has surely created images which Mao Tse-tung, Lin Piao, and Chen Yi transferred to their assessment of the outside world.[2] In substance, both for Russia and for China these are the ingredients that make up the respective "models" which each seeks to peddle to the non-Communist world.

Special attention should be drawn to the danger of "presentism." It is particularly relevant to the present topic, because of the widespread temptation to absolutize the momentary policies or approaches of either power. The "immutability" school has had far too many converts in various corners: those who see the

[2] On this point, see Tang Tsou and Morton H. Halperin, "Mao Tse-tung's Revolutionary Strategy and Peking's International Behavior," *The American Political Science Review*, Vol. LIX, No. 1 (Mar., 1965), pp. 80–99.

powers pursuing permanent national objectives; those who consider communism essentially a single and static phenomenon; and those who see the divergent perceptions in Moscow and Peking as, simply, functions of the different stages of socio-economic development attained by the two states. Whatever the degree of soundness of each of these contentions, the fact remains that such determinism (especially when monistic) has all too often misled the pundits and prophets.

As one reviews the half-century of Soviet foreign-policy strategy, the zigzags of perception and policy between "left" and "right" strike the observer as an outstanding feature. A generation ago Stalin was telling a credulous West that the Chinese Communists were but "agrarian reformers," and soon American commentators developed the theory that the farther east it went, the more "watered down" Marxism-Leninism would be. While this proved to be accurate with regard to the proletarian, or class, element of Communist appeals in the non-Western world, it was decidedly wrong insofar as it implied a moderation of Communist strategy and tactics. A decade later, things had changed to the point that one heard the opposite hypothesis—to the effect that, as one moved east, communism was bound to become more intransigent or "leftist." Yet not only are there more exceptions from, than examples of, this law, but it is also well to remember that in both periods—say, 1950 and 1960—China was at a lower stage of socio-economic development than Russia, and the "national" characteristics of either were presumably unchanged —both when China was to the "right" of Russia and when it was to the "left" in its perception of the world scene.

One final warning need perhaps scarcely be voiced: the disparity between word and deed. Time and again Moscow and Peking have accused each other of failure to live up to its commitments and obligations. When the Chinese, for instance, blamed the Soviet leadership for its failure to provide the requisite support for the "liberation" of Quemoy and Matsu and, more important, of Taiwan, the Russians pointed to Chinese caution regarding the "liberation" of Hong Kong. More recently, the credibility of Peking's threats has suffered markedly from its failure to act on its warnings regarding Vietnam and its threats against India during the Indo-Pakistani war.

While both have manifested a capacity for erring (which could be both disconcerting and comforting to the rest of the world), both the Soviet and the Chinese leaders have shown themselves able to refrain from acts that would have amounted to suicide even if a narrow-minded implementation of their own programs and prognoses should have called for them. They have, by and large, been remarkably rational in assessing the limits of the possible (though Khrushchev's overconfidence in his ability to pull off the impossible, at home and abroad, led him into such lunatic endeavors as the dispatch of missiles to Cuba). But by no means does it follow herefrom that all the "extremist" pronouncements from Communist sources are no more than propaganda and can be dismissed from an analysis of Chinese or Soviet views.

Looking at them from afar and outside, we have often been inclined to see Communist pronouncements as cunningly rounded, systematic statements revealing an enviably simple and orderly (if often mistaken) view of the world. This simplicity is deceptive, for with the benefit of hindsight one may assert that we have generally underestimated the difficulties which Soviet and Communist theorists have had in systematizing their own views. Not only has the world not conformed to their earlier expectations (let alone to the formulae of the Marxist "classics"), but— the Soviet leaders have been frank to acknowledge—currently the process of correctly assessing rapidly-changing events and unfamiliar phenomena is fraught with great difficulties and risks of error, inviting repeated disagreements in their own midst.[3] Another reason, then, for what Peking calls Soviet revisionism and betrayal of the faith—and what Moscow likes to see as "creative Marxism" adapted to new needs and conditions. But also another reason why once should not be surprised if the world view of either elite turns out to be less homogeneous, less clear-cut, less unanimous—if it reveals more inconsistencies and incongruities —than has commonly been believed. As one of the discussants pointed out, some of the uncertainty of the current Soviet posture stems precisely from the strain between the traditional adherence to a revolutionary perspective and the newly-discovered interest in maintaining the status quo.

Since they are genuine and stimulating contributions to the general effort of crystallizing common and divergent elements in the Soviet and Chinese world views, the following papers elicited lively comment and discussion. The participants would agree, no

[3] See, e.g., Boris N. Ponomarev (ed.), *Mezhdunarodnoe revoliutsionnoe dvizhenie rabochego klassa* (Moscow, 1965), p. 401.

doubt, that there is room for further discussion of certain facets of Soviet and Chinese policies, such as

—their relative rationality;

—their respective appeals to other states, groups, and individuals;

—the relevance of their experience to others;

—the distortion of reality due to ideological blinders;

—the compatibility of "proletarian" and "colonial" strategies of revolution in a Communist framework;

—the relative flexibility and ability to adjust to new situations and opportunities;

—the roots of each elite's perception to be found in the frustrations and objectives of the national intelligentsia.

The comparison of Communist outlooks and policies remains a fruitful and challenging area of inquiry. It deserves and needs further work.

Soviet and Chinese Communist World Views

RICHARD LOWENTHAL

THE FOREIGN policies of any sovereign power are shaped, to a considerable extent, by the view its rulers take of the outside world—by their ideas about the strength of other powers and the motivating forces of their policies, about the compatibility of the objectives of those other powers with their own or among each other, and about the tendencies toward a change in these factors and the power constellations determined by them. One reason why the concept of the "national interest" is so often liable to widely differing interpretations is precisely that the requirements of the military security and the economic and political stability of a given state can never be determined by looking at the geographic situation, the resources and needs of that state alone—that the evaluation of those requirements must always depend on an estimate of the strength and an interpretation of the objectives of other powers. The classic formula according to which foreign policy is dictated by national interest is thus strictly true only in the tautological sense that it depends on the view of that interest taken by the government in power, and therefore in a large part on its views of the outside world.

Any attempt to understand, predict, and possibly modify the policies of a foreign power therefore presupposes an effort to understand the "world view" of its government in the sense defined above. In the case of Communist powers, the specific character of their ideological regime both provides an easier approach for such an effort and besets it with certain pitfalls. The Communist parties legitimate their rule by a coherent system of doctrinal beliefs, including explicit public statements of their views about the forces at work in world politics and the inherent "laws" shaping the development of world affairs; those doctrinal statements thus offer a ready-made starting point for the student investigating the world views of a Communist power. The pitfalls lie, of course, in the fact that the doctrinaire statements are unlikely to be identical with the actual operative views of the rulers of Communist states, and that for at least two main reasons. One is that, precisely owing to the legitimating function of the ideology in Communist regimes, their spokesmen seek to create an exaggerated image of their doctrinal consistency, to minimize the practical importance of adjustment to unforeseen events, to describe as the pursuit of principle what may in fact have been the outcome of contingent necessity. The other is that no fixed political doctrine can provide in advance for all the dilemmas with which its ruling practitioners may one day be faced; hence situations are bound to arise in which different aspects of the doctrine may serve as arguments for different decisions, while the actual decision is determined by preferences that were not explicit in the doctrine—which is subsequently "reinterpreted" accordingly. In either case, the explicit statements and their claim to doctrinal consistency have to be critically evaluated in the light of the actual conduct of policy over time in order to arrive at the really operative world views of Communist powers.

Because of the pitfalls inherent in an uncritical acceptance of the Communist claim to doctrinal consistency in foreign policy, it is often suggested that the student of international affairs should confine himself to observing the practical behavior of Communist governments, ignoring their ideological verbiage as a mere cloak used to cover the nakedness of their power politics, or as the pious Sunday talk of statesmen who in their workaday practice have long settled down to the agnostic pursuit of the national interest. Yet we have pointed out that a statesman's concept of the national interest depends on his view of the outside world; and in the case of a Communist government, it would be absurd to deny that Communist ideology is at any rate *one* major factor determining that view—indispensable, even though not by itself sufficient, for its understanding. Moreover, even when Communist doctrinal statements reflect a policy decision rather than motivate it, they frequently furnish, once properly decoded, early and important clues for perceiving the decision and its causes. To deprive ourselves of this kind of clue in the name of the exclusive observation of Communist behavior from the outside would mean that we should gratuitously renounce the advantage of the fact that we are not dealing with the incomprehensible actions of some sort of Martians but with articulate human beings whose language and thought processes, however strange, are intelligible to us in principle.

In seeking to derive the operative world views of the Soviet and Chinese Communists from their official formulations on world affairs, we have above all to watch out for three major sources of distortion. First, we must expect that until the emergence of major conflict between the two Communist powers, both sides would have tended to use common formulas even where their views actually differed on important specific issues, and that the Chinese in particular would have clung to the Soviet model more closely in their public statements than in their actual thinking. Second, after the emergence of open differences, each side had an interest in presenting its own views as a continuation or at least a logical development of the former common orthodoxy, and in minimizing the departure from that orthodoxy implied in the innovations it had adopted in response to new conditions. Third, each side had a corresponding interest in magnifying the deviation from orthodoxy committed by the other and in distorting its views accordingly, so that once the conflict had passed a certain point, the formal statements were likely to give an exaggerated picture of the gulf between the actual views of the Soviet and Chinese Communist leaders. In attempting to trace, in the following pages, the divergent development of Soviet and Chinese Communist world views from their common roots in Stalinist orthodoxy, and to analyze the factors that have caused this divergence, we shall seek to bear these reservations in mind.

THE COMMON FRAMEWORK

For a long time, both Soviet and Chinese Communist world views developed within the framework of the official "Marxist-Leninist" doctrine laid down by Stalin. While it is true that this doctrine grew out of Lenin's thought and action with a high degree of continuity, it was only Stalin who created a fixed and frozen system out of the flux of that thought and action, eliminating some of the contradictions in Lenin's thinking and putting one-sided emphasis on those of its elements that could serve as the official ideology of a totalitarian state.

This Stalinist version of "Marxism-Leninism" became for many years the basis of the political education not only of Soviet Communists but of all "orthodox" foreign Communists, including the leading cadres of the Chinese Communist Party. That applies without reservation for the period of total Soviet control of the Chinese party leadership, roughly from the fall of Ch'en Tu-hsiu in August 1927 to the takeover of Mao Tse-tung in January 1935. Even after Mao's assumption of the leadership had led—not without several years of underhand struggle—to the growing emancipation of the Chinese Communist Party from Soviet control in matters of their own strategy, tactics, and organization, Mao and his team remained sincerely loyal to Stalin's general doctrine and more particularly to his interpretation of world affairs. During the Yenan period, the same campaign for the retraining of the party cadres which served to consolidate Mao's independence in Chinese affairs was used for the intensive study of Stalin's writings, and massive efforts to popularize these writings continued after the creation of the Chinese People's Republic and even beyond Stalin's death. The effect of these writings on the world view of the Chinese Communists must have been all the more profound because they lived and fought in practically complete isolation from the outside world between 1935 and 1945, and to a large extent right up to 1949; and it was reflected in their unquestioning acceptance of such crucial Soviet actions as Stalin's pact with Hitler and—more important to them—Soviet wartime diplomacy toward Japan.

It will be sufficient for our purpose merely to sketch the broad outline of this common standard version of "Marxist-Leninist" doctrine. Its core is the view of the world as divided into two irreconcilable "camps," representing respectively the capitalist and proletarian classes or the capitalist and socialist systems and their allies. The capitalist world is viewed as inevitably declining in political cohesion and material power as well as in productive growth potential and ideological creativity and attractiveness, owing to the progressive unfolding of its internal contradictions —the conflicts among the imperialist powers, between those powers and the oppressed colonial peoples, and between the capitalist exploiters and the productive classes led by the proletariat within the imperialist countries. The socialist world is seen as rising and expanding with equal inevitability thanks to the superiority of its economic and social system, the scientific leadership of its ruling Communist parties, their international solidarity, and their alliance with the struggling proletarian classes and colonial peoples. The conflict of the two camps can only end with the final victory of socialism on a world scale, but according to the Stalinist version of Marxist-Leninist orthodoxy, this will not come about by a single blow and need not, and preferably should not, be the result of a final world war: by exploiting the conflicts among the imperialists and mobilizing the desire of the peoples for peace, the socialist powers may prevent a united imperialist attack on them again and again until the declining enemy has become too weak to risk it. Since the historical forces work in any case in favor of the socialist camp, steadily shifting the relation of forces to the disadvantage of its opponents and offering ever new chances for exploiting the crises of the capitalist system by successful revolutions, the Communists have no interest in precipitating a general showdown and may content themselves with seizing these revolutionary opportunities as they arise. In that sense, "peaceful coexistence," or the strategy of protracted worldwide conflict with controlled risk, is good traditional Stalinist doctrine.

As far as we can judge, the concrete application of this common framework of analysis to the interpretation of the world situation by Soviet and Chinese Communists also developed on roughly parallel lines until 1957. For instance, both had by 1946 come to the conclusion that after the defeat of Germany and Japan, the United States with its atomic monopoly was seeking to unify the capitalist camp under its leadership and had become their main enemy; but both Stalin and Mao argued at the time in authoritative interviews[1] that an American-led all-out attack on the Soviet Union was unlikely, despite the temptation offered by that atomic monopoly, owing to American preoccupation with inter-imperialist conflicts. There are some indications that around 1948, at the height of the East-West conflict in Europe, the

[1] Cf. Stalin's interview with Alexander Werth, *Bolshevik*, No. 17/18, Sept., 1946, and Mao's talk with Anna Louise Strong of August, 1946, printed in *Amerasia*, Apr. 1947, and in Mao's *Selected Works*, Vol. V (New York, n.d.), p. 97. Though Stalin is more diplomatic about American intentions, both agree in belittling both the atom bomb and all talk about the imminence of a new war.

Chinese leaders may have come to believe in the imminence of major war,[2] as some other Communist leaders did and even some Soviet leaders may have done, but Stalin certainly did not. But by the time of the Korean War, both Soviet and Chinese actions were clearly based on a rejection of the "war perspective." Again, both Soviet and Chinese Communists were prevented by doctrinaire blinkers from grasping the authenticity and significance of the beginning of decolonization when Britain started the process by granting independence to India, Pakistan, Burma, and Ceylon in 1947/48—though Peking, being geographically and psychologically closer to the phenomenon, gave earlier indications than Moscow of recognizing the fact of Indian independence and its possible diplomatic usefulness.

Even after the death of Stalin, Soviet and Chinese Communists at first proceeded more or less in step in adjusting the common doctrine to new realities. Both now turned eagerly to an effort to keep the new, ex-colonial nations at least neutral and thus incorporate them in a "zone of peace" around their borders, a policy that presupposed acceptance of the independence of the new nations from the "imperialist camp" and understanding of the strategic value of their anti-imperialist outlook. Both also came to agree on the need to transform the Soviet bloc into a "Socialist Commonwealth," based on continued Soviet leadership in foreign policy and in the interpretation of the doctrine but allowing considerable domestic autonomy for all member governments; here again, Peking was somewhat ahead in its "revisionism" in the Polish case, but full harmony was preserved during all phases of the Hungarian crisis, and the two parties presented a common formula on the issue at the Moscow conference of November 1957. Finally, both interpreted the development of a thermonuclear stalemate and particularly the growing vulnerability of the United States after the invention of intercontinental missiles as a major shift in the world balance of power offering increased chances for new advances of the socialist camp. It was only at this point that serious differences arose about the extent of the shift and the best strategy for exploiting the new opportunities.

[2] Reports about a disagreement on these lines in the summer of 1948 appeared first in *The World Today* (London), June, 1950; they were used by C. P. Fitzgerald, *Revolution in China* (London, 1952), and judged trustworthy by Max Beloff, *Soviet Policy in the Far East* (London, 1953).

THE DIFFERENT BACKGROUND

Yet while Soviet and Chinese Communists for many years professed a common world view, they had long been conscious of the differences in their own role in the world; and that awareness inevitably led to less conscious differences of emphasis in the use of the common doctrine. In the light of the later open disagreements, we may discern three major, interconnected differences in the historic background of the two parties: they concern the importance of anti-colonial nationalism as a revolutionary factor, the role of armed force in the struggle for power, and the relative weight of the "subjective" and "objective" elements of strength—of revolutionary determination against economic and technological maturity—in the class struggle.

Anti-colonial nationalism was recognized as one of the major revolutionary forces of our time by Lenin. It was he who first conceived the strategic idea of a grand alliance uniting the oppressed colonial and semi-colonial peoples with the proletariat of the advanced industrial countries and with the young Soviet state in a common struggle to overthrow the imperialist order. But in the view of Lenin and his successors, the anti-colonial nationalist movements (the "bourgeois-democratic revolutions" of the East) were ultimately auxiliaries; the Communist movements of the industrial working class (the "proletarian revolutions" of the West) would have to provide the hard core, even though the auxiliaries might conceivably decide the final battle by their sheer bulk.

This was not simply a matter of strategic doctrine but of identity and experience. The Russian revolutionaries in general, and the Bolsheviks in particular, did not regard themselves as members of an oppressed, but of an oppressing, nation; desperately impatient as they were with Russian backwardness, it did not occur to them to blame the Western imperialists for causing it. Though the Bolsheviks eventually came to inherit the Narodniks' dream of leading Russia to socialism along a new road that would spare her the evils of Western capitalist society, they were never consciously anti-Western before the conquest of power. It was only after that victory had been followed by the futile intervention of the Western imperialists and the defeat of the Western Communists that the Bolsheviks reluctantly settled down to fulfill the Narodniks' testament in isolated Russia. When Lenin talked about former colonial peoples taking the "non-capitalist road of development" with the help of the proletarians of the advanced countries, he saw the young republics of Central Asia as examples of such former colonial peoples, but Soviet Russia as representing the advanced proletarians.

In Russia, in short, anti-Western nationalism arose only as a by-product of the victory of the Bolshevik revolution—it had not been among its motivating forces. Chinese communism, by contrast, may be said to have arisen as a by-product of anti-colonial nationalism. It had its immediate origin in the atmosphere of the May Fourth Movement of national protest against the Versailles transfer of Chinese territory from one imperialist power to the other, and in the consequent desperate search for means to overcome national weakness and humiliation. In a longer perspective, it has been described as the final outcome of the quest for identity pursued by an intelligentsia that had to break with its cultural tradition to achieve modernization, yet had first set out to achieve modernization in order to recover its national dignity.[3] Though the founding fathers of Chinese communism were by no means anti-Western in a cultural sense and had turned to Marxism as an advanced Western message that seemed relevant to their problems,[4] the influence of those Westernizing intellectuals from the coastal cities has been increasingly replaced by that of profoundly anti-Western backwoodsmen like Mao Tse-tung and his Hunan clan, until China's spiritual climate today has become much closer to that of Mao's youthful tract about the patriotic value of physical jerks[5] than to that of the early writings of Li Ta-chao or Ch'en Tu-hsiu. Before its final postwar bid for power, the two periods that saw the greatest expansion of Chinese Communist influence were that of the struggle for national unification

[3] For this interpretation of the place of the Communists in Chinese intellectual history, see above all Joseph R. Levenson, *Confucian China and Its Modern Fate* (3 vols.; Berkeley and Los Angeles, 1958–65).

[4] On the origins of Marxism-Leninism in China, see the opening chapter of Benjamin I. Schwartz, *Chinese Communism and the Rise of Mao* (Cambridge, Mass., 1951).

[5] See Stuart L. Schram's French translation: Mao Ze-dong, *Une Étude de l'Éducation Physique* (Paris, 1962), and the same author's English extract and comments in his *The Political Thought of Mao Tse-tung* (New York, 1963).

up to 1927, and that of the national resistance against Japan after 1937; while the decisive struggle after 1945 was accompanied by unceasing denunciations of American imperialist intervention.

The Chinese Communists' view of themselves and of the world has been profoundly marked by this history. Lenin believed that he had creatively applied Marxism to Russian conditions; but if he had been told that he had "Russified" it, he would have rejected the phrase as an insult. Mao began to boast of his "Sinification" of Marxism in 1938, in his address to the first plenary session of the Central Committee after the coup that had given him leadership of the party[6]—the session that marked the final legitimation of that leadership and its acceptance by the Comintern; and within a year, he formally claimed that the "New Democracy" he was creating must become a model for the revolutions in all colonial and semi-colonial countries.[7] Subsequently, "Sinification" became an essential part of the Cheng Feng movement for the retraining of party cadres, while the claim for a model role of the Chinese revolution for all revolutions in colonial and semi-colonial countries was repeated on the morrow of Communist victory on the whole Chinese mainland by Liu Shao-ch'i from the international platform of the Peking conference of Asian and Australasian trade unions.[8]

Against this different background, it appears natural that the two parties should have reacted differently to one of the basic experiences of the international Communist movement in the past half century: I mean the decline in revolutionary tensions in the advanced industrial countries, and the mounting evidence of

[6] The report, given in November, 1938, was first published in English under the title "On the New Stage" by the New China Information Committee in Chungking. For different translations of the relevant passage, see *Selected Works*, Vol. II (London, 1954) (where it appears as "The Role of the Chinese Communist Party in the National War"), p. 260, and Stuart L Schram, *The Political Thought of Mao Tse-tung* (New York, 1963), pp. 112–15.

[7] "This kind of revolution is developing in China as well as in all colonial and semi-colonial countries, and we call it the new-democratic revolution." *Selected Works*, Vol. III (London, 1954), p. 96. The passage occurs in Mao's Yenan textbook, *The Chinese Revolution and the Chinese Communist Party*, written in December, 1939, directly preceding his more widely-known *On New Democracy*.

[8] Text of the speech in *For a Lasting Peace, for a People's Democracy*, Dec. 30, 1949.

the revolutionary potential, or at any rate the social and political instability, of the underdeveloped countries both before and after decolonization. To the Soviet Communists, whose own successful industrialization increased their sense of community with the advanced nations, this experience posed the problem of whether there might not be other roads to Communist power than violent revolution; to the Chinese Communists it has suggested that the underdeveloped continents are becoming the main "storm centers" of the world revolution, and that they themselves, being the model and guide for these national liberation movements, are destined to become the leaders of world communism.

A second difference of background concerns the role of armed force in revolutionary strategy. Lenin taught his followers that the true revolutionary must in principle be ready to use all means of struggle—legal and illegal, violent and peaceful—according to criteria of political expediency. He believed that final victory could be won only by an armed insurrection, started on a signal from the political leadership once conditions were ripe for it, and that any truly revolutionary party must therefore maintain at least the nucleus of a military organization in being at all times, in order to study the techniques of insurrection and train its cadres for rapid expansion as the revolutionary crisis approached; and he imposed those principles on all parties that wished to join the Communist International. But while he regarded the use of armed force for revolutionary purposes as legitimate at all times and as crucial in the hour of decision, he never viewed it as a means of gaining mass influence or of *bringing about* the revolutionary crisis. In his experience, a revolutionary military organization could go into effective action only when the masses were ready to follow it, and when the cohesion and loyalty of the army and police of the bourgeois state had been undermined by other factors, such as defeat in war. In the fifteen years of revolutionary struggle that preceded the Bolsheviks' seizure of power, their military organization saw only two brief phases of armed insurrection—in December 1905 and in November 1917—and a comparatively short period of minor violent actions of the "expropriation" type; major civil war came only *after* political victory, and not until then was a revolutionary army created to defeat the uprisings of the "Whites" and to consolidate the new power.

This pattern of a small, secret military organization "in being" that is quickly expanded for overt action at a time of (real or supposed) revolutionary crisis was also followed, on Bolshevik advice, by the European Communist parties: it may be studied in detail, for example, in the history of the abortive Communist risings of 1921 and 1923 in Germany.[9] In China in the twenties, the Bolsheviks were helping the Kuomintang to build up a political army and instructing the Chinese Communists to occupy positions of influence in that army as well as in the Nationalist Party and government machines; but when the Chinese Communists proposed to set up independent military units of their own, Stalin repeatedly turned down their suggestion.[10] To many of those Chinese Communists who survived the debacle of 1927, when Chiang Kai-shek turned on their party and crushed it, and to Mao Tse-tung in particular, this failure to build up an independent military force during the period of the "bloc within" appeared as one of the decisive causes of their defeat, as the subsequent creation of such independent forces, on however small and shifting a territory, became the decisive precondition of their political survival.[11] From this experience starts the development of Mao's new, radically different view of the role of armed force in revolutionary struggle—the view that "political power grows out of the barrel of a gun."[12]

Mao's own power certainly did. It was as the political leader most trusted by the Red Army commanders that he first gained control of the party in 1935. It was as the exponent of a policy of maintaining that army's *de facto* independence within the framework of the anti-Japanese united front with Chiang that he defeated Stalin's emissary Wang Ming and finally legitimated his

[9] For a full, scholarly account, see Werner T. Angress, *Still-born Revolution: The Communist Bid for Power in Germany, 1921–1923* (Princeton, N.J., 1963).

[10] In the summer of 1926 and again at the 7th Plenum of the Comintern Executive in November of that year; see Conrad Brandt, *Stalin's Failure in China* (Cambridge, Mass., 1958), pp. 76, 100–101, where Ch'en Tu-hsiu, then general secretary of the Chinese party, and T'an P'ing-shan, who represented it at the 7th Plenum, are quoted as sources.

[11] Cf. Mao Tse-tung, *Why Can China's Red Political Power Exist?*, written for a party conference in 1928, *Selected Works*, Vol. I (London, 1954), and above all his *Problems of War and Strategy*, extracted from his winding-up speech at the Central Committee Plenum of November, 1938, *Selected Works*, Vol. II (London, 1954).

[12] *Ibid.*, p. 272.

leadership of the party in 1938.[13] It was for the sake of preserving this military independence that he was prepared to let the coalition talks fail after the defeat of Japan. Altogether, the Chinese Communists' experience has been victory after a quarter century of continuous armed struggle, of civil war interrupted only by war; and Mao's interpretation of that experience is not only that military independence is the key to survival, but that unceasing armed struggle, even if begun by small minorities on severely limited territory, is the sure way to undermine the stability of an apparently strong hostile regime and to *bring about* a revolutionary crisis.[14] Not, of course, that Mao would regard armed terrorism as sufficient to achieve this *by itself;* he has never tired of pointing out that to be successful, armed struggle must always be combined with policies designed to secure popular support for the guerrillas and prevent their isolation. But given such policies, the struggle may be begun locally, without waiting for a nationwide revolutionary situation, and be protracted indefinitely. It may be started with vastly inferior forces opposing a strong enemy, and may gradually weaken his manpower, resources, and morale until the relation of strength is finally reversed. Armed struggle is thus the highest form of revolutionary struggle, because it is the most effective way of increasing the "contradictions," that is, the difficulties and divisions, of the hostile regime, and thus turning a dangerous, real tiger into a "paper tiger."[15]

[13] At the 6th plenary session of the sixth Central Committee, held in Yenan in November, 1938. It is characteristic that his report and winding-up speech at this session, quoted in notes 6, 11, and 12 above, marked both the first statement of his claim to the "sinification" of Marxism and the first full development of his view of the primacy of the military struggle in Chinese conditions. In September, 1965, the crucial importance of Mao's 1938 victory over Wang Ming for maintaining the independence of the Red Armies was made even more explicit in Marshal Lin Piao's famous speech on the twentieth anniversary of victory in the "People's War" against Japan.

[14] The importance of protracted armed struggle in Mao's political strategy as a means for reversing an originally unfavorable relation of forces between a revolutionary minority and an apparently strong regime has been brilliantly brought out by Tang Tsou and Morton H. Halperin, "Mao Tse-tung's Revolutionary Strategy and Peking's International Behavior," *American Political Science Review,* March, 1965. The present discussion owes much to their analysis, the central thesis of which has been strikingly confirmed by Lin Piao's speech.

[15] The 1946 interview with A. L. Strong (cited in note 1 above) in which the phrase first occurred has recently been reprinted in pamphlet form under the heading "Imperialism and All Reactionaries Are Paper Tigers."

In the view of the Chinese Communists, based on the experience of their own victory after decades of fighting against originally overwhelming odds, the crucial importance of armed struggle is thus linked with their belief in the fundamental instability of all "reactionary" regimes. Their successful resistance against the Japanese until their final participation in the Allied victory over them, and their postwar victory over Chiang Kai-shek despite initial American support for him, has enabled them to persuade themselves that foreign imperialist powers are as basically unstable as the Kuomintang regime was in its later phase, and may likewise be brought down by the appropriate, that is, tactically cautious but unceasing, use of armed violence. Their tendency to see the defeat of Japan as primarily their own work and the defeat of Chiang as a victory over the military might of the United States has probably been reinforced by the experience that their massive intervention in the Korean war resulted in a quick growth of their military prestige without damage on their own territory.

By contrast, the Soviet experience of international affairs has been as different from the Chinese as that of the two parties' rise to power. In the half century since the October revolution, the comparative stability of the "capitalist" order in the advanced industrial nations, despite war, economic upheavals, and decolonization, has been the source of repeated major disappointments to the Russian leaders; and it is the advanced industrial nations which have been their main concern—as potential threats to their own security no less than as revolutionary targets. The risk of war with one or more of these powers has always appeared serious to the Soviets, and its avoidance—by exploitation of their mutual conflicts but also, if necessary, by appropriate compromises—has been a major goal of their diplomacy under Lenin and Stalin as well as later. The one major war they were unable to avoid, Hitler's attack, came close indeed to destroying the Soviet Union, and its human and material cost certainly prolonged the period of deprivation and sacrifice by which the present military and economic strength of the Soviet Union was built. In Soviet experience, then, major war has been a terrible risk to be avoided if possible, even before the nuclear age, and its revolutionary effects have been uncertain at best.

A third historic difference between Soviet and Chinese Communists arises from the different degree to which they have been willing to give priority to political and ideological over economic considerations. All Communists do this to some extent: Lenin broke with the Marxian tradition in establishing the dictatorship of his party in the name of of the proletariat, even though Russia lacked the economic preconditions of an advanced industrial society, and its industrial working class was very much a minority; and Stalin even defined the need *first* to seize political power and *then* to use it to create the missing economic basis for a new social order as the characteristic distinguishing the proletarian revolution from the bourgeois-democratic one.[16] But the Russian Bolsheviks, at any rate, found their main support in the struggle for power among the industrial workers, and once in control they took it for granted that both the strength of their country and its approach towards socialism would depend on rapid industrialization and technological progress. However many errors of economic policy they may have committed, however many setbacks they suffered, at no time after the end of the civil war have they been willing consciously to sacrifice economic efficiency to ideological principle. On the contrary, when Stalin became convinced that increased income differentials and privileges for scarce leading personnel and good foremen were a condition for quick economic results, he strained ideology to prove that egalitarianism was not a socialist principle. During his five-year-plans, statistics of industrial production with special emphasis on heavy industry became the official yardstick for socialist progress, a view still reflected in the formulation of the "basic economic law of socialism" in his final pamphlet; while the great purges of the thirties resulted in the massive replacement of revolutionary veterans by bureaucrats and technicians who had won their entrance into the party by their merits in the management of "socialist industry." In the view of this new ruling elite, it was largely the degree of industrialization achieved by 1941 that accounted for the Soviet Union's ability to survive and finally defeat Hitler's assault, and to fill so large a part of the resulting power vacuum. The same kind of thinking has continued under Stalin's heirs, with the difference that they have felt the need to grant improved economic incentives not only to managers and foremen but to the masses of

[16] Cf. J. V. Stalin, *Problems of Leninism* (Moscow, 1947), pp. 129–30.

workers and kolkhoz peasants, thus increasingly replacing a climate of enforced sacrifice with a climate of recognized consumer claims, and that the discussion has moved from the characteristics of socialism to those of the "higher stage" of communism—defined in (Marxist) terms of the most highly productive technology and of abundance for all to be achieved on this basis.

The Chinese Communists did indeed, like their Russian teachers, start with a largely urban composition and with a similar admiration for economic progress. But after their urban strongholds had been destroyed, the surviving intellectual and working-class cadres had to recruit a new following in the rural fastnesses to which they had been driven, and to fall back on the economic resources of these isolated regions; the result was a type of "war communism" based on a near-subsistence agriculture and primitive craftsmanship organized under military discipline. The experience that prolonged survival and gradual expansion of an armed community inspired by an ideological faith is possible under such conditions is deeply imprinted on the thought and emotions of an entire generation of Chinese Communist militants —all the more so since the ideologically formative period of emancipation from exclusive dependence on the Soviet model, the Yenan "thought reform," took place in these conditions, and since the final outcome was total victory; and in contrast to Russia, this veteran generation has never been purged during the later years but is still desperately clinging to its control of the party on all levels. True, the Chinese Communists, too, after the end of the civil war endeavored first of all to rebuild economic life, and indeed did so with remarkable flexibility and success in the early years; but they never concentrated so one-sidedly on industry as Russia had, and their own criterion of success was at least as much the remolding of the consciousness of the various petty-bourgeois strata as the production figures achieved. Hence when the inevitable difficulties of development arose in China by 1957/ 58, the true underlying priorities turned out to be different from Russia's: the Chinese Communists' first choice was not all-out industrialization but a new version of their "war-Communist" methods in the People's Communes, not material advantages for the privileged few but equality, moral enthusiasm, and military discipline. Though the grave economic crisis produced by this experiment has forced the Chinese Communists to correct some of the specific policies of the communes and the Great Leap

Forward, the attempt to change the fundamentals was rejected in 1959.[17] Equality is still preferred to income differentials, moral incentives to material ones, political reliability to expert training, military discipline with "politcs in command" to economic rationality, which is suspected as a tool of the class enemy. In Chinese communism, political stability and ideological consistency remain more important than general industrial progress; apart from specific war industries, the Chinese leaders seem convinced that maintenance and even expansion of their power may be assured for as long as necessary even on the basis of a comparatively low level of economic performance.

THE ROAD OF DIVERGENCE

The differences noted above between the Soviet and Chinese Communist views of their own role, and the resulting differences of emphasis in their views of the contemporary world, did not lead to explicit ideological disputes between the two parties so long as there was no practical conflict between their policies. But within the last decade, such conflict has been brought about by the divergent development both of their national interests and of the requirements of their internal self-preservation; and at the same time, the decline of Soviet doctrinal authority in the post-Stalin cra has made it possible for the Chinese leaders to express their disagreement with Soviet policies in the form of an open ideological challenge. As a result, the original common world view has been explicitly "reinterpreted" in two opposite ways, with each side naturally developing its new interpretation out of its earlier specific emphasis.

The divergence of national interest between the two leading Communist powers may be viewed as a consequence of their different levels of economic development, of military strength, and of freedom for diplomatic maneuver. The Soviets have a capacity for steady and all-sided economic advance, for deterring any deliberate attack on their territory, and for influencing the behavior of their opponents by graduated moves in a world-wide field of diplomatic action which was and is still denied to the

[17] At the Lushan session of the Central Committee. The account of this crucial decision and the struggle preceding it first given by David Charles, "The Dismissal of Marshal P'eng Teh-huai" in *China Quarterly,* Oct.–Dec., 1961, has been confirmed in its essentials by repeated references to these events in the course of the 1966 purge of the CCP.

Chinese. As long as the alliance functioned, this situation led to a one-sided material dependence of Communist China on Soviet economic, military, and diplomatic support; and one-sided dependence within an alliance inevitably leads to disagreement about the degree of priority to be granted by the stronger ally to the needs of the weaker, and about the burdens and risks to be assumed on his behalf. Moreover, the different capacities for international action of the Soviet and Chinese Communists combined with their different traditions and experiences to inspire different concepts of the strategies to be followed in fighting the imperialist enemy, and particularly the United States, in dealing with uncommitted, ex-colonial countries and their nationalist governments, and in supporting and guiding the revolutionary movements of the underdeveloped world and the Communist parties of the advanced capitalist countries respectively. As the point was reached where Moscow was no longer willing to appease the Chinese demands by compromise and Peking was no longer willing to submit to Soviet leadership in silence, the Chinese Communists began to argue publicly for the adoption of their own strategy and to develop in justification their view of the decisive forces and tendencies of the contemporary world. The Soviets had to respond to this challenge to their ideological authority by making their own divergent view more explicit.

The core of the strategic dispute concerned the relative importance of violent revolution, including in particular the "wars of liberation" in the underdeveloped, colonial or ex-colonial countries, on one side, and of diplomacy, economic competition, and other methods aimed at directly influencing the policies of the advanced imperialist countries on the other, for ensuring the survival of the Communist states and shifting the world balance of power in their favor. Around this core a series of in part real, in part pretended differences of analysis has been built up, dealing with the "chief contradiction" of the present epoch; the existing relation of forces between the two "camps"; the character of imperialist and particularly United States policy in the nuclear age, the possibility of avoiding wars before the disappearance of imperialism, and the consequences of not avoiding them; the chances of further consolidating and increasing the power of the "socialist camp" without further revolutionary advances abroad; the degree of economic and political instability in the advanced imperialist states and the consequent chances of violent revolution there; the chances of Communist parties in these states of winning a share of power by non-violent means and of influencing their foreign policies even before transforming their social structure; the role of economic progress in the "socialist camp" in improving the attraction of those parties in the West and their chances of success; the possibilities of influencing the foreign policies of the imperialist powers by the pressure of neutral opinion and the mechanism of the United Nations; the role of revolutions in the underdeveloped continents, including wars of national liberation, in increasing or diminishing the risk of world war and in shifting the balance of world power in favor of the "socialist camp."

Parallel with the growth of the dispute on strategy caused by the divergence of national interest between the two leading Communist states, their different stages of economic development have also led them to adopt sharply divergent internal policies and to justify them by conflicting views on the nature of socialist construction after the elimination of the exploiting classes. The nationwide outburst of criticism of the regime that occurred in China when controls were tentatively relaxed in the later part of 1956 and the first half of 1957—the period when a hundred flowers were supposed to bloom and contradictions among the people to find legitimate expression within the framework of the socialist order—has convinced the Chinese Communist leaders that the efforts and sacrifices they must demand from their people during the long and difficult period of industrialization that lies ahead of them are incompatible with such relaxation. As a result, they have returned to a concept of "uninterrupted revolution" and unceasing vigilance in the class struggle on the home front; and this concept has survived the partial retreat from the policies of the Great Leap Forward with which it was originally connected, and has even been given a more extreme doctrinaire form in the context of later polemics with the Soviets.

Conversely, the Soviet experience under Khrushchev has not only generally confirmed the need for a more relaxed internal climate, based on the renunciation of mass terror and the increasing use of material incentives at the stage of industrial maturity reached by Russia; it has also shown that the attempt to bring about further upheavals in the social structure even by non-terrorist means, as initiated by Khrushchev at the 21st Congress in 1959, must at this stage lead to setbacks in economic performance which are incompatible with the power competition with the advanced Western countries, and must therefore be abandoned. In the new party program adopted at the 22nd Congress in 1961, recognition of this fact has found expression in formulations that, in announcing the end of the internal class struggle and of the "dictatorship of the proletariat," are diametrically opposed to the Chinese Communists' concept of their own regime. As a result, rival interpretations of the process of socialist and communist construction and of the role of the ruling Communist Party in this process have also led to different views about the relations between such ruling parties and between them and the revolutionary movements in the non-Communist world; and this difference has greatly contributed to the elaboration of the divergent world views of the two sides into complete rival systems.[18]

THE RIVAL WORLD VIEWS TODAY

Both these systems are presented by their authors as orthodox applications of the common framework to the present world situation; each is attacked by its opponents as totally heretical and incompatible with the essence of the common tradition. What matters to the outsider is that they are incompatible with each other because their interpretations of the contemporary world have developed the tradition in opposite directions. For our purposes, it will be convenient to summarize these rival views under three main headings. The first concerns the forces shaping the policy of the imperialist powers in the nuclear age, the impact on them of the various "contradictions," the relation of strength between the two camps, and the consequences for the danger of world war. The second concerns the problems of construction within the socialist states and the relation between their solution and the victory of revolutionary movements elsewhere. The third

[18] For documentation of these rival systems in a mature state, see on the Soviet side the "Open Letter from the CC of the CPSU," *Pravda*, July 14, 1963, and the report made to the CC by M. A. Suslov on Feb. 14, 1964, *Pravda*, Apr. 3, 1964. On the Chinese side, see above all "A Proposal for the General Line of the International Communist Movement," July 14, 1963, and the nine "Commentaries" on the CPSU "Open Letter," issued jointly by the editorial staffs of *Red Flag* and *People's Daily* on Sept. 6, 13, and 26, Oct. 21, Nov. 18, and Dec. 12, 1963, and Feb. 4, Mar. 30, and July 14, 1964. All these were issued in English by NCNA on the dates cited, and also as pamphlets by the Foreign Languages Press, Peking.

concerns the prospects and forms of such revolutionary victories in the advanced imperialist countries and the underdeveloped world respectively.

a. The Imperialist Camp and Its Contradictions

Both in the Soviet and Chinese views, the basic nature of imperialism has not changed: it continues to depend on exploitation and oppression at home and abroad and to seek to expand its basis by all means including aggressive war. The Chinese polemical charge that the Soviets have abandoned this view is demonstrably untrue; the Soviet statements that "general and complete disarmament" was possible, used by the Chinese to substantiate that charge, were of a propagandist character and not part of serious Soviet analysis. But Soviet and Chinese views differ in their estimate of the factors that may modify this inherent aggressive and warlike tendency of imperialism, and of the manner of their operation.

In the Soviet view, the most important modifying factor is the military strength of the "socialist camp" and above all of the Soviet Union. The socialist camp is said to have become the decisive factor in the development of mankind, with the conflict between it and the imperialist camp constituting the "main contradiction" of our epoch. The strength of the Soviet Union is viewed as sufficient to deter any deliberate imperialist attack on its territory and that of its immediate sphere of influence, and to act as a major limiting factor on the scope and forms of imperialist aggression elsewhere, because it is now on the same scale as the power of the United States and historically bound to grow faster than the latter. But it is not yet regarded as by itself sufficient to prevent every imperialist aggression or decide every conflict in its favor, let alone to win offensive objectives at will,[19] because the use of Soviet socialist strength is limited by the same nuclear balance as that of United States imperialist strength.

A second factor modifying the aggressive tendencies of imperialism is seen in the continuing contradictions among the imperialist powers. This factor was far less stressed in Soviet analysis during the Khrushchev era than it had been under Stalin

---

[19] That this view is still held by Khrushchev's successor was brought out with remarkable clarity in A. Rumyantsev's article on "The Decisive Factor of the Development of Human Society," *MEMO* (World Economy and International Relations), 1/1966.

(and continued to be in China), but it was never entirely written off and has again received more emphasis under Khrushchev's successors.

A third modifying factor of great importance both in Soviet thinking and Soviet practice is the impact of "peace-loving" neutral opinion, as embodied chiefly in the uncommitted new states and exercised in part through the United Nations, on the policies of the imperialist powers. While many of the states in question are ruled by governments of the "national bourgeoisie" and not by representatives of revolutionary movements, their interests in the preservation of peace and national independence are seen as conflicting with the plans of the imperialist aggressors, and their role in the balance of power as capable of hampering these plans.

A fourth modifying factor is constituted by the class conflicts and other conflicts of interest within the advanced imperialist countries. This is seen as underlying not only the activity of working-class movements but also all kinds of opposition to "the aggressive plans of the monopoly capitalists" which the various Peace Councils are striving to mobilize, and indeed as effectively dividing the capitalist classes themselves. The modifying factors from outside the imperialist countries, including Soviet diplomacy and propaganda, are indeed viewed as influencing their policies through their impact on such "reasonable" elements within them and on their political spokesmen even among the ruling class.

Last not least, the fifth modifying factor is, of course, the resistance of the semi-colonial and ex-colonial peoples to "neo-colonialist" imperialist aggression, which makes such aggression more costly and, owing to the support of that resistance by the socialist camp, more risky and uncertain in its outcome than it would otherwise be.

According to the Soviet view, then, imperialist aggression may be "checked" by the operation of all these factors, of which the strength of the "socialist camp" under Soviet leadership is by far the most important one. The means for checking it, that is, for influencing the policy of the imperialists and foiling their aggressive plans, range all the way from violent revolutionary action and nuclear blackmail to peace propaganda and diplomatic compromise. Again, the Chinese charge that the Soviets have come to reject the use of violent means in principle, and that this is the meaning of their "general line" of "peaceful coexistence," is demonstrably untrue; but it is true that in the Soviet view the scope of such violent conflicts must be kept under strict control so as to avoid at all cost their escalation into nuclear world war, in which the Soviet Union itself might be destroyed along with its imperialist opponents. Because of the common realization by both sides of the risk of nuclear destruction, the avoidance of world war and the reduction of its risk by mutual agreements, for example, on the limitation of the arms race, are definitely possible in the Soviet view. But this implies that the danger of escalation sets limits not only to imperialist but also to Soviet action: rather than risk the destruction of the main stronghold of socialism, the Soviet leaders may have to accept the occasional success of peripheral imperialist aggression whenever the latter cannot be stopped by means short of general war.

The Chinese view is far more sceptical about the chances of checking imperialist aggression without war, and generally of influencing the policy of the imperialist powers by any means short of armed resistance. Aware of Soviet unwillingness (and, without admitting it, of their own) to risk direct armed resistance to imperialist aggression against third parties, the Chinese conclude that the "main contradiction" of our epoch is not that between imperialism and the "socialist camp" but that between imperialism and the national liberation movements of the underdeveloped peoples, which constitute at present the main reservoir of revolutionary violence, hence in the Chinese view the "main storm center of the world revolution."[20]

The Chinese do, of course, recognize that other contradictions may play a secondary role in defeating imperialist aggression. The states of the "socialist camp," the world peace movement, and the working-class movements in the advanced imperialist countries may aid the peoples engaged in armed struggle against the imperialists; the conflicts among the imperialist powers and within their leadership may hamper the effectiveness of their action and at times even paralyze them. But in the Chinese view, the imperialists cannot be influenced by diplomatic compromise or by neutral offers of mediation or by maneuvers in the United Nations, which they dominate, but only by uncompromising support for their fighting opponents. Meaningful agreements with

[20] This formula made its first appearance in the *Red Flag* and *People's Daily* joint editorial "More on the Differences between Comrade Togliatti and Us," *NCNA*, Mar. 4, 1963.

the imperialists can only come about as the result of a clear victory over them.

It does not follow from the rejection of compromise that the Chinese actively wish to bring about a nuclear world war, as the Soviets have charged, or even that they regard it as inevitable. But they do not consider such a war a catastrophe which their own system could not survive and which must therefore be avoided at all costs;[21] they deny that the two camps have a common interest in preventing a nuclear catastrophe and *a fortiori* in agreed limitations of the arms race; and they do not believe that any political strategy on the part of the "socialist camp" could eliminate the danger of world war while imperialism exists. Their view is that a policy of uncompromising support for all armed liberation struggles, by forcing the dispersion and attrition of imperialist strength, offers also the best chance to avoid world war, but still an uncertain chance. Hence they oppose to the priority of risk control—the "general line of peaceful coexistence"—the priority of support for armed, anti-imperialist struggle.

b. Socialist Construction and International Solidarity

According to the Soviet view, the liquidation of the old exploiting classes of capitalists and landowners and the transformation of the former individual peasants into members of collective farms have created a socialist society, that is, a society not yet free from class differences but free from exploitation and class struggle. The further transformation of that socialist society into a truly classless, communist society depends primarily on technological progress leading through growing abundance and leisure to a steady improvement in the material and cultural standard of the working people. True, the elimination of class differences between state-employed workers and collective farmers and between both and the groups engaged in intellectual, administrative, and directing labor will still constitute a major change in the social structure; but this change will not be brought about by another revolution from above that would impose it on its presumed opponents by political force, but will be a by-product of the

[21] This was made clear by Mao Tse-tung even during the Moscow conference of ruling Communist parties in November, 1957; cf. now the slightly different versions of the arguments used by him on that occasion in the Chinese government statement, *NCNA*, Sept. 1, 1963, and the Soviet government statement, *TASS*, Sept. 21, 1963.

steady increase in productivity that will change the conditions of all the working people and give them increasingly identical interests.

One consequence of this happy state of affairs is that, in the view of its leaders, the Soviet Union has ceased to be a dictatorship of the proletariat and has become a state of all the toilers, because there is no hostile class left over which a dictatorship would have to be exercised. The Communist Party itself is no longer a working-class party engaged in class struggle against internal enemies, but a party of all the toilers engaged in constructive tasks of social administration and guidance. In this new capacity, it is supposed to continue its leading role among the social organizations long after the state, owing to the disappearance of its oppressive functions, has withered away.[22]

Nor does, in this view, further progress toward the higher stage of communism depend in any basic sense on the international class struggle—on the expansion of the socialist camp or on the disappearance of the imperialist enemy. Of course, international tension, acute crises, or even local wars may temporarily tie down an important part of the resources of the socialist camp and thus delay its productive progress, while Communist victories in advanced industrial countries could accelerate it. But nothing short of direct involvement in nuclear war could reverse the progressive trend of the socialist economic development, and this risk can be eliminated by the deterrence of deliberate attack and the control of accidental escalation in the manner described above. From a Soviet point of view, further advances in the "world revolution," that is, the expansion of the Communist system, however likely and desirable in themselves, are therefore not a vital precondition of the domestic stability and productive growth of that system.

It follows from this analysis that the constructive tasks of the ruling Communist parties and the revolutionary tasks of the nonruling parties are different in kind: they are allies, but their situations are so far apart that each can be of only limited assistance to the other in achieving its goal. The main contribution of the ruling Communists to the cause of their struggling comrades *in partibus infidelium* consists, in the Soviet view, in making their own system more attractive by improving their domestic productivity and standard of living, with direct support

[22] This point is fully developed in the new program of the CPSU adopted at the 22nd Congress in 1961.

for the international struggle playing a secondary role.[23] Conversely, the main contribution of the non-ruling Communists to the cause of the socialist camp consists in defending its security by means of the peace movement, that is, in seeking to influence the foreign policy of the imperialist governments without waiting for the conquest of total power. For the Soviets, economic progress is the best form of international solidarity; for the non-ruling parties, international solidarity with the Soviets is the most important form of political struggle—in Moscow's view.

The Chinese view of the relation between the Communist tasks within and without the socialist camp is diametrically opposed to all this. According to Peking, the internal class struggle will continue until the achievement of full communism; the danger that corrupt, selfish elements and degenerate bureaucrats may attempt a restoration of capitalism with the support of the imperialist enemy will be ever present right up to that moment—in the Chinese case for "five to ten generations or one or several centuries."[24] Hence the state must remain a dictatorship of the proletariat as long as it exists at all, and the ruling Communist Party must maintain unceasing class vigilance for this entire period. The fact that the "revisionist" Soviet Communists have "abandoned" the class dictatorship and the class character of the party itself appears to the Chinese Communists as proof that in Russia the supporters of a capitalist restoration have come to power and the process is far advanced.

It follows that in the Chinese view, the link between socialist construction and the international revolutionary struggle is far closer than in Soviet eyes—as direct and inseparable, indeed, as it was in Trotsky's vision. The process of building socialism at home is seen as one of uninterrupted revolution,[25] carried on as part of

[23] This priority was formulated with particular clarity in M. A. Suslov's report to the CC, CPSU, cited in note 18 above. For a post-Khrushchev statement, see the editorial of *Pravda*, Oct. 27, 1965.

[24] See for this the Ninth "Commentary" on the CPSU "Open Letter," entitled "Khrushchev's Phony 'Communism' and the Historical Lessons for the World," *NCNA*, July 14, 1964, the last part of which gives an authoritative fifteen-point summary of the "main content" of Mao Tse-tung's ideas and policies. This document must be regarded as a kind of "political testament" of Mao.

[25] The phrase came to the fore in China in 1958, during the "Great Leap Forward" and the creation of the "People's Communes," but has not been abandoned since. Its history and significance are studied and documented in Stuart R. Schram, *Documents sur la Théorie de la Revolution Permanente en Chine* (Paris, 1963).

a world-wide, irreconcilable struggle against the class enemy: defeat of its agents within the socialist base may depend in part on the blows that are inflicted on it abroad, as the survival of a besieged fortress may depend on the action of relieving forces. Moreover, since the Soviet Union has "changed color" under its revisionist leadership, the territory of the fortress has shrunk; in the Chinese view, Russia has joined the ranks of the besiegers, collaborating with the United States imperialists on a basis of solidarity between their ruling classes.[26]

Since the Chinese Communists believe that their own fate depends on the course of the world-wide struggle, "correct" ideological direction of that struggle appears to them as a vital necessity; hence the example of their militancy is judged by them a more important contribution to the international movement than the example of their economic progress could possibly be. True, they deny any intention of setting up a new Communist world party under their own centralistic discipline, and such an attempt would indeed be hopeless under present conditions; but in contrast to the Soviets they continue to insist that one and only one interpretation of the doctrine must be right for all Communist parties, and that they are its exponents. The Chinese emphasis on international revolutionary solidarity does find a limit in the fact that they are no more willing than the Russians to stake the existence of their own state in order to aid a "people's war" beyond their frontiers, an attitude expressed in the formula that any people must win its freedom primarily by its own strength.[27] But while they refuse to sacrifice their power, they are prepared to sacrifice both economic progress and comfort to purity of ideological principle in a manner not hitherto encountered in any Communist state.

c. *The Prospects and Forms of Revolution*

Soviet and Chinese Communists agree about the evident fact that the prospects of violent revolution in the contemporary world are in the main confined to the underdeveloped regions of Asia, Africa, and Latin America. But they differ profoundly about the

[26] This view has been brought out most clearly in the Chinese documents rejecting Soviet offers of a "united front" for the defense of North Vietnam, see, e.g., the joint *Red Flag* and *People's Daily* editorial of Nov. 11, 1965 (*NCNA*, same date) and subsequent similar statements.

[27] See, e.g., the *People's Daily* editorial of July 10, 1966, *NCNA*, July 11, 1966.

significance of this fact for the future of communism and of the world.

In the view of the Soviet leaders, both their present security and the future of world communism depend mainly on developments in the advanced industrial countries. Communist revolutions in the underdeveloped regions may be useful in weakening the imperialist opponents, but they cannot decisively change the world balance of power by themselves; on the contrary, their victory depends in every case on the support and protection of the socialist camp, which can only be rendered within the limits of controlled risk. To separate the cause of the national liberation movements in those countries from that of the main forces of the socialist camp and the industrial proletariat of the advanced capitalist countries can, in the Soviet view, only lead to their defeat; hence, the usefulness of a Communist bid for power in an underdeveloped country and of other forms of violent struggle there must always be judged in terms of their effect on the overall world situation at the given moment.

In the advanced capitalist countries, on the other hand, most of which are "bourgeois democracies," the Communists are in the Soviet view now more likely to come to power without violent revolution, by a peaceful or parliamentary road. As seen from Moscow, this does not imply a weakening of the doctrine that total power, that is, a single-party dictatorship, is a precondition for the building of socialism, as the examples given at the 20th Congress of the CPSU and since have made clear.[28] But victory by the peaceful road presupposes a possibly prolonged period during which the Communists in the capitalist democracies join in the parliamentary game and abide by its rules in order to get hold of the machinery of government; and this could have the— to the Soviets—important by-product that their political allies in those countries would gain a chance effectively to influence their national foreign policies even before the conquest of total power.

[28] These examples included the peaceful victory of "socialism" in the course of the annexation of the Baltic states, in Soviet-occupied Eastern Germany, and above all in the Prague coup of February, 1948. However, a much more "revisionist" interpretation of the "peaceful road," including pledges of continued legal operation for opposition parties under a Communist government, has in recent years been adopted by the Italian CP, and even the French CP has at least flirted with similar views since the death of Thorez. The CPSU has been more interested in facilitating the return of these fraternal parties into the democratic political game, even short of the conquest of power, than in correcting these "deviations."

Both Soviet diplomacy and Soviet policy toward the Western Communist parties are therefore partly geared to improving the chances for this type of development.

To the Chinese Communists, all this is anathema. As the class conflict is absolute, a peaceful or parliamentary road to power is as dangerous an illusion as peaceful competition or diplomatic compromise with the imperialists; and as chances of violent revolution in the advanced capitalist countries do not at present exist, it follows that the progress of the world revolution now depends primarily on the violent movements of the underdeveloped peoples. It is only their struggle which, by straining the resources and the political cohesion of the advanced imperialist countries, will gradually undermine their present political stability and make them ready for a revolutionary assault, just as in the Chinese revolution the great cities, which were the traditional strongholds of imperialist influence, had to be encircled by the progress of revolution in the countryside before they could be taken. The formula of the underdeveloped "countryside of the world" that has to be revolutionized before the advanced, industrial "world cities" will fall to their proletariat thus sums up the Chinese view of the prospects and forms of the world revolution.[29]

CONCLUSION: ROOTS AND TRENDS

In elaborating their rival interpretations of the world and of the common "Marxist-Leninist" tradition to justify their divergent domestic and international policies, both Soviet and Chinese Communists have to a striking degree fallen back on their historic differences of outlook and emphasis. Yet while formerly, under the pressure of their desire for unity, they were trying to reduce the importance of these differences to the mere expression of national peculiarities, the impact of open conflict has made the same differences appear to both as the expression of different

[29] The formula was first used by the late leader of the Indonesian CP, D. N. Aidit, in his pamphlet *Set Afire the Banteng Spirit! Ever Forward, No Retreat!* (English ed. Peking: Foreign Languages Press, 1964). It was quoted with approval in the speech of the former Chinese Politburo member P'eng Chen at the Djakarta celebration of the 45th anniversary of the Indonesian party (*Peking Review*, June 11, 1965) and taken over in the speech of his successful rival, Lin Piao, at the 20th anniversary celebration of China's victory over Japan ("Long Live the Victory of the People's War," *Peking Review*, Sept. 3, 1965).

general principles. As an example of this transformation, it is instructive to recall that when Mao Tse-tung first discovered the supreme importance of independent military forces for the fate of the Chinese revolution, he tied it explicitly, and correctly, to the near-anarchic conditions of a semicolonial country, in which neither a national government nor a colonial power was strong enough to maintain an effective monopoly of armed force.[30] Yet today, the Chinese present their doctrine of the revolutionary "people's war" as an international model without any qualifications of this kind.

As we look back on the historic differences between Soviet and Chinese Communists regarding the importance of anti-colonial nationalism and of protracted military struggle and the relative priorities of political struggle and economic construction, and on their generalized reappearance in their present rival world views, one single root becomes manifest as common to them all: the greater or lesser distance from Western experience and Western values in the two nations and the two parties. The early identifications of the Chinese Communists with the revolutionary movements of the colonial peoples and of the Russian Communists with those of the European proletariat have reappeared in their present strategies and world views. The different importance attributed to "peaceful" and violent political struggle is directly linked to the same contrast of Western and non-Western conditions. Finally, the growing emphasis on economic strength and economic progress, on material comforts and material incentives in the Soviet Union, which takes the ideological form of a shamefaced rediscovery of the Marxian link between the state of the productive forces and the possibility of socialism and communism, is also a reflection of the growing impact of Western

---

[30] "The phenomenon that within a country one or several small areas under Red political power should exist for a long time amid the encirclement of White political power is one that has never been found elsewhere in the world. . . . It can exist and develop only under certain conditions. First, it cannot occur in any imperialist country or in any colony under direct imperialist rule, but can occur only in such an economically backward, semi-colonial country as China which is under indirect imperialist rule. . . . Two things account for its occurrence, namely localized agricultural economy (instead of unified capitalist economy) and the imperialist policy of division and exploitation by marking off spheres of influence . . ." From Mao Tse-tung's 1928 resolution "Why Can China's Red Political Power Exist?" *Selected Works*, Vol. I (London, 1954), pp. 64–65. Footnote 7 to this text, *ibid.*, p. 345, emphasizes that Mao has since changed his views in this respect.

materialist values on the mature industrial society of the Soviet Union, while the stubborn rejection of this development by the Chinese Communists as a form of "bourgeois decadence" and their recurrent insistence on the primacy of moral enthusiasm and military discipline in economic life seem to express an increasingly radical rejection of those values—even at the price of rejecting the entire Marxist contribution to Leninism which is Western in essence.

One question raised by this analysis concerns the prospects for China's successfully solving her tremendous problems of economic development under the present Communist leadership. The usual attitude to Western values of non-Western regimes that are engaged in a political effort to "catch up with and overtake" the industrial West is highly ambivalent: they wish to acquire the Western techniques for achieving wealth and power, yet to preserve as much as possible of their own different traditions in the process. Yet while such ambivalence, for all its problems, may be a powerful stimulus to achievement, the present Chinese Communist attitude to Western values appears to be less and less ambivalent and more and more predominantly negative; hence it seems, to the present writer at least, increasingly doubtful whether success in economic development will prove compatible with this fanatical rejection of the motivations of "economic man" and of the concept of economic rationality based on them. As of now, Communist China cannot seriously be regarded as a possible model for the economic development of other countries—but rather as a possible model for non-development under the imperatives of political stability and ideological purity.

Another and final question we have to ask ourselves turns on the different ways in which the Soviet and Chinese world views, and the patterns of international conduct linked with them, have responded to changes in the outside world. We have seen that both have moved some distance from "classical" Marxism-Leninism under the impact of experience, particularly of the nuclear balance of terror, of the prolonged absence of revolutionary crises in the advanced Western countries, of the transformation of the international scene by near-universal decolonization, and of the emergence of major differences of national interest among the Communist powers. But while the effect of this changing outside reality has in the Soviet case combined with the effect of long-term internal changes to cause a marked weakening of the Soviet leaders' commitment to active policies designed to foster the world-wide expansion of Communist rule and an acceptance of looser ties to other Communist movements, in the Chinese case the same changes in the outside world have combined with very different internal trends to imbue the present leaders with an increasingly fanatic belief in the overwhelming historic importance of the armed "liberation struggles" of the underdeveloped peoples, and in their own mission of providing ideological leadership for that struggle. To a Western observer, it would appear that Soviet views have on the whole responded to changing reality with a gradual if limited adjustment, Chinese views with a frantic attempt at denying it.

This suggests that the responsiveness of an ideological regime to changes in the outside world depends both on the stage of its internal development and on cultural factors facilitating or hampering perception of the change. From the point of view of Western policy, it would seem to follow that the chances of influencing the Soviet outlook, in the sense of reviving or reducing the acuteness of our conflicts with the Soviet Union, by Western action are at present very much better than the chances of similarly influencing the outlook and conduct of the Chinese leaders. The fact that in recent years the Chinese leaders have reacted to Western threats and Western offers of conciliation, to Soviet polemics and Soviet proposals for a "united front" with equally militant statements appears in this context as characteristic rather than surprising. Of course, this pattern of ideological self-isolation from reality may change if the Chinese Communists should overcome the present difficult stage of their internal development and the obsessively tense ideological climate that goes with it; yet the ability of their present leaders to surpass this stage must be considered an open question. Pending that, the scope for Western efforts to influence the direction of change in Communist views and conduct is likely to remain far greater on the Soviet than on the Chinese side.

Russia, China, and the New States

DONALD S. ZAGORIA

ON A superficial level there appears to be very little difference between Soviet and Chinese revolutionary strategies in the underdeveloped areas. Both Russia and China give economic aid to "bourgeois nationalist" regimes. Both are prepared to sacrifice the interests of local Communist parties to their own interests. Both give support to liberation movements in those parts of Africa still under colonial rule. Both seek to reduce Western influence in the underdeveloped areas.

The fact remains that there are important differences of strategy, and in this paper I want first to try to define the most important of these differences, then to show how these differences are reflected in the splits in local Communist parties, with the Indian party as a case study, and finally to assess the objective merits and limitations of Soviet and Chinese strategy respectively.

As Kautsky has pointed out, one of the principal hallmarks of Communist strategy is its attitude towards alliances and its identification of the main enemy. In the colonial areas, there have been three distinct strategic models. The classical "left," and now obsolescent, strategy considered capitalism its main enemy, saw the socialist revolution as the immediate goal, eschewed cooperation with the nationalist leaders, and sought rather to induce the rank and file of the nationalist parties to desert their leaders and join with the Communists in a "united front from below." In line with this strategy, nationalist leaders were denounced as imperialist stooges. The classical "right" strategy considered feudal-

A shorter and earlier version of this paper was presented to the Academy of Political Science at Columbia University and was published in the *Proceedings* of the Academy.

ism and foreign imperialism—not capitalism—to be the main enemy, gave higher priority to bourgeois national and democratic goals than to radical social demands, and sought alliances at the top with the nationalist leaders. It was accordingly called a "united front from above."

The essential difference between the two classical strategies is that the "left" strategy—envisioning as it did a one-stage revolution—emphasized Communist-type social demands even at the expense of failing to gain non-Communist nationalist allies; while the "right" strategy—envisioning a two-stage revolution—subordinated social to national demands in order to gain as many allies as possible for the intermediate national-democratic stage of the revolution.

The classical left strategy has by and large been abandoned since the end of World War II because few Communists believed after that time that there was much likelihood of a one-stage revolution anywhere in the underdeveloped areas. The question since World War II was not whether a one-stage revolution would work but rather, accepting the need for a two-stage revolution, how the Communists could get themselves into a strategic position during the first stage and how the socio-economic and political prerequisites for the second stage could be prepared during the first.

One answer to this was given by Mao and the Chinese Communists who pioneered a third strategy, what Kautsky calls neo-Maoism,[1] and what I would call the Maoist, or independent-right as opposed to the classical, or coalition-right. The Maoist right strategy borrows elements from both the classical left and classical right. From the right it takes the idea of a two-stage revolution in the first stage of which Communist-type social demands are subordinated to national and democratic goals. The social appeal of the Maoist right strategy, like that of the classical right, is thus to all anti-imperialist groups and classes, including the national bourgeoisie, and even to "patriotic" landlords. But from the classical left strategy, the Maoist right borrows the idea of a united front from below. And—unlike the classical right strategy, which is prepared to tolerate nationalist leadership of the anti-imperialist united front during the first stage—it insists on the

---

[1] John Kautsky, *Moscow and the Communist Party of India* (Cambridge: Technology Press of M.I.T., 1956). In his first chapter Kautsky provides a taxonomy of Communist strategies similar to that offered here.

need for Communist hegemony in the first stage of the revolutionary process.

Both the classical and the Maoist-right strategies are designed to bend the nationalist movement to Communist purposes during the first stage, but there are differing assumptions as to how this goal can best be achieved.

The Maoist-right strategy, a product of Chinese Communist revolutionary experience, seeks to transform the nationalists primarily by putting pressure on them from below, although it does not rule out uniting from above so long as the Communists maintain a base of power independent from that of the nationalists. Heavily influenced by the debacle they suffered in 1927 at the hands of the Chinese nationalists, and the successes of their united front policy after 1936, the Maoists reject the classical, or coalition right strategy, which, they believe, makes the Communists vulnerable to nationalist betrayal because it deprives them of an independent power base. Alliances between Communists and nationalists are possible, say the Maoists, but they can only be supplementary; what is fundamental is that the Communists must put forward a program of their own rather than tail along behind the nationalists and must attach primary importance to winning over the peasants rather than to manipulation of the nationalists at the top.[2]

Equally important, the Maoist-right strategy asserts that Communist leadership of the national front is necessary at the earliest opportunity during the first stage of the revolutionary process or else "no real or thorough victory in the national democratic revolution is possible, and even if victory of a kind is gained, it will be impossible to consolidate it."[3] Common to these two strategic imperatives—an independent power base and early leadership of the national front—is a basic distrust of the nationalists which is, of course, the result of thirty years of CCP experience with the Kuomintang.

This experience was decisive in shaping Chinese Communist revolutionary strategy. From the 1927 debacle the CCP concluded that coalition or fusion with the nationalists is a road to disaster.

[2] See Li Wei-han, *The Struggle for Proletarian Leadership in the Period of the New-Democratic Revolution in China* (Peking: Foreign Languages Press, 1962), esp. chap. 1.

[3] "The CCP's Proposal concerning the General Line of the International Communist Movement, June 14, 1963," in William E. Griffith, *The Sino-Soviet Rift* (Cambridge: M.I.T. Press, 1964), Document 2, p. 267.

From the successes of the united front policy after 1936 the CCP concluded that a united front can work provided it is a limited and not an unconditional alliance and provided the Communist Party maintains its independence and autonomy. As Tang Tsou has pointed out, throughout the period of the second united front, the CCP maintained exclusive control over the Communist base areas even though non-Communist nationalists were welcomed as individuals into those areas.[4] In short, the leading role of the party was never abandoned. Moreover, Mao's conception of the united front did not even exclude limited armed struggle against his Kuomintang "allies," although this struggle was always kept within certain limits. The Maoist "united front" was thus never a classical, coalition united front in which the Communists fused with the nationalists or acquiesced in even temporary nationalist leadership of the front. It was from the outset a Communist-manipulated coalition resting on a multi-class base whose appeal was primarily nationalist.

The classical right strategy, on the other hand, attaches primary importance to infiltration and manipulation at the top rather than to pressure from below. It sees major exploitable divisions at the top of the nationalist movement between more and less radical groups and leaders and, in order to exploit these divisions, it minimizes pressure from below which, it fears, can only alienate the nationalists prematurely. The coalition rightists are relatively more optimistic than the Maoists about the revolutionary potential of the nationalists during the first stage of the revolutionary process and, for this reason, are willing for the Communists to play second fiddle and even, under certain conditions, to allow organizational fusion.

Since 1959 there have been two basic differences between Soviet and Chinese revolutionary strategy in the underdeveloped areas. The first has been the much greater emphasis placed by the Chinese on armed struggle, particularly in areas still under colonial or semicolonial control or in countries allied to the United States. The second has been the Chinese insistence on the Maoist-right strategy in the newly independent and non-aligned nations while the Soviets follow the classical, coalition-right strategy in a new dress called "national democracy."

[4] Tang Tsou and Morton Halperin, "Mao Tse-tung's Revolutionary Strategy and Peking's International Behavior," *The American Political Science Review*, Vol. LIX, No. 1 (Mar., 1965), pp. 80–99.

The "national democratic" strategy evolved at the Moscow Conference of 81 parties in 1960 has been much discussed.[5] Suffice it to say in this context that it has classical rather than Maoist roots. Local Communists are instructed to acquiesce in nationalist leadership of a broad, anti-imperialist united front for the indefinite future and to struggle for hegemony in the front largely by manipulation at the top rather than by pressure from below.

Since 1960, the Soviets and their allies in the international Communist movement have held extensive discussions and debates on various aspects of this "national democratic" strategy, and although there has been and continues to be considerable controversy on several aspects of that strategy, its basic outlines have not changed. There have, however, been two major innovations, both of which have the effect of moving the strategy even further to the right. The first has to do with Communist strategy in those one-party states—mostly but not exclusively in Africa—in which local Communists cannot legally maintain a separate organization. Clearly the Communists cannot hope to pursue a coalition-right strategy when they do not exist as a legal entity. In these circumstances Moscow has developed a strategy of what has been aptly called by Lowenthal "licensed infiltration." This strategy makes it the task of local Communists in one-party states to join the ruling nationalist party, to seek to influence its decisions, and to turn it in a more radical direction. Thus a Nigerian Communist has written:

In some of the African states like Ghana, the UAR, Algeria and Mali the question has been raised whether there is a need to found a purely Marxist-Leninist party as distinct from the popular nationalistic governments. In some of these countries existing communist parties that have played leading roles in the national liberation movement have been banned and their leaders jailed.

As Marxist-Leninists, we must admit that we are capable of making mistakes, if we become dogmatic, if we feel that we are the only chosen people to herald scientific socialism and that the move towards socialism not necessarily based on scientific socialism must be opposed. If, rather than using our knowledge to guide others towards our goal, we create the impression that as individuals, we are the only group to rule the people, then we are bound to end up in isola-

[5] See in particular Richard Lowenthal, "On National Democracy," *Survey*, No. 47, Apr., 1963.

tion. The realistic application of Marxist-Leninist tactics by the Cuban communist party is worthy of very close study.

It follows therefore that in countries where the national leadership is not necessarily Marxist but simply anti-feudal and anti-imperialist, it is the duty of true Marxist-Leninists to place their services at the disposal of such a government.[6]

What, however, if Communist activities within the ruling nationalist party are greatly obstructed or limited so that the Communists have no opportunity to exercise influence? Or what if the ruling nationalist party turns away from revolution and seeks to compromise with the imperialists? In such cases the local Communists should leave the nationalist party and set out on their own. Thus, another African Communist cautions, after bestowing much praise on the leaders of African one-party states, particularly Algeria, Ghana, Guinea, and Mali, that there

can be no mechanical and blind acceptance or rejection of the concept and the system of single-party states as such. . . . If the workers find that their activities are limited within the single party: that, should the emerging capitalist forces join with imperialism, no matter how indirect, and assume dictatorial control of the party, then it is as inevitable, as it becomes necessary, that the working class would seek to establish a new front of the progressive anti-imperialist forces to defend their own interests and those of the nation and work for real freedom and independence. On the other hand, where the anti-imperialist forces join together and maintain a popular dictatorship through a single party system, the working class will not only participate but undoubtedly become the central and leading core of the struggle forward. . . .[7]

In other words, the strategy of infiltration is to be continued only so long as there is increasing influence of local Communists. The clear implication of these two African statements is that, for the time being at least, the Communists in one-party states will not seek to organize separate Communist parties underground, but they must be ready to do so should the nationalists turn "reactionary." This probably presumes some kind of skeleton underground organization.

[6] *The African Communist*, No. 19, 1964, pp. 57–58.
[7] *Ibid.*, p. 76.

The second innovation in Soviet colonial strategy since 1960 is an ideological *rapprochement* with the nationalists, that is, a partial acceptance of national socialist ideologies. As recently as 1961, the Soviet Draft Party Program attacked "socialism of the national type" as "variations of the petty bourgeois illusion of socialism . . . which rules out the class struggle."[8] But by the spring of 1963, a prominent Soviet theoretician was saying that although some of the nationalist ideologies were in fact "petty bourgeois blundering," illusory and even demagogic, nevertheless "they contain a sound democratic core, a still-latent germ of the future. Indeed they resolve into a program of national-democratic revolution."[9] By December 1963, the full ideological seal of approval was given to several of the nationalist regimes when former Premier Khrushchev, in an interview with Algerian, Ghanian, and Burmese newspapermen, warmly praised "revolutionary democratic statesmen" who "sincerely advocate noncapitalist methods for the solution of national problems and declare their determination to build socialism. We welcome their declarations . . . we fully support their measures."[10] This was a far different attitude from the one Khrushchev had displayed a few years earlier when he lectured a visiting Egyptian delegation to Moscow on the virtues of "scientific socialism." In the spring of 1964, Khrushchev went a step further in the direction of giving approval to some of the nationalist leaders when he referred to both Egyptian President Nasser and Algerian leader Ben Bella as "comrades."[11] At the same time Egypt and Algeria were among several countries prominently mentioned by Soviet writers as moving towards a noncapitalist path.

The ideological *rapprochement* with the one-party states has, moreover, clearly continued since the ouster of Khrushchev. Writing in the authoritative pro-Soviet organ of the international Communist movement, the *World Marxist Review*, Pietr Keuneman, head of the Ceylonese Communist Party, said in December 1964 that although most of the socialist programs put forth by the nationalists were "variations of utopian and petty bourgeois

[8] Program of CPSU (draft), part 1, chap. 7, 1961.
[9] A. Sobolev, "National Democracy—The Way to Social Progress," *World Marxist Review*, Apr., 1963, p. 42.
[10] *Pravda* and *Izvestia*, Dec. 22, 1963.
[11] For Ben Bella, see *Pravda*, May 2, 1964. The paragraph above is based on Uri Ra'anan, "Moscow and the Third World," *Problems of Communism*, Vol. XIV, No. 1 (Jan.–Feb., 1965), pp. 22–31.

socialism" and were "a long way from scientific socialism," nevertheless "communists should adopt a positive attitude" to them and "seek to guide them in the right direction.[12] Keuneman argued that these diverse socialist ideologies owed much to the impact of the Soviet example and to the realization that capitalism could not ensure rapid development. Moreover, he pointed out, many of these national-socialist theories arose during the anticolonial struggle—the implication being that they could be turned increasingly against the West. For all of these reasons, Keuneman said "we should search out and support all that is democratic and rational in these theories and use them to help the progressive forces in the fight for revolutionary social, political and economic reforms."

The main significance of this development seems to be that it reflects a new and genuine belief in Moscow that the various socialist programs adopted by the modernizing nationalists in the one-party states will eventually bring the social structures of these countries to resemble those of Communist states. Since the nationalist leaders of the one-party states already have exclusive power, so the reasoning goes, the only problem is to get them to change their politics and to convert to communism.[13] This, say many Soviet writers, will not be difficult because of: the growing political, economic, and military might of the Soviet Union, the fact that Marxism offers the nationalists a scientific theory of modernization towards which some of them are already groping, and the existence of Communists in many of these countries, who can, as individuals, help push the nationalists in the right direction. The Soviets and their Communist allies therefore proclaim that "socio-economic changes have at the present become the main content of the national liberation movement."[14]

Peking's objections to Moscow's revolutionary strategy have already been suggested. Although the Chinese Communists did not publicly object to Moscow's reversion to the classical right strategy in 1955, it may be presumed that the Chinese have all

[12] *World Marxist Review*, Dec., 1964, p. 8.

[13] See Sobolev, *op. cit.*, who predicts that many of the radical nationalists will eventually "come over to the positions of scientific socialism." See also the article by G. Mirski in *Mirovaia ekonomika i mezhdunarodnaia politika*, No. 2, 1963. See also the glorification of "popular dictatorships" in recent issues of *The African Communist*.

[14] Kh. Bagdash, "Some Problems of the National-Liberation Movement," *World Marxist Review*, Aug., 1964, p. 550.

along regarded the strategic model by which they came to power as the correct one. Indeed, Chinese spokesmen have over the years persistently claimed that the Chinese model for gaining power is valid for all colonial and semicolonial countries. The Chinese definition of this revolutionary model has, moreover, consistently remained the same since 1949. That is, at the time of coming to power, the Chinese Communists advanced a doctrine for the seizure of power based on their own revolutionary experience, and this doctrine has remained unchanged. It has been suppressed during periods of consolidation but has come to the fore whenever there was a prospect of revolutionary advance.[15] The doctrine maintains that three basic elements account for Chinese Communist success: a Leninist party, a revolutionary army controlled by the party, and a correct policy on the united front. Mao's creative application of Marxism-Leninism it is said had to do with the second and third elements and it is on these two elements that the controversy with Moscow turns.

The Chinese attitude on the united front can be summed up as follows: the Communists in the front should under all circumstances strictly maintain their ideological, political, and organizational independence; otherwise the enemy could "butcher us at will."[16] There should be a combination of unity with and struggle against the national bourgeoisie, who, it must be constantly remembered, tend to vacillate. The alliance between Communists and the national bourgeoisie is not nearly so important as Communist control of the workers and particularly the peasants. The stronger this control, the easier it is to win over the national bourgeoisie.[17] Finally, Communist leadership of the front is necessary from the beginning to ensure final victory.

The Chinese have no objection to the creation of a broad anti-imperialist front, including "even certain kings, princes, and aristocrats who are patriotic."[18] But the local Communists must not content themselves with the role of second fiddle in the front;

[15] A. M. Halpern, "Foreign Policy Uses of the Chinese Revolutionary Model," in DeVere Pentony (ed.), *China the Emerging Red Giant* (San Francisco: Chandler Publishing Co., 1962). For the latest restatement of this revolutionary model, see Marshal Lin Piao's "Long Live the Victory of People's War," *Peking Review*, Sept. 3, 1965. See also my analysis of Lin Piao in *Commentary*, Nov., 1965, "China's Strategy: A Critique."

[16] Li Wei-han, *op. cit.*, p. 53.

[17] *Ibid.*, p. 2.

[18] Griffith, *op. cit.*, p. 267.

they must strive to build up an independent base of power among the peasants and to take over leadership of the front at the earliest possible opportunity to avoid the danger of being squeezed out by the nationalists.

In some places, the opportunity for local Communist seizure of the leadership of the revolution will not arise in the foreseeable future. In Africa, for example, the Chinese strategy is based on a long view.

Some places in Africa are like China at the time of the Boxer rebellion, some are at the stage of the 1911 Revolution, some at the period of the May Fourth (1919) movement. They are far from the 1949 era of China. What matters now in Africa is anti-imperialism and anti-colonialism; anti-feudalism is not yet important. It is time not for social revolution but for national revolution, time for a broad United Front. In Africa there are many rightists, not many leftists in power; the rightists must lose their prestige and position; then others will come forward and carry out the national revolution. We must explain the revolution from the Taipings onwards . . . they must act for themselves, foreign assistance being secondary . . . if there were one or two among the independent countries which would effect a real nationalist revolution their influence would be great and a revolutionary wave would roll up the African continent.[19]

It follows from this revealing insight into Chinese thinking about Africa that Peking, like Moscow, wants to encourage local Communists to enter into broad, anti-imperialist fronts in which social demands will be subordinated to national demands during the first phase of the revolutionary process. It also follows that the Chinese expect the national, anti-imperialist phase of the revolution in Africa to continue for the indefinite future. Their expectation is that in the course of this process more moderate African leaders will give way to more radical nationalist leaders.

But to judge from Chinese writings previously cited, Peking—unlike Moscow—will advise African Communists to maintain ideological and organizational independence throughout the first stage so that they will be in a position to seize control of the revolution from the radical nationalists at the earliest opportunity.

A second basic difference between Soviet and Chinese strategy

[19] *Bulletin of Activities,* No. 17, 1961.

towards the revolutionary nationalists has to do with the question of armed violence versus socio-economic change. Peking has persistently been skeptical about the effectiveness of nonviolent revolutionary methods, and it rejects the current Soviet contention that primary emphasis in the new states should be placed on fostering radical socio-economic reforms.[20]

Thus, on the tenth anniversary of the Algerian revolution, while Moscow emphasized the sweeping social and economic reforms of the Algerians, Peking emphasized that the lesson of the Algerian rebellion for revolutionaries everywhere was "to hold rifles tightly in their hands." Similarly, while Peking is evidently seeking to convince the Arab ultras that the Israeli problem can be solved only by war, pro-Soviet Arab Communists are arguing that armed conflict in the Middle East would "only threaten the gains of the national liberation movement of the Arab peoples who want the problem settled peacefully in conformity with N. S. Khrushchev's proposal concerning the peaceful settlement of territorial disputes."[21]

These differences between Soviet and Chinese strategy in the underdeveloped areas arise in part from differences in national interest, but they should not be understood exclusively in those terms or as mere ideological superstructures erected to justify national rivalries for world leadership. Obviously the Soviet strategy, which emphasizes internal socio-economic change as the key to revolutionary advance, is designed to obtain maximum advantage with minimum risk of war. The Chinese preference for violence is also rooted in part in its particular national situation. But these differing strategies are also the results of differing revolutionary traditions and experiences. The Chinese revolutionary model, it should be recalled, was not advanced in order to justify a dispute with Moscow. It has a history which long predated, and contributed to, the Sino-Soviet Conflict.

The strategic differences between Moscow and Peking will be clearer perhaps if we look at how they are manifested in a particular country. I have chosen India although it should be borne in mind that the situation in India is by no means typical of situations elsewhere in the underdeveloped areas. Still, the Indian situation lends itself to an examination of Sino-Soviet strategic

[20] Bagdash, *op. cit.*
[21] *World Marxist Review*, Sept., 1964, p. 63.

differences because there are now two rival Indian Communist parties with distinctly different programs. One of these is supported by and looks towards Moscow; the other is supported by and looks towards Peking.

The strategic differences between the two Indian Communist parties are in fact the differences between a Maoist-right and a classical-right strategy. The pro-Peking Indian party wants to return to the Maoist-right strategy used successfully by the Indian Communists in the early 50's. That is, it wants to pursue a united front from below against the ruling Congress party rather than cooperate with Congress in a united front from above. The "Pekingese" argue that the Congress government is dominated by the "big bourgeoisie" and therefore hopelessly reactionary in both domestic and foreign policy. They see no possibility for exploiting differences among the Congress leaders. They call instead for a "people's democratic front" under Communist leadership which will carry out the anti-feudal and anti-imperialist program by pressing for radical agrarian reforms and the elimination of foreign capital from the economy. The core of this front will be the worker-peasant alliance, but every effort will be made to win the national bourgeoisie to it as well. In short, the strategy calls in typically Maoist-right terms for the Communists to form a multi-class front under their own leadership and to concentrate on organizing the peasants under independent Communist control. The "agrarian revolution . . . is the axis of the democratic revolution according to the Indian Pekingese and "any failure to grasp its full significance and import is to miss the very essence of the democratic revolution."[22]

The pro-Moscow Indian Communists, on the other hand, argue that the Congress party is dominated not by the reactionary "big bourgeoisie" but by the national bourgeoisie which, while wavering, still has revolutionary potential. They assert that the national bourgeoisie in the Congress is divided between more and less radical leaders and that the Communists must support the left Congressmen to bring about a more radical Congress in which the Communists would have considerable influence. While they do not deny the significance of the worker-peasant alliance and the need for radical agrarian reforms, they place more emphasis on

[22] "Draft Program of the CPI Left" (undated, mimeographed).

the "contradictions" among the national bourgeoisie.[23] The pro-Moscow CP thus accepts the Soviet slogan of national democracy and seeks to form a united front from above with the left wing of Congress.

At the root of this dispute over strategy is essentially the question whether the Communists have more to gain by cooperating with or subverting the Congress party. More specifically, the question is whether Indian communism should continue to play the national game in alliance with Congress or whether it should return to the regional strategy of opposition to Congress used so fruitfully in the early 1950's. At that time, when they considered the nationalist leaders to be imperialist stooges, the Indian Communists successfully exploited regional resentments against the central Congress government, particularly regional demands in several south Indian states for linguistic autonomy. In several of these southern states, Kerala, Andhra, Bengal, and Madras, the Communists became the successful spokesmen of regional sub-nationalism.[24]

This regional strategy was abandoned after Stalin's death when his successors decided, in line with the new Soviet foreign policy of supporting the nationalists, that more could be gained by wooing Nehru and the Congress party than by trying to exploit regional resentments against them. So the Soviets and local Communists adopted a national strategy of a united front from above. This meant, among other things, support for Congress against regional and anti-Congress communal parties such as the Muslim League, for the Hindi language against regional languages, etc.

The Indian Communists obediently followed this shift in Soviet strategy, but there was much resentment over it, particularly on the part of south Indian Communist leaders with large mass

[23] See the political resolution adopted by the 7th Congress of the CPI on December 22, 1964, in *New Age* weekly, Dec. 27, 1964. See also the Draft Program of the CPI, *Information Bulletin,* issued by *World Marxist Review,* No. 18, Sept. 11, 1964. See also the various answers to readers' questions by Mohit Sen which appeared in *New Age* weekly throughout 1964. Most of these questions obviously came from members of the rival Communist Party, e.g., "Why Does CPI Prefer National Democracy?," *New Age* weekly, Aug. 30, 1964, p. 8.

[24] See Selig Harrison's *India, The Most Dangerous Decades* (Princeton: Princeton University Press, 1960); also Donald Zagoria, "The Roots of Communism in Asia," *Commentary,* Feb., 1965.

followings. These mass leaders well understood that their following was in large part a result of their opposition to what is
regarded in the south as a north Indian Congress government.
For these leaders, the classical coalition-right strategy based on
exploiting Indian nationalism never looked promising, and it is no
accident that the pro-Peking Communists are strongest precisely
in those areas where regional feeling is strongest.

On the other hand, the new national strategy did appeal to
many Communist intellectuals, trade union leaders, and others
without strong regional bases of their own who could not hope to
come to power regionally. For them, the only road to power was
on the Congress coattails nationally.

This issue of nationalism versus regionalism has smoldered
beneath the surface for the past decade. It was greatly accelerated
by the Sino-Indian border conflict. The "national Communists"
saw that conflict as an opportunity to establish their nationalist
bona fides and to consolidate their alliance with the Congress left
by taking a strong anti-Chinese line. But the regional Communists
were more interested in weakening Congress; they consequently
took an ambiguous position on the border conflict.

In 1964 the issue finally came to a head when the regional
militants formed their own party. They are now returning to the
anti-Congress regional strategy. Their party program claims that
the Hindi language is being imposed in place of English on the
non-Hindi-speaking people, that the central government has too
much power at the expense of the states, and that India needs
greater regional autonomy. Moreover, the regional Communists
are seeking to make regional alliances against the Congress: in
the Punjab with the Akalis who stand for a separate Sikh state, in
Kerala with the Muslim League and the rebel Congress, and
generally with any and all anti-Congress parties and groups.

The left Communists seem to believe that there is no chance to
come to power nationally because Congress is too well entrenched. Their apparent expectation is that they can come to
power regionally in a fragmented India. The pro-Moscow Communists, on the other hand, with no regional base of their own—
it is appropriate that their leader is S. A. Dange, a trade union
leader with no base in his own state of Maharashtra, where the
Communist Party is very weak—are optimistic about pushing
Congress further to the left and coming to power in a coalition

government. They believe that the classical-right strategy is the only way to power in India, even though it may require a long and protracted political struggle. As one of their leaders told me in private conversation, the only mass-based Communist Party in Asia is the PKI in Indonesia, and for all of its pro-Peking noises, it has pursued an opportunist strategy of vulgar collaboration with Sukarno.

It should be apparent by now that the differences between the left and the right in Indian communism are rooted in differing interests and perspectives that predate both the Sino-Soviet conflict and the Sino-Indian border war. It should also be apparent that neither Indian Communist Party is a docile satellite of Moscow or Peking. What unites the two local parties with their allies in Moscow and Peking are common or at least overlapping interests.

Moscow and the pro-Moscow Indian Communists support Congress but for different reasons—the Russians for reasons of foreign policy, the local Communists because they believe such a policy is their only route to power.

Peking and pro-Peking Indian Communists both oppose Congress but also for different reasons. China is increasingly disillusioned with India's foreign policy of friendship with both the revisionist Russians and the imperialist Americans, with India's moderating influence on the non-aligned countries, its recalcitrance on the border issue, its real or alleged role in encouraging Tibetan revolts, etc. China therefore wants a weak, Balkanized India. Such an India is also the object of the regionally based local Communists, who believe that it is their only road to power.

Let me conclude by trying to answer two questions concerning Sino-Soviet competition in the underdeveloped areas. First, what are the general advantages that Russia and China each have in waging the battle for influence in these areas? And second, what are the advantages and the limitations of their differing strategies for revolutionary advance?

The first general point in Peking's favor is that socialists and Communists in many underdeveloped countries are more enthusiastic about the Chinese economic example than the Russian. The reasons are not hard to find. There is great admiration for the bootstrap nature of Chinese economic development and a widespread feeling that the Chinese began from a point closer to their own than the Russians did.[25] Many of the socialists and Communists also feel that China has had to contend with a similar problem of mobilizing a mass of unskilled, uneducated peasants for the tasks of development. The mass-mobilization techniques that China employed in the Great Leap Forward attracted great interest, for example, in Guinea and Mali. To the intellectual and political elite in the underdeveloped areas, the Soviet Union, on the other hand, is an advanced industrial society with many resemblances to the United States; its economic methods are therefore increasingly irrelevant to their problems.

Peking undoubtedly also attracts support of the underdeveloped areas by its violently anti-colonial line. It accuses Moscow of giving greater priority to an accommodation with the West than to support of colonial liberation movements, and for many non-Communist Afro-Asians to whom anti-colonialism still is the most pressing issue this is an effective argument.

Finally, it is quite likely that Peking has been somewhat successful in its efforts to portray the Russians as a white, European power which colonized Asians and grabbed portions of Asian territory during the nineteenth century.

The Russians, on the other hand, have the considerable advantage of being able to give much greater economic aid to the new states[26] and of being more valuable trading partners than China. The level of Chinese trade with most of the underdeveloped countries has been insignificant, and there is little prospect for an increase in that trade. Russian trade with many of the new states, on the other hand, is significant.

The very fact that states such as Cuba and Algeria have adopted a neutral position in the Sino-Soviet dispute is an indication of some Soviet success. In the case of Cuba, Soviet economic pressure is probably the main reason for the recent decline of the pro-Peking forces, led by Che Guevara, who appear to have been

[25] The comparison has been made directly by Leopold Senghor, President of Senegal: "The social problem today is less a class struggle within a nation than a global struggle by the 'have' nations (including the Soviet Union) and the proletarian nations (including the Chinese People's Republic), and we are one of these 'have-not' nations." *On African Socialism* (New York: Praeger, 1964), pp. 132–33.

[26] In 1965, however, Soviet economic aid to the underdeveloped areas declined sharply—reflecting both a new pessimism about the political value of such aid and rising domestic demands for scarce economic resources.

overtaken by the pro-Moscow group. The former were apparently pushing for a program of self-reliant industrialization as advocated by Peking. The pro-Soviet group was apparently urging an emphasis on increasing sugar production, Cuba's main cash crop, and the shelving of industrial projects not related to the sugar industry. The emphasis on sugar would facilitate the integration of Cuba's economy into the East European system, which is based on a division of labor, and thereby it would make Cuba politically more dependent on the Soviet Union. This is precisely what the Chinese have been trying to prevent by stressing to the new states the virtues of self-reliant economic development.

Soviet military power also gives the Russians certain advantages over the Chinese in competing for the loyalties of the newly independent states. For one thing, the Russians are in a better position than the Chinese to provide military equipment and training to these states. For another, Moscow can provide a more credible deterrent against Western intervention. The Indonesian armed forces are, for example, heavily dependent on Soviet military aid. And the North Vietnamese have recently adopted a more neutral position in the Sino-Soviet dispute, in part because they realize that Soviet support would be more critical than China's in any showdown with the United States.

Let us now turn to the advantages and limitations of the specific Chinese and Soviet revolutionary strategies. The Maoist-right strategy worked in China under conditions of a protracted war and the erosion of authority of the nationalist regime. The strategy has been successful recently in South Vietnam, again under conditions of civil war in a country in which national authority never penetrated down to the village level. The Chinese strategy of creating a broad national front under Communist leadership has thus depended for success on a protracted military struggle in which the authority of the national government erodes or collapses.

It is possible, indeed likely, that in the fragile, divided, amorphous societies in many parts of the underdeveloped world, where national governments lack effective political organization, such situations will arise again. The Maoist strategy should be particularly promising in those areas of Asia and Africa where there are deep ethnic, tribal, and communal cleavages that inhibit the consolidation of national authority. In these areas, it should be possible to wed Communist organization to tribal grievances.

Moreover, there is the danger in all of the new states—even in those where national authority is relatively strong—that modernization efforts will fail. In such conditions the Communists might be able to capitalize on mounting frustration in order to form a broad national front under their own leadership.

The Maoist-right strategy does, however, have some serious limitations. First of all, it is difficult to see how the Chinese will be able to ride two horses simultaneously. On the one hand, they will seek to form a broad, anti-imperialist united front with the nationalists while on the other they will encourage and support Communists or crypto-Communists to undermine the nationalists from below. The inherent contradictions in the dual strategy is not so great in the first, anti-imperialist, stage of the revolutionary process if Peking is prepared to sacrifice local Communists to the nationalists during this first stage.[27] But as the revolutionary process deepens, and Peking begins to insist on Communist leadership, the contradictions must grow. This two-sided activity has already got Peking into trouble in several parts of Africa.[28]

Moreover, the dual strategy will be particularly difficult to implement in the one-party states where the ruling nationalist parties refuse to allow independent Communist activity. If the Chinese adhere to their present strategic line and advise local Communists to pursue such independent activity anyway, they are bound to clash with the nationalists.

Also, we should not lose sight of the fact that the Maoist strategy has failed even in many countries where there was prolonged armed violence and a weak national authority. It failed in Malaya largely because the local Communists were almost exclusively overseas Chinese, a fact which turned the vast majority of the indigenous Malays against them. In the Philippines it failed when a new nationalist leadership under Magsaysay gave strength to the nationalist cause. It has failed in Burma, appar-

[27] Moroccan Communists were going on trial at the very time Chou En-lai was visiting Morocco and hailing its anti-imperialist position. Nor did the Chinese protest the banning of the Algerian Communist Party and its forced integration into the FLN.

[28] At a recent conference of French-speaking countries in Mauretania, Chinese activities in Africa were discussed at length. Several of the heads of state—notably the Presidents of Ivory Coast, the Malagasy Republic, and Niger—have outspokenly attacked Chinese Communist ambitions in Africa in recent public statements. See "New Directions for French-Speaking Africa," *Africa Report,* Mar., 1965.

ently because the Communists have been unsuccessful in uniting the various minority groups which are hostile to the central government. The absence of an active sanctuary for the local Communists was of course an important factor in their defeat in both Malaya and the Philippines. In Burma, although such a sanctuary exists, the Chinese Communists have been reluctant to make use of it for fear of antagonizing the Ne Win government.

Finally, the Chinese strategy is probably least promising in those few countries such as India where national authority does effectively penetrate to the villages. In India, the pro-Chinese Communists must hope for a breakdown of Congress authority. In fact, they are trying to bring it about. They are mainly pursuing a strategy of regional alliances against Congress with the idea that eventually India can be broken up. Whether such a strategy can work is a moot question.

The Soviet strategy also has advantages and serious limitations. One advantage is that it seeks to combine the interests of the Russians, the nationalists, and the local Communists in the new states and has a good chance of succeeding in this. It has the effect of assuring the nationalists that local Communists will help build a national front under nationalist authority. In return, the Soviets ask that the nationalists grant the local Communists greater freedom of action. If they do, they can get greater Soviet aid and support. This may in fact be an attractive proposition to some of the nationalist states. Egypt, for example, has already amnestied many of its formerly imprisoned Communists. India may be prepared to give greater prominence to its pro-Moscow Communists in return for increased Soviet support. Such a strategy also removes some of the potential sources of friction between the Russians and their Communist allies in the new states, inasmuch as the Soviets can plausibly argue that the greater influence and freedom of action allowed the Communists is a direct result of Soviet power and influence with the nationalist governments.

The strategy of infiltration may also have some success. Algerian Communists who are now integrated into the FLN were reportedly influential in drafting parts of the Tripoli Program and subsequent far-reaching social and economic programs adopted by the FLN. In Burma some former members of the Communist Party have been given key advisory roles in the Ne Win government. In Egypt, Nasser has allowed some Communists into advisory positions in government. In fact, in many of the new states, there are persons in important positions who are either Communists or crypto-Communists.

While the local Communists may therefore exert an increasing degree of influence in the new states by following the Soviet strategy, it is by no means clear how they will be able to take power in their own right. The Soviet strategy deprives the local Communists of any effective independent base. This puts them more or less at the mercy of the local nationalists, as Peking points out. The Soviets seem to be betting on the possibility that some of the nationalists may imitate Castro and convert to communism. But Castro did what he did for reasons not at all typical in the new states. Indeed, the Algerians, for whom the Soviets evidently have big hopes, have privately been very critical of Castro precisely because they feel that he should have avoided committing himself so closely to the Communist camp.*

The Communists' influence may in some cases increase as a result of an infiltration strategy, but they will have difficulty taking over by such a tactic a party modeled on Leninist lines. Their pupils may have learned their lessons too well. Moreover, in many countries the task will be not only to infiltrate the ruling party but, more important, to infiltrate the army. Although the Communists have had some success in infiltrating the Indonesian army for reasons peculiar to that country, they must expect to meet anti-Communist sentiment on the part of army leaders generally.†

In the last analysis, there are no prefabricated roads to Communist victory in the underdeveloped areas. Conditions vary too much for general prescriptions based on differing national circumstances to be universally valid. Apart from the Vietcong, whose success is due in part to the existence of an active sanctuary in North Vietnam, the only relatively successful, mass-based Communist Party in Asia was the Indonesian party, which—until the recent premature effort to take power—had successfully adapted its strategy to the unique conditions it faced.

While Peking and Moscow both pay lip service to the need for a

---

* This was written prior to the coup in Algeria which overthrew Ben Bella and that in Ghana which ousted Nkrumah, both of which have disillusioned the Russians and cast doubt on the "infiltration" strategy.

† This was written prior to the Army takeover in Indonesia.

flexible and differentiated approach taking into account national peculiarities, there are built-in constraints on each. The Chinese, for their part, have frozen their own revolutionary model into a dogma while the Russians have national interests that generally dictate support of the "bourgeois nationalists" regardless of their internal policies.

PART SEVEN

Russia and China in a Modernizing World

Russia and China in a Modernizing World:
A Concluding Note

HAROLD D. LASSWELL

IN ONE perspective the revolutions in Russia and China are part of the larger transformation characterized by the accelerated rise of science and technology, a movement that gained shape and strength in Western Europe and has been expanding throughout the globe. One obvious criterion for the appraisal of Communist developments in the two countries is the magnitude of their influence on spreading or restricting the mastery of science and technology. However evident the suitability of the criterion may be, its application is beset with complexity, a point that was abundantly underscored in the papers and deliberations of the conference. True, the two revolutions swept away institutions that stood in the path of scientific and technological modernization. At the same time they destroyed or crippled institutions that were favorable to innovation. Many of the policies supported by the political elites of communism through the years have worked against, rather than for, the full use and encouragement of science and technology. The relationship is patently interactive, not onesided. Hence it is important to direct further inquiry, by the use of all appropriate procedures, to the impact of communism on the dimensions of scientific and technological innovation, diffusion, and restriction; and, conversely, on the effect upon communism of degrees of exposure to, or command over, these component elements of modern civilization.

One aim of the present commentary is to bring into the open

With no desire to incriminate Professor John M. H. Lindbeck for the final product, I nevertheless express my appreciation for his time in commenting on a rough outline of the proposed essay.

and render more explicit some hypotheses that were partly explicit, partly implicit in the conference, and which bear immediately on the interplay of science, technology, and politics. The policies of the two revolutions, in so far as they affect science, are the outcome of two sets of factors: the predispositions existing at the time of the seizure of power, as modified by the experience of seizing power; and the environing circumstances in the arena of world politics during and after the takeover period. We shall focus on these factors.

Running through the proceedings of the conference was a certain tension between the demand to explain and the demand to guide scholarly efforts at explanation by raising evaluative questions. An objective of the present comment is to develop some implications of a value-oriented approach.

In harmony with the overriding goal of the conference, the commentary is concerned with the policy questions that face the individual scholar and the scholarly community. These questions go beyond the choice of topic and method by the particular scholar for the conduct of his own research. As a member of the community of scholars the individual has a tacit, and often a formal, vote in shaping the course of research, teaching, and advice in the universities, professional associations, and other official or unofficial organizations.

THE INCORPORATION OF SCIENCE AND TECHNOLOGY

a. The Degree of Pre-Revolutionary Incorporation

The incorporation of science and technology in any society is indicated by the degree to which every sector of the society is adapted to the cultivation and use of scientific perspectives and modes of operation. At the level of subjective outlook much more is involved than an affirmative evaluation of empirically oriented theory, or of the innovation of new materials and energies. The intellectual operations themselves—the problem-solving procedures—must be realistically harmonized with science and technology. Although the Russian and Chinese revolutions were indubitably Communist, in any unforced interpretation of the term, it is generally agreed that they differ in many ways. The Chinese revolution seems less "Western" than the Russian. The contrast appears valid even when we limit comparison to cross-sections taken at corresponding years after the seizure of power (1965 is sixteen years after 1949; hence comparisons can be made with 1933, which is sixteen years after the October revolution). The difference is more explicit than is suggested by the dismissive remark that after all the revolutionaries in Peking are "Chinese." The significant contrast seems to lie in the persistence of patterns of mind and behavior that are widely distributed among "traditional," "prescientific" societies. The interpretation can be generalized for purposes of research (not only on Russia and China) as follows: *The revolution is most realistically encouraging to science and technology which occurs where science and technology are most fully incorporated at the time of the revolution.* A corollary is that pre- or at least non-technoscientific values and institutions are stronger among the people where the incorporation is relatively low.

It is frequently noted, for example, that outstanding among Chinese objectives and strategies has been reliance on the omnipotence of thought. A trait of this kind is in no sense peculiar to Chinese tradition. On the contrary, confidence in the potency of the mind as an instrument for obtaining immediate, external effects is widely, if not indeed, universally distributed among all societies, especially pre-machine cultures. A technology that depends on impersonal sources of energy and on the use of machines gradually modifies the world view of modern populations. A man-machine combination is perceived as essential to achieving and sustaining the level of resource modification and accumulation that is indispensable to high levels of wealth, power, and other value outcomes. By 1949 the Chinese had been less disciplined than the Russians by exposure to, and incorporation of, the new pattern.

Closely connected with the stress on subjectivity is the reliance by the Chinese on a deeply imbedded pedagogical and small group pattern of persuasive pressure. The pedagogical component is distinctively Chinese; the Confucian emphasis on change through education and example, institutionalized through centuries, presumably left a residue of sanguine expectation that minds mold conduct, and conduct imprints mind. Accompanying this distinctive element, however, was a mode of control that is not unique. There is nothing new among traditional societies in isolating the doubter or rejector in the family or neighborhood and subjecting him to a barrage of "coercive persuasion," "thought control," "group suasion," or opportunities for "voluntarism" in a return to the fold.

Subjectivism and personalism are expressed in traditional Chinese opposition to reliance on the use of written contracts, enforcible by public authority in case of dispute among the parties. Although the central government has relied for centuries on a vast bureaucracy thoroughly accustomed to paper work, there has been reluctance to bind the discretion of magistrates at the primary level of contact with the population by detailed public codes of authoritative prescription. The traditional preference for ambiguity in written formulations is one element in the frequent assertion that Chinese civilization traditionally devalued law and lawyers. The Russians were more accustomed than the Chinese in prerevolutionary days to rely on courts, prosecutors, and a private legal profession. In the early revolutionary days the Russians undertook to exalt the lay component in the settlement of controversies; and subsequently, under the impact of semi-cyclical demands for a return to revolutionary orthodoxy, have made new and only partially effective, gestures in the direction of strengthening the lay element in the administration of justice.

It is well understood that the perpetual innovations in the division of labor that are connected with modern technology have the effect of undermining the clarity of mutual expectation among producers and purchasers (or barter partners) in traditional economies. The resulting substitution of "contract" for "custom" is an attempt to reduce the costs to public order of waste in production and conflict in the community.

In view of the seeming incompatibility of many assertions that have been made (also at the conference) about the role of law, it should be observed in passing that some scholarly controversies seem to depend on different definitions of law. According to one usage a legal prescription is solely to be understood as an *explicit rule* purporting to establish norms and sanctions for conduct which is *formulated by public authorities and enforced by officials specialized to the task.* Such a conception reflects the viewpoint of one of the several schools of jurisprudence developed in our own civilization. Some legal scholars have modified this approach to *include customary practices* that are *expected to be enforced,* and are *actually enforced,* by *severe sanctions* in the community, *whether the enforcement officers are "officials" or "specialists" or* not. ("Mild" sanctions can be regarded as part of the civic order rather than the public order.)

In any case the prerevolutionary exposure of Russian society to a division of labor affected by the technology of the internal combustion engine and of electricity appears to have created resort to the use of written agreement and instruments designed to reduce the role of "personal" factors in social life. Even when we limit comparison to 1965 in China and 1933 in Russia, the conclusion seems tenable.

b. The Subsequent Effect of the Seizure of Power

Any revolutionary movement perceives itself as having successfully passed the greatest of all reality tests when it has toppled the established regime and outlasted its rival claimants to the seat of formal and effective power. The strategies that are supposed to have been crowned with victory are deeply imbedded in the repertory of the revolutionary generation and therefore exercise a profound effect on successor generations. Hence any attempt to account for the more positive attitude of the Russians (when compared with the Chinese) toward science and the machine must go beyond the hypothesis of difference in initial levels of incorporation to emphasize the subsequent effect of the seizure and early retention of power.

These effects are somewhat ambivalent, hence partly favorable and partly unfavorable, to further rapid incorporation. The Bolsheviks were a corps of professional revolutionaries who prepared for the day of glory by living as journalists, lecturers, and conspirators. They perfected a technique of calculated coercion for use against their rivals in the revolutionary movement as a whole and depended, among other strategies, on counter-conspirative measures to protect themselves from overthrow. The Bolsheviks were conspicuously lacking in administrative, scientific, and technological skills; hence they sought at first to consolidate their rule by de-emphasizing professional know-how and sacrificing efficiency in factories or offices to revolutionary zeal. But the hard realities of their situation plainly showed that enemies from within and without could not be dealt with successfully unless the new power wielders were willing and able to mobilize military and administrative talent from prerevolutionary formations. Since they perceived themselves as alone in a threatening world of counterrevolutionary powers, the most potent of which were

industrialized, the obvious need of modernization burned itself
into the creed of the Kremlin.

Chinese experience was in many ways contrasting. The take-off
occurred after years of struggle outside the cities, during which
the party leadership was welded into a notably unified instrument
of authority and control. The long struggle was perceived as a
history-shaking triumph of man over machines. Possessed of
revolutionary determination and illumination, the Chinese Communists simply took the engines of war away from the decaying
forces of the established order. Guns were turned against the
gunsmiths.

The predispositions of the Chinese elite as shaped by the
seizure of power were corroborative of pre-scientific and pre-
technological world views. Hence the extraordinary lack of mat-
ter-of-fact realism in devising and executing policies related to
modernization. The Great Leap Forward was a grandiose expression of this cavalier approach to the built-in rhythms and limitations of nature and man. Some experts are even willing to predict
that the Chinese elite may quite possibly attempt another Leap in
future years, anticipating that the discipline of contact with
science and technology will not be sufficient to overcome the
intensity of commitment to the strategy of zeal. That it would
succeed is most unlikely; hence the forecast is a slow but sure
triumph of "the reality principle."

The same combination of determining factors applies to such
sophisticated instruments of war as nuclear weapons. If the
potential impact of nuclear devices has been perceived in somewhat off-hand fashion, the allocation of resources to build a
substantial capability can be expected to have educational side
effects. But no analyst-observer rests too securely in his confidence that in the immediate future, reversing the traditional
sequence, material mountains can move faith.

In this context the problem of elite succession comes prominently into view. It was generally conceded by conference discussants, for instance, that the Russian elite is transforming its
outlook and its strategies to overcome the adverse consequences of
some of its traditional policies for the value-shaping processes
of Russian society. Even if we assume an occasional resumption
of Stalin-like technique, the cumulative transformation of the
public and civic order strengthens the weight of factors in support
of science, technology, pluralization, and individuality.

The prognosis for China, on the other hand, is complicated by the age gap that will implacably produce a sharp change in the composition of Peking's power-holders. The phenomenal stability of China's government by a board of elders in revolution has thus far had a unifying and reassuring impact on politics and society. However, the old men are plainly apprehensive. The great revolution was in the hands of intellectuals and semi-intellectuals who were remarkably self-isolated from their families, and indeed from effective functioning in the framework of the prerevolutionary social system. Presumably the rising leadership is less alienated from primary circles and is more accustomed to thinking in terms of continuing the established order rather than subverting it. If the postrevolutionary generation is less full of bitterness and hate, less committed to a life of perpetual reaffirmation of intense destructiveness, what then? Even the most cautious commentators usually find themselves inclined to concede the strength of defanaticizing factors. Hence the possibility is not to be overlooked of a comparatively rapid reversal of outlook if the "hard line" becomes a target of accumulated resentment against the elders.

c. *The Imprint of External Factors*

Any attempt to account for the contrasting emphases on science and technology in the two chief Communist powers must go beyond predisposing factors, such as the prerevolutionary incorporation of science and technology, or the stereotyping effect of the strategies that are credited with the seizure of power, to assess the subsequent impact of the world political environment. The Russian elite had to face counterrevolutionary action from outside; and much of the fighting was closer to the format of front-line conflict than to the fluid, guerrilla-like operations in which Mao excelled. Armored trains, tanks, and heavy artillery were more conspicuous in Trotsky's campaigns than in the Long March or during operations on the borders of Yenan. Petrograd was a city with many huge plants and a disciplined labor, technical, and managerial force; Peking, on the contrary, could be the capital of a new state that felt at some distance from such bases of wealth and power.

Moscow was alone in a hostile world arena. Peking, on the contrary, could count on the deterrent effect, and the support, of Moscow. Although a younger brother role could not be permanently satisfactory, the protecting shadow of Russia, particularly after the achievement of nuclear capability by the Russians, was vitally important. It made possible a timetable that could defer realistic programs of modernization, and give preference to costly strategies intended to cultivate Redness over expertness. Today, the cadres of Peking, when compared with their opposite numbers in contemporary Moscow, are both undertrained and underspecialized. The difference remains, though less noticeably, if we examine the Russia of 1933.

Among the long-term factors that can be expected to modify the Chinese picture is the probable growth of economic and cultural exchange with other members of the Communist Bloc. As the Bloc loosens, and the predominance of Moscow is cut down, rivalry for trade, investment, and cultural ascendancy gives a premium to participation in a wider division of labor, and to an accelerated pace of realistic technoscientific transformation.

THE APPRAISAL OF REVOLUTION IN TERMS OF HUMAN DIGNITY

The foregoing discussion has brought together some of the principal hypotheses that are available to explain the different roles of the Russian and Chinese revolutions in spreading or restricting the world revolution of science and technology, variously called the rise of the machine, the rise of industrialism, or modernization. The relative lag in China appears to confirm the broad proposition that the modernizing effect of revolutionary movements is a function of the degree of incorporation of science and technology at the time of the revolutionary upheaval; of the strategies that meet success in the seizure and early confirmation of power; and of the threats and opportunities afforded by the world arena.

As noted above, the conference sustained a degree of tension between the task of explaining and of evaluating the two Communist powers. There was no doubt about the fundamental criterion that members of the conference were concerned with using. The key question was: What significance have the revolutions had for expediting or retarding movement toward the realization of human dignity? The policies of both Communist systems are totalitarian, hence devastatingly suspicious and intolerant of spontaneous human choice. Whether the rulers relied on the mind-freezing effect of terror or the mind-sterilizing impact of indoctrination, perpetual busy-ness, and the abolition of privacy, the ruling elites of communism have obviously sought by cultivating rituals of unanimity to protect themselves from the anxieties of free discussion, debate, and inquiry.

But the human personality is notoriously difficult to discipline into utter conformity, especially when the societies subjected to totalitarian strategies possess a complex tradition in which many forms of free expression have been firmly implanted. The conferees often raised questions about the intensity and mode of free expression in Russia and China, and about the continuing influence of the predispositions carried over from prerevolutionary times. The latent and partially explicit hypothesis appeared to be that both the modes and intensities of the freedoms found in postrevolutionary years could be predicted from the strength and character of the modes and intensities prevailing in the earlier period. There was the further hypothesis that the growth of a specialized society would foster freedom; and that chronic crisis in external affairs would work against free institutions.

The principal topic of inquiry in the effort to appraise the fate of freedom was poetry and scholarship as a sample of the role of the intellectual classes. In Russia the novelists and poets were sufficiently disaffected from the old regime, and strongly enough identified with the cry for justice, to meet the revolution with hope and to play no insignificant part in its consummation. Hence the connection between the ideological features of the change and the literary class was relatively intimate. As the revolution became more totalitarian, intellectuals felt betrayed; *their* revolution had been taken away from them. Hence many literary figures continued the struggle to redirect the revolution. The degree of freedom that has been achieved in recent years would suggest that they have not been without success. At the very least, they can be interpreted as having seized promptly on every potential mood and circumstance favorable to free expression.

The Chinese intellectuals included a powerful sector whose role in undermining the hold of ancient tradition and opening the door to innovation was decisive for the revolutionary movement. They, too, evidently experienced a sense of betrayal. But perhaps the richness of Chinese tradition in providing examples of how to live through a time of trouble and dynastic innovation has influenced the conduct of disaffected intellectuals. They appear to have adopted personal strategies of seeming conformity, and to have executed these maneuvers with so much finesse that the top leadership was itself misled. Hence the Hundred Flowers; hence, too, the early blight. To date, at least, the evidence is that the Chinese poet has soared on a broken wing. There is some difference of view about the success of the historical and analytic intellectual in protecting the integrity of the scholarly enterprise. It would be revealing to compare novelists as a group with dramatists, choreographers, painters and sculptors, architects and musicians. The nonverbal arts may safely exhibit signs of nonconformity before the verbal arts can run the risk of explicitness.

The subtleties involved in the conception of individuality, of freedom of mind and spirit, came explicitly into view in the discussions of the conference. Working definitions or exemplifications were offered; and some of the most absorbing contributions brought out traditional differences in individuality as "withdrawal" (in Russia) and as "congenial small group expression" (in China).

It must be conceded that as knowledge stands at present we are in much uncertainty and confusion about the effect of the spread of science and technology on freedom. There is no doubt in anyone's mind that the power elite of a totalitarian regime is ambivalent about science and scientists. On the one hand the elites are eager to have at their disposal the forces of production and destruction that are made available by scientifically generated technology. On the other hand the rulers are apprehensive of the consequences of the scientific outlook for the continuity of the political system, and especially of the proliferation of groups of distinctive perspective and skill in a transformed structure of society.

Outside observers hypothesize a state of growing tension between the party and the other value-institution sectors of Russian society. They regard the party as in a more or less clearly perceived crisis in which the agonizing issue is whether party dominance and party strategies of repression have outlived whatever usefulness they once had, and are now strangling the productive potentialities, not only of science and technology, but of the whole society. The Chinese leadership acts as though it were cognizant of an eventual tie between science and freedom, but is willing to settle for somewhat retarded modernization, an option that seems more open to Peking than it was to the Russians, given the quantitative weakness of the prerevolutionary component of scientific technology.

Pertinent data on many critical factors have been remarkably difficult to come by in either society. It is established, for example, that the authorities in Peking dislike differential incomes. Yet there are indications of the important part that is already played by these differences. How they affect the outlook and behavior of those affected is obscure.

Much more information is needed to confirm the quantitative significance of the aggregate losses that are to be attributed to the strategies by which human beings seek to maintain their integrity against constant pressure. If we can possibly examine absenteeism (alleged illness), spoilage, and withholding (of harvests, for instance), we can add to our scanty knowledge of fundamental trends.

We are no less in the dark about the connection between the growth of specialization, as modern technology advances, and the resulting political and civic involvement of the specialists. Is the implication that these skill groups will almost inevitably contribute to the growth of a bi-party or multiple-party system, a free press, and an active system of pressure and interest groups designed to influence both the parties and official organs of government? Certainly the appearance of totalitarian movements and parties in relatively modernized societies is a contrary fact that must be accounted for. Perhaps it is to be satisfactorily explained by the impact of external factors such as humiliating defeat in war; and perhaps there are grounds for predicting that sooner or later the pluralistic tendencies reassert their strength. Doubt presently arises from lack of information about the factor-combinations that affect the direction and timing of such responses.

DIRECTIONS AND STRATEGIES OF INQUIRY

The conference was planned as a means of fostering individual and joint scholarly effort to study the two greatest Communist powers. The present comment has emphasized the manifest and latent contributions that were made to the appraisal of these developments in two frames of reference of world importance: the timing of the spread of science and technology toward universality; the timing of the impact of Russian and Chinese developments on the realization or frustration of human dignity.

Many other themes might have been chosen, such as the problem of the timing and arrangement of factors internal and external to a given society that precipitates *revolution,* or, more specifically, a *Communist* revolution. Or what accounts for the degree of likeness and difference to be found at various phases of the history of self-designated "Communist" revolutions?

The choice of theme is affected by several considerations emphasized in a problem-solving approach to the context of world politics. There is for instance, the question of goal, and the deliberate selection of the postulate of human dignity as the overriding criterion. How can scholars contribute to the clarification of such a value goal? Can they improve the body of historical and contemporary knowledge concerning movement toward or away from the realization of a defined conception of human dignity? Will they be able to add to our knowledge of the combination of factors that explains the timing and characteristics of the trends toward or away from the goal? Is it possible to locate strategic problems of inquiry by critically projecting contemporary trends into the future and locating the zones of crisis? And, finally, is it possible to draw attention to broad strategies that promise to further the realization of human dignity?

The connection between science and technology, on the one hand, and the dignity of man is far from the status of a foregone conclusion, especially when precise questions are raised about either the timing or the character of the response. One purpose of the present discussion, therefore, is to put forward definite hypotheses regarding the interplay of science and revolution in undermodernized countries. The hypothesis about the connection between realistic revolutionary policy and the degree to which scientific technology is incorporated in the prerevolutionary society (and the strategies credited with the seizure of power) is a relatively straightforward quantitative assertion. It can be applied in principle to all cases of partial incorporation of the techno-scientific components of European civilization. For example, it predicts that the more science is taught in the schools, the more science is pushed in universities and research agencies, the more scientists and technologists are found in the population, the more agricultural and nonagricultural operations are conducted by an advanced technology, the greater the likelihood that a Communist revolution will seek to further the transformation of society in realistic ways that include and encourage science and technology. Ultimately the hypothesis calls for an inventory at the prerevolutionary phase of every sector of society. A working model of the social process of any society conceives of it in terms of "man" striving to optimize his "values" (preferred events) through "institutions" using "resources." To those for whom science is a prime value (a scope value) it is a mode of enlightenment. For those who regard science as a means (a base value), it is evaluated as a contributor, for instance, to power, wealth, well-being, skill, and respect. It also possesses implications for intimate relationships and large group loyalties, and for religious and ethical achievement (affection, rectitude). Scientific practices (perspectives and operations) are part of the institutions of enlightenment, and when the scientific pattern spreads throughout a society it modifies the institutions specialized to every value (the institutions of government, law, and politics; of production, distribution, investment, consumption; of health, safety, and comfort; and so on).

The hypothesis assumes—and this is open to empirical refutation in concrete instances—that the prerevolutionary introduction of science and technology, despite particular adverse effects, has had relatively value-indulgent rather than value-deprivational impacts from the standpoint of those who make and consolidate revolution. Hence the revolutionary elements will take an affirmative attitude toward science and technology, even though limited incorporation leaves them with limited understanding and capability for adopting policies that are relatively contributory to its further incorporation.

It seems probable that established methods of scholarly investigation into world processes need to be supplemented in various ways. It may be pertinent to underline the possibilities, not infrequently mentioned, of paralleling the work of the economists by extending analytic and quantitative procedures to non-economic sectors of the social process of Russia and China before and after communism. If the social and historical flow of events at all times and places is described in the same fundamental categories, it becomes possible to evaluate the relative magnitude of developments in more critical and realistic terms than otherwise can be done. The economist who defines such terms as production, income, saving, investment, and consumption is able to search for usable indices with which to compare Russia or

China with themselves or with any other nation at any selected time.

A further suggestion is inspired by experience of the intellectual advantages of *prediction* and of *critical discussion*. If the intellectual tools at the disposal of scholars were adequate, it would be possible to make highly accurate estimates of the timing and the character of future developments. Prediction exercises are usually thought of, or engaged in, as part of a policy-advisory or policy-executing task. This view is too limited; prediction can also be a scholarly and scientific tool when properly adapted to the purpose. If scholars make intermittent estimates and candidly consider the bases of inference that led them previously to make accurate or inaccurate predictions, the results would be various: greater insight by scholars into chronically "sanguine" or "pessimistic" biases on their part; the focusing of historical inquiry on neglected factors; the planning of field research to provide for better recording of anticipated developments; the discovery of the time span within which the scholarly observer can make the best specific forecasts.

If joint ventures in the gathering and processing of data are accelerated, it will be useful to utilize and guide these efforts by continuing seminars that convene intermittently and explore the most advantageous means of audio-visual presentation of simulated models of past, present, and future events.

The age of science and technology does not supersede the creativity of the scholarly imagination or the self-discipline essential to the acquisition and application of a particular skill. The technoscientific age provides a test of creativity by making available instruments of observation, analysis, and presentation that can change the level of reality on which the disciplined mind is free to operate.

Contributors

S. II. CHEN
Professor of Chinese
University of California, Berkeley

JEROME ALAN COHEN
Professor of Law
Harvard University

ALEXANDER DALLIN
Professor of International Relations
Director, Russian Institute
Columbia University

VICTOR ERLICH
Bensinger Professor of Russian
  Literature
Chairman, Department of Slavic
  Languages and Literatures
Yale University

MERLE FAINSOD
Carl H. Pforzheimer University Pro-
  fessor
Director, Harvard University Li-
  brary
Harvard University

MARK G. FIELD
Professor of Sociology, Boston Uni-
  versity
Associate, Russian Research Center,
  Harvard University

GREGORY GROSSMAN
Professor of Economics
University of California, Berkeley

HAROLD D. LASSWELL
Edward J. Phelps Professor of Law
  and Political Science
Yale University

J. M. II. LINDBECK
Associate Director, East Asian Re-
  search Center
Harvard University

LEON LIPSON
Professor of Law
Yale University

RICHARD LOWENTHAL
Professor, Otto-Suhr-Institute
Free University of Berlin

SIDNEY MONAS
Professor of History
University of Rochester

RICHARD PIPES
Professor of History
Harvard University

LUCIAN W. PYE
Professor of Political Science
Massachusetts Institute of Technol-
  ogy

443

FRANZ SCHURMANN
Professor of History and Sociology
Chairman, Center for Chinese
 Studies
University of California, Berkeley

GEORGE E. TAYLOR
Professor of Far Eastern History and
 Politics
Director, Far Eastern and Russian
 Institute
University of Washington

DONALD W. TREADGOLD
Professor of Russian History
University of Washington

EZRA F. VOGEL
Lecturer in Social Relations
Harvard University

K. C. YEH
Economist
The RAND Corporation

DONALD S. ZAGORIA
Professor of Political Science
Columbia University

Index